English G Neue Ausgabe

Band C4

für das 10. Schuljahr
an Schulen mit Englisch
als 2. Fremdsprache

Cornelsen

English G · Neue Ausgabe
Ausgabe C
Band 4 für das 10. Schuljahr an Schulen mit Englisch als 2. Fremdsprache

Im Auftrage des Verlages erarbeitet von

Carl Taylor MA, Maidencombe, Devon · StD Udo J. Hennig, Neuwied

in Zusammenarbeit mit der Verlagsredaktion

Cedric J. Sherratt (Projektleitung); Kirsten Bleck, Uwe Tröger (verantwortliche Redakteure);
Karl Brehmer, Ph.D., Susanne Döpper, Dr. Gunther Weimann *sowie* Rebecca Robb, MSc
mit Unterstützung des Redaktionsbüros Victor Dewsbery, Berlin

Weitere Mitarbeit

David Bolton, Bristol · Karen Carlson-Kreibohm, Berlin · William C. Flowe, Konstanz · StR Mervyn Whittaker, Bad Dürkheim

Beratende Mitwirkung

RLin Sylvia Anna Behet, Blieskastel · StD Burkhard Dammann, Nürnberg · OStRin Louise Raetzell, Kiel · OStR Heiner Ratsch, Würzburg · StR Albert Rau M.A., Brühl · StRin Susanne Schroeder-Thürauf, Erlangen · StD Dr. Michael Schulz, Oldenburg · Prof. Hellmut Schwarz, Mannheim · StD Heinz Thillosen, Krefeld · Prof. Franz Vettel, Heppenheim · StD Dieter Weis, Hochspeyer · OStR Harald Weißling, Mannheim *sowie* StRin Dagmar von Arnim, Hanau · OStR Winfried Braun, Göttingen · OStD Hans-Günter Kruppa, Osnabrück · OStR Wolfgang Schild, Bielefeld

Grafik

Hewett Street Studios, London: David Graham, Graham Humphreys, Liz Roberts; Mike Mosedale *sowie* Robert Broomfield, Tunbridge Wells, *und* Gabriele Heinisch, Berlin

Design und Layout

David Graham · Susanne Meyer

Technische Umsetzung

Susanne Meyer

Bild- und Textquellen

s. Verzeichnis auf S. 201

Zusatzmaterialien zum vorliegenden Schülerbuch:

Workbook (Best.-Nr. 52680)
1 Cassette zum Schülerbuch (Kurzfassung für Schüler 71081) · 2 Cassetten (Vollfassung für Lehrer 71065)

Auf weitere Bestandteile des Lehrwerks wird im Lehrerhandbuch (71049) verwiesen.

1. Auflage 1995

Alle Drucke dieser Auflage können, weil untereinander unverändert, im Unterricht nebeneinander verwendet werden.

Druck Cornelsen Druck, Berlin

ISBN 3-464-05267-2
Bestellnummer 52672

Contents

Pflichtbereich: Units

Wahlbereich: Options

Obwohl die *Options* einzelnen Units thematisch zugeordnet sind, können sie beliebig im Laufe des Unterrichtsjahres eingesetzt werden.

Units and Options at a glance

	"Text" Options	"Skills" Options	"Grammar" Options
Unit 1	1, 2, 3	13, 14	19
Unit 2	4, 5, 6	13, 15	19, 20
Unit 3	7, 8	13, 16	19, 21
Unit 4	9, 10, 11, 12	13, 17	19, 22
Unit 5		18	

R *Revision* – Abschnitte, die der Wiederholung und Festigung des Lernstoffes dienen.

☞ Leitfragen für die Bearbeitung, die vorab gelesen werden sollten.

Kurze, zusätzliche Hörverstehenstexte. Die mit einem „L" gekennzeichneten Texte sind nur auf den Cassetten für Lehrer/innen enthalten. Alle anderen befinden sich auch auf der Cassette für Schüler/innen.

Introduction

American high schools • Washington, D.C. • Blacks in the USA • American Indians • The world of literature – these are the topics of the five units in this book. The small pictures in the last panel tell you about some of the options at the back of the book.
First of all, with a partner, choose two pictures.
Then, each of you, write down for yourself …
– what comes into your mind when you look at the pictures
– why you chose them.
Finally, compare notes with your partner and, together, write a short text about each of the topics you have chosen.

Unit 1 American high schools

First read this page from the Dunlap High School newspaper. What does it tell you about this high school in Dunlap, Illinois? Then work with a partner and try to recall what you have learned so far about American high schools.

DUNLAP HIGH SCHOOL NEWS

School info

There will be a Career Day on TUESDAY, April 26. We have invited different speakers to talk about topics from *Biotechnology* to *Working for an airline.* If you are interested in any particular job, you can talk to the individual speakers later.

Erin Spirropoulos, Sarah Cruz, and Kevin Metz, Guidance Counselors

I would like to remind all students who drive to school that they must park on the north side of the building. I would also like to remind you again to drive carefully and slowly. And please remember that smoking in the parking lot is not allowed.

Wayne Holmes, Assistant Principal

Father-Daughter Dance

The next Father-Daughter Dance will be held at the Raffestry Center on April 16 from 8:00 to 11:00 p.m. If you can't bring your father, bring an older brother, uncle, etc. Tickets are $10. Soft drinks and snacks will be provided. The couples will dance to music from the 60s.

Your ads

Tired of spending money on car repairs? Join our auto mechanics club. Tuesdays 4-5 p.m. If interested, get info from the office.

I'm quitting my job at the PIZZA PLACE. It's two afternoons a week (Tuesdays and Fridays) from 4 p.m. to 7 p.m. Information is in the office for anybody who is interested.

Craig Rosetti

We regret to say that Debbie Frank is leaving our school, so we need somebody to fill her place as a CHEERLEADER. If anybody is interested, just come to the gym for a try-out on Tuesday after school when we have cheerleader practice and talk to Joanne Rigby.

Found in the town paper

DUNLAP GIRLS 71 – O'CONNELL 63

by Pat Lanigan, Sports Editor

The Dunlap girls' basketball team is having a great season under new coach Pam Eastman. The team has won all its games so far. At the start of the season nobody expected them to be very successful, but as Captain Suzie Miller said, "We are not cowards. We play hard and we never give up, no matter what the score is or how good the other team is."

Focus on GRAMMAR Participles I

1 Read the text on the right and the eight statements below to find out about the links between Dunlap High and a German *Gymnasium*.
Then discuss in class which blanks must be completed with the present participle and which ones with the past participle of *organize*. – Start with the sentences that you are quite sure about.

Links …

Dunlap High has had an exchange with Max-von-Laue-Gymnasium in Koblenz for over ten years now. Not long ago they started a computer link. Via modem the students can now communicate directly and very quickly with each other.

organizing or organized

1. The teachers … the exchange are Mr Weitzel in Dunlap and Herr Altenkamp in Koblenz.
2. Whenever groups from Dunlap and Max-von-Laue meet, they have a well-… party on the first night.
3. One of the highlights at the party are the … games which the students play to get to know each other.
4. During the exchange they make trips to places of interest. Those … by the students themselves are always a real success.
5. For several years Dunlap students have helped with the programme. Last year four days were … by one of Mr Weitzel's classes.
6. The second German teacher at Dunlap High is Mr Stoyak. At the moment some of his students are … part of the exchange programme for this year.
7. Mr Stoyak is also the … teacher for the new computer link with Koblenz. He has … everything with Frau Hartmüller at Max-von-Laue.
8. Anybody … such a link can easily turn into a 'forever-…' teacher. Mr Stoyak and Frau Hartmüller are aware of this. So they want to ask some students to help.

As you can see, participles can be used in different places in a sentence.
Look at the sentences again and decide in which of them *organizing* or *organized* is used as …

- an adjective
- part of a compound adjective
- part of a progressive form
- part of a perfect form
- part of a passive form
- part of a clause that is similar to a relative clause.

On p.17 you can learn more about participles used as compound adjectives.
Here you will learn some more about <u>participle clauses</u> that are similar to relative clauses.

→ Grammar 1: 1 (p.128) → Exercise 1

2 Participle clauses that are similar to relative clauses

The following sentences give you four more examples of participle clauses. If you look at them closely, you will see that these participle clauses are very similar to relative clauses.

The computer club **run by Frau Hartmüller** is for students of all ages.
The ten students **working with Frau Hartmüller** would like to send their letters as soon as possible.
Anybody **interested in information** about the computer link can join the club.
Those **taking part in the exchange** will also get a chance to use the computer link.

To show that you have understood the participle clauses properly, change them into relative clauses.
Try to remember what you have learned about the function of relative clauses. Then explain what participle clauses have in common with relative clauses.
Finally, find <u>two</u> German translations for each example sentence, one with a relative clause and one with a participle construction that is similar to the English one.
Compare the word order of each English sentence with the word order in your translations. What do you notice?

→ Grammar 1: 2 (p.128) → Exercise 2

A letter via the computer

Hardly had the link been established when a group of Max-von-Laue students started to send letters via the computer. They waited excitedly to see who would send an answer to their letters. The following day a reply came for two of the German pupils.

Dear Sylvia and Patricia,

We received your letter yesterday. We are two students at Dunlap High School. We're in two different grades of high school. My name is Jeremy Glass (my friends call me 'the Jerm'). I'm 15 and in the 10th grade. I'm a sophomore. My hobbies are listening to music, playing football, basketball and baseball, playing computer games, watching TV, and trying to solve my friends' social problems.
My friend's name is David Wu. He's 16 and he's in the 11th grade. He's a junior. He has his own car and drives to school every day. His hobbies are listening to music, running, reading books, looking for girls, playing guitar, watching TV, and writing poems.
David is also a member of SADD (Students Against Driving Drunk). This club was founded by teenagers who were upset about the deaths of two of their friends who were hit by drunk drivers. The students meet about once a week to discuss problems related to alcohol, and they try to find ways to handle these problems.
In our school there are only about 735 students. We start school at 8:00 in the morning and leave at 3:00. We have a lunch break about 25 minutes long (from 12:35 to 1:00). The school food is OK. We have a salad bar and a snack bar. The cafeteria serves a main meal every day.
We have hardly any problems with violence or drugs in our school, but I know that in some inner-city schools it can be real bad.
Your next question: Yes, we have homework almost every day. How much we have depends on the teachers. *We* have lots of homework.
For subjects I have: English, German, Algebra, Biology, Afro-European Literature, Jazz Ensemble, and P.E. David has: U.S. History, American Literature, German, Chemistry, Band, Algebra, and Art. Our teachers are very nice and we enjoy all our classes.
We've really enjoyed writing to you and it would be great if we could write each other regularly.

Jeremy and David

P.S.: Why don't you send us some photos of yourselves via 'snail mail'? David would like to know what you look like.

☞ Find out from this page who Sylvia, Patricia, Jeremy and David are and how they got to know each other.
To get a better picture of the boys, make notes about each of them and arrange the information in the form of two networks.
Then write what you think the girls' first letter was *or* what their reply to the boys' letter might be.

→ Option 1: What to say in the USA
→ Option 14: Writing practice: formal letters
→ Option 19: A mixed bag of grammar

How an American high school is organized

In group work, pair work or on your own, use the information you have from the first three pages of the unit and from this page to develop an American high school quiz. It should consist of about 20 questions. Then use your quizzes to test your knowledge of American high schools.

List of activities at school

- Black Students' Association
- Chess Club
- Cheerleading
- Debate
- Drama Club
- French Club
- Math Team
- Music Ensemble
- Newspaper
- Science Club
- Spanish Club
- Yearbook

age	grade		
17	12	seniors	senior high school
16	11	juniors	
15	10	sophomores	
14	9	freshmen	junior high school
13	8		
12	7		
elementary school			

Info box Each student has his or her own personal schedule. In many schools the schedule is the same every day from Monday to Friday. That means the students do the same subjects in the same order at the same time.

- Teachers in an American high school have their own rooms, so students move from classroom to classroom to their different teachers. There are often only three to five minutes between lessons.
- Students don't repeat a year as some students have to in Germany, but they can repeat a class in a certain subject. If students fail a subject, they can do additional work in summer school during the summer vacation and then pass the subject.
- Subjects are divided into requirements and electives. Requirements are subjects students have to take. Electives are subjects students can choose to take. These are often subjects like Art, Shop, Music, Drama, or Computer Applications.
- Sports and extra-curricular activities are very important in American schools. There is often a large choice of activities throughout the year. However, students do different sports in different seasons. Practice takes place after school.

SPORTS PROGRAM DUNLAP HIGH SCHOOL

FALL	WINTER	SPRING
Cross-country	Basketball	Track and field
Football	Gymnastics	Baseball
Volleyball	Wrestling	Lacrosse
Soccer	Swimming	Tennis
	Hockey	Golf

Project Prepare a wall display: school life in the USA – school life in Germany. Here are some aspects to consider: subjects, schedule, time spent at school, the age of students, extra-curricular activities, importance of sports, role of guidance counselors, free-time activities.

L

→ Listening comprehension, p. 20 → Option 2: Schools in Britain

Focus on WORDS Talking about people

In their letter Jeremy and David told the girls quite a lot about their hobbies, their interests and their opinions about certain things. From what they wrote you can imagine that they are both active and athletic. David might be quite a sensitive person if he writes poems. They're probably both popular with other students. However, they didn't say anything about their +appearance. From the photograph on the left you can see what they actually look like, what kind of clothes they wear, the kind of hairstyles they have.
You might also be able to say a few things about their character, whether you think they are +outgoing, +casual, or friendly. But until you meet them, you won't know what they are really like.

1 Collecting words

Collect words and phrases that are related to people and put them in one of the four groups a-d. The text above will help you.

a How can you describe people?

Somebody has short brown hair, wears glasses, …

Somebody is	tall, +slim, +gorgeous, lively, … +familiar to, popular with, married to, … sb. a friend, a relative, a stranger, … a student, a teacher, …

b How do people behave towards other people?

They	love argue with admire …	other people.

c +Traits of character

People are	shy, confident, +self-conscious, polite, impatient, funny, +spoiled, …

d Abilities and interests

Some people	enjoy sport, like skiing, … write poems, +paint pictures, … are +fond of music, …

2 Words in use

a Say what you think these four people are like. Why do you have this impression of them?

b How would you describe yourself and how would you like to be?

c Some people think 'shy' is a positive trait of character, others think it is a negative one. Choose other traits of character and decide whether they are positive or negative for you.
Then compare your lists of 'positive' and 'negative' words with a partner's lists. Give reasons for your decisions and discuss the differences.

– Find out from the text on the right what THE DUNLAP STUDENT VOICE is.
– Then read the sentences below.
– The phrases next to the sentences will help you to say what pupils working for THE STUDENT VOICE think about their work.

THE DUNLAP STUDENT VOICE NO. 1

"I do not agree with a word you say, but I will defend to the death your right to say it." Voltaire

THE STUDENT VOICE. At last students will be able to express their opinions freely. We are not under the heavy thumb of the principal and the teachers. Will it last, or will we have to give up like so many other student organizations that started with so much hope? It's up to you, and you, and you! ...

1. We needed an organization and a magazine **run** by students only.	The first pupil feels that they needed … **which** are …
2. **Encouraged** by a number of seniors, we decided to produce THE STUDENT VOICE.	The second pupil believes that they decided … **because** they were …
3. We had a lot of fun **planning** everything, **talking** to people and **writing** the articles.	The third pupil mentions they had … **while** they were …
4. **Having produced** the first number, we felt quite proud.	… says they felt … **after** they had …
5. **Not being** sure about the reactions of the teachers and the students, we were a bit worried.	… mentions that they were … **because** they weren't …
6. **Although not considering** ourselves an environmental group, we will try to discuss environmental issues.	… that they … **although** they don't …
7. Josh found out about reusable cups **before speaking** to the principal about the styrofoam cups in the cafeteria.	… Josh found out … **before** he …

As you can see, the participle clause in the first sentence is similar to a relative clause – like the ones on p.9. What does it give additional information about?
From the column on the right you can see that the participle clauses in sentences 2-7 are similar to <u>adverbial sub-clauses</u>. Decide for each of the six participle clauses whether it is similar to a clause of reason, a clause of time, or a clause of concession.
Now look at sentences 4-7 and find out from the forms in bold print: What can you do to express that one action took place before another? How do you make a participle clause negative? How are the clauses in sentences 6 and 7 different from the ones in sentences 2-5?

→ Grammar 1: 3a, b (p.129) → Exercises 3-6

Turbo brain*

Finally compare the following three sentences:

Having complained about the cups in the cafeteria before, Josh hoped to be successful soon.
The cafeteria manager **having complained** recently, too, Josh now had a partner in his fight.
With more and more students **complaining**, the principal finally got rid of the cups.

Who had complained in the first sentence? Who had complained in the second sentence, and who was complaining in the last sentence?
– How did you come to your decision?
Now try to translate the three sentences into German. Be careful: You must find a conjunction for the 'with' in the last sentence.

→ Grammar 1: 3c (p.130)

A break from grammar

Look at the motto of THE STUDENT VOICE and discuss it in class.

*Diese Struktur muß lediglich verstanden, nicht angewendet werden.

1 First prize: Ice-cream for two at Enrico's Ice-cream Parlor

Present participle or past participle?

a After the summer vacation the Dunlap students found the following competition on the school notice-board:

Can you guess ...? *Enrico's vacation competition for seniors*

Your answers should be handed to Desiree Vance before October 10th.

1. ... the names of the two people who were (sunbathe) on the beaches of California?
2. ... the name of the girl who was (invite) to go to Mexico by her grandma?
3. ... the titles of the soap operas (watch) during the vacation by most students?
4. ... the addresses of two people (see) regularly hand in hand at the ice-cream parlor?
5. ... the store (offer) the prettiest dresses for our Father-Daughter Dance?
6. ... whose car was (drive) more than 5,000 miles in only three weeks?
7. ... the places (visit) by the students that took part in the foreign-language trips?
8. ... the number of movies (see) by the 'average' Dunlap student?
9. ... whose eyes were (glue) to a computer monitor for more than 6 hours a day?
10. ... who has been (send) lots of letters from Germany via modem?

b *Make up a similar competition in which you try to use a number of present and past participles as in the sentences above.*

2 The good old days ...

a One of the letters from Dunlap told the German pupils about ...

Look at the *Rules for teachers* and the column on the right. Then complete each rule with a participle clause.

Rules for teachers · 1872

1. *Teachers ... should clean the chimneys every day.*
2. *Teachers ... will get lower wages at the end of the week.*
3. *Teachers ... normally have one evening a week for this purpose. Those ... may have two evenings.*
4. *In their free time teachers should read The Bible or other books ...*
5. *Women teachers ... will have to give up their job at once.*
6. *A good sum of money ... is absolutely necessary for the time when a teacher is no longer able to teach.*
7. *Any teacher ... is seen as unfit to carry out the job any longer.*
8. *Teachers ... will be paid 25 cents more per week.*

work at this school
forget to bring coal to school
look for a wife
go to church regularly

write to improve their behavior
show an interest in marriage
save from the weekly wages

smoke, drink alcohol or visit public places of amusement
do their job to the expectations of the community for five years

b *Make up some rules which you think teachers today should follow.*

Just for fun

Just for fun

What's the definition of 'illegal'? – An eagle feeling bad and unable to fly.
Why is 'u' the unhappiest letter? – It's the letter stuck in the middle of all trouble.
What lies on the ground with one hundred feet up in the air? – A centipede lying on its back.

3 Read the following part of a manuscript for THE STUDENT VOICE and exchange opinions on the topic.
The editors who saw the manuscript decided to ask the author to make it more formal.
Imagine you were the author: Identify the sub-clauses and see if you can change them into participle clauses for your article in THE STUDENT VOICE.

A violent society by Kimberley Porch

Violence in our society seems to be increasing all the time. When I read a new survey on violent behavior among young people, I found several explanations for this development. Here are some of the things that are mentioned in the survey:
When they talk to each other, adults usually look at each other and smile. But when they talk to children, many adults don't smile. And they also often ignore children's questions. That means they don't have proper conversations with their children. These children don't learn to talk about problems, and in later life they might try to solve problems through violence.
A number of adults hit their children. Although they know that this doesn't really help, they pretend that physical punishment is necessary. And because they see all the violence in their families, young people often behave violently outside their home. ...

4 In English, please: A notice-board at a German school

Wherever possible, use a participle clause.

[1] picture frames [freɪmz]

5

Samuel Morse (1791-1872), an American artist and inventor

Today it is computers and modems, 150 years ago it was the telegraph and the Morse code.
Read the text and then put the words in brackets in the right form. Use participle clauses where it is possible.

Samuel Morse (become) an inventor after (try) unsuccessfully to be a professional painter. (Return) from Britain, where he (study), he quickly realized that he couldn't sell his pictures on the US market.
(Know) this, one fact (seem) surprising today: Morse (think) of himself as a painter even after (successfully invent) a new way of sending messages quickly from one place to another. (Work) harder than ever before in his life, Morse finally (succeed) in sending his first message from Washington, D.C. to Baltimore in 1844. His Morse code, a system of dots and dashes, (make) him a rich man.
About one hundred years after his death, in 1982, people suddenly (become) interested in Morse's paintings – one of his paintings (sell) unexpectedly in Paris for $3.2 million.

6 From different letters sent to Dunlap (Participles – special uses)

Read the following texts carefully. Although there are some grammatical forms in the texts that you don't know, you should be able to understand them. – Try to explain what the texts have to do with a kitchen and a classroom. Don't look at the texts while you are doing this.

1. … At the moment our school **is having** *some classrooms modernized*. So far we **have had** *new windows and a new floor put in*. Originally our principal wanted **to have** *everything done* by firms. But now he has decided that we **won't have** *the walls done* by a firm. We'll paint our classroom ourselves together with Frau Hartmüller. I'm sure that'll be fun. …

2. … Last week Herr Helms, a maths teacher and an expert in Asian cooking, cooked a Chinese meal with us in our small school kitchen. First we **observed** *him doing* the preparations. Then we took over and he only gave us instructions. He seemed very pleased with our work – while we were cooking, you couldn't **see** *anyone making* a mess, you couldn't **hear** *people complaining* and, what is also very important, you couldn't **smell** *anything burning*. …

You will have seen that all the verbs in bold print are in some way followed by a present or a past participle. Look at each text again separately. What is the infinitive of each verb in bold print? What exactly is each verb followed by?
Try to translate the sentences that have a verb in bold print. Compare the English and the German sentences. How did you translate the participle into German? Compare and discuss different solutions.

→ Grammar 1: 4 (p.130-131)

Now try to put the words of these sentences in the right order:

1. I – over there – can – out of the window – somebody – climbing – see. 2. have – had – repaired – your CD-player – you? 3. something – burning – smelled – in the kitchen – Susie. 4. they – into the classroom – came – laughing. 5. for help – he – shouting – ran away.

6. becoming excited – could feel – Alan – the crowd. 7. recently – have had – checked – our heating – we. 8. reading – on the floor – lay – she. 9. Jenny – can – hear – practising – you – the guitar? 10. what to do – in the shop – thinking about – they – were standing.

R 7 But didn't you say …? *Check if you can still use reported speech correctly.*

1. My new neighbour is terrible. – But didn't you say last week he *was* very nice? (be)
2. Susan loves working in the garden. – But she told me she … working in the garden. (not like)
3. Tom went to the theatre last weekend. – But yesterday you said he … to the cinema. (go)
4. Perhaps we'll buy a new car. – Oh, I thought you … to buy a new one. (not want)
5. I built a cupboard for our kitchen last week. – Well, yesterday you said you … anything. (not do)

Cornelsen

Hinweise für Eltern und Lehrkräfte

Mit dem Recorder und dem Computer lernen

Textcassetten

Britische und amerikanische Sprecher/-innen geben Aussprachemodelle für den aktiven Gebrauch des Englischen. Um die wichtige Fertigkeit des Hörverstehens auch weiterhin regelmäßig zu schulen, enthalten die Cassetten zusätzlich eine Reihe von *Extra Listening* – Hörverstehenstexten, deren mögliche Einsatzorte im Schülerbuch gekennzeichnet sind. Für das vierte Englischlernjahr sind wahlweise folgende Cassetten lieferbar:

(Fortsetzung nächste Seite)

1 Cassette zum Schülerbuch (Kurzfassung)

Die Cassette umfaßt alle Lieder und Haupttexte, eine Reihe zusätzlicher Hörverstehenstexte (Extra Listening) sowie einige Abschnitte aus dem A-Teil.
Der Cassette ist ein Übungsheft zu den Hörverstehenstexten beigefügt.

2 Cassetten zum Schülerbuch (Vollfassung)

Dieser umfangreichere Cassettensatz enthält außerdem die Hörverstehenstexte am Ende der Units, alle zusätzlichen Hörverstehenstexte (Extra Listening), zahlreiche Texte aus dem A-Teil der Units und den *Options.* Das Übungsheft ist ebenfalls beigefügt.

Diskette zum Schülerbuch

English Coach ist ein Computerprogramm, mit dem sich Vokabeln abwechslungsreich üben lassen. So kann man den Wortschatz nach Lektionen, nach Wortarten, nach Schwierigkeitsgrad, für einen oder mehrere Lerner wiederholen. Das Programm „merkt sich" gewußte und nicht gewußte Vokabeln und führt durch ein ausgeklügeltes Verfahren zur Beherrschung des bearbeiteten Wortschatzes.
Sofort abrufbare Informationen zum Arbeitsstand, ein Testmodus und ausdruckbare Vokabellisten runden das Programm ab.

Bitte in Druckschrift ausfüllen

Name / Vorname

Straße / Hausnummer

Postleitzahl / Ort

Ort / Datum

Unterschrift der / des Erziehungsberechtigten

Bitte freimachen

Antwortkarte

Cornelsen

Verlagskontor

33598 Bielefeld

a Trouble spot Infinitive or gerund after certain verbs

You already know that there are verbs which can be followed by a gerund or an infinitive with little or no change in meaning: *She likes playing tennis./She likes to play tennis.*

A few verbs, however, can be followed by **a gerund or an infinitive** with **different meanings**:

(to) **remember doing** sth.	sich daran erinnern, daß/wie man etwas getan hat
(to) **remember to do** sth.	daran denken, etwas zu tun
(to) **forget doing** sth.	vergessen, daß/wie man etwas getan hat
(to) **forget to do** sth.	vergessen, etwas zu tun

⚠ Be careful: *(to) stop* is followed by the gerund when it means "mit etwas aufhören", e.g.
He stopped buying newspapers. (= Er hörte auf, Zeitungen zu kaufen.)
But, like other verbs, *(to) stop* can be followed by a *to*-infinitive ("…, um zu …"), e.g.
He stopped (in order) to buy newspapers. (= Er hielt an, um Zeitungen zu kaufen.)

Fill in the correct form of these verbs and an infinitive or a gerund to make sentences. Then translate the sentences into German.

1. Tina can't wash her hair. She (forget / buy) some shampoo when she went to the supermarket. 2. I've (stop / read) that magazine. It's boring. 3. David will never (forget / be) in Los Angeles during the last earthquake. 4. When I phoned Liz last night, I (forget / tell) her what time the concert started. 5. It gets quite cold in the evening, so (remember / take) a warm pullover. 6. Can you please (stop / do) that? It makes me really angry. 7. Whose drink is this? I don't (remember / order) it. 8. My watch has stopped. I must (remember / get) a new battery. 9. How can David say he hasn't got the book? I (remember / give) it to him. 10. I'm hungry. Can we (stop / eat) our sandwiches, please?

→ Vocabulary (p.145)

b Word builder's corner Compound adjectives from participles

Compound adjectives from present participles:

hard + working	→ **hard-working**	**Hard-working** people often suffer from stress.
adverb + present participle	→ compound adjective	*(**Schwer arbeitende** Menschen …)*

Compound adjectives from past participles:

carefully + planned	→ **carefully-planned**	It was a **carefully-planned** trip.
adverb + past participle	→ compound adjective	*(… eine **sorgfältig geplante** Reise)*

Compound adjectives can also consist of **adjective** + present/past participle *(good-looking, long-planned)* or **noun** + present/past participle *(oil-exporting, man-made)*.

Use the words from the boxes and translate the following German phrases into English.

langsam fließender Verkehr ➤ fleischexportierende Unternehmen ➤ ein krank aussehendes Tier ➤ weizenanbauende Landwirte ➤ ein gutaussehender Junge ➤ die schnell wachsende Bevölkerung ➤ eine unendliche Geschichte ➤ ölproduzierende Länder ➤ ein handgemachter Korb ➤ ein neugeborenes Kind ➤ ein gutorganisiertes Team ➤ ein hochentwickeltes Land ➤ ein schlecht gekochtes Essen

badly – fast – good – highly – never – new – sick – slow – well

(to) be born – (to) cook – (to) develop – (to) end – (to) export – (to) grow (2x) – (to) look (2x) – (to) make – (to) move – (to) organize – (to) produce –

animal – baby – basket – boy – company – country (2x) – farmer – hand – meal – meat – oil – population – story – team – traffic – wheat

Now make sentences. Example: The streets are always full of slow-moving traffic.

WAITING...

Take some time to look at the photos and speculate about what story they might tell. (Consider the title, the girl's behaviour, the expressions on her face, what is going on around her, and what might be going through her mind.)
Make notes for an outline of the story and compare different outlines before you read Eleanor Meek's story.

I hate this milkshake. I'll take chocolate next time. I push the half-full glass across the table. If there *is* a next time, that is. The way things are going, it doesn't even look like there's going to be *this time*.

I look at my watch – 7:36. OK, so he's only six minutes late; nothing to worry about ... Perhaps he missed the bus, or maybe he's as nervous as I am and is still at home, making himself look extra-gorgeous. That would be difficult though – Jake's already a "ten", as far as I'm concerned, with his thick dark hair and those beautiful green eyes.

I wonder what he'll be wearing tonight. I've only ever seen him in his school clothes. My friend Kate said she saw him in town one weekend in jeans and an old leather jacket. My heart races at the thought.

"Hey, dreamer! Wakey, wakey!"

I look up. The voice belongs to Andy. He's smiling and waving his hands in front of my face, playing the fool again. I smile back weakly, thinking, not for the first time, how silly he looks in his waiter's uniform. Tomato red trousers and a bow tie, his red hair under a white hat. Not very attractive.

"Another kiwi shake?" he asks. "I can see you enjoyed the last one."

I try to laugh but I can't. It's 7:42 and there's still no sign of Jake.

"I'll have a chocolate one," I say, wondering how long I can make it last. Andy goes to the kitchen. I'm feeling a bit self-conscious now. The diner is filling up with couples and groups of friends. Nobody I know, thankfully. Still, I'm sure they're wondering why I'm alone. There's a boy and girl at the next table. They're a bit older than me – about 16 or 17 – and they're laughing and holding hands across the table. Soon that'll be me and Jake.

"He likes you – I'm sure he does," Kate had said to me on Tuesday in the schoolyard.

I'd smiled across at him and he'd smiled back.

"A good sign," Kate had said, "Go and ask him out."

So I did. Right there and then. I asked Jake out. He said nothing for a moment, and that moment seemed like a lifetime to me. Then he spoke.

"OK," he said simply.

So here I am, waiting, at 7:56.

I'm uncomfortable now, I have to admit. Suddenly, I think of the horror of tomorrow at school. What will I say when my friends ask me how the evening was? "He didn't come." I imagine saying it, trying to sound casual, as if it doesn't matter. But however I say it, their faces are the same. There's pity in their eyes and Kate is saying, "He wasn't worth it, Em. Don't worry about it – there are lots more fish in the sea." But I don't want a fish. I want Jake.

The news will get around our whole year and people will laugh at me for the rest of my life. Everyone will think I wasn't good enough for him. It will be so embarrassing!

A familiar face appears opposite me.

"Cheer up. Here's your chocolate milkshake. It's on the house."

"Thanks, Andy," I say. I wish he'd stop being so nice to me. If he continues like that, I'll be crying into my milkshake in no time. "Listen …," he says, putting his hand over mine. "I finish in about five minutes. We could go out somewhere if you like."

I can't refuse. Andy's a clown but he knows when I need somebody to cheer me up. And at 8:09, it doesn't look as if anyone else will join me for the evening.

The diner is beginning to empty as people leave for the movies, or the skating-rink, or to go bowling. I feel silly now, dressed up like this. I even bought a new lipstick on the way home from school. Pink Passion, it's called. Tragic.

Andy goes away, then comes back from behind without his bow-tie and wearing a pair of jeans.

"You don't *have* to take me out, you know," I say. "I can handle it." But I'm just trying to sound confident – and Andy knows it.

"It's OK," he grins. "I'm not doing anything." He smiles playfully and I stand up and slowly pull on my coat.

"It's 8:15," I say, as if the time has some special meaning.

"Don't worry about it," replies Andy. "He'll regret it one day."

"But why did he say he'd meet me?" I'm thinking out loud. "Why, when I asked him out, did he say 'yes'? I don't understand."

Andy puts his arm around me. "Some guys just aren't able to say what they mean," he explains. "They're afraid of being honest. They say 'yes' when they mean 'no' and get into all kinds of unpleasant situations."

That's news to me, but I suppose it makes sense, and suddenly I find myself really losing interest in the gorgeous Jake. I stop by the door and turn to Andy. "So you think he's just a coward?" I ask.

"Yes," he replies. "Either that or he's crazy. I mean, what guy in his right mind wouldn't want to go out with my pretty little sister?"

I smile – my first real smile of the night.

"Right!" I say confidently, and link my arm through Andy's.

We'll go somewhere nice tonight, I think to myself. Because big brothers – especially those as kind and thoughtful as Andy – deserve to be spoiled sometimes.

(adapted from a story by Eleanor Meek, in *Just Seventeen*)

How close is your outline to E. Meek's story? (Where are the similarities/the differences? What in the photos on page 18 gave you the right clues? What led you in a different direction?)

Working with the text

1 A closer look at the characters in the story

a Go through the story and find out as much as possible about the narrator, especially about her feelings during the 40-minute wait in the diner. Draw a graph of her emotions. Add to it how she feels at different times, what explanations the text gives, and your explanations for her feelings. Use this information and what you have learned from the Focus on Words-page (p.12) to give an oral or written character portrait of the narrator.

b The text gives quite a lot of information about Andy, but hardly any about Jake. What kind of person does Andy seem to be for the largest part of the story? How does the author of the story use him to make the story interesting? What kind of person do you think Jake is? (Think of different reasons for his behaviour. What was he doing/thinking while the girl was waiting for him? Do you think he will talk to her the next day?)

2 Beyond the text

a The story could – without a major change to the storyline – have a boy as its main character. Obviously some things would have to be changed – others might be changed – if the story was told from a boy's point of view. Rewrite the whole story or part of the story from a boy's point of view. See if the changes made by the girls in your class are different from those made by the boys. – If so, try to find explanations for the differences.

b 'Kitsch' is the word used for low quality art and literature that tries to appeal to popular taste only. – What do you think? Is this story from a young people's magazine 'kitschy'? Why/Why not?

→ Option 3: Charles

L Listening comprehension The last dance of the year

You already know that apart from academic and practical work, social activities are very important at American high schools. One of these social activities is a dance called the 'prom'.
Try to make sense of the words in the box. This will help you to imagine what the 'prom' is. – Don't worry about unknown words; wait and see if listening to the tape will help you to understand them.
Exchange ideas in class about what you imagine the 'prom' to be.

> 11th grade   12th grade   formal clothes
> tuxedos   casual clothes   prom committee
> three fundraisers   tickets   dinner
> ushers   9:00   11:00   1:00   5:30   coronation
> 'afterprom'   movies   volleyball   bowling
> donuts   prizes

Now listen to the tape – if necessary more than just once – to find out exactly how 'The last dance of the year' is organized and what happens on the day of the prom.
Finally try to say what is illustrated in the little pictures on the right.

→ Option 13: Interpreting and translation practice

Unit 2 Washington, D.C.

"Knowledge will forever govern ignorance; and a people who mean to be their own governors must arm themselves with the power knowledge gives."
James Madison, 4th president of the USA (1809 to 1817)

WASHINGTON, D.C. – the center of political power in the USA

- *The capital of the world's most powerful nation*
- *The home of the president*
- *The seat of the federal government*
- *The place where Congress meets and the nation's laws are made*
- *The seat of the Supreme Court, the nation's highest court*
- *The headquarters of the FBI (Federal Bureau of Investigation)*
- *Also the home of America's military headquarters (the Pentagon)*
- *A city of magnificent buildings, national monuments and museums*

Facts about Washington, D.C.

- *The population of Washington, D.C. is about 610,000. The population of the Washington metropolitan area is nearly 4 million.*
- *Almost three-quarters of the city's population is non-white.*
- *Washington, D.C. is not a state and it is not in a state. It is an independent federal district (District of Columbia).*
- *There are few factories. Most people in Washington work in offices.*
- *The United States government is the largest employer in the city.*
- *No building can be taller than 13 stories (about 40 yards) so that the Capitol and the important monuments can be seen above everything else.*
- *Washington has a larger variety of trees than any other city in the world.*
- *There are over 600 parks in the city.*

Look at the information on this page about Washington, D.C. What is new to you, what did you know before?
In the bottom right-hand corner you can see the logo of the **Close Up Foundation**, an organization based in Washington. – Looking at the whole page, what kind of organization do you think it might be?

CLOSE UP FOUNDATION

→ Option 4: Creating a nation and a society

Focus on GRAMMAR Using sub-clauses

a First read the excerpt from a newspaper article. Then read the nine excerpts from Senator Dawson's talk.
In the senator's opinion: What is wrong with education in the USA? How can things be improved?

THE WASHINGTON NEWS, FRIDAY, JANUARY 21, 1994

In his talk to the National Conference of Teachers, Senator Dawson talked about the president's planned education reform and many of the problems we have in education today. He finished his talk with two questions which will have to be answered by the nation as a whole: "How can we make sure that our children have the knowledge they need to understand the society in which they live? How can we help our children to become active participants in American democracy?"

1 All of us have, at one time or another, met students **who** couldn't find our capital on a map, or **who** didn't know why our Constitution was written. …

2 Too many young people don't know enough about the men and women, the places and the events **that** have made our past and created our present. …

3 Our schools have, **although** our teachers are doing their best, too often failed to meet the expectations of the American people. …

4 Our democracy is in danger **because** our people don't know or understand enough about American history, government and geography. …

5 Of course, not all is bad. **When** I read the latest government report on education, I was very pleased. We are doing better than in the 1980s. …

6 But our country can only survive **if** we all learn from the fine schools, teachers, principals, parents and the good students of every race, class and background. …

7 Students need to take more courses in basic subjects **so that** they will have a better understanding of the world around them. …

8 The president's education reform mustn't be watered down **as** so many reforms **which** also started hopefully have been in the past. …

9 **Wherever** schools have high standards, students' results have improved a lot, **which** gives me hope for our future. …

b Work with a partner. Then compare and discuss your results in class:
- On the right you can find some of the senator's notes for his speech. Compare them with excerpts 1-4: As you can see, the senator used ➤ as a 'linking symbol' in his notes. How did he actually link his ideas in his speech?
- Identify all the sub-clauses in the excerpts and decide which of the following grammar terms is the right one for each sub-clause. – Start with the ones you are sure about:

conditional clause – clause of place – relative clause – clause of purpose – clause of time – clause of reason – clause of comparison – clause of concession

Notes for talk to NCT
– students ➤ not find capital – ➤ not know why Constitution written …
– not know enough – people, places, events ➤ make our past – create our present …
– schools – too often fail – meet expectations of the American people ➤ teachers – do their best …
– democracy – in danger ➤ people not know or understand enough – American history – government – geography …
…

- You will have noticed that sub-clauses can be put in different places in a sentence. Look carefully at all the sentences and find out where sub-clauses can be put. Then compare the punctuation in sentences where the sub-clauses are in different places. – How is it different from the punctuation in German?
- Finally, look again at excerpts 8 and 9. What does the 'which' refer to in excerpt 8? What does it refer to in excerpt 9? How is the difference shown in the punctuation?

→ Grammar 2: 1, 2 (p.132-134) → Exercises 1, 2

One answer to the questions asked by Senator Dawson is offered by the **Close Up Foundation**. The aim of **Close Up** is to help young people to understand more about the society they live in. **Close Up** hopes that this will also help them to become active participants in American democracy.
Here are some comments from **Close Up** participants.

1 I didn't realize that Close Up **brings** over 22,000 students to Washington every year.

2 Comparing programs from different years we discovered that the Close Up instructors **are improving** the courses all the time.

3 We heard from different people that Close Up **has** always **been** very objective about all political issues.

4 We learned that Close Up **has been bringing** students to Washington since 1970.

5 By the end of our one-week course we realized that we **had learned** a lot about the US system of government.

6 I noticed in our daily seminars and discussions that a number of students **knew** very little about the American political system.

7 Our instructor was pleased that most students **were working** really hard in the seminars.

8 In the weeks before my trip I was thrilled by the thought that I **would meet** young people from all over the States.

9 It wasn't quite clear to some students that the week **was going to be** an educational course, not a holiday.

These comments tell you, directly and indirectly, a lot about **Close Up** and about how the organization tries to help young people to become active participants in American democracy. What do you now know about the organization?

If you look again at the nine comments, you will notice that each consists of one complex sentence. The verb form in all the main clauses is the simple past. In each of the nine sub-clauses you can see a different verb form. – Decide for each sub-clause what the speaker wanted to refer to …

- a state that was valid in the past
- an activity that takes place regularly
- a state that started in the past and continues up to the present
- a 'future'-activity in the past
- an activity that started in the past and continues up to the present
- an activity that took place before a point in the past
- an activity that was in progress in the past
- an activity that is in progress

Ex *Here are some more complex sentences. Complete each sub-clause with the correct verb form.*

1. It was no problem for me to speak in front of our group although I (never / speak) in front of so many people before. 2. Our instructor talked about some important political issues with us so that we (be) well prepared for our discussion with the senator the next morning. 3. In one of our seminars we wrote letters to scientists who, at the moment, (work) on environmental projects. 4. We actually received some answers because we (be allowed) to use the Close Up fax machines. 5. On the first day our group listened to a talk that the instructors (give) to all students when they (arrive) in Washington. 6. We were taken to the Capitol, which (be) the home of Congress since the early 19th century. 7. In the seminar called 'Women in politics' we heard from Senator Petonita that she (fight) for the rights of minorities for more than twenty years.

→ Grammar 2: 3 (p.135) → Exercises 3, 6 L 9

Washington – a planned capital

- On arriving in Washington **Close Up** students first get to know the city. Look at this map of a section of Washington and find places that you have heard about.
- Now read the texts to find out what the Close Up instructor is telling the students about Washington.

"Washington is one of the few capital cities in the world whose site was actually chosen and developed to be a capital. The city is divided into four parts: Northeast, Northwest, Southeast and Southwest, with the Capitol as the central point. Most of the government buildings and monuments are in Northwest. The layout of the city reflects the system of government. The White House is connected directly to the Capitol, where Congress meets, and to the Supreme Court by a long wide avenue, Pennsylvania Avenue."

"The Vietnam Veterans Memorial is one of Washington's most recent monuments. For many Americans it is also the most moving one. The Vietnam War deeply divided the country. Many felt the United States should not be involved, others felt it was the duty of the United States to fight there. Written on the Memorial are the names of the 58,132 men who either lost their lives or who are still missing. The average age of the young men who fought in that war was 19."

"The White House is, of course, the home of the most famous government employee. The president and his family live at 1600 Pennsylvania Avenue. The White House is the oldest public building in Washington. Every president has lived here except George Washington, who was president before it was built. Until 1834 the White House had no running water, and gas lamps were only installed in 1848. The White House is open to visitors for two hours each day from Tuesday to Saturday. However, as you can imagine, one can't actually visit the president or go into the Oval Office, the room where he works."

"We will now look at some of the places tourists don't normally visit. I suppose you have heard that Washington has one of the highest murder rates in the United States. A lot of those murders are drug-related and take place in southeast Washington. Anacostia, which we are going to visit now, is an area where mainly poor black families live. It seems that few people know that some of the poorest areas in the city are less than a couple of miles from the White House."

Which German city would you choose for a group of American students visiting Germany? What would you tell them about it?

Project Make a poster, similar to these two pages, with pictures and texts about the German city you have chosen.

→ Exercise 5 → Listening comprehension, p.33 → Option 19: A mixed bag of grammar → Option 20: Linking ideas, linking sentences

During their seminars, Close Up students find out how the political systems in the USA and in other countries work.
The political life of a country is strongly influenced by its leaders. In the United States the most powerful politician is the president, in the United Kingdom it is the prime minister, and in Germany it is the +chancellor. The power these leaders have depends, however, on the country's political institutions.
In democracies the politicians +representing people in parliaments are +elected in free elections. The US parliament is called Congress and consists of two houses: the Senate and the House of Representatives. The UK parliament consists of the +House of Commons and the +House of Lords. In Germany it consists of the *Bundestag* and the *Bundesrat.*
Before elections politicians give speeches, appear on TV, and give interviews to newspapers and magazines. They try to explain their political views on certain issues and the policies of the party they represent.

1 Collecting and arranging words

Collect all the words related to politics in the text above and add them to one of the groups a-d. Go through pages 21-25 again and find more "political" words. Also add the words from the box.

> +abolish/introduce laws – +capitalism – civil rights – +communism – Democrats – +dictatorship – +equality – fight for free elections – freedom of speech – govern a country – government – Greens – join/leave a party – Liberals – +opposition – party leader – Republicans

a Political systems and institutions
- democracy, +monarchy, …
- parliament/congress, …

b People in politics
- president, +minister, …
- Christian Democrats, Social Democrats, Socialists, …
- voter, +candidate, …

c Political activities – what politicians do/what political parties do
- try to come into power/stay in power, form a +coalition, convince the voters of …/to …, …
- have debates on …, make laws about …, …
- protect the environment, +reform the educational system, …

d Political activities – what citizens do
- vote for a candidate/a party, support/… a party, work in community projects, …
- fight for the rights of minorities, fight for/against …, …

2 Words in use

a "Only the most brilliant people should be sent to parliament, and they should all have been to a university." What do *you* think?

b Choose a political issue which is being discussed locally or throughout the nation. Collect opinions about the issue in your class and talk about them. Then write a letter to an English-speaking pen-friend, telling her or him about the issue and your opinions on it.

→ Option 15: Making notes – developing a network

1

THE WASHINGTON NEWS

Washington – city of writers

by Patricia Davis

★ you can imagine, Washington is full of men and women ★ job it is to write about all kinds of subjects. ★ it is often necessary for them to get information quickly, a group of writers ★ call themselves *Washington Independent Writers* have now produced **A Writer's Guide to Washington.**
Here is an excerpt from the guide about the most important library in Washington, the *Library of Congress:*

"*The Library of Congress (LC),* ★ is the largest library in the world, has about 100 million items. More than 25 million of them are books. Every year about 1.5 million items are added to the library. ★ you looked at each item for one minute and worked for eight hours a day, five days a week, it would take you about 780 years to see everything.

The library is so busy ★ *LC* librarians strongly advise people to use other libraries in the city first ★ they come to the *LC*. And they ask everyone to remember the following: ★ *LC* books can't be borrowed, you will have to use them in one of the reading rooms.

You will sometimes have to wait as long as two hours ★ you have your books, ★ it is good to bring other work for the time you are waiting.
★ it sometimes takes so long to get a book, many writers prefer the *LC* to any other library. ★ you can make an informed decision, you should read the free guides to the library in the Main Reading Room. At the library shop you can buy a *Guide to the Library of Congress,* ★ is also very useful. And finally: ★ you don't know how to find material, ask the librarians, they are always very helpful."

Read this newspaper article to find out about an important institution in Washington.

Give a short summary of the article, then try to fit these linking words into the text:

because – who – before – which – so that – if – although – if – that – because – until – as – so – whose – which

2 Questions asked by visitors to the Library of Congress

So many visitors ask the same things that a brochure has been produced which answers the 25 questions most often asked by people who are in the library for the first time. Here are six of these questions.
Read the questions on the left and the incomplete answers in the middle. Then complete each answer with a sub-clause from the jumbled list on the right.

1 When was the library opened?	The first real library building was opened in 1897, ★.	whereas most of the other materials are in the Madison Building
2 Are there any guided tours of the library?	Yes, and ★, visitors can watch a film about the library.	where about 5,000 people work
3 Where are the books and the other materials?	About 500 miles of books are in the Jefferson Building and the Adams Building, ★.	if you want to have a proper meal
4 How can I find out about public events in the library?	★, there is a free monthly Calendar of Events.	before they go on a tour
5 Where can I get something to eat in the library?	There are snack bars in every building. The cafeteria in the Madison Building is best ★.	so that everyone is well-informed about the events
6 How many visitors does the Library of Congress serve?	Every year the library, ★, serves 2.5 million people.	after the library had been in the Capitol for about 100 years

3 Preparations …

Here is a conversation between two Close Up students. Read it to find out what the preparations are for, then choose the right form for the verbs in brackets. Sometimes there is more than one solution.

We (prepare) everything tomorrow afternoon so that we (not have) anything to do in the evening.

(you / invite) all the instructors we (have) so far, and (you / inform) all the students in the course yet?

Yes, so far everyone (accept) our invitation although some of the instructors (seem) to be very busy.

I (make) a list of what still (have to) be done. Here it (be). I'm sorry if it (look) quite long.

If we (not find) some people to help us, we (probably / not be able) to do everything in time.

I (not think) people (mind) if we (still / be busy) when they (arrive). Nobody (expect) us to be a professional party service.

True. The most important thing (be) to bring people together so they (get) to know each other better.

I'm sure it (make) a difference to the rest of the week. People (feel) freer to express their opinions in the seminars after our welcome party.

4 Political decisions

a To learn how far-reaching a political decision can be, the Close Up students had to take the role of advisers to the US government in one of their seminars. Their task was to find out what would happen if the government raised the tax on gasoline by 100%.

Look at the 'network of possible effects' that the students produced. Then try to add a few more possible effects.
Finally, present your thoughts to *your* 'government', the class. This is how you can start:
"If we raised the tax on gas/petrol, fewer people might use cars. And if fewer cars … . But we also have to consider other effects: If …"

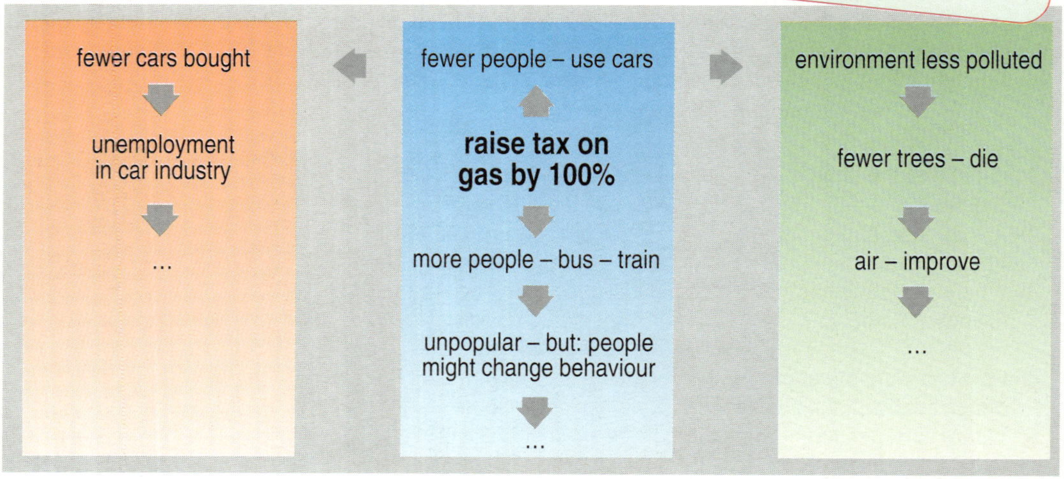

b Here is another, perhaps less serious problem which 'your government' has to solve: "Pupils should be allowed to finish their school education whenever they like."
Make a network together with a partner, then present your thoughts to the class.

→ Option 13: Interpreting and translation practice

5 Heard on the Close Up coach

If this was a German dialogue, these words would be missing: *hoffentlich – vermutlich – gern – wahrscheinlich – leider.* Here are the English words *am afraid – are likely to – enjoy – hope – suppose.* Find the right place for them. What are the matching German words?
What do you notice about the word classes in the two languages?

Do you … going on guided tours of a city?

I … not. But I … it's a good way to get a first impression of a city.

Do you think we'll have any problems going through Anacostia with our coach?

I … not. Did you know it was once a very high-class part of the city?

I didn't. All I know is that you … get killed if you go there on your own. Many taxi-drivers refuse to take people there.

What would these sentences be in English?

1. Ich würde morgen lieber ins Kennedy Center gehen. (prefer) 2. Wahrscheinlich werden wir weniger sehen als wir möchten. (be likely to) 3. Spazierst du auch gern durch Kaufhäuser in großen Städten? (like) 4. Wenn ich die Wahl hätte, würde ich vermutlich lieber in New York leben. (suppose / prefer) 5. Ich habe meine Eltern noch nicht angerufen. Hoffentlich machen sie sich keine Sorgen. (hope) 6. Anscheinend sind wir jetzt schon in Anacostia. (seem)

→ Vocabulary (p. 151)

6 The Smithsonian Institution

When the Close Up bus turned into Constitution Avenue, the guide said, "The area between Constitution Avenue and Independence Avenue is called the Mall. You may be surprised to hear that the Mall was influenced by an Englishman more than by anybody else. …"

Continue the guide's explanations. Wherever you find the symbol ➤ in the prompts, the linking word from the box on the right is needed.

The original Smithsonian Institution Building

In the 1820s – English scientist ➤ name – James Smithson – give – all his money – US government / he – think – Britain – be – class society ➤ USA – be – democratically governed country / that's why – believe ➤ money – be spent best – USA / the Americans – not want – accept – money ➤ offer – to them, – but finally – Congress – accept – present / 1846, ➤ be seventeen years after Smithson's death, – Smithsonian Institution – found / original building – still – see – western part – Mall / ➤ look – on the Mall, – see – a Smithsonian museum / altogether, – thirteen Smithsonian museums, ➤ twelve – be – Washington / out of these twelve, – nine – Mall / one – New York /
you – have – one afternoon – free ➤ can visit – National Air and Space Museum, – perhaps – most popular museum – Washington / every year – more than nine million people – visit – this museum / there – see – Apollo 11, ➤ carry – first astronauts ➤ walk – moon / ➤ you – there, – touch – real moon rock – visit – Skylab, – first American space station – ➤ astronauts – live – work in / ➤ interested – history of flying, – see – some of – early flying machines, – e.g. – plane ➤ carry – Wright brothers – distance – 300 meters – 1903 / also – special cinema – museum ➤ see – different films on flying / ➤ watch – these films, – feel ➤ you yourself – fly – plane

whose
whereas
that
when
which

wherever
of which

so that

which / who
while
which / if
that
where
while / as if

Words Words Words

a **Which is "bigger"?**

Put together pairs of words from the box. One word must be "bigger" than the other.

road – skyscraper – cathedral – sword – church – country – village – house – hill – county – CITY – knife – van – motorway – mountain – lorry

b **Trouble spot** Pronunciation *Odd one out. Which word has got a different vowel sound?*

1. [ʌ] once – done – gone – worry – enough
2. [e] bed – said – threat – say – men
3. [ɜː] girl – heard – world – hurt – preferred – heart
4. [ʊ] push – butcher – foot – pull – front
5. [ɑː] chance – aunt – laugh – because
6. [ɒ] bottle – comb – watch – cough – cost

c **Word builder's corner** Negative prefixes

un-, in-, dis- and *non-* are the most common negative prefixes. *un-* is used more often than any other. But it is not possible to predict which prefix is used with a particular word. The correct forms must simply be learned. (For those of you who know Latin or French: *in-/im-/ir-* are used almost exclusively with words of Latin origin.)

un-	**in-**	**im-** *(before p)*	**ir-** *(before r)*	**dis-**	**non-**
unborn	incomplete	impatient	irregular	disadvantage	non-fiction
unfriendly	independent	imperfect	irresponsible	disagree	non-profit-making
unhealthy	indirect	impersonal		disappear	non-returnable
unmarried	informal	impolite		discontinue	non-stop
unnatural	inhuman	impossible		dishonest	non-violent
untidy	intolerant	improbable		dislike	non-white

Find a word that fits in.

1. I've been waiting for 20 minutes and I'm beginning to get … . 2. I see things differently. That's why I … with you. 3. When the police arrived, the gang had already … . 4. Did you know that "(to) steal" is an … verb? 5. The railway link to Clayton was not very popular, so it was decided to … it. 6. Julia likes her job, but she … getting up so early. 7. No, you don't have to wear a tie. It's just an … meeting with a few friends. 8. In wars people often behave like … monsters. 9. You have done well in all your tests. It is highly … that you will fail this one. 10. Charities are … organizations. 11. It's 8.30 now, so it's almost … to catch the 8.40 train. 12. The climate in that region is so … that it doesn't attract any tourists.

Use a dictionary and write down words with the prefix "un-" whose roots you already know. You'll be surprised how many there are. – Example: uncertain – certain, …

In English, please *Translate the following phrases and sentences and make similar ones using the words from the list above.*

1. ein unfertiger Roman 2. ein unordentliches Zimmer 3. ihr unverantwortliches Verhalten 4. eine unhöfliche Antwort 5. große, unpersönliche Institutionen 6. eine unvollständige Sammlung 7. sein unehrliches Verhalten 8. Es ist verantwortungslos, Einwegflaschen zu kaufen. 9. Mein Bruder redet ununterbrochen. 10. Gewaltfreie Proteste können viel erreichen.

One sentence in the following story says, "… he had forgotten that you can only climb to the top on the backs of other people and sooner or later they would hold out their hands."
What do you think this sentence means, and what do you expect the story will be about?

How will you vote, Senator?

"Senator, what are your feelings about the president's plans not to send military aid to the Middle East?"

The girl who had asked the question was sitting at the front of the Close Up group in Senator Young's office. She was a serious-looking student, who had asked a number of interesting questions during the seminar. "I think the president is saying what a lot of Americans feel," the senator said. "There are quite a lot of people here in Washington who say that as a nation we should stop selling weapons altogether and retrain the people in those industries to do other jobs. I personally have never been convinced that military aid is the best solution to a political problem."

He was pleased to see that the students were smiling at his comments. He liked to present himself as a popular, friendly politician who was able to communicate with his nation's youth. That was not difficult for the students to accept. The senator was tall, good-looking and appeared to be quite youthful, although he was surely old enough to be the father of any one of them.

"And how will you vote after this afternoon's debate in the Senate?"

The senator smiled at the young girl. "You don't give up easily. Are you sure you aren't from the *Washington Post*?" The group laughed. "As you have learned in your seminars, it is important to look at all aspects of an issue very carefully before you make a decision. And that's exactly what I'll do."

"Yes, but Senator, what's your opinion about …"

The girl tried to continue with another question, but Senator Young looked at his watch. "Well, thank you for attending this seminar. I hope you enjoyed it as much as I did." "Thank you," came the reply from several of the participants as they got up from their seats.

"You're more than welcome," smiled Senator Young. With a warm smile he watched the group of young Close Up students walk out of his office, their seminar papers under their arms.

Senator Young checked his watch again. Luckily the meeting hadn't gone on too long, so he still had enough time for lunch before the debate on the president's plans started. One thing was certain: the debate in the Senate wouldn't be as simple as a student seminar. The vote would be close, very close indeed. At that moment everybody was being lobbied heavily to vote one way or the other.

"Senator, don't forget you have a meeting at one o'clock," said his secretary, coming into his room with several documents for him to read.

"I do?" He checked his diary. "Who with?"

"Lloyd Maunders. At the Georgetown Inn."

The senator checked his watch again. "I still have a few things to do. Could you call a cab for me? I'll be ready in about twenty minutes."

"Yes, sir. I'll do it at once," she said and left the room. The senator sat down at his desk. So Lloyd Maunders was in Washington and wanted to see him for lunch. The senator knew the name. He came from a family of industrialists. They built vehicle and machine parts and employed several thousand people in his state. Lloyd Maunders had also been a major financial supporter of his campaign. The senator remembered that Maunders had tried to see him the week before, but he had been too busy.

Senator Young called his secretary. "Did he mention what he wanted to see me about?"

"No, Senator," she replied.

Senator Young left the Capitol and took a taxi to Georgetown. It was a beautiful warm day, although fall was clearly in the air. The summer heat was over and the leaves were beginning to turn brown. The summer crowds of tourists had also grown thinner, although many were still looking at the sights. At the Kennedy Center the cab driver drove along Wisconsin Avenue and into Georgetown. "The Georgetown Inn," said the cab driver as they stopped. Senator Young saw the hotel and paid the driver.

They met in a private dining-room. The senator shook hands with Lloyd Maunders and was introduced to another man, whose name was Carl Peterson. The name was familiar to him from his home state. Petersons were large employers, also industrialists, not the largest, but certainly powerful enough to make employment figures a political issue. He wondered what had brought them together. And why they wanted to speak to their senator. "We are still waiting for our third guest," said Maunders, the youngest of the group. "His flight must be late. But we can certainly start with a cocktail and a look at the menu. I believe the fish is especially good today." The senator accepted his drink and began to relax. He hoped it would be nothing more than a social meeting. Local businessmen have to meet their senator when they are in Washington to give themselves the feeling they are important. And these people had supported his campaign with large amounts of money. To have lunch with them was the least he could do.

Just then the door opened and their last guest arrived. Warren Mitchell held out his hand to the senator. The senator felt the old hand in his. It was still powerful, still healthy. The old man must be eighty, Senator Young thought to himself. But then the names came together, and he knew why they were there. They were all in the weapons industry. Every one of them. Individually, it hadn't made sense. Together, it did. Maunders vehicle parts, Peterson machine parts, but Mitchell – military equipment. The man who put the parts together.

"First, may I offer you my congratulations on reaching the Senate," said the old man, shaking Senator Young's hand warmly. "I'm sure the state will be very proud of you."

"Thank you," said the senator. "It's very kind of you to say that."

Then, like an old Civil War general, Warren Mitchell waved a hand and the four men sat down at the table.

* * *

Lunch was served and the men ate without discussing anything of importance. During coffee, Warren Mitchell sat back in his chair and said, "We are worried about the debate in the Senate over the president's plans."

"So is everybody else," said the senator. "It will be a very close vote."

"I feel we should send those weapons," said the older man. "I believe we should show that America has a clear foreign policy and is prepared to support a government we can do business with."

"Guns are not a solution to a political problem," replied the senator.

"There is another issue," said Carl Peterson. "It is jobs. If the Senate supports the president, we could lose millions of dollars in lost contracts. We need those contracts. Without them it will mean that thousands of jobs will have to go. Those jobs will be in factories in your state, Senator."

"And if they don't buy weapons from us," said Lloyd Maunders, "they will only buy them from some other government."

"The president has a lot of support," said the senator. "His plans to retrain the workers in the weapons industries are popular with a number of senators."

"They would be popular with me if I had a sausage factory," said the old man.

"The president's plans are certainly interesting," said Carl Peterson. "But he is moving too quickly. We need time to adapt and restructure."

"And we can't do that from one day to the next," said Lloyd Maunders. "Your vote could help to make sure that a large number of men and women in your state will enjoy full employment for some years until we have restructured. We need time."

"I would say a large number of *voters* in your state will enjoy full employment," said Warren Mitchell. "And there aren't many alternative jobs in some areas. If they lose their jobs, they might remember that Senator Young was the man who shut down their factories and left his own people unemployed."

The senator remained thoughtful while the conversation continued. In his fight to get to the

Senate he had forgotten that you can only climb to the top on the backs of other people and sooner or later they would hold out their hands. He also enjoyed the privileges of his office. The thought that he could lose that office was unbearable.
The meeting came to an end and the four men left the hotel to take separate cabs. Before he left, Lloyd Maunders put his hand lightly on the senator's arm and said, "Senator, it may help to remember that you would never have gotten to the Senate without our financial help. Without it, you will not return to the Senate. I'm sure it is worth a vote in our favor to make sure you stay there. And you can always be certain of our future support."
Later that day the senator listened to the debate. At the end of it came the vote. As their names were called out, one after the other, and each gave their reply, Senator Young thought of the answer he had given to the young student earlier that morning, "It is important to look at all aspects of an issue very carefully before you make a decision."

Carl Taylor

- How do you think the senator should vote? What speaks for supporting the president, what speaks for voting against his plans?
- What impression do you get of the senator from the meeting with the Close Up students? What impression do you get of him from the meeting with the industrialists?
- What exactly does the sentence mean that you read in the box at the beginning of the text?

Working with the text

1 A closer look at the main characters

Go through the text and make notes on how …

1. … the three industrialists proceed step by step until they finally tell the senator what they want him to do. Why do you think they proceed in this way? 2. … the senator behaves in the meeting with the Close Up students and in the meeting with the industrialists. Why do you think he behaves differently? Why do you think it takes him such a long time to realize what they want?

2 Beyond the text

1. Imagine you have heard about the senator's vote. Write a letter to his office praising or criticizing him for his decision. 2. What questions would you like to ask a politician who represents your area in parliament? 3. Politicians are more often criticized than praised in the media. – Rightly so?

Listening comprehension **The birth of a capital**

You now already know quite a bit about Washington, D.C. Without locking at the book again, recap what you have learned so far about the US capital.

The tape you are going to listen to now will tell you …

… what July 4th means to Americans;
… where George Washington, the first president, accepted the job as leader of the new country;
… why none of the existing cities were chosen as the capital of the USA;
… why Jefferson and Washington chose the banks of the Potomac for the new capital;
… what this area looked like in the early 1790s;
… how Pierre L'Enfant, the architect chosen by Washington, wanted to connect the buildings for the three branches of government;
… when John Adams, the second president of the USA, and Congress moved to Washington;
… what the capital looked like then;
… how the city was saved in the war of 1812 between England and the USA;
… how the White House got its name.

Make notes while you are listening. If necessary, listen to the tape more than once. Then compare your notes in class.

→ Option 5: Different roles for Britain: From Empire to European Union → Option 6: Monarchy and Parliament in Britain

Unit 3 Blacks in the USA

The white man's ideal slave

1619 The first 20 Africans are brought to work as "servants" in Jamestown, Virginia. During the next two hundred years thousands more are brought as slaves to work on the tobacco and cotton fields in the South.

1808 Congress passes a law making it illegal to import slaves, but it is generally ignored.

1820 Slavery is declared legal in the South, but illegal in all states north of Missouri.

1861 Abraham Lincoln becomes president of the United States. The number of slaves in the USA has reached 4 million. Eleven southern "slave" states leave the Union, afraid that Lincoln will abolish slavery, which is the basis of their economy. The Civil War breaks out.

The eleven slave states and their flag

1865 The North defeats the South. Slaves are freed throughout the nation.

1868 Blacks officially become American citizens. But it is made difficult if not impossible for blacks to vote in the South.

1896 The Supreme Court says any state can have facilities for blacks and whites, as long as they are "separate, but equal". In some southern states there are separate schools for blacks and whites, separate theatres, restaurants, hotels, taxis, and seats on buses.

Free at last

Free at last, free at last,
Thank God Almighty I'm free at last;
Free at last, free at last,
Thank God Almighty I'm free at last.

1. Way down yonder in the graveyard walk,
Thank God Almighty I'm free at last,
Me and my Jesus goin' to meet and talk,
Thank God Almighty I'm free at last.

2. On my knees when the light passed by,
Thank God Almighty I'm free at last,
Thought my soul would rise and fly,
Thank God Almighty I'm free at last.

3. Some of these mornings, bright and fair,
Thank God Almighty I'm free at last,
Goin' to meet King Jesus in the air,
Thank God Almighty I'm free at last.

☞ Before you read through all the dates on these two pages …
- look at the pictures and read the words of the spiritual on this page: What does the speaker say – directly and indirectly – about his/her situation? How does the speaker feel? – Why do you think this kind of song was popular with slaves in the 18th and 19th centuries?
- read the excerpt from Martin Luther King's speech: How is his idea of freedom different from the idea of freedom in the spiritual?

Segregation

I have a dream ...

... that one day, on the red hills of Georgia, sons of former slaves and the sons of former slave owners will be able to sit down together at the table of brotherhood. [...]
I have a dream that my four little children will one day live in a nation where they will not be judged by the color of their skin, but by the content of their character. [...]
Let freedom ring from the mighty mountains of New York; [...] let freedom ring from every hill and molehill of Mississippi [...] until one day all God's children will be able to join hands and sing in the words of the old Negro spiritual: "Free at last! Free at last! Thank God Almighty, we are free at last!"

Martin Luther King, August 28, 1963

- What does Martin Luther King's speech tell you about the situation of blacks in 1963?
- Now read through the dates on both pages to get an idea of black history from 1619 on. Then write a short essay: What was the situation of blacks at the end of the 19th century? What seems to be their situation today?
- Look at Germany's history and at the history of some other countries: What other groups of people have, like black people in the USA, had to fight for their rights?

→ Listening comprehension, p. 47

From 1919 on Thousands of blacks move to cities in the North, looking for work.

1954 The Supreme Court changes its 1896 decision: Schools must be desegregated in all states. Some areas in the South don't accept this.

1956 The Supreme Court declares: Segregation on public buses is against the Constitution.

1963 Dr Martin Luther King leads 250,000 people to Washington, D.C. in the largest protest march in US history to that date. His speech is the climax of the Civil Rights Movement. Civil rights leaders meet President Kennedy.

1964 Congress passes a civil rights law which makes discrimination illegal in hotels, restaurants and at the workplace.

1965 Congress ends voting discrimination, so that all blacks are finally able to vote.

1967 Carl Stokes of Cleveland, Ohio, and Richard Hatcher of Gary, Indiana, are elected as the nation's first black mayors of major cities.

1968 Martin Luther King is assassinated. Riots break out in many American cities.

1973 Thomas Bradley is elected mayor of Los Angeles.

1988 Jesse Jackson is the first black with a serious chance of being chosen as a candidate for president.

1989 David N. Dinkins becomes mayor of New York City.
General Colin L. Powell becomes main military adviser to the president.

1990 Douglas Wilder, grandson of slaves, becomes governor of Virginia.

1992 Carol Moseley-Braun becomes the first black woman to be elected to the US Senate.

1993 Novelist Toni Morrison is the first black American to win the Nobel Prize for Literature.

L

Focus on GRAMMAR Modals and their substitutes

a What do the following comments by different people tell you about the situation of black people in the USA over the last forty years?

1 Did you know that until 1956 black people **couldn't sit** on the same seats as white people in public buses in some states?

2 Schools, hotels and restaurants **were allowed to discriminate** against black people, too, and there was nothing they **could do**.

3 Luckily, the Civil Rights Movement of the 1960s **was able to convince** politicians that something **had to be done**.

4 It seems public opinion was so strong that Congress **had to pass** the civil rights law and the voting rights law. This meant new chances in many fields of life.

5 Freedom and equality for everyone seemed realistic goals in the 1960s. For many blacks the American dream **could** at last **come true**.

6 From the 1970s on, the economic situation slowly got worse again. And from what I've seen, life today **must be** much harder again for most blacks.

7 The country **should do** more for all its minorities. If we don't, we **might have** more riots like the ones in Los Angeles.

8 I've heard that the most common form of death for young black men is being shot. Congress **should have passed** stricter gun laws long ago.

9 Black people, too, **must have started** to worry about the violence in their communities. In New York some well-known black people recently offered $100 for each gun which a black youth gave to the police.

b You have already learned that modals can be used to express …

ability • permission • possibility • obligation.

There are two more functions modals are often used for …

deduction • suggestion.

Make a list, one column for the six functions and one column for the verb forms.
Then go through all the comments again and decide for each verb form in bold print which of the six functions it is used for. – What translations into German are possible for the different verb forms?
Finally, check your list against the list in the appendix on p. 136.
As you can see, modals and their substitutes aren't so difficult to understand. Two things do, however, often cause problems for pupils: the forms of the different tenses, and the decision whether a simple or a progressive form is best.
The following exercise deals with these two problems.

Ex **Voices from across the USA**

After the 1992 race riots in Los Angeles a leading newspaper asked people about the state of race relations in the USA.
Read their comments and complete the statements with one of these forms:
be able to forget – be making – have gone – have been doing – have realized – be to blame – be allowed to make – be created

Sherri Goodrum, 33: Race relations may … slow progress, but they are progressing. I feel sad about all the violence. Job opportunities must … for young people.
Jo Santi, 23: Racism isn't getting better or worse. Why? The government may not … enough to give minorities hope for the future.
Janice Sharpe, 40: I feel there is no more progress. Our politicians may not … the changes that have taken place in our society; the education system might …; people might not … their feelings of mistrust.
Jack B. Evett, 50: I think the majority of people of different races get along well on a day-to-day basis. The media shouldn't … a sensational story of everything that might … wrong in the past.

→ Grammar 3: 1 (p. 136) → Exercises 1, 2

Find out from the text why the woman below was quite ordinary and yet somehow very special.

Mary Elizabeth Bowser

An unusual example of race relations in the 19th century

"Being black, a slave, and a woman was reason enough for my birth and death to remain unknown. I have, however, been called a brave woman, prepared to risk my life in the Civil War, which divided the South and the North.
I was a slave in the South until I was freed in 1851 by Elizabeth van Lew, the wife of my owner. It was Elizabeth, too, who helped me to become a spy for the North more than ten years later. She arranged for me to work as a servant in the home of Jefferson Davis, the president of the southern states.
"Through a network of people we both gave information to General Ulysses S. Grant and so helped the North. – Here are some things that went through my mind one day when I worked for President Davis:

1. "Davis **might be** with his officers *now* and they **may be talking** about their plans *at this moment*.
2. "They **should be meeting** *tonight* at the latest. So they **could talk** about their plans *tonight*, too.
3. "Davis **must have decided** on the new plan *yesterday*. He **can't have discussed** it with his officers *yet*.
4. "Who knows – they **may have changed** their plans again *by tomorrow morning*.
5. "Elizabeth **must have been expecting** a message *all day yesterday*.
6. "General Grant **may have been waiting** to hear from us *since Monday*.
7. "*By the end of next year* I **may** already **have been living** up North *for several months*."

– If you reread the seven statements carefully, you will see that in each of them the speaker is somehow deducing information and speculating about situations in the past, the present, or the future. In some of these statements she is more certain than in others.
Try to arrange the verb forms on a scale from 'almost certain' to 'not very certain'.
– Now go through the statements again and organize the verb forms into four groups of identical forms. Write the adverbials next to each form and add what time the sentence refers to. Looking at the verb forms and the adverbials, explain why the adverbials are necessary to understand the sentences properly.
– Finally, translate the seven statements into German and try to explain what the difficulties might be for German learners of English.

→ Grammar 3: 2 (p. 137) → Exercises 3-5

Some facts and figures: The situation of blacks today

Look at the statistics and then explain: Why does the first group of charts give a picture that is different from the one suggested by the charts showing family incomes?

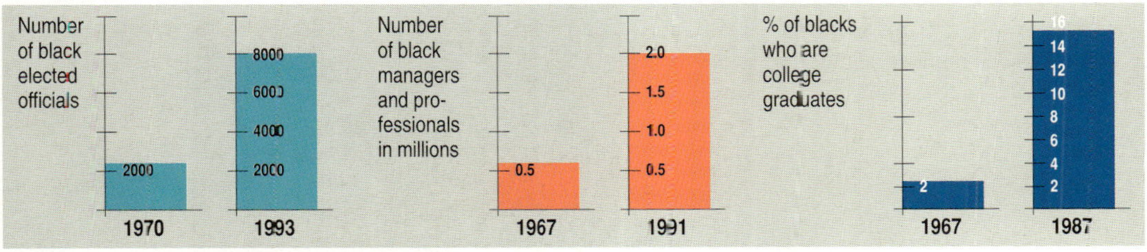

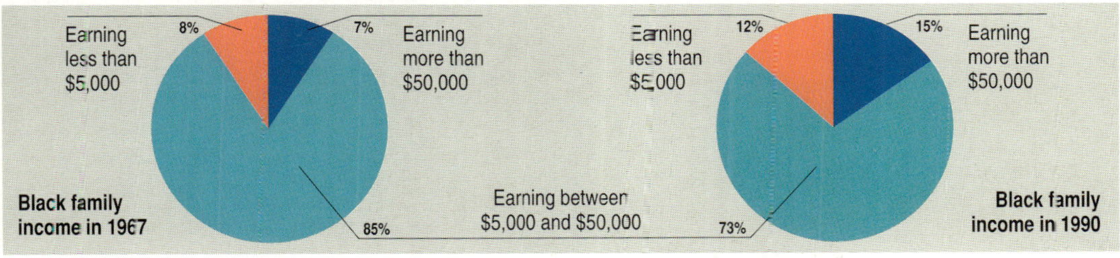

- Before you start with these two pages, try to recall what you already know about the situation of black people in the USA today. What general impression of the situation of black people do you have?
- Look at the titles, the pictures and the captions that go with them. What do you expect the people to tell you?
- Read what they say about themselves and their families. Then work with a partner: Arrange in a network what *you* find important about 'Black America in the 90s'. Compare some of the networks.
- Then turn to the Info box at the bottom of this page and the newspaper article on p. 39 and add the information you find there to your network.
- One group of black Americans has been left out here: the extremely successful. What very successful blacks do you know and what do you know about them?

Info box

- Only 12% of the total population of the USA are blacks. About 53% of them live in the eleven southern states. Large numbers live in the big industrial cities of the North, such as Chicago, Detroit or New York.
- Black and white Americans have more contact than before, especially at work and at school. However, in their free time they often go their separate ways.
- Segregation can still be found in the places where Americans live. One third of all blacks live in neighbourhoods which are almost totally black. Six out of ten whites live in mainly white areas.

Black America in the nineties

Successful, but still not equal

Leon Brooks is a lawyer. His wife Cora is a manager at an electronics company. They have a comfortable home in a mostly black middle-class area in Washington. Their children can expect to go to college and have successful careers.

Making ends meet

Gail Rand works in a department store in Washington. Her husband Charles is a waiter in a small restaurant. They live in an apartment in northeast Washington.

The poverty trap

Linda Roberts works as a secretary for a Washington company. She has two children aged two and four.

"Unfortunately, many whites have not yet gotten used to a successful black middle class. Some feel threatened. They seem to believe that the good life is for whites only. Of course I want to live in a nice area and I want my kids to go to a good school. But the feeling we often have is that we're not allowed to enjoy the things we have worked so hard for. As a successful black I'm also likely to experience annoying insults that few whites will ever face. Being ignored by taxi drivers as I wait on the street is one example of what can happen when I travel to other cities on business. You have to learn to accept it, and it reminds you that no matter what we achieve as individuals, we will always be judged by what people see first – our color."

"We've come a long way since the civil rights marches of the 1960s. A black president could soon become a reality. But we still have a long, long way to go. If you went into a good restaurant here in Washington, you wouldn't think you were in a city with a population that's 70% black, because you would hardly see any blacks at the tables. Only a minority has really made it. And yet the people who work in this city, the people in the department stores, the people who serve in the restaurants, drive the buses, build the homes – they are all black people.

"We couldn't live on what Charles and I earn. We both have second jobs to help pay the bills and make sure we can save enough to send our daughter to college."

"I live with my mother in Anacostia. If she didn't look after my children during the day, I couldn't possibly go to work. There aren't enough day-care facilities for working women in the United States, and on my salary I would never be able to pay for private day care. My husband Floyd lives with his mother. He used to work for a construction firm till he lost his job. Now there is no way we can afford the rent for an apartment together. If I didn't have a job, we'd have nothing at all, and I'd have to live on welfare. Although I have a full-time job, the salary I get is so low that I am still living under the poverty line. I worry myself sick about the future of my children, who are growing up in an area like this. Many of the friends my husband grew up with are already dead or in prison. I don't want that to happen to my kids, but I don't know how to protect them from it, either."

Friday, September 23, 1994
THE WASHINGTON CHRONICLE

Rich-Poor Gulf Becoming Wider Among Blacks

By FELICITY BRENNMEIER
Special to *The Washington Chronicle*

WASHINGTON, Sept. 22 – The Civil Rights Movement of the 1960s helped those black Americans who were talented, educated and skilled, or already had qualifications – those who really had been held back by race.

One important development from this period has been the appearance of an authentic black middle class, better educated and better paid than any group of blacks before.

For other blacks who were not in this group, however, very little has happened. In general, black workers are still badly paid even today, and many families need two salaries to survive. Furthermore, as well-off blacks move to better neighborhoods in search of a better life for themselves and their children, they have left behind a socially disabled group of poor people who have become the underclass. Once caught in such a situation, it is almost impossible for families to escape.

A major problem in black America and one that contributes to the continuation of the underclass is the huge increase in one-parent households. About 58% of all black households are headed by single black females. Their children often live in poverty. The dangers they face in the ghettos where they grow up are drugs, violence from street gangs, and other crimes.

→ Option 19: A mixed bag of grammar

Focus on WORDS Talking about feelings and emotions

Linda Roberts has mixed feelings and emotions when she talks about her situation. She feels +frustrated that she cannot live with her husband. She is obviously pleased that she still has a job, but she is annoyed that there aren't enough day-care facilities in the United States.
She is quite fond of her work and she gets a lot of +satisfaction from it, but she feels very angry that her salary still leaves her below the poverty line.
Linda loves her family like any mother. She gives her children a lot of +affection, but she is worried that her children are growing up in an area like Anacostia. She is terrified that her son might join a local gang one day and get into serious trouble.
She tries to look at things positively, but a feeling of helplessness often comes over her when she thinks about what the future might bring.

1 Collecting words

Collect the words which express Linda's feelings and add them to the following word lists. If you go through pages 38 and 39 again, you will find more words. (If they don't fit into one of the groups a-d, why not open a new group?)

a Words expressing happiness or sadness
– be/feel happy, pleased, …
– satisfaction, +joy, …
– be/feel unhappy, helpless, …
– unhappiness, loneliness, …

b Words expressing love, dislike or hate
– like, love, be fond of, …
– love, affection, …
– dislike, be fed up with, …
– hate, …

c Words expressing worry and fear
– worry, be/feel afraid, …
– +anxiety, nervousness, …

d Words expressing anger
– be/feel annoyed, fed up with, …
– +rage, …

2 Arranging words

a There are several ways to arrange words. You can look for
– word families (to disappoint – disappointing – disappointment – …),
– opposites (boring – exciting; to like – to dislike; love – hate)
– or "word thermometers" like the one on the right.
Take the "feeling" words you have collected and try to find other word families, opposites and word thermometers.

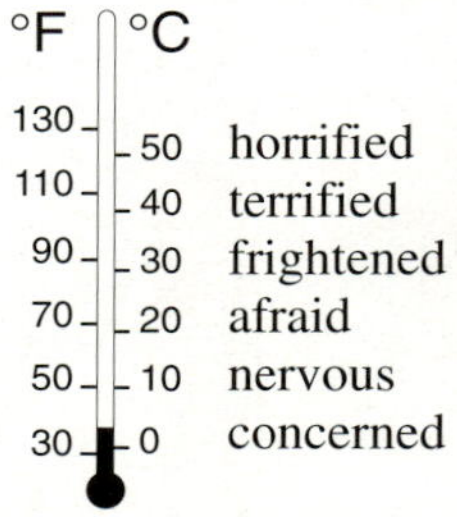

b Make a network of your own free associations. Here is an example of how somebody started such a network. You can either complete the example in your exercise-book or choose a different starting word.

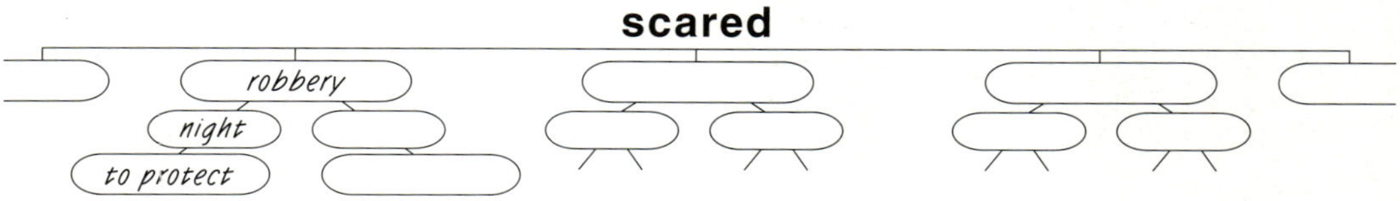

3 Words in use

Ask one of your classmates for her/his network and find out together why one word has led to another. (Look at the dialogue in the box for help.)

Why do you think *scared* has led to *robbery*?
– Perhaps there's just been a robbery somewhere near.
What about *robbery* and *night*? …

→ Option 7: The All-American Slurp → Option 16: Using a monolingual dictionary

1 Read the following text and find out what is special about Placer County in California. Then work out with a partner what verb form must follow each modal verb. Be careful: there are active and passive forms. (In some cases a simple *or* a progressive form is possible.)

Racial Pioneers

In 297 places black households earn more than white households

In a country where the average white family income is about $40,000 and the average black family income about $26,000 many people *may* (not yet realize) that there are communities like Placer County in California.
About 400 black households in this almost totally white area *can* (call) 'special'. They are among the 20,000 black households throughout the nation (0.2%) that earn more than the average white family in their community.
Altogether, there are 297 communities like Placer County and their number *should* (increase) from day to day. "We are pleased about this development," say Carol and Ray Beale, one of the black couples living in Placer County. "But we believe that for the last 30 years the country *should* (do) more to help all minority groups. Here in Placer County local politicians noticed long ago that we need help; the government in Washington *must* only (notice) this very recently. This development *must* (continue) so that even more *can* (achieve) by black Americans in the future than has been in the past."

2 One statement – different ways of reacting

a Depending on the context and on what is important to a speaker, she/he can react in many different ways to a certain statement. Look at the statement in the middle and then read how six different people react to it.
Finally, work out what the correct form is for the verbs in brackets. Be careful: there are active and passive forms.

"Since 1965 black Americans (be able to vote) in all elections."

1. They (should / be allowed to vote) a hundred years earlier.
2. Who knows. A black candidate (may / soon / elect) president.
3. More support (must / give) to black candidates in all elections. We (might / have) many more blacks in important positions years ago if we (be able to convince) more black people to use their right to vote.
4. Until 1965 they (have to pass) tests before they (be allowed to vote) in some southern states.
5. They (have to fight) a long time to get the right to vote.
6. There are still many countries in the world where certain groups of people (not be able to vote).

b *Two extreme reactions to the statement might be "Can't we talk about something else?" and "Do we have to talk about this topic for so long?" – Can you think of two or three other reactions to the statement?*

Project Find out from history books or from an encyclopedia how, from the 19th century on, people slowly got the right to vote in what is now Germany.
Make notes and prepare a short talk which you could present to a group of young people from another country.

→ Option 13: Interpreting and translation practice

3 When will you …?

Imagine an American friend asked you about your opinion on the development of the European Union. – How certain are you about the things in the circles?
Here are some verb forms and some adverbials you can use:
will/won't – should – could – may – might
soon – in a few/ten … years – before/after the year 2020 – never

- **live in one European nation**
- **elect a European parliament with real powers**
- **have a president elected by the people**
- **decide on a European capital**
- **speak one European language**
- **introduce a single European currency**
- **have a European police**
- **have more than twenty member states**
- **elect a female European president**

I think we could soon … .
As I see it, we should … in a few years.

4 Advice for black graduates

Read what Marian Wright Edelman said to a group of students leaving Howard University, a university for black students. What do you think of Edelman's ideas, not just as advice for young black people, but for young people in general?

"Every responsible black adult **ought to tell** young blacks what she or he has learned from life. The education students receive at Howard University **is intended to do** just this. That's why it **is said to be** among the best universities for black students.

"I want to add some lessons to the ones you have received here before you leave this place. Here you were first taught and then tested. In life, the tests and consequences come before the lessons.

1. You **should never take** anything for granted. There is no magic carpet to success.
2. Pay attention to detail. People who are careful in little things **are supposed to be** careful in big things, too.
3. Don't think you have a right to get anything even if others act as if they have. Our society believes that blacks **are meant to sweat** for everything.
4. Don't wait for others to discover you. You **should be able to build** your own life.

"One day you might say: I **should not have forgotten** what I learned at school and I **ought to have remembered** Frederick Douglass's words: 'People may not get all they pay for, but they must certainly pay for all they get.' …"

Translate the sentences that contain verb forms in bold print. There is one German word that you could use in all your translations. What is it? Go to the vocabulary box on p. 157 to find out more about the English expressions and their German translations.

Now translate the following sentences.

1. Es sollte nicht das höchste Ziel im Leben sein, teure Kleider zu tragen. *(should)* 2. Ihr solltet jetzt gelernt haben, wie man für sich selbst Ziele findet. *(be supposed to)* 3. Arbeit soll nicht nur dazu da sein, uns mit Geld zu versorgen. Sie sollte auch Spaß machen. *(be intended to / be meant to)* 4. Booker T. Washington hat seinen Vater nicht kennengelernt. Sein Vater soll ein Weißer gewesen sein. *(be said to)* 5. Was, glaubt ihr, sollte eine Schule lehren? *(should)*

→ Option 21: Ways of expressing the future

5 Perhaps some of you have heard of the film *Gone with the Wind* or have even seen it. What is it about?
Read the German text and try to say in a few English sentences what it tells you about the film. Then translate the text.

In English, please:
Filme können manchmal wie Träume sein …

Leute, die nach Atlanta, Georgia reisen, sollten wissen, daß sie dort die Schauplätze nicht finden können, die sie aus David O. Selznicks Film *Vom Winde verweht* kennen.
Leider gibt es viele Touristen, die glauben, daß der Film den amerikanischen Süden zeigt, wie er zur Zeit des Bürgerkriegs vielleicht war. Die Fremdenführer und Fremdenführerinnen müssen diesen Leuten dann erklären, daß der Film ein Produkt der Traumfabrik Hollywood ist.
Als Margaret Mitchells Roman 1936 herauskam und ein Bestseller wurde, sagte Selznick sofort, er könne aus diesen 1000 Seiten einen Film machen. Viele Film-Fachleute sollen ihn angeblich ausgelacht haben. Sogar für Fachleute muß es unmöglich gewesen sein, sich vorzustellen, wie das zu machen sei. Und niemand hat wissen können, wie erfolgreich der Film sein würde. Heute, fast 60 Jahre später, darf man den Film den beliebtesten aller Zeiten nennen: 1939 gewann er acht Oscars, und bis heute mögen ihn fast 300 Millionen Menschen gesehen haben. Seit Juni 1987 können Touristen den Film im CNN Cinema 6 in Atlanta täglich sehen.

6 Read the following text and then see how much you can remember about Frederick Douglass (1817-1895) without looking at the text again. Then go through the text again, sentence by sentence, and decide on the right forms for the verbs in brackets. Be careful: there are active and passive forms.

From slave to politician

In 1877 a family named Douglass (move) into the part of Washington, D.C. which (be) now Anacostia and which (then / call) Uniontown. The fact that the home of the Douglass family (be) a historical monument today which (can / visit) by everybody, (show) that somehow they (be) a 'special' family.
From about 1840, Frederick Douglass, the father of the family, (become) known as an author, a fighter for civil rights and a politician. In 1877 he (make) US marshal for Washington, D.C., and later in his life he (have) several other government jobs.
His wife Helen (found) the Frederick Douglass Memorial Association after his death. That is why his name (not forget) up to this day and why important events in Frederick Douglass's life (can / reconstruct):
He (be) a slave, but he (be able to) escape to the North in 1838. In 1845 he (have to) leave the USA and (go) to England. He (be able to / return) after some of his friends (pay) his former owner $710. In his anti-slavery newspaper, *The North Star*, which Douglass (start) in 1847, he not only (continue) his fight for the freedom of black people, he also (fight) for the rights of women. Today Frederick Douglass's work for more equality in American society (recognize) by all Americans. In schoolbooks that (use) all over the USA, Frederick Douglass (mention) next to such a great black leader as Martin Luther King.

Words Words Words

a **Trouble spot** Words that can easily be mixed up

Choose the correct word from the following pairs of words to complete the sentences.

foreigner/stranger – fault/mistake – meaning/opinion – bring up/educate – narrow/small – murder/murderer – check/control – take place/sit down – strict/strong – pension/rent

1. I'm sorry I can't tell you the way, I'm a ● here myself. 2. The accident was your own ●. 3. What is your ● of the new history teacher? 4. Did you know that Martin Luther King was ● at Morehouse College? 5. I'm afraid this street is too ● for our lorry. 6. The ● may be sent to prison for his crime. 7. When we crossed the border, our passports were ●. 8. Please ●. Mr Brown has just left the office, but he'll be back in a minute. 9. Teachers who are too ● are usually not very popular. 10. Mrs Middleton's ● is not enough to live on.

Now form sentences with the words you haven't used.

b **Trouble spot** Tricky words

become/get   aloud/loud   remind/remember   hear/listen   go/walk

Fill in the right words in their correct form to complete the following sentences.

1. Sorry. I can't ● the title of the book. 2. Karin, would you please read the poem ●? 3. If I forget to give it back, please ● me. 4. I'm sorry I didn't ● to phone you. 5. Where can I ● more information? 6. He's got such a ● voice. You can ● him talking in the whole house. 7. I ● this anorak for Christmas. 8. Did you ● what I said? 9. You should ● by bus, it's too far to ●. 10. She never ● to what you tell her. 11. At the age of 30 she ● an architect. 12. What has ● of Angela? Do you know?

c **Word builder's corner** Suffixes and prefixes to make verbs

You can understand many "new" verbs that you have never met before if you know their stem and the suffix and prefix that has been added:

1.	(to) modern**ize**:	modern + **-ize**	(modernisieren)
	(to) short**en**:	short + **-en**	(kürzen, verkürzen)
2.	(to) **re**build:	**re-** + build	(wiederaufbauen)
	(to) **mis**use:	**mis-** + use	(mißbrauchen, zweckentfremden)

-ize: terrorize, fertilize, symbolize, legalize, generalize, civilize, nationalize
-en: widen, deepen, blacken, ripen, flatten, harden, weaken, deafen, soften
re-: rearrange, redo, reappear, re-elect, refill, renew, rename, reorganize
mis-: mislead, misinform, misbehave, mistreat, misspell

Work in groups: Look up the "new" words in an English-English dictionary. Check if you know how to pronounce them correctly, then write down their meaning and examples which show how they are used. Examples:

terrorize: (to) fill sb./sth. with terror – *(to) terrorize the neighbourhood*
widen: (to) make or become wider – *(to) widen a road/one's knowledge*
rearrange: (to) arrange sth. in a different way – *(to) rearrange the furniture*
misspell: (to) spell sth. incorrectly – *(to) misspell sb.'s name*

Read the story and then try to explain what the title means.

Two ways to 16th Street

It was an unbearably hot night. Calvin got out of bed and walked to the open window. A gentle breeze seemed to come through, not much, but enough to tell him that the street might be cooler than his bedroom. He pulled on his jeans and moved quietly through the living-room towards the front door.
"Calvin, is that you?" his mother asked from another room.
"Yeah."
"Where you goin'?"
"I need some fresh air. I can't breathe in here."
"Do you know what time it is?"
But Calvin was already outside.
The street was almost as hot as his bedroom, but at least he could hold his face towards the gentle breeze, although he knew it would never dry the sweat on his body.
Suddenly a car stopped in front of him. "Hey, want a ride? We're going into town."
Calvin recognized the driver. Ray Johnson was a friend of his brother's. "Come on, get in," he said with a big smile. A door opened. Inside were two other black teenagers, both drinking from cans. Music almost drowned their voices.
"Get in," said Ray. "I want to talk to you."
Calvin did as he was told – you didn't argue with Ray Johnson – and the car drove away through the dark streets.
"Meet Ed and Louis," said Ray. Calvin knew their faces. Two more from his brother's group of friends.
"How's Sonny?"
"He's OK," said Calvin. "He might be out next year. For good behavior."
And back again a few months later, a guidance counselor had once said in an angry moment. That was all any of them could look forward to.
"How would you like to do a few jobs?" asked Ray. "You know, not a lot of work, but good money."
"What kind of jobs?"
"You know, just taking something someplace, or collecting something. Maybe a message, maybe a little package or two."
Calvin had a good idea what would be in those packages.
"Money counts in this world and I'm telling you, there's lots to be made."

They drove downtown. It was still alive with cars and taxis and people who hadn't yet gone home. They cruised the streets, music playing loudly out of the open windows. At one point a police car shot past, its siren screaming through the dark night. Later they saw the same police car; it was parked at the side of the road. The policemen had forced the passengers out of another car, and they were now standing with their hands on the top of the car. Calvin could imagine the questions, fast, aggressive, "Where are you going? Got a driver's license? What's that in your pocket? Come on, keep your hands on the car."
"Where are we going?" Calvin asked as they left the downtown area and drove towards the quieter, more expensive neighborhoods.
"We're going to visit a wealthy man," said Louis. "Only he ain't home and he don't really know we're coming."
The others laughed. Calvin looked out of the window. It was going to be a robbery, and there was no escape for him.
"Don't worry," said Ray. "Louis is a real expert. Nothing will go wrong."
"Man. I don't want to break in anywhere. I came onto the street because I couldn't sleep."

They stopped on a quiet street in a part of town that was very much the opposite of his own neighborhood. The houses were big and comfortable. The cars in the garages were the kind of car he would like to drive one day, but he knew that only one type of career brought that kind of money to his world. And his brother was already paying the price. His mother had screamed at

him never to do the same thing. And here he was now in a car with the same guys who had gotten his brother into trouble. Louis got out of the car first.
"I'm not coming," said Calvin.
"Look, man," said Ray. "This is easy. We walk in, look around, and leave."
"And in between?"
"Maybe when he comes home, some things are missing. This guy's got big bucks. He ain't going to notice. Come on."
Calvin got out. The group walked along the empty street. Nobody was sitting on the sidewalks here. These houses had air-conditioning to keep out the heat.
Moving quietly in the darkness, they climbed quickly into the yard and without making a noise, walked along the path to the back of the house. Within seconds Louis had opened a window, and they were climbing into a large, cool living-room.
Nobody spoke as Ray switched on a flashlight and let the thin light go around the room, from tables, to shelves, to chairs. Calvin had never been in such an expensive house before. He looked, hardly believing what he saw, while the others moved noiselessly between the furniture. Just then the light went on and a tall black man in pajamas stood in the open door. Before he could say anything, Louis jumped forward and hit him, and the silence was suddenly broken.
"Let's get out of here," said Ray as they climbed quickly out of the window.
Calvin stayed where he was, too shocked to move, too surprised by the sudden violence, too amazed to see it was a black family whose house they had broken into.

The tall man had fallen against a cupboard. Slowly he stood up, holding his hand to his head. The man and the boy looked at each other for what seemed an endless period of time.
"Why didn't you go with the others?" the tall man said, as if he had been thinking about something and had finally made up his mind. Outside they both heard the car engine start and the vehicle drive away. "They've left you," he continued. "You could have gotten away with them. Why didn't you go?"
He wasn't talking angrily, simply asking questions in a quiet voice. Calvin started to shake. Then, nervously, almost in a panic, he started to talk, "I didn't want to come. I didn't want to do this. I ..., I ...," and he explained what had happened. The whole time the tall man kept his eyes on him.
Then the door bell rang.
"It's the police," said the man. "I called them before I came down. As usual they get here ten minutes after everybody's gone." Calvin almost saw a smile on his face. "The kitchen's down here," he said. "Go and wait in there." He stopped and turned to look at Calvin. Calvin's eyes were moving towards the window. "Go into the kitchen," said the man. "It's safer."
Inside the modern, clean kitchen Calvin heard the conversation at the front door. "Yes, I frightened them away. No, they didn't hurt me. I'll be okay. Nothing has been taken." And the door shut. The man hadn't mentioned Calvin. The police hadn't come in to arrest him. The man returned a moment later. He had changed into jeans and a T-shirt. "How old are you?"
"Fifteen," said Calvin.
"Got any brothers or sisters?"
"A brother. But he's ..."
"Go on."
Calvin sighed. "In jail. Mom said if I ever got into trouble like him, never to come home."
"And your father?"
Calvin said nothing.
The man nodded. "Where do you live?" he asked suddenly. "Southeast?"
Calvin looked at the floor. "Yeah," he said.
Again the man nodded. "I think you'd better go home. I'll call a cab for you. Tell your friends people sometimes come back early from vacation. I had some business to do in town."
The man picked up the phone and ordered a cab in a calm and quiet voice, then he put the phone back, and the two sat without speaking until the man looked at his watch and suggested they should wait outside. "You know, I grew up in Southeast, too."
"How did you make it to 16th Street?" asked Calvin, surprised to hear what the man had said.
The man thought a moment, then he said, "Hard work ... and luck." When the cab arrived the man gave the driver several dollar bills to take Calvin home. "Life doesn't give you many chances," he said. "When you get one, take it, and don't mix with those characters if you can help it."

Carl Taylor

Working with the text

1 A first look at the story

1. Without looking at the text again, how much do you remember about …
   – Calvin (his age, his home, his family)
   – the time when all the events take place and the places mentioned in the story
   – the other people in the story?
2. What situation in the story is illustrated in the picture on p. 45?
3. What do you think will happen when Calvin sees Ray again?

2 A closer look at the story

1. Go through the story, make notes, and check if you have remembered everything about Calvin. Imagine that Calvin is ten years older now and through luck and hard work he has been successful in society. – Use your notes and write a text as he might tell the incident to a friend. Don't forget to add his feelings then and some comments that express what he thinks about the incident today.
2. Try to show that the following statements about stories in general are true for this story, too.

> In the introductory passage of a story there is often a situation in which there is some 'instability', something which, later on, will be responsible for a conflict.
> In the development of a story different forces struggle with each other.
> A certain 'stability' is achieved at the end of a story.

3 Why do you think …

1. … Ray wants someone to do some jobs for him? 2. … Ray asks someone like Calvin to do these jobs? 3. … Calvin is too shocked to run away with the others? 4. … Calvin doesn't say anything when the man asks him about his father? 5. … the man doesn't give Calvin to the police?

4 A point for discussion

How do you think young criminals should be treated? (Find one or two cases in a newspaper, present them to the class, together with the sentence that was given, and then discuss the cases.)

L 9 Listening comprehension

The history of the blues

Have a look at the pictures and speculate on what they might have to do with the history of the blues.

South Carolina

Chicago, around 1920

Big Bill Broonzy, 1893-1958

Arthur Crudup, 1905-1974

Elvis Presley, 1935-1977

Listen to the tape and check where you were right or wrong.
In addition, find out …
1. … what the spirituals and work songs of the slaves have to do with the blues. 2. … why the guitar is such a good blues instrument. 3. … how the blues reached the big cities. 4. … how the topics of the songs changed. 5. … how rhythm and blues is different from traditional blues. 6. … why the blues is still so popular today.

→ Option 8: Black music

Unit 4 American Indians

A long time ago a famous hunter was going home with some birds he had shot, and he saw a little snake by the side of the trail. It was a beautifully colored snake, and it looked friendly, too. The hunter stopped and watched it for a while. He thought it might be hungry, so he threw it one of his birds before he went home. A few weeks later he was coming past the same place with some rabbits he had shot, and he saw the snake again. It was still very beautiful and seemed friendly, but it had grown. He threw it a rabbit and said "Hello" as he went on home. Some time after that, the hunter saw the snake again. It had grown very big, but it was still friendly and seemed to be hungry. The hunter was taking some turkeys home, so he stopped and gave the snake one. Then, one time, the hunter was going home the same way with two buck deer on his back. By this time, that pretty colored snake was very big and looked so hungry that the hunter felt sorry for it and gave it a whole deer to eat. That night the people were dancing around the fire and singing the old songs when the snake came and started moving around the fire, too, outside of where the people were dancing. The snake was so big and long that it stretched all around the people. The snake was covered with pretty colors and it seemed friendly, but it looked hungry, too, and the people began to be afraid. They told some boys to get their bows and arrows and shoot the snake. They all shot together and they hit the snake. That snake was hurt. It thrashed its tail all around and killed a lot of people. They say that snake was just like the white man.

☞ What ideas about American Indians do you have? Where do your ideas come from? How do they compare with those on the right?
- Make a poster, perhaps with a network, so you can later go back to your original ideas.
- Now read the sayings at the top of page 49. Explain what you think they mean.
- Which of the sayings and which of the facts in the Info box on page 49 support your ideas? Which contradict what you originally thought?
- Find out from the legend on this page how American Indians see the beginnings of their relationship with the 'white man'.

"I guess there are no longer any real Indians in the USA. What few there are live somewhere out in the West. Some live in big cities, others just hang around on reservations. They're mostly lazy alcoholics who live off the monthly welfare checks they get from the government. From what I understand they're superstitious. They have strange religious ceremonies and they don't believe in God."

Info box

About 1.6 million American Indians live in the United States today. They belong to more than 500 tribes.

Half of all American Indians live in large cities like Los Angeles or San Francisco. The other half live on reservations. These are special areas of land that belong to the tribes.

Many of the names on maps of the USA are Indian words: Massachusetts ("near the great hill"), Mississippi ("great water"), Kansas, Manhattan, Lake Huron. Even the word 'okay' may have been borrowed from American Indians.

American Indians are very religious people who try to live in harmony with nature. For American Indians life is religion. They cannot understand why so-called civilized nations are destroying Mother Earth and Father Sky.

Many American Indians have learned to survive in a white man's world. There are successful Indians in well-paid jobs in American companies. There are Indian teachers, lawyers, doctors, writers and sports stars. There was once a vice-president of the United States who was part Indian (Charles Curtis, from 1928 to 1933).

Most American Indians fought only when they had to defend themselves and their land. The majority lived in villages. They were excellent farmers who showed the first settlers how to grow and use many different plants. For example, the plant from which aspirin was first made was known to the Indians. And they introduced Europeans to maize, potatoes, beans, tomatoes and tobacco.

Project

– Rewrite the legend from the snake's point of view. Include the snake's thoughts and feelings and its view of the hunter and 'the people'.
– Compare your versions. Perhaps you can publish one of them in your school magazine.

→ Option 9: Strangers in a distant land → Option 10: The tall stranger

Focus on GRAMMAR Tense and aspect in different types of texts

- Look at the cartoon for a few moments. Then explain what the ranger on the right wants to express with the inscription.
  What message might the other ranger prefer?
- Read the three texts on this page. Then imagine and describe a situation in which each text might have been produced.
- Which of the texts do you think is mainly a narrative text (a text that tells a story), which one is mainly a descriptive text (a text that 'paints a picture with words') and which one is mainly an argumentative text (a text that discusses an issue)?

"That is not the mood we're trying to get across out here, Parker!"

1. There **are** two rangers in this cartoon. They **are** somewhere in the USA, perhaps in a national park.
One of them, his name **is** Parker, **is kneeling** in front of a memorial. In his left hand he **has** a chisel, in his right hand he **is holding** a mallet. He **has** just **finished** an inscription which he **has** probably **been working on** for some time. It **says**, ***1856 – SITE OF THE SENSELESS MASSACRE OF SEVERAL HUNDRED INDIANS.***
The other ranger **looks** annoyed. He **is looking at** Parker and the inscription, which he **must** just **have read**, and **is saying**, "That is not the mood we're trying to get across out here, Parker!"
As he **is** probably Parker's boss, he **will make** Parker take the sign down again. Most likely Parker **is going to say** that he **is** sorry for what he **has done**. I can imagine that he **will be writing** a new inscription at the same time again tomorrow. …

2. … A few days ago I **was kneeling** in the grass next to a memorial in our park when my boss **appeared**. I **was** just **finishing** a new inscription on it.
He **read** the words that I **had written** and I **could see** at once that I **had made** a mistake. He **looked** quite angry.
I **completed** the last word while he **was looking at** the memorial. "That is not the mood we're trying to get across out here, Parker!" he **shouted**. – He often **shouts** when he **is** angry. – I **realized** then that I **would be sitting** there again the next day and I **would be writing** a new inscription. I **wasn't** sure what exactly **was making** him angry.
I **had been working** on the inscription for several hours. I **thought** he **would be** pleased with it. At least it **tells** the truth. …

3. Hicktown Gazette, July 14 — Letters to the Editor

Dear Sir or Madam:

We all **know** that our government **has** often **treated** the native population of this continent miserably. However, until yesterday I **had not seen** a memorial which **says** this openly. I **must admit**, though, that our schoolbooks **have been telling** our children the truth about the settlement of the West for some time. I personally **am** very happy with what our schools **are doing** …
Still, if we **admit** in more public places how we **have** sometimes **treated** all our minorities, we **might avoid** confrontations in the future. If we **had done** this earlier, we **would** perhaps **have avoided** some of the riots of recent years.

Look again at text No. 1

– First look at the verb forms in bold print. Make a list of those verb forms which are used to describe all the things that you can actually see in the picture.
If you have done this correctly, you will see that some are progressive forms, others are simple forms. Try to explain why the simple forms and the progressive forms are used.
– Look at the text again. What are the present perfect forms used for?
What verb forms are used for the things which will probably develop out of this situation?
Again you can see that there are simple and progressive forms. Why?

Before you start with the tasks on this page, try to remember what you have learned about state verbs and activity verbs so far. Consider also those verbs that can be used as both state and activity verbs.

Now turn to text No. 2

– Think again of the situation in which Parker might have told this story to a friend. Then explain why Parker, except for three simple present forms, only uses different past forms? – What are the reasons for the three simple present forms?
– Which of the forms refer to something that took place before some other event in the past? Which forms refer to the 'future in the past'?
– Look at the progressive forms and explain why they have been used.

Turbo brain And now read this task and then go back to text No. 3.
You will notice that there is a greater mix of tenses in this text than in the other two texts. Taking into consideration the way the writer approaches the issue and what he or she might want to achieve, try to explain why there is such a mix of tenses.

Have a good look at the cartoon on the right. Then write two of the following texts:
– a mainly descriptive text (it should, however, also contain some explanation.)
– a narrative text (You may choose one of the people in the cartoon as the narrator of this incident.)
– an argumentative text (Somebody discusses the issue of integration of minorities into society.)
As you'll have to write two texts, they obviously needn't be too long.

"Why can't you be like other people?"

→ Grammar 4: 1-4 (p. 138-139) → Exercise 1 → Option 17: A question of style

The Navajo – an American Indian tribe

The Navajo reservation is the nation's largest. It is located in the northeast corner of Arizona, but it also covers parts of Utah and New Mexico. The population of the Navajo reservation is about 170,000. The capital is Window Rock. The reservation contains some of the most beautiful scenery in the USA. There are mountains, lakes, deserts, deep canyons and forests. The most famous sight, Monument Valley, has been the setting for countless Hollywood westerns. Over 97% of the population speak Navajo. Within the reservation the Navajo have a system of self-government. They organize their own schools, their own hospitals, and their own police.

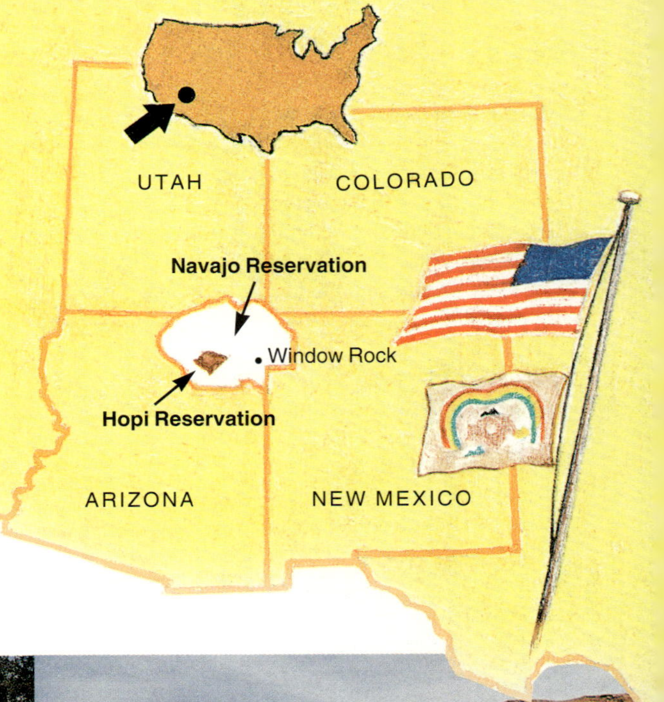

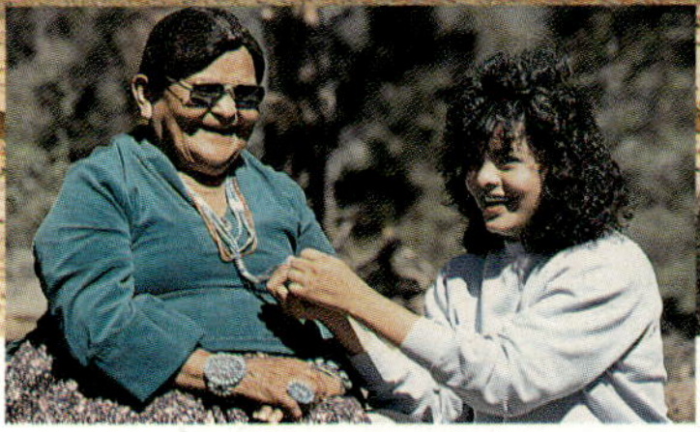

A Navajo family

"My name is Angela Blackburn and I live with my family on the Navajo reservation. A lot of people are surprised when they drive onto the reservation for the first time. There are no fences or walls around it and no big signs. And our capital, Window Rock, looks like any other American town – gas stations, supermarkets, a movie theater, fast-food places. I go to the high school in Window Rock, and my life is probably not very different from that of other American teenagers – except that I'm also a Navajo.

"Traditionally, the Navajo don't like living in towns or villages. They prefer living together with their relatives, scattered over all parts of the reservation. Many Navajo people today live in normal American houses, but next to the house you can often see a hogan. This is the traditional Navajo home. It has eight sides, and the front door faces east, where the sun rises. We get up early with the sun, so we always start the day with beauty. Few people live in hogans today, but we still use them for religious ceremonies."

Angela's father – working for the Navajo

"Our reservation is one of the nation's poorest, with a huge unemployment problem. Our land is dry and we don't have a lot of water, so it isn't very good for farming or keeping cattle. We are also a long way from the jobs in the big cities and main industrial areas. That means we have to find ways of creating jobs on the reservation itself. And that is part of my work for the tribal government.

"Actually, the reservation does have a lot to offer. We have very beautiful scenery. One possibility would be to improve the tourist industry. We also have huge amounts of coal, natural gas and oil under the ground. We could exploit those. Our people are clever with their hands, they have very good eyes and they want to work. We would like to develop industries which make use of these qualities and abilities. We are trying to encourage our people to produce local arts and crafts and we have also invited electronics industries to open factories that make computers or televisions. However, we must consider very carefully what all these developments mean, for the land and for our people. In our culture it is the people who decide what we do. And of course, although we have ideas, we don't have the money to build hotels, factories or stores."

☞ Find out as much as possible from the texts and the map about the people and the places in the photos.

– Develop your poster from page 48 further by adding information (in words and in pictures) about life on the Navajo reservation.
– Why could one say that the reservation, with its unemployment problem, is in a situation similar to that of the hunter in the legend on page 48?

Project Prepare a presentation – similar to the one on these two pages – to be given to a young person from an English-speaking country. You should introduce the area where you live and an imaginary family (mother a teacher, father working for the local government, teenage daughter or son).

Angela's mother – a Navajo teacher

"All Navajo children go to school, either on the reservation or to a school outside. In the reservation schools students are taught by both Indian and non-Indian teachers. The children learn the same subjects as in any white American school, but they do extra classes in Navajo language and culture. The Navajo also have a lot of respect for older people. That is why we sometimes invite the grandparents or even the medicine men to teach the children about our traditions."

L

→ Option 11: Reservations
→ Option 12: Nature: the core of Navajo religion
→ Option 13: Interpreting and translation practice
→ Listening comprehension, p. 61

Focus on WORDS Talking about different attitudes and +values

We all have different attitudes and values. One person might +attach great importance to owning a +fancy sports car. Another person might believe it is important to use only public transport.
It is always dangerous to generalize, but if you travel abroad, you will notice some attitudes and values that are shared by a lot of people in a particular country.
Many Americans, for example, think it is important to look fit and healthy. For many British people it is important to own your own home. In French culture, food plays a central role. And in other countries you will find that people prefer living in large families under one roof.
Obviously, different American-Indian societies have different attitudes and values, too. What they all have in common is a culture that is a mixture of Indian tradition and western influences. Of course there are TVs and fast-food places on many reservations, and many Indian teenagers do have the same or similar values as "Anglo"-American teenagers. Traditionally, however, the values of American-Indian societies are quite different from those of western societies.

1 Arranging words

Here is a collection of words and phrases. Make two lists, one with the +items you think belong to the cultural values of American Indians and one with the items which you associate with western societies. Compare some of your lists in class. Perhaps you found that some of the items could easily be put into one of the lists while others that "caused problems". Discuss why this might have been the case.

live	in harmony with nature each day as it comes
be afraid of	silence age and getting older
believe in	competition youth and youthfulness the future +individuality doing things only when they need to be done
believe that	only people are important there is life in all things we have power over nature we are in control of the +elements only the biological family is important

don't believe in	making plans for the future
attach importance to	time +material things a person's +status somebody's +personality large homes patience advice from older people +extended families
share	wealth with others homes with other people
respect	elderly people all life on earth individual +achievements people who are +punctual

2 Words in use

a Work in groups or with a partner: In three lists, collect a few values which you believe are typically German, British or American. Compare your lists and identify those values which are most likely only prejudices about the countries.

b Through travelling or reading, you may have come into contact with different cultures. Talk about those things which you believe a traveller to Germany, Britain or the USA ought to be aware of.

c Which things do you yourself value? What about your friends, classmates or older people you know?

d Looking at the world in general and/or at personal relationships, what conflicts may come up when groups of people or individuals value different things?

→ Option 19: A mixed bag of grammar

1 Stereotypes of the West

a Indians

Look at the picture and read the text about Indians. – What type of text would you say it is? Try to link it up with the information you got on pages 48 and 49.
Then find the right forms for the verbs in brackets.

Even today, there … (be) many people who … (associate) the word 'Indians' with films and novels which present two types of people: There … (be) the bad Indian who … (fight) white settlers, who … (drink) a lot of whiskey, and you … (can / not / believe) a word he says. If you … (look) at the picture on the right, you … (see) that these Indians … (be) aggressive. In the picture they … (ride) across the plains; perhaps they … (attack) some innocent settlers. They … (probably / even / kill) them. This kind of Indian … (can / often / find) in 'cheap' books and films. The second type … (be) the good Indian. For Germans, it … (be) Karl May's *Winnetou*. He … (see) as a man who always … (do) the right thing, who … (be prepared) to help the weak and risk his life for others.
Until about 40 years ago American Indians themselves … (not / openly / fight against) this black and white picture of their culture. However, during the 1960s, while the Civil Rights Movement in the USA … (fight) for the rights of blacks, the Indians, too, … (start) telling the truth about the lives of their ancestors. They … (draw) attention to the miserable

conditions their ancestors … (force) to live in. Suddenly a wider public … (find out) that the Indian tribes and the early settlers … (live) together peacefully before the waves of settlers … (arrive). For many tribes, fishing, hunting and farming the land … (be) most important then.
Since the 1960s more and more American Indians … (live) again according to their old traditions, in harmony with nature and the land.

b Cowboys: The Virginian

"… the Virginian – come – West – 1870s – where – work – Judge Henry's ranch / he – quiet – strong – honest – peace-loving – and – he – like – by most people / one day, – while – visit – town not far away, – hear – how Trampas, – strange character, – tell lies – Molly Wood / Molly – our local schoolteacher – who, like the Virginian, – come – from – East / Virginian – force – Trampas – take back – what – say / from this moment on – Trampas – Virginian's deadly enemy / I could see clearly – how – end – one day: Trampas – provoke – Virginian; – there – be – showdown – which – one of them – die / it – happen – sooner – I – expect / fortunately – Virginian – draw faster / to this day – I – remember – Molly – find – difficult to understand – that – a peaceful life – be – something – you – have to – fight for – in the West / some time later – accept – Virginian's proposal to marry her."

Info box Owen Wister's novel *The Virginian: A Horseman of the Plains* was published in 1902. It became a bestseller and several films have been based on it. Later, many authors used it as a model for romantic cowboy stories that had nothing to do with the real, quite miserable life of cowboys.

2 "Hyphenated" Americans

R a Scottish-Americans – Scottish traditions in the USA

First read the complete text and then decide whether you need an adjective or an adverb.

Many descendants of immigrants to the USA have (strong) links to their mother country. At the Scottish Games in Alexandria, Virginia, for example, you can see quite (clear) how (close) these links are.

Alexandria was founded in 1749 by two Scotsmen, J. Carlyle and W. Ramsey, and was named after John Alexander, a (successful) Scottish businessman in the area.

Haggis hurling[1] is just one of the (unusual) competitions that you can watch at the Virginia Scottish Games in Alexandria. Scottish-Americans throw their haggises as (good) as native Scots. And they toss the caber[2] as (good) here as at the Highland Games back in Scotland. You can enjoy Scottish dances and listen to music (traditional) played in Scotland. The National Scottish Fiddling[3] Competition (regular) attracts so many (good) players that it is not (easy) to decide who is best.

The games have now been held (successful) every summer since 1974, when they started as a one-day event. Over the years they have become a (popular) two-day event which fascinates both young and old.

The price for a two-day ticket: $18.00
For further information about the games, dial (703) 504-7208

[1] haggis hurling *Haggisschleudern (Haggis = schottisches Gericht aus gehackten Schafsinnereien und Haferschrot, im Schafsmagen gekocht)* [2] toss the caber *den Baumstamm werfen* [3] fiddling *Geigen, Fiedeln*

b *Imagine you have to organize a German day for exchange students from the USA or Britain. What activities would you choose?*

R c In English, please

Portuguese-Americans – explorers and settlers in Massachusetts

Wenn wir Zeit haben, sollten wir Fall River besuchen. Es ist etwa 50 Meilen südlich von Boston. Dort sollen Portugiesen mehr als 100 Jahre vor den *Pilgrims* gelebt haben.

– Gute Idee. Wir sollten die Stadt und die Gegend gesehen haben, bevor wir heimfliegen.

Nördlich von Fall River liegt Dighton Rock. Das ist ein Felsen, der beweisen soll, daß Portugiesen bereits 1511 hier siedelten.

– Was genau soll der Beweis dafür sein?

Der Felsen ist voller Graffiti. Zum Beispiel steht die Zahl 1511 darauf. Außerdem findet man auf dem Felsen ein Kreuz, das ein portugiesisches Kreuz sein soll.

– Das hört sich gut an. Wir sollten Tom und Susan auch mitnehmen.

3 How do you think they felt?

Read the quotations and then say how you think the people felt when they said these things:
upset – angry – sad – full of hope – proud – happy – confident (Choose which adjective you think is best. There is no right adjective.)
Examples:
1. I think Tuekakas felt sad when he said that the country of the Indians would soon ... and that the white men had ... . He told him never to ...
2. Lavelle probably felt angry when he said that ...

1. *Tuekakas, a 19th century Indian chief, to his son, Chief Joseph:*
   "Our country will soon hold my body. The white men have their eyes on our land. Never sell the bones of your father and your mother."
2. *John Lavelle, an Indian chief today, when he heard about a group of middle-class whites who are practising Indian rites:*
   "First whites took our land and now they are after our religious traditions."
3. *Tim Severin, who with four friends crossed the Atlantic in a boat made of leather, as the Irish monk Saint Brendan is said to have done around 600 A.D.:*
   "Our boat may have looked like a floating bird's nest, but she has brought us safely to America. We have proved that Brendan could have sailed to the New World long before the Vikings and Columbus."
4. *Ex-US Supreme Court Justice Louis Brandeis, when asked about the high number of immigrants to the USA:*
   "I don't fear political change because of immigration. Like the people who won independence for the United States by revolution, Americans today will not call for order at the cost of liberty."
5. *Marian Wright Edelman, who in 1965 became the first black woman lawyer in Mississippi:*
   "Many women are dreaming of a world which will be better not only for themselves, but for future generations, a world where character and ability will count more than color and gender."
6. *Los Angeles professor Victoria Valle on the situation of Mexican-Americans today:*
   "A number of medium-size firms owned by Mexican-Americans are growing fast in southern California. There were times when the future looked dark for us, but now we are looking ahead to a brighter future."
7. *Francis Lieber, a German immigrant to the USA in the early 19th century:*
   "It will be easy for our children to learn two languages at once. Few things will help them more than the knowledge of two languages."

4 Interviews with people from the past

a Choose two famous people from history and explain why you would like to interview them and what questions you would ask them.
Here is how you could start: *If I could choose, I would interview ...*

b Which two people from German history would you advise an American student to interview? Give reasons why you chose these two people.

5 How do you see the USA?

Get together with a partner and – in a network – collect words and phrases that you associate with the USA. Perhaps your class can also make a collage that expresses your views of the USA.

→ Option 22: The passive

Words Words Words

a Words in combinations

(to) agree	criminal	(to) fight	(to) hurt	neighbour	(to) protect	(to) suggest
(to) attack	(to) damage	free	injured	neighbourhood	right	suggestion
beautiful	danger	freedom	(to) kill	peace	safe	thief
(to) break	dangerous	(to) hit	law	peaceful	(to) save	(to) throw
careful	(to) destroy	home	(to) miss	police	(to) steal	war
(to) catch	(to) disagree	homeless	music	powerful	strange	weapon
crime	(to) escape	hooligan	musician	prison	stranger	wrong

Here are some suggestions how to put new and old words together into combinations. Can you think of any other possibilities yourself?

1. dangerous – danger	2. right or wrong	3. beautiful	4. strange – stranger
free – ?	agree or ?	careful	crime – ?
peaceful – ?	war or ?	?	steal – ?
suggest – ?	catch or ?	?	music – ?

5. If you have no home, you are … . – I like the neighbours in our … . – A weapon can … or even … people. – The police keep law and order, they … . – Criminals …/Thieves …/Hooligans … .

b Words which sound similar

Use the words from the box in the following sentences:

(to) accept [ək'sept] – aspect ['æspekt] – except [ɪk'sept] – (to) expect [ɪk'spekt] – expert ['ekspɜːt] – excerpt ['eksɜːpt] – respect [rɪ'spekt]

1. You needn't read the whole book. An ••• will be enough. 2. I can't go to the meeting tonight. We're •••ing an exchange student from abroad. 3. Tom is very good at repairing broken TV sets. In fact, he's a real •••. 4. Credit cards are •••ed in most hotels and shops these days. 5. The way Jenny behaved is really un•••able. 6. If people had more ••• for nature, all of us could lead a better life. 7. Everybody •••ed Arthur as the real king, ••• the Black Knight. 8. At our next meeting all •••s of this problem should be discussed.

c Trouble spot *gehen* – go, walk, leave, be, work

Translate the following sentences.

1. John *geht* noch zur Schule. 2. Wo *gehst* du denn hin? 3. Du kannst den 33er Bus nehmen oder zu Fuß *gehen*. 4. Wann *geht* der nächste Bus zum Flughafen? 5. Zwischen 22 Uhr und 5 Uhr *gehen* keine Busse. 6. Die Klingel *geht* nicht. 7. Wie *geht's* deinem Bruder? *Geht's* ihm wieder gut? 8. Deine Uhr *geht* falsch. 9. Wenn ich jetzt nicht *gehe*, verpasse ich meinen Zug. 10. Mach dir keine Sorgen! Mir *geht's* gut.

d Trouble spot hear/listen (to) – see/look (at)/watch

Fill in the correct verb form to complete the following sentences. Add "to" or "at" if necessary.

1. ● where you're going. 2. I could ● the monkeys for hours. 3. Are you ● the radio, or shall I switch it off? 4. Tommy never ● what you tell him. 5. The thief became nervous because he felt he was being ●. 6. I'm sure the accident was the driver's fault. He should have ● more carefully. 7. Steve, ● the board, please. 8. Although we ● carefully, we couldn't ● a word of what they were saying. 9. ● ! Somebody is knocking at the door, I think. 10. On our way to the cinema we ● Helen on the other side of the street. She was ● us and shouting something we couldn't ● very well. 11. We look forward to ● from you.

- "Belonging to two worlds isn't easy." – This is what a teacher says in the following story to Lynn, a Navajo teenager. What do you think he wants to tell her?
- Where do you think problems can arise when a young person belongs to or, for one reason or another, has to belong to two 'worlds'?
- Read the story about Angela's cousin Lynn and find out what exactly Lynn's problem was and how she solved it.

A question of identity

When Lynn was 16, her teachers told her about a new government program for minority high school students – blacks, Hispanics, American Indians – who were good at school. If they were chosen, these students would be given the chance of going to some of the best schools in the US, where they could prepare for college.
"We hope that you will try to win a place in the program," said one of Lynn's teachers. "The competition will be great, but we feel that you have a good chance of being chosen."
Lynn began to feel nervous. "And if I win a place, where will I go? Will it be far from the reservation?"
"We don't know," another of her teachers said. "But most of the schools are in California and on the East Coast."
Lynn listened carefully while her teachers explained the program to her and finally, after talking to her parents, she agreed to apply and take the exam. "I know I won't pass," she thought, "so there's nothing to worry about." A short time later, she took the exam. It was difficult, as she had imagined it would be. She was sure she had done terribly and soon forgot the whole thing. And then one day, she was called into the principal's office. He smiled when she walked in and held up a piece of paper.
"Congratulations, Lynn," he said. "You've been chosen. You're going to Brandermill School in Vermont. It's one of the best schools in the country. You're very lucky."
Lynn suddenly felt weak and afraid. "But it's so far away," she said.

In June there was a special summer program to prepare the students before they left for their new schools. That gave Lynn just two weeks to be with her family, just two weeks to look again at the red earth of the reservation, at the desert and the wild strange rocks that the winds and water had made into fantastic figures over thousands of centuries.
During those two weeks she visited her relatives, sat in her grandparents' hogan, got water for them as they had none in their home. She helped to make bread and look after her grandfather's sheep. And at night she lay on the ground outside and watched the stars in the dark sky, felt the cool wind against her face. "It will be so different," she thought.

Brandermill was a school for the children of rich parents. It cost more money to go there than Lynn could imagine. The school could afford the best teachers in the country and the students' results were among the best. Everybody had told Lynn how lucky she was to go to such a school.

But two weeks after school had started, Lynn felt completely miserable. She was lonely and homesick for her family and her Navajo friends. She hated September in New England. She missed the warmth of Arizona and wished to be home among the great rocks and deep canyons.

So Lynn sat quietly in all her classes, afraid of saying the wrong thing; she felt she could not compete with her classmates. They seemed to be much more intelligent. In her English class they talked about books and writers she had never heard of. Lynn was also having problems with her English. On the reservation she had learned both English and Navajo, but she had always thought in Navajo. Now she had to think in English. During the following weeks, Lynn felt that she was surely failing.

And Lynn made no friends. A few of the students talked with her sometimes, but it was usually about homework. Lynn did not try to make friends either. "I am not part of their world," she thought. "They just don't notice me." By the middle of October Lynn was sure that she should leave Brandermill and go back to the reservation. She went to the counselor to tell him of her decision. He listened quietly while she told him about her problems.

"I'm not good in class," she said. "I can't follow. I'm unhappy with the life here. I'm really a Navajo. I should be back where I belong."

"You *are* a Navajo," said her counselor. "That's right. And right now you belong here."

"But I'm failing," said Lynn.

"Have any of your teachers said you are failing?" the counselor asked.

"No," said Lynn. "I just know it."

The counselor smiled. "You just *think* you know it. I've talked with your teachers. They say you're doing just fine in everything. You have to improve your written English, but you're certainly not failing."

"But I'm not happy," said Lynn.

"That's a different thing," said the counselor. "What you're doing is very difficult. Belonging to two worlds isn't easy. You have come from your own special world into one that is very different. There are few people who could do what you are doing and succeed. That's why you were chosen, because somebody believed you could do it."

"But I can't," said Lynn.

The counselor looked at her. "You *can* do it. Believe me. If you go back to the reservation now, you won't feel good about yourself or about leaving here. You'll feel that you have failed. You will feel that you have let down your tribe, your family, and your friends. Stay here until Christmas. You'll be able to go home then. Don't leave before that. Make a calendar, count the days on the wall – do anything, but don't leave now. When you get back to the reservation, then you can decide whether you want to come back to Brandermill. That's the place where you have to make the decision."

The conversation with her counselor helped her. She threw herself into her work. She studied harder and spent more time in the library. She forced herself to speak in class, she forced herself to talk to the other students – and some even became more friendly. And time flew by, until suddenly it was Christmas and she was on her way back home.

On her first night at home Lynn sat with her mother and her grandparents in their hogan. During the day she had ridden with her father and grandfather. She had looked again at the mountains and canyons. She felt at home, felt that these were her people and this was her life. Now a cold winter wind was blowing outside, but inside it was warm and comfortable. Lynn told her family about the school, how big and expensive it was, how good the teachers were – and she talked about her problems.

"What if I turn into a white person?" she said. "If I learn white ways and how they think, if I learn their language and read their books, if I spend most of my time with them – won't I become a white person?"

Her grandmother answered in Navajo. "You should learn the ways of the white people. You can help all of us in the tribe by acquiring the white man's knowledge. But the ways of your own people are deep inside you. I don't think you will forget who you are."

And her mother said, "Nothing can make you a white person unless you want to be one."

In that moment her decision was made.

(Based on "Lynn, a Navajo" from *To live in two worlds* by Brent Ashabranner)

Working with the text

1 Check if you can remember some important points of the story

Each of these sentences is only partly right. Identify what is right, and correct what is wrong.

1. Lynn was worried before the exam because she was weak in some subjects. 2. There was a new government program for sons and daughters of rich parents. 3. Lynn changed schools and felt happy in the weeks before leaving. 4. The climate in Vermont made her unhappy. 5. The guidance counselor said a final decision must be made by Lynn's parents on the reservation. 6. After the conversation everything was suddenly OK for Lynn. 7. Her grandmother and her mother made the decision for her.

2 A poem to go with the story

The poem on the right is by some students.
How can it help to understand Lynn's situation better?

It Is Not!

The Navajo Reservation
a lonesome place?
It is Not!
The skies are sunny,
Clear blue,
Or grey with rain.
Each day is gay –
In Nature's way.
It is not a lonesome place at all.
A Navajo house shabby and small?
It is Not!
Inside there's love,
Good laughter,
And *Big Talk.*
But best –
It's home
With an open door
And room for all.
A Castle could have no more.

3 A letter home

Before Lynn visited the guidance counselor, she wrote to one of her teachers in Window Rock. Finish her letter.

Dear Mrs. Hopp,
How I miss the reservation. I've only been here for a few weeks and I feel terrible. ...

Listening comprehension Canyon de Chelly

- Read the sentence on the right and the words in the box below it.
- Listen to **Part I** of the text. Then try to reconstruct the first part of the text with the help of the words in the box.
- The information below will give you the historical context for **Part II**.

Part I

"In the northeast of Arizona, in the heart of the Navajo nation, lies one of the most beautiful canyons in the United States, the Canyon de Chelly. ..."

2000 years hundreds of feet 14th century
water, food from trees, animals the Navajo's return
the Spanish/over a hundred years later live outside

Part II

by about 1860	The railroads from the East have reached cities like St. Louis and Memphis.
in 1860	Congress passes a law giving settlers free land in the West.
from 1861 to 1865	The Civil War is fought mainly in the East, but also in some areas of the West.
in 1862	A large number of northern 'Bluecoats' arrive in New Mexico. The soldiers fighting for the South flee to Texas and leave the Bluecoats with nothing to do.
from 1863 to 1869	A transcontinental railroad is built. The tracks meet in the Utah desert.
in 1891	The last Indian revolt ends in a tragedy. Chief Sitting Bull is killed. Ten days later almost three hundred Sioux men, women and children are killed in the Wounded Knee massacre in South Dakota.

Now listen to **Part II** and find out what happened to the Navajo in the time from 1863 to 1868.
In 1868 Manuelito, a famous Navajo chief, said, "When we saw the top of the mountain, we wondered if it was our mountain, and we felt like talking to the ground, we loved it so, and some of the old men and women cried with joy when they reached their homes." What do you think he was talking about?

Dreams

Hold fast[1] to dreams
For if dreams die
Life is a broken-winged[2] bird
That cannot fly.

Hold fast to dreams
For when dreams go
Life is a barren[3] field
Frozen[4] with snow.

Langston Hughes

DREAM

1 sequence[5] of scenes and feelings happening in the mind during sleep
2 state of mind in which things happening around one seem unreal
3 ambition[6] or ideal

(adapted from the *Oxford Advanced Learner's Dictionary*)

DREAMS

Everybody has dreams; whether or not the dream is remembered depends on how quickly after it the sleeper wakes up. The new combinations of ideas produced in dreams can be creative and valuable.

(adapted from the *New Webster's Universal Encyclopedia*)

DAYDREAMS

Some psychologists believe that daydreams are a kind of wishful thinking[7] that happens when inner needs cannot be expressed in real behavior. We daydream, they claim, when the world outside us does not meet our needs, or when we are motivated to do something but cannot achieve our goal.

(adapted from *Psychology* by Charles G. Morris)

*Not all the new words in this Unit are explained. Still, you should be able to understand the texts. Only the key words are explained at the foot of the page. The new words from the questions can be found in the

[1]hold fast to *festhalten an* [2]wing [wɪŋ] Flügel [3]barren ['bærən] *öde, leer, unfruchtbar* [4]frozen [frəʊzən] *gefroren*
[5]sequence ['si:kwəns] Reihenfolge [6]ambition [æm'bɪʃn] *Ehrgeiz* [7]wishful thinking *Wunschdenken*

Look at the picture on these two pages for a few moments and then, slowly, read the poem[+].

Why do you think this particular picture was chosen to go with the poem?
Who could the speaker in this poem be? Who might she/he be addressing?
What might a possible situation be, quite concretely, in which she/he is saying this?

When I look at the picture, I think …/feel …/have the impression …; and when I read the poem, I … . The speaker could be … or … . She/He might be addressing …/Perhaps she/he is addressing … I could imagine a situation …; or maybe …

Try to read the poem aloud to yourself several times, and then present it to the class.
Listen to different pupils and compare the effect different presentations have on you.
What do you think is the function of the repetition in the two stanzas?

I feel the way Y read the poem fits the spirit of the poem very well because …/doesn't fit so well because … . Somehow it seems that through the repetition … . Langston Hughes might want to stress/show … .

Look again at the poem and find out what exactly the differences are between the two verses. Pay particular attention to Langston Hughes' choice of words and the central image in each verse.

The first difference is …; secondly, L. Hughes chose to write … in the first verse and … in the second verse. The image in lines three and four … . If you compare what the images mean, you could say …

Looking at the complete poem, what do you think dreams and dreaming mean to different people?
Langston Hughes (1902-67) was a black American. What do you think dreams and dreaming meant to him?
Why does/doesn't the poem appeal to you?

Read the information about dreams and dreaming in the three texts on the left. It might help you when you are talking about the following four texts.

Vocabulary on pages 165-168.

[+] → Option 18: Literary terms and their collocations (Words underlined in this Unit are listed and explained here.)

Look at the illustration and the moral at the end of James Thurber's fable. Then try to answer the following questions:
What do moths normally do when there is a light? What happens to them quite often? Why does this moth seem to be different from the 'average moth'?
Read the fable and find out about this moth's life.

The moth and the star

A young and impressionable[1] moth once set his heart on[2] a certain star. He told his mother about this and she counselled him to set his heart on a bridge lamp instead. "Stars aren't the thing to hang around," she said; "Lamps are the thing to hang around." "You get somewhere[3] that way," said the moth's father. "You don't get anywhere chasing[4] stars." But the moth would not heed[5] the words of either parent. Every evening at dusk when the star came out he would start flying toward it and every morning at dawn he would crawl[6] back home worn out[7] with his vain endeavour[8]. One day his father said to him, "You haven't burned a wing in months, boy, and it looks to me as if you were never going to. All your brothers have been badly burned flying around street lamps and all your sisters have been terribly singed[9] flying around house lamps. Come on, now, get out of here and get yourself scorched[10]! A big strapping moth like you without a mark[11] on him!"

The moth left his father's house, but he would not fly around street lamps and he would not fly around house lamps. He went right on trying to reach the star, which was four and one-third light years, or twenty-five trillion miles, away. The moth thought it was just caught in the top branches[12] of an elm[13]. He never did reach the star, but he went right on trying, night after night, and when he was a very, very old moth he began to think that he really had reached the star and went around saying so. This gave him a deep and lasting pleasure, and he lived to a great old age. His parents and his brothers and his sisters had all been burned to death when they were quite young.

Moral: Who flies afar[14] from the sphere of our sorrow[15] is here today and here tomorrow[16].

James Thurber

– What is the story of the moth's life and what does it have to do with dreams and dreaming?	→ From an early age on, the moth … . One could say that the moth was trying to get away from …
– What kind of 'person' was the moth in his younger years, what was he like in his later years?	→ The author characterizes the young moth as someone who … . Later, he is characterized as … .
– What unwritten laws in 'moth country' doesn't the moth want to follow?	→ If you look at what the mother/father says, one such law must be …
– As in all fables, the animals here are similar to people. What kinds of people might the different moths represent? What might such symbols as the star or the street lights suggest to a reader?	→ For me the young moth represents different people. … . The father/mother could be … To me the star is …, but I could imagine that to someone else it might …

– Work with a partner: Together, make up an interview for the 'Moth Times' in which the moth, in his old age, talks about his life and his opinions on the life of 'average moths'. (The interview should include a critical question about the fact that the moth obviously lost all touch with reality at one point in his life.) Add a comment to the interview with your opinion on the question: Was this dream worth dreaming?

[1]impressionable *leicht zu beeindrucken* [2]set one's heart on – set – set *sein Herz hängen an* [3]get somewhere (infml.) *Fortschritte machen* [4]chase [tʃeɪs] *nachjagen* [5]heed *beachten* [6]crawl [krɔːl] *kriechen* [7]worn out *erschöpft* [8]vain endeavour [ɪn'devə] (fml.) *vergebliche Anstrengung* [9]singe [sɪndʒ] *versengen, ansengen* [10]scorch [skɔːtʃ] *versengen* [11]mark *Markierung, Mal* [12]branch [brɑːntʃ] *Zweig* [13]elm *Ulme* [14]afar [ə'fɑː] *weit (weg)* [15]sorrow *Kummer, Leid* [16]*eine Abwandlung der Redensart* 'here today and gone tomorrow' *(= von kurzer Dauer)*

Look at the illustration that goes with the following short story. Look at the faces of the two men and at the way they are dressed.
Who could they be? What might they be talking about? Why do you think the younger man is not looking at the older man?

The Winner

Wordman stood at the window, looking out, and saw Revell walk away from the compound[1]. "Come here," he said to the interviewer. "You'll see the Guardian[2] in action."
The interviewer came around the desk and stood beside Wordman at the window. He said, "That's one of them?"
"Right." Wordman smiled, feeling pleasure. "You're lucky," he said. "It's rare when one of them even makes the attempt[3]. Maybe he's doing it for your benefit[4]."
The interviewer looked troubled[5]. He said, "Doesn't he know what it will do?"
"Of course. Some of them don't believe it, not till they've tried it once. Watch."
They both watched. Revell walked without apparent haste, directly across the field toward the woods on the other side. After he'd gone about 200 yards from the edge[6] of the compound he began to bend[7] forward slightly at the middle, and a few yards farther on he folded his arms across his stomach as though[8] it ached him. He tottered[9], but kept moving forward, staggering[10] more and more, appearing to be in great pain. He managed to stay on his feet nearly all the way to the trees, but finally crumpled to the ground, where he lay unmoving.
Wordman no longer felt pleasure. He liked the theory of the Guardian better than its application. Turning to his desk, he called the infirmary[11] and said, "Send a stretcher[12] out to the east, near the woods. Revell's out there."
The interviewer turned at the sound of the name, saying, "Revell? Is that who that is? The poet?"
"If you can call it poetry." Wordman's lips[13] curled in disgust[14]. He'd read some of Revell's so-called poems; garbage[15], garbage.
The interviewer looked back out the window. "I'd heard he was arrested," he said thoughtfully.
Looking over the interviewer's shoulder, Wordman saw that Revell had managed to get back up onto hands and knees, was now crawling[16] slowly and painfully toward the woods. But a stretcher team was already trotting toward him and Wordman watched as they reached him, picked up the pain-weakened body, strapped it to the stretcher, and carried it back to the compound.
As they moved out of sight, the interviewer said, "Will he be all right?"
"After a few days in the infirmary. He'll have strained[17] some muscles."
The interviewer turned away from the window. "That was very graphic," he said carefully.
"You're the first outsider to see it," Wordman told him, and smiled, feeling good again. "What do they call that? A scoop[18]?"

[1]compound ['--] *Gefängnishof* [2]Guardian ['gɑːdɪən] *Wächter* [3]attempt *Versuch* [4]for your benefit *Ihretwegen* [5]troubled *beunruhigt* [6]edge *Rand* [7]bend – bent – bent *(sich) krümmen* [8]as though *als ob* [9]totter *wanken* [10]stagger *taumeln* [11]infirmary [-'---] *Krankenstation* [12]stretcher *Bahre* [13]lip *Lippe* [14]disgust [-'-] *Empörung, Abscheu* [15]garbage ['gɑːbɪdʒ] (infml.) *Schund, Mist* [16]crawl [krɔːl] *kriechen* [17]strain *zerren* [18]scoop *sensationelle Erstmeldung*

"Yes," agreed the interviewer, sitting back down in his chair. "A scoop."

They returned to the interview, just the most recent of dozens Wordman had given in the year since this pilot project of the Guardian had been set up. For perhaps the fiftieth time he explained what the Guardian did and how it was of value to society. The essence of the Guardian was the miniature black box, actually a tiny radio receiver, which was surgically inserted[1] into the body of every prisoner. In the center of this prison compound was the Guardian transmitter[2], perpetually[3] sending its message to these receivers. As long as a prisoner stayed within the hundred-and-fifty-yard range[4] of that transmitter, all was well. Should he move beyond that range, the black box inside his skin[5] would begin to send messages of pain throughout his nervous system. This pain increased as the prisoner moved farther from the transmitter, until at its peak[6] it was totally immobilizing.

"The prisoner can't hide, you see," Wordman explained. "Even if Revell had reached the woods, we'd have found him. His screams would have led us to him."

The Guardian had been initially[7] suggested by Wordman himself, at that time serving as assistant warden[8] at a more ordinary penitentiary[9] in the Federal system. Objections[10], mostly from sentimentalists, had delayed[11] its acceptance for several years, but now at last this pilot project had been established, with a guaranteed five-year trial[12] period, and Wordman had been placed in charge[13].

"If the results are as good as I'm sure they will be," Wordman said, "all prisons in the Federal system will be converted to the Guardian method."

The Guardian method had made jailbreaks[14] impossible, riots easy to quell[15] – by merely turning off the transmitter for a minute or two – and prisons simplicity[16] to guard. "We have no guards here as such," Wordman pointed out[17]. "Service employees only are needed here, people for the mess hall[18], infirmary and so on."

For the pilot project, prisoners were only those who had committed crimes[19] against the State rather than against individuals. "You might say," Wordman said, smiling, "that here are gathered[20] the Disloyal Opposition."

"You mean, political prisoners," suggested the interviewer.

"We don't like that phrase here," Wordman said, his manner suddenly icy. "It sounds Commie[21]."

The interviewer apologized for his sloppy use of terminology, ended the interview shortly afterward, and Wordman, once again in a good mood, escorted him out of the building. "You see," he said, gesturing. "No walls. No machine guns in towers. Here at last is the model prison."

The interviewer thanked him again for his time, and went away to his car. Wordman watched him leave, then went over to the infirmary to see Revell. But he'd been given a shot[22], and was already asleep.

Revell lay flat on his back and stared at the ceiling. He kept thinking, over and over again, "I didn't know it would be as bad as that. I didn't know it would be as bad as that."

Mentally, he took a big brush of black paint and wrote the words on the spotless white ceiling: *"I didn't know it would be as bad as that."*

"Revell."

He turned his head slightly and saw Wordman standing beside the bed. He watched Wordman, but made no sign.

Wordman said, "They told me you were awake."

Revell waited.

"I tried to tell you when you first came," Wordman reminded him. "I told you there was no point[23] trying to get away."

Revell opened his mouth and said, "It's all right, don't feel bad. You do what you have to do, I do what I have to do."

"Don't *feel* bad!" Wordman stared at him. "What have *I* got to feel bad about?"

Revell looked up at the ceiling, and the words he had painted there just a minute ago were gone already. He wished he had paper and pencil. Words were leaking out of him like water

[1]surgically inserted [ˌsɜːdʒɪklɪ‿ɪn'sɜːtɪd] *operativ eingesetzt* [2]transmitter *Sender* [3]perpetual [pə'petʃʊəl] *fortwährend* [4]range *Reichweite* [5]skin *Haut* [6]peak *Höhepunkt, Gipfel* [7]initial [ɪ'nɪʃl] *anfänglich* [8]warden (AE) *Gefängnisdirektor/in* [9]penitentiary [ˌ--'---] (AE) *Gefängnis* [10]objection [-'--] *Einwand* [11]delay [-'-] *verzögern* [12]trial ['traɪəl] *Erprobungs-* [13]place sb. in charge *jm. die Leitung übertragen* [14]jailbreak *Gefängnisausbruch* [15]quell *(Aufstand) unterdrücken* [16]simplicity [-'---] (infml.) *hier: die einfachste Sache der Welt* [17]point out *klarmachen* [18]mess hall *Speisesaal* [19]commit a crime, -tt- *ein Verbrechen begehen* [20]gather *versammeln* [21]commie (infml.) *kommunistisch* [22]shot (infml.) *Spritze, Injektion* [23]no point *sinnlos*

through a sieve[1]. He needed paper and pencil to catch them in. He said, "May I have paper and pencil?"

"To write more obscenity? Of course not."

"Of course not," echoed Revell. He closed his eyes and watched the words leaking away. A man doesn't have time both to invent and memorize, he has to choose, and long ago Revell had chosen invention. But now there was no way to put the inventions down on paper and they trickled through[2] his mind like water and eroded away into the great outside world. "Twinkle, twinkle, little pain," Revell said softly, "in my groin[3] and in my brain[4], down so low and up so high, will you live or will I die?"

"The pain goes away," said Wordman. "It's been three days. It should be gone already."

"It will come back," Revell said. He opened his eyes and wrote the words on the ceiling.

"It will come back."

Wordman said, "Don't be silly. It's gone for good, unless you run away again."

Revell was silent.

Wordman waited, half-smiling, and then frowned[5]. "You aren't," he said.

Revell looked at him in some surprise. "Of course I am," he said. "Didn't you know I would?"

"No one tries it twice."

"I'll never stop leaving. Don't you know that? I'll never stop leaving. I'll never stop being, I'll not stop believing I'm who I must be. You had to know that."

Wordman stared at him. "You'll go through it *again*?"

"Ever and ever," Revell said.

"It's a bluff." Wordman pointed an angry finger at Revell, saying, "If you want to die, I'll let you die. Do you know if we don't bring you back you'll die out there?"

"That's escape, too," Revell said.

"Is that what you want? All right. Go out there again, and I won't send anyone after you, that's a promise."

"Then you lose," Revell said. He looked at Wordman finally seeing the blunt, angry face. "They're your rules," Revell told him, "and by your own rules you're going to lose. You say your black box will make me stay, and that means the black box will make me stop being me. I say you're wrong. I say as long as I'm leaving you're losing, and if the black box kills me you've lost forever."

Spreading his arms, Wordman shouted, "Do you think this is a *game*?"

"Of course," Revell said. "That's why you invented it."

"You're insane[6]," Wordman said. He started for the door. "You shouldn't be here, you should be in an asylum[7]."

"That's losing, too," Revell shouted after him, but Wordman had slammed the door and gone.

Revell lay back on the pillow. Alone again, he could dwell[8] once more on his terrors[9]. He was afraid of the black box, much more now that he knew what it could do to him, afraid to the point where his fear made him sick to his stomach, but he was afraid of losing himself, too, this a more abstract and intellectual fear but just as strong. No, it was even stronger, because it was driving him to go out again. "But I didn't know it would be as bad as that," he whispered. He painted it once more on the ceiling, this time in red.

Wordman had been told when Revell would be released from[10] the infirmary, and he made a point[11] of being at the door when Revell came out. Revell seemed somewhat leaner[12], perhaps a little older. He shielded his eyes from the sun with his hand, looked at Wordman, and said, "Good-bye, Wordman." He started walking east.

Wordman didn't believe it. He said, "You're bluffing, Revell."

Revell kept walking.

Wordman couldn't remember when he'd ever felt such anger. He wanted to run after Revell and kill him with his bare hands. He clenched his hands into fists and told himself he was a reasonable man, a rational man, a merciful[13] man. As the Guardian was reasonable, was rational, was merciful. It required only obedience[14], and so did he. It punished only such purposeless defiance[15] as Revell's, and so did he. Revell was antisocial, self-destructive, he had to learn. For his own sake[16], as well as for the sake of society, Revell had to be taught.

[1]sieve [sɪv] *Sieb* [2]trickle through *sickern durch* [3]groin *Leiste(ngegend)* [4]brain *Gehirn* [5]frown *die Stirn runzeln* [6]insane *wahnsinnig* [7]asylum [ə'saɪləm] *Irrenanstalt* [8]dwell on *nachdenken über* [9]terror *(panische) Angst* [10]release (from) *entlassen (aus)* [12]make a point of doing sth. *Wert darauf legen, etwas zu tun* [12]lean *mager* [13]merciful *barmherzig* [14]obedience [ə'biːdɪəns] *Gehorsam* [15]defiance [dɪ'faɪəns] *Trotz, Widerstand* [16]for his own sake *um seinetwillen*

Wordman shouted, "What are you trying to *get* out of this?" He glared[1] at Revell's moving back, listened to Revell's silence. He shouted, "I won't send anyone after you! You'll crawl back *yourself*!"

He kept watching until Revell was far out from the compound, staggering across the field toward the trees, his arms folded across his stomach, his legs stumbling[2], his head bent forward. Wordman watched, and then gritted his teeth, and turned his back, and returned to his office to work on the monthly report. Only two attempted escapes last month.

Two or three times in the course of the afternoon he looked out the window. The first time, he saw Revell far across the field, on hands and knees, crawling toward the trees. The last time, Revell was out of sight[3], but he could be heard screaming. Wordman had a great deal of trouble concentrating his attention on the report.

Toward evening he went outside again. Revell's screams sounded from the woods, faint but continuous. Wordman stood listening, his fists clenching and relaxing at his sides. Grimly he forced himself not to feel pity. For Revell's own good[4] he had to be taught.

A staff doctor came to him a while later and said, "Mr Wordman, we've got to bring him in."

Wordman nodded. "I know. But I want to be sure he's learned."

"For God's sake," said the doctor, "*listen* to him."

Wordman looked bleak. "All right, bring him in."

As the doctor started away, the screaming stopped. Wordman and the doctor both turned their heads, listened – silence. The doctor ran for the infirmary.

Revell lay screaming. All he could think of was the pain, and the need to scream. But sometimes, when he managed a scream of the very loudest, it was possible for him to have a fraction of a second for himself, and in those fractions of seconds he still kept moving away from the prison, inching along the ground, so that in the last hour he had moved approximately seven feet. His head and right arm were now visible[5] from the country road that passed through these woods.

On one level, he was conscious[6] of nothing but the pain and his own screaming. On another level, he was totally, even insistently, aware of everything around him, the blades of grass near his eyes, the stillness of the woods, the tree branches high overhead. And the small pickup truck, when it stopped on the road beyond him.

The man who came from the truck and squatted beside Revell had a lined and weathered face and the rough clothing of a farmer. He touched Revell's shoulder and said, "You hurt, fella?"

"Eeeeast!" screamed Revell. "Eeeeast!"

"Is it okay to move you?" asked the man.

"Yesssss!" shrieked Revell. "Eeeeast!"

"I'd best take you to a doctor."

There was no change in the pain when the man lifted him and carried him to the truck and lay him down on the floor in back. He was already at optimum distance from the transmitter; the pain now was as bad as it could get.

The farmer tucked[7] a rolled-up wad of cloth into Revell's open mouth. "Bite on this," he said. "It'll make it easier."

It made nothing easier, but it muffled[8] his screams. He was grateful for that; the screams embarrassed him.

He was aware of it all, the drive through increasing darkness, the farmer carrying him into a building that was of colonial design on the outside but looked like the infirmary on the inside, and a doctor who looked down at him and touched his forehead and then went to one side to thank the farmer for bringing him. They spoke briefly over there, and then the farmer went away and the doctor came back to look at Revell again. He was young, dressed in laboratory white, with a pudgy face and red hair. He seemed sick and angry. He said, "You're from that prison, aren't you?"

Revell was still screaming through the cloth. He managed a head-spasm[9] which he meant to be a nod. His armpits felt as though they were being cut open with knives of ice. The sides of his neck were being scraped by sandpaper. All of his joints[10] were being ground back and forth, back and forth, the way a man at dinner separates the bones of a chicken wing. The interior of his stomach was full of acid. His body was stuck with needles[11], sprayed with fire. His skin was being peeled off[12], his nerves cut with razor blades, his muscles pounded with hammers.

[1]glare at sb./sth. *jn./etwas wütend anstarren* [2]stumble *stolpern* [3]out of sight *außer Sicht* [4]for his/her own good *zum eigenen Wohl* [5]visible *sichtbar* [6]be conscious of sth. ['kɒnʃəs] *sich einer Sache bewußt sein* [7]tuck *stecken* [8]muffle ['mʌfl] *dämpfen* [9]spasm *Zuckung* [10]joint *Gelenk* [11]needle *Nadel* [12]peel off *abschälen*

Thumbs were pushing his eyes out from inside his head. And yet, the genius of this pain, the brilliance[1] that had gone into its construction, it permitted his mind to work, to remain[2] constantly aware. There was no unconsciousness for him, no oblivion[3].

The doctor said, "What beasts[4] some men are. I'll try to get it out of you. I don't know what will happen, we aren't supposed to know how it works, but I'll try to take the box out of you."

He went away, and came back with a needle.

"Here. This will put you to sleep."

"Ahhhhh."

"He isn't there. He just isn't anywhere in the woods."

Wordman glared at the doctor, but knew he had to accept what the man reported. "All right," he said.

"Someone took him away. He had a confederate out there, someone who helped him get away."

"No one would dare[5]," said the doctor. "Anyone who helped him would wind up[6] here themselves."

"Nevertheless," said Wordman. "I'll call the State Police," he said, and went on into his office.

Two hours later the State Police called back. They'd checked the normal users of that road, local people who might have seen or heard something, and had found a farmer who'd picked up an injured man near the prison and taken him to a Dr Allyn in Boonetown. The State Police were convinced the farmer had acted innocently.

"But not the doctor," Wordman said grimly. "He'd have to know the truth almost immediately."

"Yes, sir, I should think so."

"And he hasn't reported Revell."

"No, sir."

"Have you gone to pick him up yet?"

"Not yet. We just got the report."

"I'll want to come with you. Wait for me."

"Yes, sir."

Wordman traveled in the ambulance in which they'd bring Revell back. They arrived without siren at Dr Allyn's with two cars of state troopers, marched into the tiny operating room, and found Allyn washing instruments at the sink.

Allyn looked at them all calmly and said, "I thought you might be along."

Wordman pointed at the man who lay, unconscious, on the table in the middle of the room. "There's Revell," he said.

Allyn glanced at the operating table in surprise. "Revell? The poet?"

"You didn't know? Then why help him?"

Instead of answering, Allyn studied his face and said, "Would you be Wordman himself?"

Wordman said, "Yes, I am."

"Then I believe this is yours," Allyn said, and put into Wordman's hands a small and bloody black box.

The ceiling was persistently bare[7]. Revell's eyes wrote on it words that should have singed[8] the paint away, but nothing ever happened. He shut his eyes against the white at last and wrote in spidery letters on the inside of his lids[9] the single word *oblivion*. He heard someone come into the room, but the effort[10] of making a change was so great that for a moment longer he permitted his eyes to remain closed. When he did open them he saw Wordman there, standing grim and mundane at the foot of the bed.

Wordman said, "How are you, Revell?"

"I was thinking about oblivion," Revell told him. "Writing a poem on the subject." He looked up at the ceiling, but it was empty.

Wordman said, "You asked, one time, you asked for pencil and paper. We've decided you can have them."

Revell looked at him in sudden hope, but then understood, "Oh," he said. "Oh, *that*."

Wordman frowned and said, "What's wrong? I said you can have pencil and paper."

"If I promise not to leave any more."

Wordman's hands gripped the foot of the bed. He said, "What's the matter with you? You can't get away, you have to know that by now."

"You mean I can't win. But I won't lose. It's your game, your rules, your home ground, your equipment; if I can manage a stalemate[11], that's pretty good."

Wordman said, "You still think it's a game. You think none of it matters. Do you want to see what you've done?" He stepped back to the door, opened it, made a motion, and Dr Allyn was led in. Wordman said to Revell, "You remember

[1]brilliance ['brɪljəns] *Genialität* [2]remain *bleiben* [3]oblivion [ə'blɪvɪən] *Vergessen* [4]beast *Bestie* [5]dare *(es) wagen* [6]wind up (at a place) – wound – wound (infml.) *(irgendwo) enden, „landen"* [7]bare *kahl* [8]singe (away) [sɪndʒ] *(ab-)sengen* [9](eye-)lid *(Augen-)Lid* [10]effort *Anstrengung* [11]stalemate *Patt, Remis*

this man?"

"I remember," said Revell.

Wordman said, "He just arrived. They'll be putting the Guardian in him in about an hour. Does it make you proud[1], Revell?"

Looking at Allyn, Revell said, "I'm sorry."

Allyn smiled and shook his head. "Don't be. I had the idea the publicity of a trial[2] might help rid[3] the world of things like the Guardian." His smile turned sour. "There wasn't very much publicity."

Wordman said, "You two are cut out of the same cloth. The emotions of the mob, that's all you can think of. Revell in those so-called poems of his, and you in that speech you made in court."

Revell, smiling, said, "Oh? You made a speech? I'm sorry I didn't get to hear it."

"It wasn't very good," Allyn said. "I hadn't known the trial would only be one day long, so I didn't have much time to prepare it."

Wordman said, "All right, that's enough. You two can talk later, you'll have years."

At the door Allyn turned back and said, "Don't go anywhere till I'm up and around[4], will you? After my operation."

Revell said, "You want to come along next time?"

"Naturally," said Allyn.

Donald E. Westlake

Who are the two men in the illustration on page 65? Where are they, and why might they be together in this situation? (From memory, collect as many details as you can.)
What exactly is the Guardian?

- Reread the short story and then, to get a better understanding of what happens, discuss with a partner how you could illustrate the story through a series of ten to twelve pictures. Describe your pictures or actually draw them and write a caption of two or three sentences for each picture.
- Look again at the three statements about the structure of stories on page 47. Try to explain what the 'instability' is in the introductory passage of this story and what 'forces struggle with each other' in the development. Then discuss whether in *The Winner* a 'certain stability' is achieved at the end or not.
- Some suggestions for speculation and for creative writing:
  What do you think the state is like where these events take place? What crime might Revell have committed? Write the interviewer's report of his interview with Wordman. Write the speech Dr Allyn made during the trial and present it to the class.
- What do you think of Revell's, Dr Allyn's and also Wordman's intention to 'hold fast' to their individual dreams? Do you think this story has any relevance today?
- What do *you* think: Is it worth 'holding fast to dreams'?

- In a test you might be confronted with tasks like the following. See if you could do them, too. (*Don't forget:* Not all important information is expressed explicitly. In all stories you will have to infer information from the context.)

Collect what you are told about …

– the main characters and the motives for their behaviour	X and Y seem to be the main characters because … . On page xx, in line xx, for example, Y says … .
– the setting	The action takes place … (and covers a time of about …). We are/are not told in detail what … looks like. But I imagine … .
– the action	The story starts with … . The reader learns/is told about … . The story continues with … . This is followed by a (short/longer) passage about … .
Write down in a few sentences what you believe the theme of the story is.	The story deals with … .

[1]proud *stolz* [2]trial *Gerichtsverfahren* [3]rid of *befreien von* [4]be up and around *wieder auf den Beinen sein*

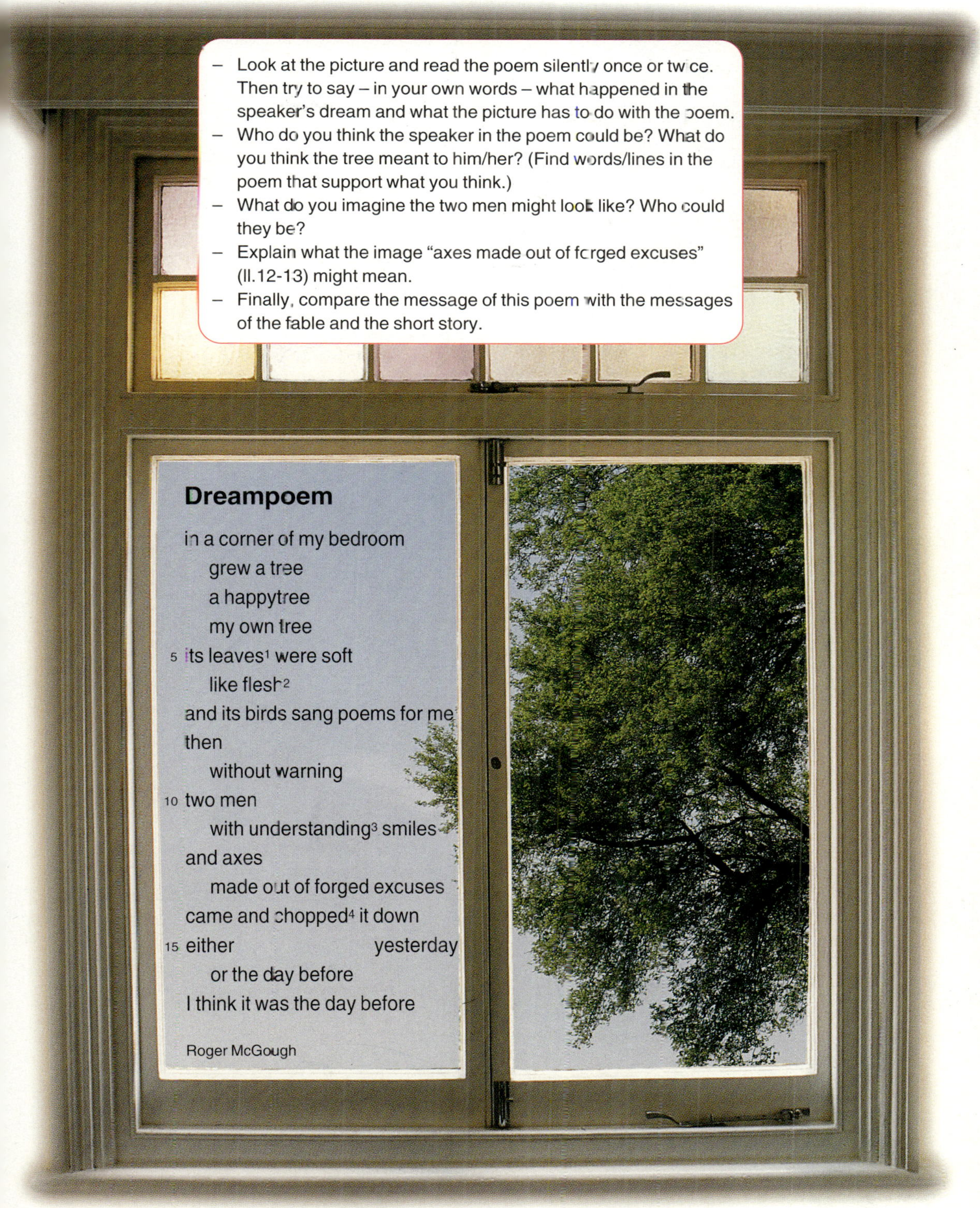

- Look at the picture and read the poem silently once or twice. Then try to say – in your own words – what happened in the speaker's dream and what the picture has to do with the poem.
- Who do you think the speaker in the poem could be? What do you think the tree meant to him/her? (Find words/lines in the poem that support what you think.)
- What do you imagine the two men might look like? Who could they be?
- Explain what the image "axes made out of forged excuses" (ll.12-13) might mean.
- Finally, compare the message of this poem with the messages of the fable and the short story.

Dreampoem

in a corner of my bedroom
grew a tree
a happytree
my own tree
its leaves[1] were soft
like flesh[2]
and its birds sang poems for me
then
without warning
two men
with understanding[3] smiles
and axes
made out of forged excuses
came and chopped[4] it down
either yesterday
or the day before
I think it was the day before

Roger McGough

[1]leaf, *pl.* leaves *Blatt* [2]flesh *(lebendiges) Fleisch* [3]understanding *verständnisvoll* [4]chop down, -pp- *fällen*

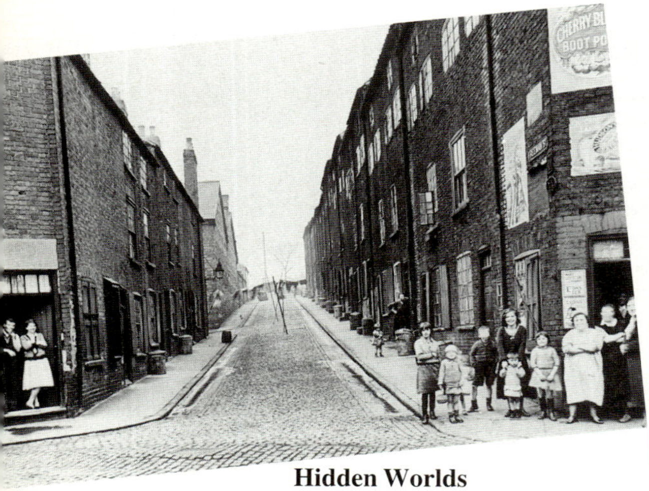

The following text is an excerpt from the novel *Key to the Door* by Alan Sillitoe, who was born in Nottingham in 1928.
The novel deals with the first 21 years in the life of Brian Seaton. The first part of the novel presents Brian's life as a working-class boy in Nottingham in the 1930s, a time of mass unemployment and great poverty. As Brian's father is unemployed, the Seaton family lives in extreme poverty, too.

Find out from the excerpt why, in this situation, *The Count of Monte Cristo*, a French novel written in the 19th century, means so much to the ten-year-old Brian. (Before you start reading look at the Info box on page 73.)

Hidden Worlds

A large atlas was opened at a map of the world, surrounded by dictionaries and foreign language books – the only section of the shop that interested him. He went in, and told a brown-dressed girl by the cash-desk[1] that he wanted to buy *The Count of Monte Cristo*, started to explain the simple financial system into which he had entered.

She left him standing with four pink receipts and the final sixpence, and came back with the manager. "I know him," he said. "He's a customer of ours." He turned to Brian, took the receipts and money and spread[2] them on the cash-desk. "*The Count of Monte Cristo*, wasn't it? Go and get it for him, will you?"

The book came, and he had only time to glimpse at the picture-cover[3] of a man holding a sword before it was taken away and wrapped up.

He opened the packet outside, flipped the hundreds of pages through his fingers, from cover to cover and back again. A posh[4] woman's voice said from behind: "You're going to be busy, aren't you?" He turned and said yes, ran his eyes up and down the formidable list of chapter[5] titles. No one was home, and he sat by the fire to read. The room had been scrubbed[6] and the table cleared, and in the congenial emptiness he sped on[7] through the easy prose of the story, had reached Edmond Dantès' betrothal[8] ceremony before his parents came in. They took off their coats.

"That looks like a nice book," his mother said.

"Where did you get it from?"

"I bought it from downtown."

"Who gen you all that money?" his father put in.

"It must 'ave cost a pretty penny," his mother said, spreading the cloth for tea.

"Nobody gen me the money," Brian told them, closing the book carefully. "I saved it up." Irritation came into his mother's voice: "How much was it?"

"Half a crown."

"Yer've wasted 'alf a crown on a book?" his father exclaimed.

He'd imagined they'd be pleased at his cleverness in bringing such a thing into the house, but it was the opposite. It was as though[9] he'd been split in half and was bleeding to death. All for a book. "It was *my* money," he cried, anguished[10] and bitter, because instead of buying the book he should have given the money to them.

"You're bloody-well silly about books," his father said, a definite threat in his voice. "You read till you're bloody-well daft[11]." His mother came back from the kitchen: "You stand need to spend half a crown on books, when you ain't got a bit o' shoe to your feet. And you're a sly little swine to 'ave money in the 'ouse all that time when I've often bin wi'out a shillin' ter buy some snap[12]."

"I didn't have the money here," he explained. "I took it bit by bit to the bookshop, like a Christmas club." This was even worse, because he'd made sure that, starving[13] or not, they

[1]cash-desk (BE) *Kasse* [2]spread [spred] – spread – spread *ausbreiten* [3]picture-cover *Bildeinband* [4]posh (infml.) *vornehm* [5]chapter *Kapitel* [6]scrub, -bb- *scheuern* [7]speed (on) – sped – sped *(weiter)jagen, -eilen* [8]betrothal [bɪ'trəʊðl] (fml.) *Verlobung* [9]as though *als ob* [10]anguished ['æŋgwɪʃt] *verzweifelt* [11]daft (infml.) *blöd(e)* [12]snap *(im nordenglischen Dialekt) (Mittag-)Essen* [13]starve *verhungern*

hadn't been able to get their hands on it. "You'd 'ave 'ad more sense to a got yoursen a pair o' shoes," Seaton cried. "I've a good mind to throw it on the bleddy fire."

" 'E's got no more sense[1] than 'e was born with," his mother said. Brian was horrified at his father's threat, saw flames already at their work.

"It's *my* book," he shouted.

"Don't cheek[2] me," Seaton said, "or you'll be for it, my lad." His tears were open, and they saw it.

"I hope there's a war on soon so's we're all killed," he raved[3].

"What a thing to say," his mother said. "I don't know where he gets it from."

A smack[4] across the head from his father. "Say one more word, and I'll show yer what I'll do wi' yer."

"Wait till I grow up," Brian cried.

But Seaton only said: "He'll be a lunatic[5] one day wi' reading so many books."

He sat by the fire while they drank tea, trying to force back the sobs, difficult because he saw too easily how he had done wrong. But hatred[6] and pity for himself surmounted[7] this, and so he couldn't stop. Vera passed him some tea: "Come on, it ain't the end o' the world." His eyes were drawn to the book cover, where a brave man held a rapier[8] as if he didn't care for anyone in the world, as though nothing could ever trouble him. And if it did, the face and sword said, it would be an easy matter to fight a duel and dispose of whatever it was.

He ate bread and jam, and went on reading. The story grafted[9] itself to him, slowly becoming him and he becoming it, and he left behind with each second the light and noise in the house, and went on wondering footsteps down into the dungeons[10] of the Château d'If with Edmond Dantès, following the guards and slipping[11] invisibly into the cell[12], and all night long he listened to the tapping and whispers[13] that came from the granite floor, heard the patient scraping[14] and scratching of freedom, was shown that even dungeons and giant prisons were unable to keep men in forever, though fourteen years was longer by four than he had so far lived: he listened to the chipping of home-made tools, and voices whispering as if from the dead, that talked of knowledge and freedom and hidden treasure[15] on the Island of Monte Cristo.

Why *does* the novel mean so much to Brian? Find some places in the text that show how he feels about the novel.

Info box

Note on the language:
"Yer" (you), "yoursen" (yourself), "bin" (been), "ter" (to), "gen" (gave), "stand need" (don't need/shouldn't), "to a got" (to have got), "so's" (so/so that) are words from the dialect of the English Midlands.

Note on the British currency up to 1971:
£1 = 20 shillings
1/2 crown = two shillings and sixpence
1 shilling = 12 pence

For sixpence you could buy a packet of tea in the 1930s; for half a crown you could buy a pair of shoes.

- Brian's father obviously has other ideas about books and reading than his son. What effects does he think they have on people? What do you think he would say to Brian in a quiet moment to explain his point of view?
- Books are only one way of experiencing other worlds. Find out how people came to know literature before the invention of the printing press. How did the situation change with the invention of the printing press, the radio, films, television, video recorders and computers? (Perhaps you can arrange the information as a table with notes.)
- When *you* want to fly 'from the sphere of our sorrow' or find 'freedom and hidden treasure' which medium do you prefer? Why?

[1]sense *Verstand* [2]cheek sb. (BE, infml.) *frech sein zu jm.* [3]rave *toben* [4]smack *Schlag, Klaps* [5]lunatic ['lu:nətɪk] *Wahnsinnige(r)* [6]hatred *Haß* [7]surmount [sə'maʊnt] *überwinden* [8]rapier ['reɪpɪə] *Rapier (Fechtwaffe)* [9]graft oneself to *sich übertragen auf* [10]dungeon ['dʌndʒən] *Verlies, Kerker* [11]slip, -pp- *(hinein-)schlüpfen* [12]cell *(Gefängnis-)Zelle* [13]whisper *Geflüster* [14]scrape *kratzen* [15]treasure ['treʒə] *Schatz*

- Read the three poems on these two pages slowly for yourself and try to understand the stories they tell.
- Exchange information in class to get a fuller picture of each 'story'. Also point out where you had problems understanding the poems so that you can solve them together.
- Which of the poems do you like best? Why?
- Look at the tasks on page 75. They may help you to get a better understanding of the meaning of each poem.

A baby sardine
Saw her first submarine[1]:
She was scared and watched through a peephole[2].

'Oh come, come, come,'
Said the sardine's mum,
'It's only a tin full of people.'

Spike Milligan

Southbound[3] on the Freeway[4]

A tourist came in from Orbitville[5],
parked in the air and said:

The creatures of this star
are made of metal and glass.

Through the transparent[6] parts
you can see their guts[7].

Their feet are round and roll
on diagrams – or long

measuring tapes[8] – dark
with white lines.

They have four eyes.
Two in the back are red.

Sometimes you can see a 5-eyed
one, with a red eye turning

on the top of his head.
He must be special –

the others respect him
and go slow

when he passes, winding
among them from behind.

They all hiss[9] as they glide[10],
like inches, down the marked

tapes. Those soft shapes[11],
shadowy inside

the hard bodies – are they
their guts or their brains?

May Swenson

[1]submarine [ˌsʌbməˈriːn] *U-Boot* [2]peephole *Guckloch* [3]southbound *in Richtung Süden* [4]freeway (AE) *Autobahn*
[5]Orbitville: orbit [ˈɔːbɪt] *Umlaufbahn* [6]transparent [-ˈ--] *durchsichtig* [7]guts *(pl.)* (infml.) *Eingeweide*
[8]measuring tape [ˈmeʒərɪŋ] *Maßband* [9]hiss *zischen* [10]glide *(dahin)gleiten* [11]shape *Gestalt, Form*

applaws)
"fell
ow
sit
isn'ts"
(a paw s

e. e. cummings

1. First look again at Spike Milligan's poem. Then try to explain how the unusual point of view and the rhyme in lines 3 and 6 create the humorous tone of the poem.
2. May Swenson, also in a funny way, uses a non-human point of view to look at human behaviour. What opinion about our behaviour and our relationship to cars is expressed in her poem? What question is raised by the visitor from outer space concerning our bodies?
3. The third poem is definitely the most difficult to understand of the three poems. It looks strange, and to many readers it doesn't make any sense at first glance. If this is the case for you, too, give the poem another chance and approach it in the following way:
   - Without letting yourself be disturbed by the actual letters/words, read the poem aloud several times, to yourself, and very slowly. Make a pause after the first bracket and before the second bracket. – What are the words in lines one and six in 'real' English?
   - Read the four lines in inverted commas quite fast, linking the 'words' as much as possible. – What two 'real' English words can you make out of these four lines?
   - Hold your right hand in front of you in the shape of a bracket and your left hand, too. – Thinking of the first line of the poem, what is suggested by this way of holding your hands?
   - Now read the complete poem, adjusting your voice to the meaning of the words you have discovered and according to the punctuation of the poem.
   - Who might be saying the two words in the middle four lines? Try to imagine a situation in which this person might say them. – What 'story' does the complete poem tell you now?
   - e.e.cummings chose to hide the meaning of the poem. Thinking about the situation presented in the poem, can you find a reason for this presentation? – What did you think of the poem when you first read it and what do you think of it now?
4. Try to write a poem in which you look at things happening on earth from an animal's, an extraterrestrial's or an object's point of view. It needn't necessarily be a poem that has a humorous tone. – Compare your work in class and choose one or two poems for publication in your school magazine or perhaps even in a youth magazine or your local newspaper.

Info box Reading may also encourage you to write your own literature. These two pages show you three types of 'home-made literature': a story that must include a number of given words, a mini-saga and a clerihew. Each of them has one or two typical characteristics.

The story that must include a number of given words was made popular through a competition in *The Spectator* magazine a few years ago. People wanting to take part in the competition had to write a story, not too long, which contained twelve words given by the editors of the magazine. The words could be used in any order.

The official birth of the **mini-saga** was 1982, when the *Sunday Telegraph Magazine* had its first mini-saga competition. Since then, mini-sagas have become very popular. The aim of the mini-saga is to tell a complete story in exactly 50 words. Additionally, the story may have a title consisting of up to 15 more words.

The **clerihew** is a humorous verse of four lines which serves as a mini-'biography' of a famous person. It was invented by Edmund Clerihew Bentley (1875-1956), whose first such verse appeared in 1905.

Make up your own story

Here are the twelve words for one of the stories in *The Spectator* and one of the winning texts:

classless – leave – mad[1] *– Kant – behaviour – carry – spelling – annoying – facilities*[2] *– goodbye – nature – struggle*

"I've decided to leave Paul," Marion said, taking off her hat.
"Are you sure it isn't the other way round[3]?" I asked, remembering how annoying her pedantic husband had found their long conversations, her bad spelling and even worse maths.
"Oh, no," she replied. "It was me. I'd accepted his strange behaviour far too long. First it was his love of philosophy; daily talks on Kant and Hegel nearly drove me mad[4]. Next, he developed an interest in social reform and creating a classless society. Then last summer he decided to go back to nature and move to an old hut[5] which was miles from anywhere and had no facilities. He expected me to struggle through the mud every morning and carry wood up a mountain path. It was either 'Goodbye, Paul' or men in white coats for me."

Now choose one of the two lists below.
Or:
Write a list of twelve words. Then get together with a partner and exchange your lists. See if you can write a similar short text in which you use all the words from the list you have chosen.

crisis – surprised – caravan – ketchup – giraffe[6] – alcohol – neighbour – introduce – intelligent – emigrate – reorganize – suggest

household – human – amazed – affection – non-returnable – responsibility – recycle – hairdresser[7] – argument – safe – survive – properly

[1]mad *verrückt* [2]facilities *(pl.) sanitäre Einrichtungen* [3]the other way round *umgekehrt* [4]drive sb. mad *jn. verrückt machen* [5]hut *Hütte* [6]giraffe [dʒəˈrɑːf] [7]hairdresser *Friseur/in*

Mini-sagas

Just One Of Many Stories In A Park

They were
sitting on a bench[1]
keeping their distances,
nothing to say.
Both reading
their books.

Suddenly her book fell down and he picked it up. What a nice surprise!

He was reading the same book as her.

They had to go.
They might
see each
other again.
Who knows?

Angeles Manzaneque

Out of the mouths of babes[2]?

“Come and meet my friend on
Sports Day, Mummy.”
Sports Day came.
“Where’s your new friend, Paul?”
“He’s sitting on the front
bench.”
There were ten on the front
bench.
“He’s wearing red shorts.”
There were three boys with
red shorts.
“His hair’s curly[3].”
“Oh, the black one,”
said Mummy.

Kathryn Clarke, age 15

Now try to write your own mini-saga. Perhaps you can even have a competition in class.

The clerihew

Look at the illustration and read the ‘mini-biography’ of E.A. Poe, a famous American writer. Then try to write a clerihew of a famous person or of one of your friends. – Perhaps you can add an illustration to your verse.

Edgar Allan Poe
Was passionately[4] fond of roe[5].
He always liked to chew[6] some
When writing anything gruesome[7].

[1]bench *(Sitz-)Bank* [2]babe *kleines Kind* [3]curly *lockig* [4]passionate *leidenschaftlich* [5]roe [rəʊ] *Rogen* [6]chew *kauen* [7]gruesome [ˈgruːsəm] *grausig*

What to say in the USA – a quiz on American customs and manners[1]

How much do you know about American customs and manners? Do this quiz and find out. Decide if the following statements are true or false. Discuss and explain the reasons for your decisions before you check the answers.

1 In the USA calling someone by their first name is like saying *du* to someone in German.

3 As a general rule Americans pay each other more compliments[2] than Germans do.

6 Guests in an American home usually offer to help with household work, including[4] working in the kitchen.

4 Americans usually wish each other "Good appetite" before they begin a meal together.

8 When you need to use a toilet in the States the polite thing to say is, "May I use your toilet, please?", "Where is your toilet?", or something similar.

7 Because of the heating and air-conditioning[5] in most American homes and offices, it is important to keep doors closed.

2 If you are invited to an American home for a meal, you should bring flowers for your host.

5 It is considered[3] polite in the US to leave a little bit of food on your plate when you have finished eating.

9 Only very old-fashioned[6] people will be shocked[7] or surprised if you use so-called 'four-letter words'[8] in everyday[9] conversation (like the 's-word' and the 'f-word').

10 When Americans ask you "How do you like the US?" they usually expect a full and honest answer, including all the things you like and don't like about their country.

[1]customs and manners [ˌkʌstəmz‿ən ˈmænəz] *Sitten und Gebräuche* [2]pay sb. a compliment [ˈkɒmplɪmənt] *jm. ein Kompliment machen* [3]be considered [kənˈsɪdəd] *gelten als* [4]including *einschließlich* [5]air-conditioning [ˈeə kənˌdɪʃnɪŋ] *Klimaanlage, Klimatisierung* [6]old-fashioned *altmodisch* [7]shocked *schockiert* [8]four-letter word *etwa: unanständiges Wort* [9]everyday *Alltags-*

Answers

1 False.
American adults use first names with each other much more often than Germans. Neighbours, colleagues at work (including the boss) as well as people you have met at a party or other social event are usually called by their first names. In banks, restaurants, stores, and other places where employees often wear name badges[1], either the first name only *(Tom)* or the first and last name *(Tom Brown)* will be printed on the badge (very rarely *Mr. Brown*). Customers usually call the employees by their first names.
But there are some people who prefer to be called *Mr. Smith* or *Mrs. Riley* or *Ms. Stokey* by people they don't know well. Many people still expect and prefer children and young people to use the more formal expressions when they talk to adults. If you are a foreign visitor in the US, most people will probably say to you, "Please call me Bob (or Kathy or Bill)", but if you are in doubt, it's best to wait until they offer.
It's not impolite to greet people without using their name ("Hi!" or "Hello" is enough), but it's a little compliment to the person if you use their name when you speak to them.
Speaking of[2] names, as a foreigner you should be prepared to pronounce your name (both first and last) in an English way. People who don't know German will find it difficult to understand and say your name if you use the German sounds – especially if you have an 'r', 'ö' or 'ü' in your name.

2 False.
Although your host would probably be pleased to receive flowers (and enjoy the 'old European custom'), bringing flowers is not too common[3] in the States and is certainly not something that is expected of a guest. However, it's never wrong to give a little present, like flowers, a box of chocolates[4], something you have made yourself, but it's not necessary. When they are invited to an informal dinner, Americans very often ask their host, "What can I bring?", which means they would like to bring part of the meal. Among friends, it is common for one person to bring the salad and another the dessert[5], for example. The host then just prepares the main part of the meal.
If you stay overnight in someone's house, you should plan to give them a little present. As a foreigner, it's nice to bring something typical of your home country. It's a 'must' to write a thank-you note to your host a day or two after you have left.

What to say	
When you give someone a present, don't say "please" (German *bitte schön*). Instead you could say …	"This is for you." "I've brought you a little present." "Here's a little souvenir from Germany for you."
When someone gives you a present, you can say …	"Oh, thank you!" "Thank you, Brian, it's beautiful!" "How did you know I loved chocolates? These really look delicious[6]. Thanks!" "Oh, you really shouldn't have – but thank you very much."
When you leave someone's home …	"Thanks, Helen, I had a great time." "I'm sorry I have to leave already, but I have to be home by midnight. This was really a wonderful party. Thanks so much."
When a guest leaves your house, you can say …	"Thanks for coming." "I'm so glad you could come."

Note: Americans don't send greetings to other people (*Schöne Grüße an die Eltern*) as often as Germans do. If you wish to do this, however, you can say, "Please give my regards to your parents", or "Say 'Hi' to Bob for me".

[1]name badge [bædʒ] *Namensschild* [2]speaking of *apropos* [3]common [ˈkɒmən] *gebräuchlich, üblich*
[4]box of chocolates *Schachtel Pralinen* [5]dessert [dɪˈzɜːt] *Nachtisch* [6]delicious [dɪˈlɪʃəs] *köstlich*

3 True.
Most Americans are very generous[1] with compliments and very careful not to make comments that are too critical. The best reaction if someone pays you a compliment is to smile and say "Thank you" and accept the compliment.

4 False.
There is no similar expression. However, you should wait for some kind of signal[2] from your host before you begin to eat. Some families hold hands or say a prayer[3] before the meal. If you are the special guest, the host will probably give the bowls of food to you first and say "Help yourself"[4]. It's polite to take at least a little bit of everything. The serving bowls are often sent around the table two or three times during a meal. Watch what the others are doing and keep passing them along.

What to say

If you want to help someone …	"Can I help you with something?" "Is there anything I can do to help?"
If someone offers to help you …	"No thanks, just enjoy yourself." "Thanks for offering. That would really be a big help."

5 False.
If you are a guest and don't eat everything, your host will probably be disappointed and think you didn't like the food. He or she will of course be pleased if you like the food – and if you say so. It's safest to take small portions[5] if you are not sure you'll like something. You will almost certainly be offered seconds[6] and then you can take more of the things you especially liked. If you are served something you really don't like and can hardly eat, you should never say "I don't like that". Try to be positive: take an extra portion of something you liked.
If you are in a restaurant and can't finish your meal, it's perfectly acceptable (even in an expensive restaurant) to ask for a 'doggy bag' so you can take home some of the food. Everyone knows that doggy bags aren't really for the dog.

What to say

If you are offered more food and would like to accept …	"Yes, please, it's really delicious." "Well, I'm getting quite full, but I'll have one more spoonful. It's so good." "Thanks. Everything tastes so good."

Note: A simple 'Thanks' or 'Thank you' by itself (without 'no' in front of it) means 'yes' in English, unlike in German, where a simple *Danke* usually means 'no': "Would you like some more coffee?" – "Thanks." (= "Yes, I would.")

And if you don't want any more …	"No, thank you." "I'm sorry. It's delicious, but I really couldn't eat any more, thank you."

6 True.
Unless[7] you are invited to a very formal dinner, it's polite to ask if there is anything you can do to help. After an informal meal, the guests often help with the dishes.
If you are staying in an American home for a few days or longer, you should always ask what you can do to help around the house. You should at least make your own bed in the morning and keep your room as tidy as possible. Your host will probably tell you to help yourself to anything you want from the refrigerator[8]. But don't forget to put things away. Don't leave a mess[9] in the kitchen!

[1]generous ['dʒenrəs] *großzügig* [2]signal ['sɪgnəl] [3]prayer ['preə] *(Tisch-)Gebet* [4]Help yourself. *Bedien dich!*
[5]portion ['pɔːʃn] [6]seconds *(pl.)* ['sekəndz] *Nachschlag* [7]unless [ən'les] *außer wenn, es sei denn*
[8]refrigerator [rɪ'frɪdʒəreɪtə] *Kühlschrank* [9]mess *Unordnung, Durcheinander*

7 False.
In American offices, schools, and private homes, room doors are usually left open. A closed door is a very clear sign that the person or persons inside want to be left alone. If you are given a room of your own in an American home, don't close the door unless you really want to be left alone. (Of course you can close it when you want to change clothes.) American families who often host[1] foreign students sometimes complain that their guests 'disappear'[2] too much into their rooms and close the doors behind them. If the family is sitting together in the living-room or kitchen, they expect their guest to be there too, at least most of the time. Bathroom doors are also left open unless someone is using the room. In fact, a closed door is such a strong signal that the room is occupied[3], that if you close the bathroom door behind you when you leave the room, the other members of the household may think someone is still in there – and wait impatiently for a long time.

8 False.
The word 'toilet' in American English is not exactly taboo[4], but it is not used very often. In private homes it's always the 'bathroom'. The question to ask is "May I use your bathroom?" – nobody thinks you plan to take a bath in there. (*Ich muß mal* is "I have to go to the bathroom".) In a public place, e.g. a hotel or restaurant, the most common word is 'restroom', and the question to ask is "Where's the restroom?", but many people call public restrooms bathrooms too, at least informally. Other possible names are 'men's room' or 'ladies' room'.
In schools, toilets are usually called the 'boys' bathroom' and the 'girls' bathroom' even though it is not possible to take a bath in them!

9 False.
Although these words are not as taboo as they used to be and you will probably hear them often in the States, there are still a lot of people who would not be pleased to hear them, especially from a foreigner. The English 's-word' has a lot stronger shock-effect than the German '*Sch*-word'. Schoolteachers are often very strict about these words and punish any student who uses them in class. Be careful.

10 False.
This is a question you will probably hear very often as a guest in the USA. Most Americans expect a short, positive answer. "I'm having a great time!" or "There are so many new things to see and do here – it's really interesting". In American newspapers and on TV you will probably read and hear lots of reports on the negative aspects of American life (drug problems, crime, homeless people, race problems, etc.) – but if an American family is kind enough to take you as a guest, they do not want to hear about all those negative things from you, the foreign guest. Americans are almost fanatical[5] about wanting other people to like them – both as individuals and as a country. Be very careful with criticism[6] and try to stress the positive.
You will probably find that most Americans are not too well-informed about Europe and most are not as interested in world politics as many Europeans are. On the other hand[7], Americans are usually open and friendly and interested in hearing about your home town and your lifestyle in Germany.

Now try to make up a similar quiz for American students who are planning to come and stay with a German family. How many 'tricky' points can you think of?

[1]host sb. [həʊst] *jn. zu Gast haben* [2]disappear [ˌdɪsəˈpɪə] *verschwinden* [3]occupied [ˈɒkjʊpaɪd] *besetzt*
[4]taboo [təˈbuː] *tabu* [5]fanatical [fəˈnætɪkl] *fanatisch* [6]criticism [ˈkrɪtɪsɪzm] *Kritik* [7]on the other hand *andererseits*

Schools in Britain

What do you remember from earlier years about schools in Britain? The photos on this page might help you. In groups, or as a whole-class exercise, do some "brainstorming" and make notes about what you can remember.

Next, try to organize your information in a network. Use the headings[1] in the circles as starting points.

At the age of 16, British pupils can follow different paths in education or employment. Before you study the example of one school on the opposite page, try to imagine what those alternatives might be.

[1]heading ['hedɪŋ] *hier: Überbegriff; Überschrift* [2]boarding school ['bɔːdɪŋ skuːl] *Internat* [3]course *Verlauf*

The Blue School in Wells, Somerset, is a comprehensive with about 1,300 pupils. Every year, about 200 of them reach the school leaving age and then have to decide what to do next. But two years before this time, in year 9 when they are fourteen, they have already made some important choices. At this age, they must put together their own timetable for the next two years. To do this they read the school's brochure, where all the subjects are described, and they take the ones they are interested in. Of course there are some subjects, like English and Mathematics, they must take, but most are optional[1]. Here are some of the symbols for the subjects in the brochure. What subjects are shown? Try to guess before you match the names and the symbols.

Child Development – Design and Technology: Food – Design and Technology: Graphics[2] – Drama and Theatre Arts – Economics – English Literature – Geography – Information Systems – Leisure and Tourism – Mathematics

What differences do you notice to the subjects on your timetable?

In year 11, the pupils at the Blue School take GCSEs in their chosen subjects. The pie chart shows how they decide to go on after that. Where do you see the advantages and disadvantages of each path? And which would be your choice? Try and say why.

39% college vocational training[3]
- business and finance[4]
- hair and beauty
- …

38% A-levels
- French and Spanish
- History and Geography
- …

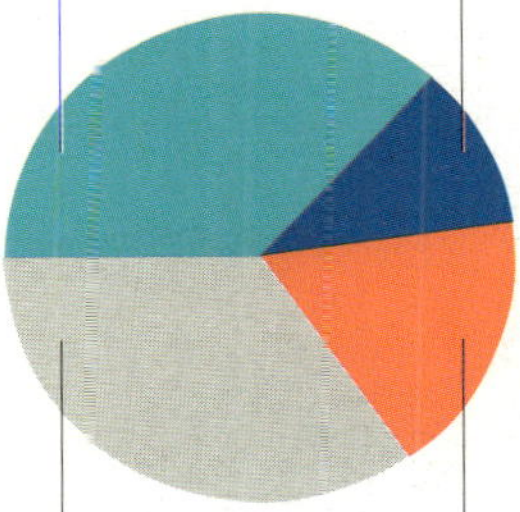

7% others
- unemployed
- leaving the area
- …

16% job or apprenticeship[5]
- tractor driver
- dental assistant[6]
- …

Here three of the 11th years explain their career decisions:

Darren Wilson
I've had enough of school and I want to start earning money soon. A newsagent where I do my paper round[7] says I can work for him, so I start there in August. I like the work and I know most of the people in the area, so I'm looking forward to it.

Helen Buck
I did quite well in my GCSEs, so I'm staying on for 2 more years to do my A-levels in politics and economics. After that, I'll take a year out[8]. I hope to go on to university and then to work in business.

Jennifer Spurgeon
I'm going to Strode College. It's not far from Wells and I can do a two-year diploma in leisure and tourism there. I liked the course at Blue School and I want to work in a travel agency[9]. The careers adviser said it should be a career with a future.

[1]optional ['ɒpʃənl] *wahlfrei* [2]graphics *(pl.)* ['græfɪks] *graphische Gestaltung* [3]vocational training (at a college) [vəʊ'keɪʃnəl] *Berufsausbildung (an einer Fachoberschule)* [4]finance [feɪ'næns] *Finanzwesen* [5]apprenticeship [ə'prentɪsʃɪp] *Lehre* [6]dental assistant ['dentl] *Zahnarzthelfer/in* [7]do a paper round *Zeitungen austragen* [8]take a year out *ein Jahr zwischen Schule und Universität aussetzen* [9]travel agency ['eɪdʒənsɪ] *Reisebüro*

Charles

Read the story and find out …
- what the illustrations on this page and page 86 have to do with the story,
- what it means 'to be or do a Charles'.

Not all the new words in the story are explained at the bottom of the page. Still, you should be able to understand the story.

The day my son Laurie started kindergarten[1] he renounced[2] corduroy overalls with bibs[3] and began wearing blue jeans with a belt; I watched him go off the first morning with the older girl next door, seeing clearly that an era of my life was ended, my sweet-voiced nursery-school[4] tot[5] replaced by a long-trousered, swaggering character who forgot to stop at the corner and wave good-bye to me.

He came home the same way, the front door slamming open, his cap on the floor, and the voice suddenly become raucous shouting, "Isn't anybody here?"

At lunch he spoke insolently[6] to his father, spilled his baby sister's milk, and remarked[7] that his teacher said we were not to take the name of the Lord in vain[8].

"How *was* school today?" I asked, elaborately casual.

"All right," he said.

"Did you learn anything?" his father asked.

Laurie regarded his father coldly. "I didn't learn nothing," he said.

"Anything," I said. "Didn't learn anything."

"The teacher spanked[9] a boy, though," Laurie said, addressing his bread and butter. "For being fresh[10]," he added with his mouth full.

"What did he do?" I asked. "Who was it?"

Laurie thought. "It was Charles," he said. "He was fresh. The teacher spanked him and made him stand in a corner. He was awfully fresh."

"What did he do?" I asked again, but Laurie slid off his chair, took a cookie, and left, while his father was still saying, "See here, young man."

The next day Laurie remarked at lunch, as soon as he sat down, "Well, Charles was bad again today." He grinned enormously and said, "Today Charles hit the teacher."

"Good heavens[11]," I said, mindful[12] of the Lord's name, "I suppose he got spanked again?"

"He sure did," Laurie said. "Look up," he said to his father.

"What?" his father said, looking up.

"Look down," Laurie said. "Look at my thumb. Gee, you're dumb[13]." He began to laugh insanely.

"Why did Charles hit the teacher?" I asked quickly.

"Because she tried to make him color with red crayons[14]," Laurie said. "Charles wanted to color with green crayons, so he hit the teacher and she spanked him and said 'nobody play with Charles' but everybody did."

The third day – it was Wednesday of the first week – Charles bounced a seesaw[15] onto the head of a little girl and made her bleed[16], and the teacher made him stay inside all during recess[17]. Thursday Charles had to stand in a corner during storytime because he kept pounding his feet on the floor. Friday Charles was deprived of[18] blackboard privileges[19] because he threw chalk[20].

[1]kindergarten *Vorschule (für Kinder ab 5 Jahren)* [2]renounce [rɪ'naʊns] *aufgeben, verzichten auf* [3]corduroy overalls *(pl.)* with a bib ['kɔ:dərɔɪ] *Latzhosen aus Cord* [4]nursery school ['nɜ:srɪ] *Kindergarten (für Kinder unter 5 Jahren)* [5]tot (infml.) *Knirps* [6]insolent ['ɪnsələnt] *unverschämt* [7]remark [-'-] *bemerken* [8]we were not to take the name of the Lord in vain *wir sollten den Namen Gottes nicht mißbrauchen* [9]spank *verhauen* [10]fresh (infml.) *frech* [11]good heavens ['hevnz] *du lieber Himmel!* [12]be mindful of (fml.) *bedenken, denken an* [13]dumb [dʌm] (infml.) *dumm* [14]crayon ['kreɪɒn] *Buntstift* [15]seesaw ['si:sɔ:] *Wippe* [16]bleed – bled – bled *bluten* [17]recess [BE: rɪ'ses, AE: 'ri:ses] (AE) *Pause* [18]deprive sb. of sth. *jm. etwas entziehen* [19]blackboard privileges *Sondererlaubnis zur Benutzung der Tafel* [20]chalk [tʃɔ:k] *Kreide*

On Saturday I remarked to my husband, “Do you think kindergarten is too unsettling[1] for Laurie? All this toughness[2] and bad grammar, and this Charles boy sounds like such a bad influence.”

“It’ll be all right,” my husband said reassuringly. “Bound to be[3] people like Charles in the world. Might as well meet them now as later.”

On Monday Laurie came home late, full of news. “Charles,” he shouted as he came up the hill; I was waiting anxiously on the front step.

“Charles,” Laurie yelled all the way up the hill, “Charles was bad again.”

“Come right in,” I said, as soon as he came close enough. “Lunch is waiting.”

“You know what Charles did?” he demanded, following me through the door. “Charles yelled so in school they sent a boy in from first grade to tell the teacher she had to make Charles keep quiet, and so Charles had to stay after school. And so all the children stayed to watch him.”

“What did he do?” I asked.

“He just sat there,” Laurie said, climbing into his chair at the table. “Hi, Pop, y’old dust mop.”

“Charles had to stay after school today,” I told my husband. “Everyone stayed with him.”

“What does this Charles look like?” my husband asked Laurie. “What’s his other name?”

“He’s bigger than me,” Laurie said. “And he doesn’t have any rubbers[4] and he doesn’t ever wear a jacket.”

Monday night was the first Parent-Teachers meeting, and only the fact that the baby had a cold kept me from going; I wanted passionately to meet Charles’s mother. On Tuesday Laurie remarked suddenly, “Our teacher had a friend come to see her in school today.”

“Charles’s mother?” my husband and I asked simultaneously.

“Naaah,” Laurie said scornfully. “It was a man who came and made us do exercises; we had to touch our toes[5]. Look.” He climbed down from his chair and squatted down and touched his toes. “Like this,” he said. He got solemnly back into his chair and said, picking up his fork, “Charles didn’t even *do* exercises.”

“That’s fine,” I said heartily. “Didn’t Charles want to do exercises?”

“Naaah,” Laurie said. “Charles was so fresh to the teacher’s friend he wasn’t *let* do exercises.”

“Fresh again?” I said.

“He kicked the teacher’s friend,” Laurie said. “The teacher’s friend told Charles to touch his toes like I just did, and Charles kicked him.”

“What are they going to do about Charles, do you suppose?” Laurie’s father asked him.

Laurie shrugged[6] elaborately. “Throw him out of school, I guess,” he said.

Wednesday and Thursday were routine; Charles yelled during story hour and hit a boy in the stomach and made him cry. On Friday Charles stayed after school again, and so did all the other children. With the third week of kindergarten Charles was an institution in our family; the baby was being a Charles when she cried all afternoon; Laurie did a Charles when he filled his wagon full of mud and pulled it through the kitchen; even my husband, when he caught his elbow[7] in the telephone cord and pulled telephone, ash tray[8], and a bowl of flowers off the table, said, after the first minute, “Looks like Charles.”

During the third and fourth weeks it looked like a reformation[9] in Charles; Laurie reported grimly at lunch on Thursday of the third week, “Charles was so good today the teacher gave him an apple.”

“What?” I said, and my husband added warily, “You mean Charles?”

“Charles,” Laurie said. “He gave the crayons around and he picked up the books afterward and the teacher said he was her helper.”

“What happened?” I asked incredulously.

“He was her helper, that’s all,” Laurie said, and shrugged.

“Can this be true, about Charles?” I asked my husband that night. “Can something like this happen?”

“Wait and see,” my husband said cynically. “When you’ve got a Charles to deal with, this may mean he’s only plotting[10].”

He seemed to be wrong. For over a week Charles was the teacher’s helper; each day he handed things out and he picked things up; no one had to stay after school.

“The P.T.A.[11] meeting’s next week again,” I told my husband one evening. “I’m going to find

[1]unsettling *aufregend* [2]toughness ['tʌfnəs] *Härte, Brutalität* [3](there are) bound to be … *es muß … geben* [4]rubbers *hier etwa: Gummistiefel* [5]touch one’s toes [tʌtʃ; təʊz] *seine Zehen berühren* [6]shrug *die Achseln zucken* [7]elbow *Ellbogen* [8]ash tray *Aschenbecher* [9]reformation *Besserung* [10]plot *etwas aushecken* [11]P.T.A. (Parent-Teacher Association) *Eltern-Lehrer-Rat (einer Schule)*

Charles's mother there."

"Ask her what happened to Charles," my husband said. "I'd like to know."

"I'd like to know myself," I said.

On Friday of that week things were back to normal. "You know what Charles did today?" Laurie demanded at the lunch table, in a voice slightly awed. "He told a little girl to say a word and she said it and the teacher washed her mouth out with soap and Charles laughed."

"What word?" his father asked unwisely, and Laurie said, " I'll have to whisper it to you, it's so bad." He got down off his chair and went around to his father. His father bent his head down and Laurie whispered joyfully. His father's eyes widened.

"Did Charles tell the little girl to say *that*?" he asked respectfully.

"She said it *twice*," Laurie said. "Charles told her to say it *twice*."

"What happened to Charles?" my husband asked.

"Nothing," Laurie said. "He was passing out[1] the crayons."

Monday morning Charles abandoned[2] the little girl and said the evil[3] word himself three or four times, getting his mouth washed out with soap each time. He also threw chalk.

My husband came to the door with me that evening as I set out for the P.T.A. meeting.

"Invite her over for a cup of tea after the meeting," he said. "I want to get a look at her."

"If only she's there," I said prayerfully.

"She'll be there," my husband said. "I don't see how they could hold a P.T.A. meeting without Charles's mother."

At the meeting I sat restlessly, scanning[4] each comfortable matronly[5] face, trying to determine which one hid the secret of Charles. None of them looked to me haggard[6] enough. No one stood up in the meeting and apologized for the way her son had been acting. No one mentioned Charles.

After the meeting I identified and sought out[7] Laurie's kindergarten teacher. She had a plate with a cup of tea and a piece of chocolate cake; I had a plate with a cup of tea and a piece of marshmallow cake. We maneuvered up to one another cautiously, and smiled.

"I've been so anxious to meet you," I said. "I'm Laurie's mother."

"We're all so interested in Laurie," she said.

"Well, he certainly likes kindergarten," I said. "He talks about it all the time."

"We had a little trouble adjusting[8], the first week or so," she said primly[9], "but now he's a fine little helper. With occasional lapses[10], of course."

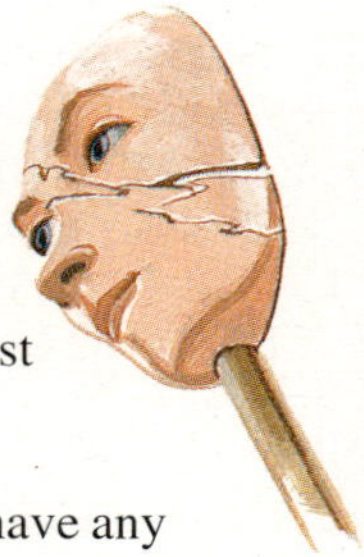

"Laurie usually adjusts very quickly," I said. "I suppose this time it's Charles's influence."

"Charles?"

"Yes," I said, laughing, "you must have your hands full in that kindergarten, with Charles."

"Charles?" she said. "We don't have any Charles in the kindergarten."

Shirley Jackson

- What do the two masks[11] in the illustrations have to do with the story?
- What does it mean 'to be or do a Charles'?
- How do you think the mother felt when she heard the kindergarten teacher's last sentence?

1. Now that you have read the story, go through the text again and find evidence in Laurie's behaviour at home which suggests that he himself is Charles. – Why do you think Laurie 'does a Charles' at kindergarten?
2. Work with a partner: Write the dialogue which might develop between the teacher and the mother, or between Laurie's mother and father, after the P.T.A. meeting.
3. What do *you* think: Why do some children/young people behave one way at home and differently at school?

[1]pass sth. out *etwas verteilen* [2]abandon [ə'bændən] *aufgeben* [3]evil ['i:vl] *böse* [4]scan *forschend ansehen* [5]matronly ['meɪtrənlɪ] *matronenhaft* [6]haggard ['hægəd] *abgespannt, kummervoll* [7]seek out [si:k] – sought [sɔ:t] – sought *ausfindig machen* [8]adjust [ə'dʒʌst] *sich anpassen, sich aufeinander einstellen* [9]prim *steif* [10]occasional lapse [əˌkeɪʒnəl 'læps] *gelegentliche Verfehlung, gelegentlicher Schnitzer* [11]mask [mɑ:sk] *Maske*

Creating a nation and a society

America – a colony

The Virginia Gazette, September 19, 1760

Dear Readers,
Today we would like to share with you two letters we received from two Europeans who are visiting the colonies. Their very different opinions about life in the New World might be of interest to you.

During a trip of 1,200 miles, I saw weaknesses which will necessarily prevent America from becoming a strong nation.
The way of farming with slaves is a very great cause of weakness. The number of Negroes[1] in the Southern colonies is nearly equal[2] to that of white men. Their condition is truly sad, their work too hard, their food bad, their treatment heartless.
The Northern colonies also have real disadvantages. They are made[3] up of people of different nations, different religions, and different languages. And they are all jealous of each other. In other words, such is the difference of character, of religion, and of interest of the different colonies, that I think if they were left[4] to themselves, there would soon be a civil war from one end of the continent to the other.

Andrew Burnaby

America is not made up as Europe is of great nobles[5], who own everything, and a majority of people who have nothing. Here are no noble families and no kings. The rich and the poor are not so far apart[6] from each other as they are in Europe.
The colonists are united by good government, all respecting the laws because they are fair. The colonists all have the will[7] to work hard.
What then is the American? He is an American who has left behind him all his old prejudices and who receives new ideas from the new ways of life he has accepted, the new government he obeys[8], and the new position he holds.
Here individuals of all nations are melted into a new race of men, who will one day cause great changes in the world.

Hector St. Jean de Crèvecoeur

Info box In the 1600s and 1700s, tens of thousands of people came to the English colonies in North America. The colonists came mainly for religious or economic reasons. By the 1750s, different ways of life had developed in the New England, Middle and Southern Colonies. This was partly[9] because of differences in climate and geography. Because of the warm climate in the South, for example, tobacco[10] and rice could be grown. For this kind of farming lots of workers were needed. To get these workers, southern planters[11] bought more and more African slaves to work in the fields.

☞ After you have read the page from the *Virginia Gazette* make a network of the ideas expressed by Burnaby and Crèvecoeur. How can one explain the fact that the two visitors had such different views about the American colonies and their future? The information given in the Info box might help you to explain.

[1]Negro, *pl.* Negroes ['ni:grəʊ] *Neger/in* [2]equal ['i:kwəl] *gleich* [3]be made up of *sich zusammensetzen aus*
[4]be left to oneself *sich selbst überlassen sein* [5]noble ['nəʊbl] *Adlige(r); adlig* [6]apart [ə'pɑ:t] *entfernt* [7]will *Wille*
[8]obey [ə'beɪ] *gehorchen* [9]partly *teilweise* [10]tobacco [tə'bækəʊ] *Tabak* [11]planter *Plantagenbesitzer/in*

The USA – a new nation

The Virginia Gazette, July 10, 1776

Independence: The Birth of a New America

Last Tuesday, on July 2, the dangerous enterprise of American independence began. When nearly 50 delegates[1] to the Second Continental Congress met in the State House in Philadelphia, everyone felt the tension. The day before, a first vote showed nine of the colonies for independence. This wasn't enough. To decide such an important question – cutting 2.5 million people free[2] from England – the Congress wanted all the colonies to support independence.

After long discussions Pennsylvania and South Carolina decided to vote for independence. New York's men still waited for instructions from home, but they would not vote against independence. Only Delaware was still undecided[3] – one delegate for, one against independence, and one back home.

When a short time later Delaware's third delegate, Farmer Caesar Rodney, arrived, the colonies finally voted to cut their 169-year-old political ties[4] with the mother country. Boston's John Adams believes: "The second day of July 1776 will be the most important day in our history."

The road to independence has been a long one. But after Patrick Henry's "Give me liberty[5] or give me death" speech in 1775 and Thomas Paine's words this year that George III was "the greatest enemy this continent has", the separation[6] from England was just a question of time.

On July 4, the Congress adopted[7] a Declaration written by Thomas Jefferson that presents the colonies' reasons for breaking away from England. He wrote that rights such as life, liberty, and the pursuit[8] of happiness should never be taken away by any government. That date and that document may be seen in the years to come as more important than the events of July 2.

After the public reading of the Declaration, Philadelphians rang their church bells all day and all night. In all this celebration we must remember that we come to independence with different interests and reasons. There are the fishermen and merchants[9] of New England, the traders and small farmers of the Middle Colonies, the planters and farmers of the South. And sometimes our regional differences have been stronger than our differences with England.

In spite of our quarrels[10], we must now stand together united as a new nation in the war against England which has already begun.

Write a dialogue with a partner. One of you takes the role of a delegate at the Second Continental Congress who supports independence and the other of a delegate who would like America to remain a British colony. For additional information look again at C3, Unit 5 and Option 14.

[1]delegate ['delɪgət] *Delegierte(r)* [2]cut free *(los-, ab-)trennen* [3]undecided [ˌʌndɪ'saɪdɪd] *unentschlossen* [4]tie *Bindung* [5]liberty ['lɪbətɪ] *Freiheit* [6]separation [ˌsepə'reɪʃn] *Trennung* [7]adopt [ə'dɒpt] *(einen Beschluß) annehmen* [8]pursuit of [pə'sjuːt] (fml.) *Streben nach* [9]merchant ['mɜːtʃənt] *Kaufmann, -frau* [10]quarrel ['kwɒrəl] *Auseinandersetzung, Streit*

The USA – a divided nation

Before you read the text below, make a survey in your class: How many think that any one of our *Bundesländer* should have the right to break away from Germany and form an independent state?
What do you think the government should do if a "state" wanted to break away?
Read the text and find out how the US government reacted in 1861.

In 1860 and 1861, 11 southern states broke away from the US and founded a new nation – the Confederate States of America[1]. Many southerners believed that states had the right to leave the Union[2]. President Lincoln, however, thought that no state could legally get out of the Union. In the Civil War that followed over 500,000 soldiers died – more than in any other war that the US has fought in.
Why did the 11 states leave the Union?
In the first half of the 1800s, the North and South had grown apart[3] as they each developed different economies. Industry and trade developed in northern cities. In the South, cotton controlled the economy. With the growth of the "Cotton Kingdom", slavery[4] also grew since many workers were needed to plant, pick[5] and clean the cotton. This meant that political views in the US developed in different directions.
By the 1850s, the issue of slavery divided the country. As people moved west, Americans had to decide if the new territories[6] should enter the Union as slave states or slave-free states. In 1850, Congress agreed that California could join the Union as a slave-free state. In the New Mexico Territory and in the Utah Territory the people would be able to decide themselves if they wanted slavery or not. About ten years later, when Lincoln became president, southerners were afraid that he would not allow slavery in the new territories. Since many believed that the South would totally lose its influence in national government, they felt that they had to leave the Union.
In 1861 the Civil War began. At first, the war went badly for the Union. The South had better generals and its soldiers had very high morale[7]. However, the North not only had most of America's factories and industries, it also had a much larger population than the South. By late 1862, the North began to win the war. At first, the North fought only to save the Union, but then many believed that the war must also lead to the end of slavery. In September 1862, Lincoln proclaimed[8] that all slaves in the Confederate States would be free in January 1863. Two years later slavery was ended everywhere in the US.

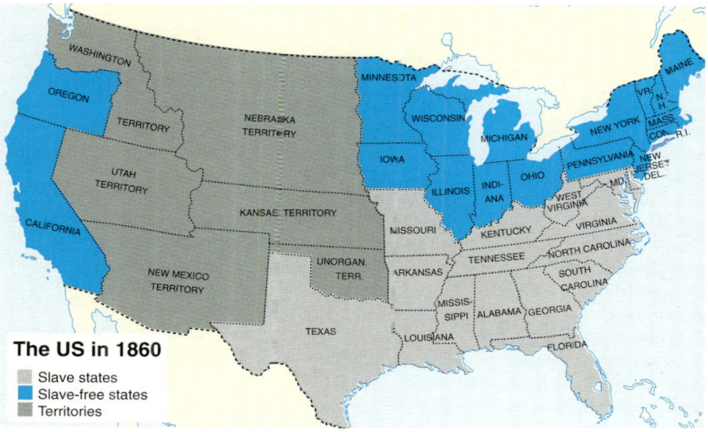

The US in 1860

The Civil War was over in 1865. The North's policy of "total war" had left southern cities, plantations[9] and homes in ruins. It took many years for the states to become truly united again.

Imagine that Burnaby and Crèvecoeur travelled through the US again in 1876. How do you think they would have viewed "100 years of independence"? Work in groups and write a letter to the *Virginia Gazette* as either Burnaby or Crèvecoeur. Before you start you should perhaps have another look at p. 87.

[1]the Confederate States of America [kən'fedərət] *die Konföderierten Staaten von Amerika* [2]the Union ['ju:njən] *die Vereinigten Staaten* [3]grow apart *sich auseinanderentwickeln* [4]slavery ['sleɪvərɪ] *Sklaverei* [5]pick *pflücken* [6]territory ['terətərɪ] *(Staats-)Gebiet* [7]morale [mə'rɑ:l] *(Kampf-)Moral* [8]proclaim [prə'kleɪm] *erklären* [9]plantation [plɑ:n'teɪʃn] *Plantage*

Different roles for Britain: From Empire to European Union[1]

Look at the different titles on pages 90 and 91, at the pictures and at the Info box. – What do they tell you about Britain's changing role in the world? Then read the three texts that go with the pictures and make a network of facts to remember.

Finally, use your network to practise an oral presentation[2] on Britain's changing role in the world. You could start like this:
"From about 1700 on, Britain started trading more and more with India. At about the same time …"

The British Empire

The loss of the thirteen American colonies came as a shock to Britain, but it did not stop the British trading round the world, nor did it stop them settling in new continents.
There were political and economic reasons for getting colonies. A growing population at home, increasing social problems, and greater economic competition from other European nations, led to the occupation[6] of more and more lands in Asia and Africa.
Many also believed it was Britain's duty to bring Christianity and "civilization[7]" to the Africans and Asians. More often than not the British government used the army to take over direct political control.
When Queen Victoria died in 1901, Britain's Empire covered a quarter of the world. She left her son an Empire "on which the sun never set[8]". English was spoken on every continent.
Not all colonies in the British Empire had the same status[9]. Most colonies were ruled directly from London. Those colonies, however, which had been settled by Europeans, governed themselves, but accepted the British king or queen as head of state[10] and Britain's leading role in foreign policy.

Info box

1600	British East India (Trading) Company is founded	1839	First British colonists in New Zealand
1607	First English colonists in North America	1876	Queen Victoria declared Empress of India
1760	British defeat French in Canada	1886-92	British Empire grows very quickly
1783	Britain loses the 13 American colonies	1921	British Empire reaches greatest size
1788	First British convicts[11] arrive in Australia	1947	India and Pakistan become independent
1795	The Cape[12] of Africa is captured	1956-65	Most colonies become independent

[1]union ['ju:njən] [2]presentation [ˌprezən'teɪʃn] [3]glory ['glɔ:rɪ] *Schönheit, Herrlichkeit* [4]lion ['laɪən] [5]mane [meɪn] *Mähne* [6]occupation [ˌɒkjʊ'peɪʃn] *Besetzung* [7]civilization [ˌsɪvlaɪ'zeɪʃn] [8]set - set - set *untergehen (Sonne, Mond)* [9]status ['steɪtəs] [10]head of state *Staatsoberhaupt* [11]convict ['kɒnvɪkt] *Strafgefangene(r)* [12]cape [keɪp] *Kap*

From Empire to Commonwealth[1]

The Queen met with the 48 leaders of the Commonwealth states yesterday to discuss economic and political matters[2]. They also talked about the next Commonwealth Games, which will take place in Vancouver. Leaders of the states meet every two years.

In the 20th century, many Britons began to think the Empire was a burden[3]. So when the colonies began to demand freedom, Britain didn't fight too hard to keep them. Between 1945 and 1965, nearly all the non-white colonies were given independence, and in most cases the change was peaceful. Most former[4] colonies chose to keep a special relationship with Britain by staying in what became known as the Commonwealth.

The British king or queen is the head of this organization, but the members are all free and equal[5].

Britain and the European Union (EU)

Britain tried to keep its international influence through the Commonwealth, but decided to take a more active role within Europe, too. In 1973 it joined what is now the European Union.

Historically, Britain has remained – partly[8] because of the Channel – cut off from the Continent. The idea of European political and economic union was generally not very attractive to many Britons. However, after much debate and protest, most leading British politicians today agree that Britain must take an active role in the development of the EU. Otherwise, they think, Britain will be isolated[9] within Europe. And, because her influence is decreasing[10] in other places in the world, on the stage[11] of world politics.

"We must make sure that the friendship[6] and respect, which we have built among ourselves, should extend[7] more widely throughout our continent."

From Queen Elizabeth's speech to members of the European Parliament in Strasbourg in 1992.

[1]Commonwealth ['kɒmənwelθ] [2]matter *Angelegenheit* [3]burden ['bɜːdn] *Last, Bürde* [4]former *ehemalige(r, s)* [5]equal ['iːkwəl] *gleichberechtigt* [6]friendship *Freundschaft* [7]extend [ɪk'stend] *sich ausdehnen* [8]partly *teilweise* [9]isolate ['aɪsəleɪt] *isolieren* [10]decrease [ˌdiː'kriːs] *abnehmen, nachlassen* [11]stage [steɪdʒ] *Bühne*

Monarchy and Parliament in Britain

In the USA the president and Congress are the most important institutions of government. In Britain it is the monarch together with the prime minister and the two Houses of Parliament. Read the following short articles from the "Royal Times". All of them deal with events in the history of the oldest British institution of government – the monarchy. Then, without looking at the text again, try to reconstruct in class what is said about the years 1215, 1649, 1658, 1689, 1789, 1873, 1936 and 1994. Finally, read the articles again to check if you have forgotten anything important.

June 30, 1215

King John I had to sign Magna Carta several days ago. Royal power is now limited[1]. In future the king will have to respect the law and the rights of the barons[2].

January 31, 1649

King Charles I was executed yesterday. England is now a republic! His fight with Parliament over taxes and religion had led to a civil war. After years of fighting he was captured and sentenced[3] to death.

September 4, 1658

The radical Puritan[4] **Oliver Cromwell**, who led Parliament's army against Charles I, is dead. He had ruled like a dictator for 15 years. Will the "republican" form of government continue or will Charles's son become the new king?

April 22, 1689

William of Orange invaded England last year to save the country from Catholic rule. William and his wife, Mary, became king and queen after they agreed to accept the Bill of Rights[5]. Britain is now a parliamentary monarchy.

November 11, 1789

George III has recovered[6] from his mental breakdown[7]. Some speculate that the war with the American colonies was one cause for the first English-born king from the House of Hanover to become mentally ill[8] last year.

June 28, 1873

Victoria became Queen 35 years ago today. However, she disappeared[9] from public life after the death of her husband, Prince Albert, in 1861. The behaviour of her son Edward has hurt the monarchy. He seems to be interested mainly in horse-racing and hunting.

[1]limited *begrenzt* [2]baron ['bærən] [3]sentence (to) *verurteilen (zu)* [4]Puritan ['pjʊərɪtən] *Puritaner/in* [5]Bill of Rights *brit. Staatsgrundgesetz* [6]recover (from) *sich erholen (von)* [7]mental breakdown ['mentl] *Nervenzusammenbruch* [8]mentally ill ['mentəlɪ] *geisteskrank* [9]disappear [ˌdɪsə'pɪə] *verschwinden*

October 8, 1936

King Edward VIII has decided to give up his throne[1] in December and marry Mrs Wallis Simpson, a divorced American woman. He is the first king to give up the throne voluntarily[2].

June 30, 1994

In a TV programme last night **Charles** said he does not want to be head of the Church of England. He also admitted that he had been unfaithful[3] to his wife, Princess Diana. Many wonder if Charles is a prince who will never be king.

Now read the Info box and use the diagram to explain today's system of government in Britain.

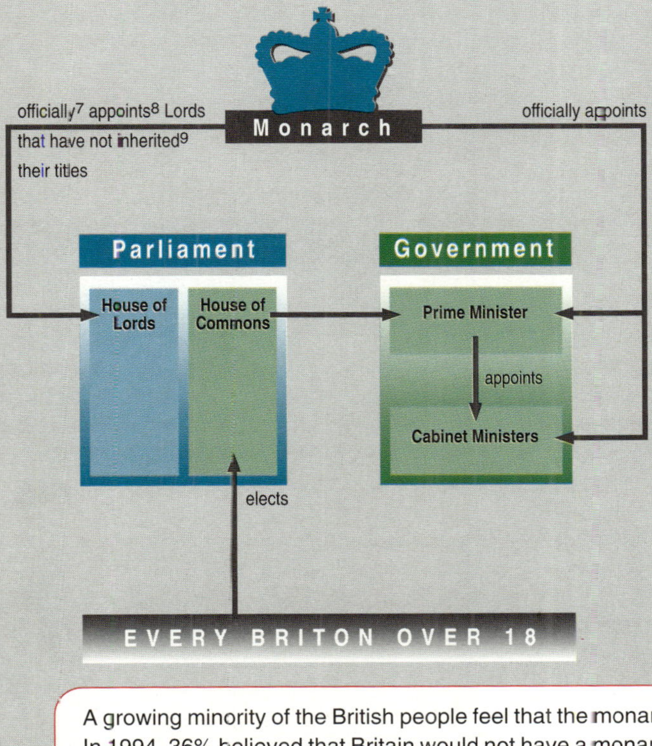

Info box The idea that the king or queen should get the advice of Parliament is very old. However, it took centuries until Britain had a parliamentary system of government. Over the years, the monarch became a more or less symbolic[4] head of state[5] with no real power. Today, the prime minister and the cabinet[6] make the important decisions on running the country. And the power to pass the laws belongs mainly to the House of Commons, which is elected by the people. Reforms made in this century mean that now every Briton over the age of 18 can help to decide who will govern the country for the following five years.

A growing minority of the British people feel that the monarchy should be abolished[10]. In 1994, 36% believed that Britain would not have a monarch in 50 years. Do you think the monarchy has a future? Or should it be abolished? Collect arguments for both sides of the issue and have a short discussion in class.

[1]throne [θrəʊn] *Thron* [2]voluntarily [ˌvɒlənˈterəlɪ] *freiwillig* [3]unfaithful [ʌnˈfeɪθfl] *untreu* [4]symbolic [sɪmˈbɒlɪk] *symbolisch* [5]head of state *Staatsoberhaupt* [6]cabinet [ˈkæbɪnət] *Kabinett*... [7]officially [əˈfɪʃəlɪ] *offiziell* [8]appoint [əˈpɔɪnt] *ernennen* [9]inherit [ɪnˈherɪt] *(er)erben* [10]abolish [əˈbɒlɪʃ] *abschaffen*

The All-American Slurp[1]

The founding fathers[2] of the USA wanted to create "One [nation] out of many ", a place where people from different countries and cultures could live together in peace. All in all the USA has succeeded in integrating[3] millions of immigrants. However, there have been times when integration into US society hasn't worked so well. In the worst cases this has led to tensions and even violence between different ethnic groups. There have been times when people have developed strong prejudices against other people because of differences in appearance, behaviour or belief[4]. Sometimes, however, when people from different cultures get together, funny situations can arise[5], and these might help to improve relationships between people.

- Look at the illustrations that go with the following story. What hints[6] do they give you about the story?
- If you look at the last picture, what do you think was the outcome[7] of everything that happened?
- Read the story to find out what actually happened to the Lin family when they first came to the USA. (Not all the new words are explained. Still, you should be able to understand the story.)

The first time our family was invited out to dinner in America, we disgraced ourselves[8] while eating celery[9]. We had emigrated to this country from China, and during our early days here we had a hard time with American table manners[10]. In China we never ate celery raw, or any other kind of vegetable raw. We always had to disinfect the vegetables in boiling[11] water first. When we were presented with our first relish tray[12], the raw celery caught us unprepared.

We had been invited to dinner by our neighbors, the Gleasons. After arriving at the house, we shook hands with our hosts and packed ourselves into a sofa. As our family of four sat stiffly in a row, my younger brother and I stole glances at[13] our parents for a clue as to what to do next.

Mrs. Gleason offered the relish tray to Mother. The tray looked pretty, with its tiny[14] red radishes, curly sticks of carrots, and long, slender stalks[15] of pale green celery. "Do try some of the celery, Mrs. Lin," she said. "It's from a local farmer, and it's sweet."

Mother picked up one of the green stalks, and Father followed suit. Then I picked up a stalk, and my brother did too. So there we sat, each with a stalk of celery in our right hand.

Mrs. Gleason kept smiling. "Would you like to try some of the dip, Mrs. Lin? It's my own recipe[16]: sour cream and onion[17] flakes, with a dash of Tabasco sauce."

Most Chinese don't care for dairy products[18], and in those days I wasn't even ready to drink fresh milk. Sour cream sounded perfectly revolting[19]. Our family shook our heads in unison.

Mrs. Gleason went off with the relish tray to the other guests, and we carefully watched to see what they did. Everyone seemed to eat the raw vegetables quite happily.

Mother took a bite of her celery. *Crunch.* "It's not bad!" she whispered.

Father took a bite of his celery. *Crunch.* "Yes, it is good," he said, looking surprised.

I took a bite, and then my brother. *Crunch, crunch.* It was more than good; it was delicious. Raw celery has a slight sparkle, a zingy taste that you don't get in cooked celery. When Mrs. Gleason came around with the relish tray, we each took another stalk of celery, except my brother. He took two.

There was only one problem: long strings ran through the length of the stalk, and they got caught in my teeth. When I help my mother in the kitchen, I always pull the strings out before slicing[20] celery.

I pulled the strings out of my stalk. *Z-z-zip, z-z-zip.* My brother followed suit. *Z-z-zip, z-z-zip, z-z-z-zip.* To my left, my parents were taking care[21] of their own stalks. *Z-z-zip, z-z-zip, z-z-zip.*

[1]slurp [slɜ:p] *das Schlürfen; schlürfen* [2]founding fathers *Gründerväter* [3]integrate ['ɪntɪgreɪt] *integrieren* [4]belief [bɪ'li:f] *Glaube, religiöse Überzeugung* [5]arise [ə'raɪz] – arose [ə'rəʊz] – arisen [ə'rɪzn] *entstehen, sich ergeben* [6]hint *Hinweis* [7]outcome *Ergebnis* [8]disgrace oneself [dɪs'greɪs] *sich blamieren* [9]celery ['selərɪ] *Stangensellerie* [10]manners *(pl.)* *Manieren* [11]boil *kochen* [12]tray *Tablett* [13]steal a glance at sb. [glɑ:ns] *jm. heimlich einen Blick zuwerfen*; glance at *einen kurzen Blick werfen auf* [14]tiny ['taɪnɪ] *winzig* [15]stalk [stɔ:k] *Stengel, Stange* [16]recipe ['resəpɪ] *Rezept* [17]onion ['ʌnjən] *Zwiebel* [18]they don't care for dairy products ['deərɪ] *sie mögen keine Milchprodukte* [19]revolting [rɪ'vəʊltɪŋ] *abscheulich, ekelerregend* [20]slice [slaɪs] *(in Scheiben) schneiden* [21]take care of *sich kümmern um*

Suddenly I realized that there was dead silence except for our zipping. Looking up, I saw that the eyes of everyone in the room were on our family. Mr. and Mrs. Gleason, their daughter Meg, who was my friend, and their neighbors the Badels – they were all staring at us as we busily pulled the strings of our celery.

That wasn't the end of it. Mrs. Gleason announced[1] that dinner was served and invited us to the dining table. It was lavishly covered with platters of food, but we couldn't see any chairs around the table. So we helpfully carried over some dining chairs and sat down. All the other guests just stood there.

Mrs. Gleason bent down and whispered[2] to us, "This is a buffet dinner. You help yourselves[3] to some food and eat it in the living room."

Our family beat a retreat[4] back to the sofa as if chased[5] by enemy soldiers. For the rest of the evening, too mortified[6] to go back to the dining table, I nursed a bit of potato salad on my plate.

Next day Meg and I got on the school bus together. I wasn't sure how she would feel about me after the spectacle our family made at the party. But she was just the same as usual, and the only reference she made to the party was, "Hope you and your folks got enough to eat last night. You certainly didn't take very much. Mom never tries to figure out how much food to prepare. She just puts everything on the table and hopes for the best."

I began to relax. The Gleasons' dinner party wasn't so different from a Chinese meal after all. My mother also puts everything on the table and hopes for the best.

[…]

Then came our dinner at the Lakeview restaurant.

The Lakeview was an expensive restaurant, one of those places where a headwaiter dressed in tails conducted you to your seat, and the only light came from candles and flaming desserts[7]. In one corner of the room a lady harpist played tinkling melodies.

Father wanted to celebrate, because he had just been promoted. He worked for an electronics company, and after his English started improving, his superiors decided to appoint him to a position more suited to his training. The promotion not only brought a higher salary but was also a tremendous boost to his pride[8].

Up to then we had eaten only in Chinese restaurants. Although my brother and I were becoming fond of hamburgers, my parents didn't care much for western food, other than chow mein[9].

But this was a special occasion, and Father asked his coworkers to recommend[10] a really elegant restaurant. So there we were at the Lakeview, stumbling after the headwaiter in the murky dining room.

At our table we were handed our menus, and they were so big that to read mine I almost had to stand up again. But why bother[11]? It was mostly in French, anyway.

Father, being an engineer, was always systematic. He took out a pocket French dictionary. "They told me that most of the items would be in French, so I came prepared." He even had a pocket flashlight, the size of a marking pen. While Mother held the flashlight over the menu, he looked up the items that were in French.

"*Pâté en croûte*," he muttered. "Let's see … *pâté* is paste. … *croûte* is crust … hmm … a paste in crust."

The waiter stood looking patient. I squirmed and died at least fifty times.

At long last[12] Father gave up. "Why don't we just order four complete dinners at random[13]?" he suggested.

"Isn't that risky?" asked Mother. "The French eat some rather peculiar[14] things, I've heard."

"A Chinese can eat anything a Frenchman can eat," Father declared.

The soup arrived in a plate. How do you get soup up from a plate? I glanced at the other diners, but the ones at the nearby tables were not on their soup course, while the most distant ones were invisible[15] in the darkness.

Fortunately my parents had studied books on western etiquette before they came to America.

[1]announce [ə'naʊns] *verkünden* [2]whisper (to sb.) ['wɪspə] *(jm. zu)flüstern* [3]help oneself (to sth.) *sich bedienen (mit etwas), sich (etwas) nehmen* [4]retreat *(n.; v.)* [rɪ'tri:t] *Rückzug; sich zurückziehen* [5]chase [tʃeɪs] *jagen, verfolgen* [6]mortified ['mɔ:tɪfaɪd] *beschämt* [7]dessert [dɪ'zɜ:t] *Nachtisch* [8]a tremendous boost to his pride [trə'mendəs] *eine ungeheure Stärkung seines Selbstwertgefühls* [9]chow mein [ˌtʃaʊ 'meɪn] *chin.-amerik. Nudelgericht* [10]recommend [ˌrekə'mend] *empfehlen* [11]bother ['bɒðə] *sich die Mühe machen* [12]at long last *schließlich, endlich* [13]at random ['rændəm] *aufs Geratewohl* [14]rather peculiar [ˌrɑ:ðə pɪ'kju:lɪə] *ziemlich merkwürdig* [15]invisible [ɪn'vɪzəbl] *unsichtbar*

"Tilt your plate," whispered my mother. "It's easier to spoon the soup up that way."
She was right. Tilting the plate did the trick. But the etiquette book didn't say anything about what you did after the soup reached your lips. As any respectable Chinese knows, the correct way to eat your soup is to slurp. This helps to cool the liquid and prevents you from burning your lips. It also shows your appreciation[1].
We showed our appreciation. *Shloop*, went my father. *Shloop*, went my mother. *Shloop, shloop*, went my brother, who was the hungriest.
The lady harpist stopped playing to take a rest. And in the silence, our family's consumption of soup suddenly seemed unnaturally loud. You know how it sounds on a rocky beach when the tide goes out and the water drains[2] from all those little pools? They go *shloop, shloop, shloop*. That was the Lin family, eating soup.

At the next table a waiter was pouring wine. When a large *shloop* reached him, he froze[3]. The bottle continued to pour, and red wine flooded the tabletop and into the lap[4] of a customer. Even the customer didn't notice anything at first, being also hypnotized by the *shloop, shloop, shloop*.
It was too much. "I need to go to the toilet," I mumbled, jumping to my feet. A waiter, sensing my urgency, quickly directed me to the ladies' room.
I splashed cold water on my burning face, and as I dried myself with a paper towel, I stared into the mirror. In this perfumed ladies' room, with its pink-and-silver wallpaper and marbled sinks[5], I looked completely out of place[6]. What was I doing here? What was our family doing in the Lakeview restaurant? In America?
The door to the ladies' room opened. A woman came in and glanced curiously at me. I retreated into one of the toilet cubicles[7] and latched the door.
Time passed – maybe half an hour. Then I heard the door open again, and my mother's voice. "Are you in there? You're not sick, are you?"
There was real concern[8] in her voice. A girl can't leave her family just because they slurp their soup. Besides, the toilet cubicle had a few drawbacks[9] as a permanent residence. "I'm all right," I said, undoing the latch.
Mother didn't tell me how the rest of the dinner went, and I didn't want to know. In the weeks following, I managed to push the whole thing into the back of my mind, where it jumped out at me only a few times a day. Even now, I turn hot all over when I think of the Lakeview restaurant.

[…]

The day came when my parents announced that they wanted to give a dinner party. We had invited Chinese friends to eat with us before, but this dinner was going to be different. In addition to a Chinese-American family, we were going to invite the Gleasons.
"Gee, I can hardly wait to have dinner at your house," Meg said to me. "I just *love* Chinese food."
That was a relief[10]. Mother was a good cook, but I wasn't sure if people who ate sour cream would also eat chicken gizzards stewed in soy sauce[11]. Mother decided not to take a chance with chicken gizzards. Since we had western guests, she set the table[12] with large dinner plates, which we never used in Chinese meals. In fact we didn't use individual plates at all, but picked up food from the platters in the middle of the table and brought it directly to our rice bowls. Following the practice of Chinese-American restaurants, Mother also placed large serving spoons on the platters.
The dinner started well. Mrs. Gleason exclaimed at the beautifully arranged dishes[13] of food: the colorful candied fruit in the sweet-and-sour pork dish, the noodle-thin shreds[14] of chicken meat stir-fried[15] with tiny peas, and the glistening pink prawns[16] in a ginger sauce.
At first I was too busy enjoying my food to notice how the guests were doing. But soon I remembered my duties. Sometimes guests were too polite to help themselves and you had to serve them with more food.

[1]appreciation [ə,pri:ʃɪ'eɪʃn] *Anerkennung* [2]drain *abfließen* [3]freeze [fri:z] – froze [frəʊz] – frozen *erstarren* [4]lap *Schoß* [5]sink *Waschbecken* [6]out of place *fehl am Platz* [7]cubicle ['kju:bɪkl] *Kabine* [8]concern [kən'sɜ:n] *Besorgnis* [9]drawback ['drɔ:bæk] *Nachteil* [10]relief [rɪ'li:f] *Erleichterung* [11]chicken gizzards stewed in soy sauce ['gɪzəd; stju:d] *Hühnermägen in Sojasoße geschmort* [12]set the table (AE) *den Tisch decken* [13]dish *Schüssel; Gericht* [14]shreds *(pl.)* *Stückchen* [15]stir-fried ['stɜ:fraɪd] *kurz angebraten* [16]prawn [prɔ:n] *Garnele*

I glanced at Meg, to see if she needed more food, and my eyes nearly popped out at the sight of her plate. It was piled with food: the sweet-and sour meat pushed right against the chicken shreds, and the chicken sauce ran into the prawns. She had been taking food from a second dish before she finished eating her helping[1] from the first!

Horrified, I turned to look at Mrs. Gleason. She was dumping rice out of her bowl and putting it on her dinner plate. Then she ladled prawns and gravy[2] on top of the rice and mixed everything together, the way you mix sand, gravel, and cement to make concrete[3].

I couldn't bear[4] to look any longer, and I turned to Mr. Gleason. He was chasing a pea around his plate. Several times he got it to the edge, but when he tried to pick it up with his chopsticks[5], it rolled back toward the center of the plate again. Finally he put down his chopsticks and picked up the pea with his fingers. He really did! A grown man!

All of us, our family and the Chinese guests, stopped eating to watch the activities of the Gleasons. I wanted to giggle[6]. Then I caught my mother's eyes on me. She frowned and shook her head slightly, and I understood the message: the Gleasons were not used to[7] Chinese ways, and they were just coping[8] the best they could. For some reason I thought of celery strings.

When the main courses were finished, Mother brought out a platter of fruit. "I hope you weren't expecting a sweet dessert," she said. "Since the Chinese don't eat dessert, I didn't think to prepare any."

"Oh, I couldn't possibly eat dessert!" cried Mrs. Gleason. 'I'm simply stuffed!"

Meg had different ideas. When the table was cleared, she announced that she and I were going for a walk. "I don't know about you, but I feel like dessert," she told me, when we were outside. "Come on, there's a Dairy Queen down the street. I could use a big chocolate milkshake!"

Although I didn't really want anything more to eat, I insisted on[9] paying for the milkshakes. After all[10], I was still hostess.

Meg got her large chocolate milkshake and I had a small one. Even so, she was finishing hers while I was only half done. Toward the end she pulled hard on her straws[11] and went *shloop, shloop.*

"Do you always slurp when you eat a milkshake?" I asked, before I could stop myself.

Meg grinned. "Sure. All Americans slurp."

Lensey Namioka

1. What do you now know about the Lins and their early days in the USA? Arrange the information in the form of a network. – Go through the story again if necessary. Then use your network to give an oral presentation.
2. Why do you think the Lin girl felt more embarrassed[12] than the other members of her family?
3. Why could Meg's last sentence be seen as the Lins' real beginning as American citizens?
4. Discuss in class: What cultural norms should people be taught who do a German course in a foreign country?
5. Try to think of situations in your life where you 'disgraced' yourself because you didn't know what the 'rules of the game' were? How did you feel?

[1]helping *Portion* [2]gravy ['greɪvɪ] *Soße* [3]concrete ['kɒŋkriːt] *Beton* [4]I couldn't bear to … [beə] *Ich konnte es nicht ertragen, zu …* [5]chopstick ['tʃɒpstɪk] *Stäbchen* [6]giggle ['gɪgl] *kichern* [7]be used to sth. *an etwas gewöhnt sein* [8]cope [kəʊp] *etwa: versuchen zurechtzukommen* [9]insist on [ɪn'sɪst] *bestehen auf* [10]after all *immerhin, schließlich* [11]straw [strɔː] *Strohhalm* [12]embarrassed [ɪm'bærəst] *verlegen*

Black music

- First look at the two photos on this page: What's going on in each of them? What's similar in the two photos and what's different? Then find out more about these two approaches[1] to music from the introductory text.
- Now look at the illustration on page 99. What do you think it shows? Finally, read texts A-F and find out which of them goes with which label on the tree.

It all started in Africa, where music played an important part in the religious events of the tribes. Musicians played drums and other instruments as singers danced and sang. Unlike in 17th- and 18th-century Europe, where the audience[2] sat and listened silently while the musicians played note for note the music of a single composer[3], there was no clear separation between the African musicians and their audience. Musicians and dancers improvised[4] and created as they played. Making music was a social event in which everyone took part.

The African approach to music was an important basis for many new genres[5] of music in the New World.

A From rhythm[6] and blues developed two very popular genres of music: **rock and roll** and **soul**. Rock 'n' roll was created when white singers, influenced by black musicians, started to sing rhythm and blues. Soul music is the further development of rhythm and blues.

B **Spirituals** were the first important genre of black music created in the New World. When African slaves were brought to America they also brought with them their approach to music. They were not allowed to practise[7] their traditional African religions, so they combined their African approach to music with Christian texts. The result was a new genre of music.

[1]approach to [əˈprəʊtʃ] *Herangehensweise an* [2]audience [ˈɔːdɪəns] *Publikum* [3]composer [kəmˈpəʊzə] *Komponist/in* [4]improvise [ˈɪmprəvaɪz] *improvisieren* [5]genre [ˈʒɒnrə] [6]rhythm [ˈrɪðəm] *Rhythmus* [7]practise *ausüben*

C **Jazz**, the most important music form of the 20th century, developed from blues. Jazz was created when black musicians played together and applied[1] their improvisational approach to the music. They combined European instruments like the trumpet[2] and the trombone[3], for example, with African instruments like drums and the banjo. As jazz evolved[4], it became one of the most complex[5] and expressive[6] forms of music.

D Like jazz, **rhythm and blues** also developed from blues. When musicians, influenced by the blues, formed bands and started to play electric guitars and drums, the music they created was more urban and reached a larger audience of black and white listeners. The songs were often the same songs that the blues singers sang, and they often had the same blues structure.

E Later, **blues** branched off[7] from spirituals and became another important genre of black music. Blues singers, who usually also played guitar, had the same approach to the music as the singers of spirituals. Both types of music are emotional, but unlike spirituals blues texts are not religious.

F From soul developed **rap**, one of the most important genres of black music today. Rap is often very political, and deals with such topics as racism and life in the inner city. In rap, the meaning of the words and their complex rhythms are very important. Rap artists often see the genre as a source of information for black people.

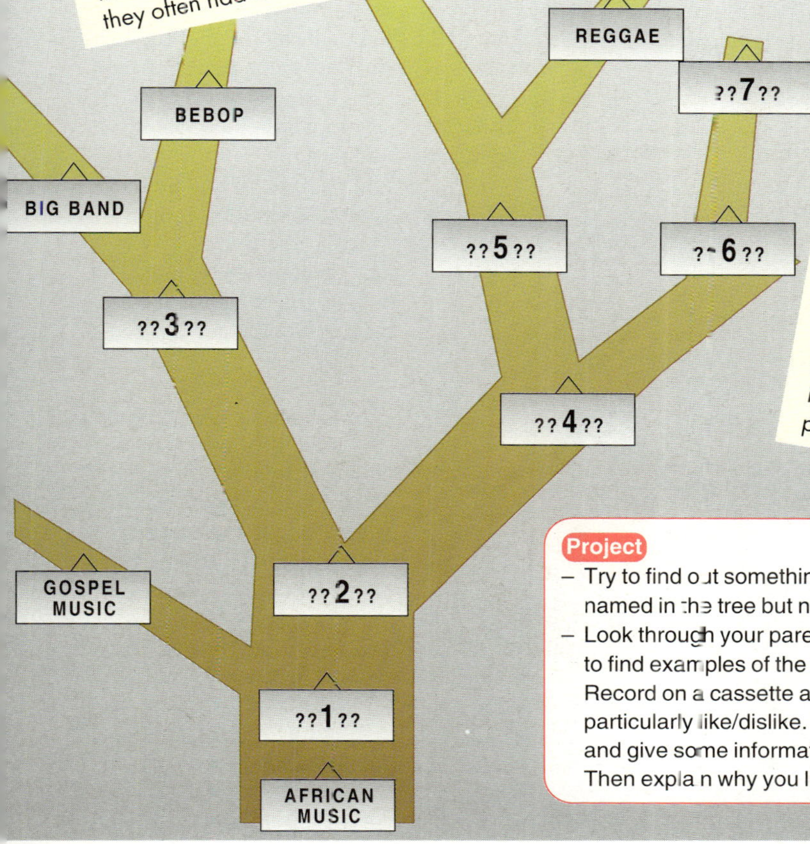

Project
- Try to find out something about the four genres of music named in the tree but not discussed in the texts.
- Look through your parents' record/CD collection and try to find examples of the different genres of black music. Record on a cassette a short excerpt of one song you particularly like/dislike. Play the cassette to the class and give some information about the singer(s) or group. Then explain why you like/dislike the song.

[1]apply to [ə'plaɪ] *anwenden auf* [2]trumpet ['trʌmpɪt] *Trompete* [3]trombone [trɒm'bəʊn] *Posaune* [4]evolve [ɪ'vɒlv] *sich weiterentwickeln* [5]complex ['kɒmpleks] [6]expressive [ɪk'spresɪv] *ausdrucksstark* [7]branch off [ˌbrɑːntʃ_'ɒf] *abzweigen*

Strangers in a distant[1] land

– Read the first four paragraphs on this page. Then try to explain what they have to do with the Indian legend on p. 48.
– Radio and television in 1856! Interview Mrs Colt for your station. – Perhaps you can even record your interview.

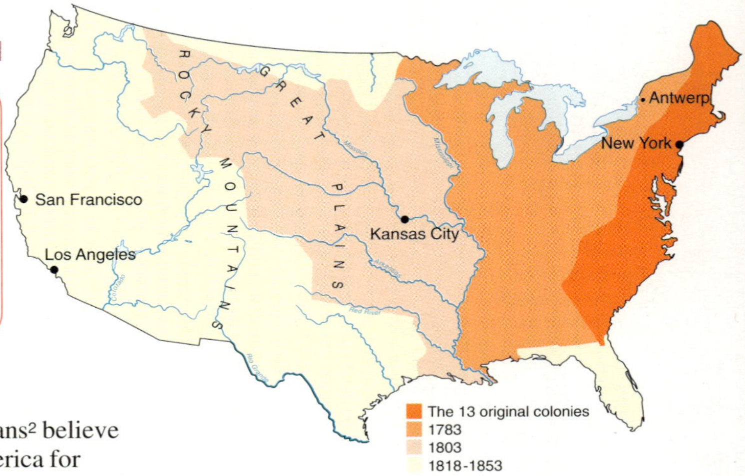

The hungry snake

Nobody knows exactly, but historians[2] believe that Indians had been living in America for almost 50,000 years before the first European settlers arrived about 1600. They lived in hundreds of separate tribes, most with their own languages and ways of life. For a short time the early settlers lived peacefully with the Indians. In fact, the colonists needed the help of the Indians to survive. But as more and more settlers arrived, the colonies on the east coast became too small. So people began to look west.

Broken promises

As settlers began to take more and more land, the Indians were forced[3] to leave. Many were killed by the white men or they died of illnesses which the white men had brought with them. The American government often promised that white settlers could not have land without the permission of the Indians, but these promises were often broken.

A permanent[4] frontier

In 1834 the government decided that the Mississippi should be the permanent "Indian Frontier". The Indians should have all the land to the west of it; white settlers should live to the east. And so the Indians from the east were forced again to leave their lands and move west. Many never survived the long journey. One in four Cherokees[5] died before they reached the Mississippi. For this reason their journey is known as the "Trail of Tears".

Gold

Fourteen years later, in 1848, gold was found in California. Travellers had also seen that on the other side of the Rockies there were wonderful valleys and rivers. So thousands of white Americans ignored the "Indian Frontier" and began to cross the Mississippi. They came in wagons, on horses and on foot. The Indians protested that so many settlers were stealing their land, but the government did nothing. Soldiers were sent to fight the Indians and protect the settlers. The Indians fought back, and sometimes they were able to beat the white men. But by 1890 the last Indian tribes had been defeated.

Pioneers

For the people who settled in the west life was not easy, especially for the women. Their lives were not recorded as the lives of many male pioneers were. However, many women recorded their own experiences in letters and diaries, and it is from these that we know what their lives were really like. Miriam Davis Colt, for example, set out[6] for Kansas with her husband and two children in 1856. Her husband's father and sister travelled in the same group. Miriam left a comfortable home for the promise of land in the west, but she was not prepared for the hard life that was waiting for her.

[1]distant ['dɪstənt] *fern* [2]historian [hɪ'stɔːrɪən] *Historiker/in* [3]force [fɔːs] *zwingen* [4]permanent ['pɜːmənənt] *fest, beständig* [5]Cherokee ['tʃerəkiː] [6]set out – set – set *aufbrechen*

April 15th, 1856
Have visited Mother. Very hard. It is probably the last visit we shall have.

April 16th, 1856
Antwerp, N.Y. Said goodbye to our friends this morning.

April 30th, 1856
Here we are at Kansas City. Went to the hotel – find it very crowded.

May 1st, 1856
Visit the city, and see that you need only a few buildings in this western world to make a city. Today is our wedding anniversary[1], … a shadow[2] comes over me, as I try to look away into the future and ask, "What is my destiny[3]?"

May 2nd, 1856
A lovely day. Our husbands are loading the wagons. … Women and children walk along up the hill out of this "great City", wait under a tree – what a beautiful country lies before us. One mile from the city, and Dr Thorn's wagon is broken; it must be sent back to Kansas City to be repaired. Fires made – women cooking – dinner eaten sitting round on the ground.

May 3rd, 1856
The women and children, who slept in their wagons last night, got wet from the heavy rain. … We women and children must sit quietly in the wagon to keep out of the rain – eat a lunch of biscuits, look at the deep, black mud in which our wagon is stuck[4].

May 11th, 1856
"Made" only a few miles yesterday. In the evening we came to a cabin[5] near a wood. … Asked the 'Lord[6] of the Castle' if some of the women and children could rest there for the night. He said we could. His lady came, with bare[7] feet, and a white sack thrown over her shoulder with some corn. I said to myself – "Is that what I have got to come to?" She seemed pleased to have company.

May 12th, 1856
Full of hope. Expect tonight to arrive at our new home. It begins to rain, rain, rain, like a shower.

May 22nd, 1856
My husband, his father, and sister Lydia have made their claims[8]. This makes 720 acres[9] of land which belongs to our family. It is next to the Osage Indian lands.

May 26th, 1856
These Indians are said to be friendly, but I cannot look at their painted faces without feeling frightened, and when they come, I sit down and take Willie, and have Mema stand by my side, with my arm around her, out of fear they might steal my children from me. They point to my boy and make signs that he is pretty. They call the boy "Chintu-chinka" and the girl "che-me chinka".

May 28th, 1856
Took my children and went with my husband to plant corn. … After we had eaten dinner in the wagon, we went and chose a site for our own cabin.

June 7th, 1856
I have cooked so much in the hot sun and smoke that I hardly know who I am, and when I look in the little mirror I ask, "Can this be me?" My hands are the color of a smoked ham[10].

June 16th, 1856
The mosquitoes have come upon[11] us. I lie awake. I try to keep my children covered.

June 17th, 1856
Our cornfield looks promising[12]. Melons[13], beans, peas, potatoes and tomatoes are growing well.

July 6th, 1856
My husband feels cold and sick.

July 16th, 1856
My husband is lying on our bed; his fever is leaving him. Father lies on a blanket, on the floor; his fever is worse. Willie lies on an Indian blanket near the door, calling for water. Just three months today since we left home.

(Based on *Women of the West* by Cathy Luchetti and Carol Olwell)

[1]wedding anniversary ['wedɪŋ ˌænɪ'vɜːsərɪ] *Hochzeitstag* [2]shadow ['ʃædəʊ] *Schatten* [3]destiny ['destənɪ] *Schicksal* [4]stick – stuck – stuck *steckenbleiben* [5]cabin ['kæbɪn] *Hütte* [6]Lord [lɔːd] *Herr* [7]bare [beə] *bloß; nackt* [8]make a claim [kleɪm] *Anspruch (auf ein Stück Land) erheben* [9]acre ['eɪkə] *Morgen* [10]smoked ham [hæm] *geräucherter Schinken* [11]come upon sb. [ə'pɒn] *über jn. herfallen* [12]promising *vielversprechend* [13]melon ['melən] *Melone*

The tall stranger

Info box The first people who moved onto the plains[3] after the Indians had left were the cattle ranchers. Cowboys now drove their herds[4] across the plains to the big cattle towns such as Dodge City, Abilene, Wichita or Topeka. From there the cattle were taken by train to the towns and cities in the east. Here – on the plains – was the Wild West with its lawless towns, its saloons, cowboys and gunmen[5], and here famous marshals[6] like Wyatt Earp and Wild Bill Hickok kept the peace.

From the Wild West came the stories and legends that later appeared in cowboy films and books. Most of them gave a false impression of the American West, but it is an impression that has never died out.

- Look at the following words: good guys, bad guys, lawless people, conflict, showdown, on the side of the law, hero, heroine[1], innocent.
  What do they have to do with westerns?
- What impression of the Wild West does one get from most westerns?
- Read the following story to find out if it conforms[2] with your idea of a typical western.

Janet stood outside the little house, alone and frightened. In front of her, high on their horses, sat two of Duke Hammond's men, confident because they knew that her husband was far away in Dodge City.

"If you know what's good for you," said one of the men, "you'll take your children and get off[7] this land."

"It's my land," she said bravely. "You can't tell me when to leave. I have the proper papers. And we have a government in Washington that says this is my land."

"The government is a long way away, lady. And I'm telling you this is Duke Hammond's land. If you want to stay here, then you'd better ask the government in Washington to send some soldiers to protect you."

"Hammond has enough land," Janet shouted. "He doesn't need this."

"Listen, if you stay, next week there'll be another family here and a week later another. Soon the whole valley will be full of you farmers. Now listen, lady, for the last time. You have 48 hours. If you're still here after that, we'll burn your house down."

In the bedroom her two children, Billy and Louise, sat on the floor under the window. Billy closed his eyes and said quietly to himself, "Dad, why can't you come back? Please. Why can't you be here? We need you." But Mike Hughes had gone to Dodge City to buy some things they needed. Now they were alone. "Dear God," he said, "please send Dad back now. Please."

He opened his eyes and looked carefully out of the window towards the trees on the other side of the valley, towards the path his father always came along.

In the distance a man appeared between the trees and rode slowly towards the house. Billy jumped up and, forgetting the danger, ran through the rooms to his mother. "It's Dad," he shouted. "He has come back." His mother had also seen the rider. But the man on the horse was not her husband. "I'm sorry, Billy," she said sadly. "It's probably another of Hammond's men."

"Now listen," said one of the cowboys. "You have 48 hours. Understand?"

Angrily, Janet lifted her rifle[8]. "I'm not going to leave. Do you understand that? And you tell that to Duke Hammond. Now get off my land before I shoot you."

She aimed her rifle, but the second cowboy threw his lasso around her shoulders and pulled it so tight[9] that she fell to her knees. "Listen, lady. I've never shot a woman before, but there's a first time for everything."

Suddenly they heard a shot[10] and a bullet[11] flew over their heads. The two cowboys turned around at once. The stranger had stopped and was sitting on his horse. The first cowboy fired[12] at him with his colt two or three times, but the stranger did not move. He just sat there. "Too far away to hit him," said the cowboy. "And he knows it."

Then the stranger took his rifle and fired once

[1]heroine ['herəʊɪn] *Heldin* [2]conform (with) [kən'fɔːm] *übereinstimmen (mit)* [3]the plains *(pl.)* ['pleɪnz] *die Prärie*
[4]herd [hɜːd] *Herde* [5]gunman *(mit einer Schußwaffe) Bewaffnete(r)* [6]marshal ['mɑːʃl] *(US) Bezirkspolizeichef/in*
[7]get off (sth.) *weggehen, verschwinden (von etwas)* [8]rifle ['raɪfl] *Gewehr* [9]tight [taɪt] *fest, eng* [10]shot *Schuß*
[11]bullet ['bʊlɪt] *Kugel, Geschoß* [12]fire *(Schußwaffe) abfeuern*

more. One of the cowboys fell from his horse, hit in the shoulder. The other raised his arms. Slowly the stranger rode towards them, his rifle aimed at the two cowboys.

Janet got up from the ground. She did not recognize the stranger. He had traveled a long way. Dust[1] was on his clothes, his shoes, his horse, and his hat was low over his face. When he got near enough, he said to the two gunmen, "I suggest you and your friend finish your business and go back where you came from."

The wounded[2] man climbed onto his horse. "We've finished here," he said. "But we've not finished with you, stranger. If you know what's good for you, keep away from[3] Deadwood and the Double-Bar Ranch. And you, lady, remember what we said. You have 48 hours to get off this land." Then they rode away.

Janet spoke first. "I'm sure[4] glad you came. Those men almost killed me." And slowly she began to relax. "My name is Janet Hughes. This is my son Billy. How can I thank you?"

"It isn't necessary," said the stranger.

"Can I at least offer you a meal and a bath?"

"That would be very kind of you. I've been riding a long time." And she looked at the stranger curiously as he climbed down from his horse. He was tall with strong shoulders, his face brown from the hot sun, his eyes blue and very clear, his age she could not say. But he was obviously a traveling man, a man of the desert, of the mountains, his home a camp fire in a lonely part of an empty region. And she thought that he was very similar to her husband.

Washed and in clean clothes from Mike's wardrobe, the stranger walked into the kitchen. The shock to Janet was even greater. He was very similar to Mike, Mike who should be back. She hoped that nothing had happened to him.

"This is a nice little farm," he said, as she sat there quietly. "You've chosen a good position."

"Thank you," she said and wondered why he had come here. It was not a part of the country for men like him. There were only cattle ranches and farms here. There was no adventure, no gold, there were no Indians to fight, no new areas to discover. The frontier[5] was further west. So what had brought him here?

"I thought you were another gunman for Duke Hammond. He seems to hire every gunman in the west."

"He didn't hire me."

Janet looked out of the window. So he was a gunman. Or was he a marshal who had finally come to bring the law into a lawless country, into a part of the world where the man who owned the most said what the law was – and that man was Duke Hammond? She sighed and wished again that Mike was there.

Suddenly Billy ran into the kitchen. "How do you like my guns?" he asked. He had a pair of toy guns made of wood. He was carrying them low, the way a gunfighter wears them.

"Where did you get those?" the stranger asked.

"Dad gave them to me."

"Billy," said Janet angrily. "Put them away." But Billy was not listening.

"Those men only came today because they knew Dad wasn't here."

The stranger looked down at the table, his face almost sad. Then he looked out of the window.

"Listen, boy," he said. "Don't ever play with guns. Guns are to kill animals, remember that." Then, angrily, he said, "Now take them off."

"And tell your sister dinner is ready," said Janet.

"Those two men," the stranger said as they ate their meal. "What did they want?"

"They work for Duke Hammond," Janet said. "He owns all the land here. Or he says he owns it. His father came here over twenty years ago. He fought the Indians and everybody else who came near him and built up a huge cattle ranch, the Double-Bar Ranch. We bought our land properly through a government office. According to the papers they gave us, we're the proper owners. Duke Hammond says he needs the land and the water for his cattle. He's afraid more farmers will come and take what he thinks is all his land."

"So he's forcing[6] you to leave?"

"That's right. He offered to buy the farm, but for so little money, it was a joke. Now he has hired some gunmen and, well, you heard what they said." Suddenly tears came to her eyes.

"I wish Mike was here. I can't fight these men alone." She breathed in deeply and said, "I'm sorry. I have no room[7] here, but you're welcome to sleep outside in the barn[8]."

[1]dust [dʌst] *Staub* [2]wounded ['wu:ndɪd] *verwundet, verletzt* [3]keep away from *sich fernhalten von* [4]sure (AE, infml.) *wirklich* [5]frontier ['frʌntɪə] *(US) Grenzland* [6]force [fɔ:s] *zwingen* [7]room *Platz* [8]barn [bɑ:n] *Scheune*

"I'll be OK."

"And …" Suddenly a strange feeling came over her. "Can you stay for a day or two until Mike returns? He should be back soon."

"I'll be glad to stay and help. I've been traveling a long time." He got up to leave the room, but she stopped him. "You haven't told me your name."

He smiled. "Few people ever ask. It's Boone, Jim Boone."

"Good night, Jim. And thank you."

"Good night," he said and left the small house.

During the next few days Jim did several jobs around the farm. At first Janet smiled to herself while she, Louise and Billy did the daily jobs, and the big man did a job here and then a job there. Until she realized that he was choosing his jobs. He only did those jobs that Mike had wanted to do before the winter came. And as a loud wind came through the trees and over the plains, it seemed that it wanted to tell her something. A cold feeling went through her. Luckily, the gunmen never came back, and so a few days later Janet decided to ride into Deadwood and go to the grocery store. Billy and Louise were already waiting in the wagon when Jim came towards them.

"I'll ride with you," he said, and before she could say anything, he climbed onto the wagon and took the reins[1]. Janet wanted to tell him that it might be dangerous for him. Duke Hammond's men were sometimes in the saloon there, and a neighbor had mentioned that a new gunman had arrived only yesterday, a man called Brodey, the most dangerous of them all. But she noticed that Jim, too, was wearing his guns. So she sat next to him and never spoke as they rode towards the small town.

When they reached Deadwood, they rode along the main street and stopped outside the grocery store. From the saloon window Brodey watched them as they got down from the wagon.

"Who's that?" Brodey asked.

"It's the Hughes family. Hammond wants to get rid of them."

"And the man?"

"No idea. He appeared a few days ago and put a bullet in Wiley's shoulder. It's your job, Brodey, to put a bullet in him." Brodey looked at Jim Boone carefully and he thought, "How can you shoot a man you've already killed?"

Outside on the street a young man ran up to the wagon and said, "Hello, Mrs. Hughes." Then he turned to the girl. "Hi, Louise. Would you like to walk with me?" Louise turned to her mother. "May I, Mother? Please?"

Janet smiled. "But stay where I can see you. We're not very popular here." The girl jumped down and walked away with the young man. Janet sighed. "It won't be long before she gets married and has her own children. It's funny. You think you're still young, but before you know what has happened, your life is over and you're a grandmother. Are you planning to do anything here in Deadwood, Jim?"

"I just want to see a few people," he said.

"Can I come with you?" asked Billy.

"No!" said Janet quickly. "You stay with me. God, I feel like a mother hen[2] when I come here. Come on, quickly, into the store with you."

Sheriff Hogan was a fat harmless man. He was the kind of sheriff Duke Hammond wanted. In fact, it was Duke Hammond who had chosen him, and Duke Hammond who made sure he stayed sheriff. Sam Hogan was happy with his job. He had little to do as Duke Hammond and his men organized the law in Deadwood. When it was necessary, he carried the bodies[3] away. He was a simple man who liked a simple life, and he was not prepared for the tall stranger. Jim Boone threw the door of his office open and said calmly, "Are you the sheriff here?"

"Yes, sir," said Hogan. "What's the problem?"

"I have some business to do. I think you should take a siesta for a couple of hours."

Sheriff Hogan looked at the clock on the wall. It was ten o'clock. "It's a little early for a siesta."

"I think it's a good time for a siesta," said Jim and left the room as suddenly as he had entered it. "Who was that?" asked the sheriff's assistant, a slow[4] youth of 17 whose main job was to make coffee and clean the office.

"I don't know, boy, and I don't like it. But you heard what the man said. Close your eyes and have a siesta."

 [1]rein [reɪn] *Zügel* [2]mother hen [hen] *Glucke* [3](dead) body *Leiche* [4]slow *begriffsstutzig*

Sheriff Hogan went to the window and looked out. The tall man was walking towards the saloon. "I don't like it," he said.

Jim entered the saloon and went to the bar. The room was not full. Men were sitting at different tables. In one corner an old black man was playing the piano. Jim recognized the song from the Civil War, but he concentrated[1] on three men sitting at a table where a card game was in progress. Two of them were the men he had seen at Janet's house. The third was Brodey, the new gunman Hammond had hired.

"Well, look who's here," said one of the cowboys from the card table. "I hear you're leaving town today. Why don't you have a drink before you go?"

Jim looked calmly at the three men. His eyes met Brodey's across the table.

"I see two cowboys with very loud mouths," said Jim. "You open them again and there'll be two dead cowboys in here."

The piano stopped at once. Nobody had spoken like that in Deadwood for a long time. The piano player left his chair and walked out of the room. Other men moved quietly from the tables out of the way. Slowly the two cowboys stood up, but Brodey said, "Sit down. This is my fight."

Brodey was not a superstitious man, but throughout the day he had had a strange feeling inside which he could not explain. When he had first ridden into Deadwood to meet Hammond, he had thought this was a town he might never leave, although no man was faster with a gun than he was. The feeling had gotten stronger during the morning. He had even written a short letter, a few lines to a relative, in which he said, "If anything happens to me, there's some money I have in the bank." But then he had thrown the letter away. Now, as he looked into Jim Boone's eyes he knew what the feeling was. "Hello, Brodey," said Jim.

People heard the shots all over town. In the store Janet dropped her bags and held Billy to her. They ran to the window and looked onto the street. Other people had come out of stores and houses and were looking towards the saloon. Minutes seemed like hours until finally Jim Boone walked out of the saloon doors.

"Jim," shouted Janet, and ran onto the street. But he did not come to her. He walked straight towards the hotel. Inside the hotel Duke Hammond was drinking coffee with a group of business friends. He had heard the shots, too, but he was smiling and confident. Brodey, he believed, had done what he had paid him to do. But when the door flew open and Jim Boone walked in, he froze[2].

Jim stopped in front of the table and aimed his gun at Duke Hammond's head. The cattle rancher began to shake. Jim took a bullet and put it on the table where Hammond could see it. "That bullet is for you, Hammond. I'm going to carry it with me wherever I go. If I ever hear that you and your men are trying to force people to leave, or you make trouble for the Hughes family, then I'm going to come and look for you, Hammond. And I'll find you."

Jim took the bullet and put it in the pocket of his shirt. "Remember that, Hammond. Leave the people in peace here. Your days are over as from now[3]."

Hammond was terrified. Then he shouted. "You can't do this. Where's the sheriff?"

"The sheriff isn't coming," said Jim. "Now get up. You're leaving town."

"You can't do this. This is my town!"

Jim fired and a bullet flew past Hammond's ear. Hammond jumped to his feet and ran to the door. Jim fired again and again as Hammond fell out of the hotel and onto the dusty[4] street; and in front of the eyes of the frightened people of Deadwood bullets hit the ground between Hammond's feet as he ran down the main street and out of the town. Again and again he shouted, "Sheriff! Brodey! Where are you?" But nobody came.

That evening when the children were in bed, Janet said, "Mike is dead, isn't he?" Jim nodded. "Did you know him?"

"We met on the way to Dodge City. I liked him. He told me about your problems. He thought it was funny that we looked like each other. But I said it's not healthy to look like me. I have too many enemies. One of them was Brodey."

"What happened?"

"Mike was sitting in a saloon one evening

[1]concentrate (on) ['kɒnsəntreɪt] *sich konzentrieren (auf)* [2]freeze [fri:z] – froze [frəʊz] – frozen [frəʊzn] *erstarren*
[3]as from now *ab jetzt, von jetzt an* [4]dusty *staubig*

during a card game when Brodey came in. Mike didn't have a chance, and he never realized that Brodey thought he was me."

"Why was Brodey your enemy?"

"I'm a U.S. Marshal. I was looking for him."

"I can't live here alone. Billy is too young. Louise is still a girl."

"Billy will soon be old enough. And Louise has a nice young man. I'm sure he can help here."

"And I finish my days as a lonely widow. I know I should thank you for what you've done, but why Mike? Why? And why didn't you stop him? He wasn't a gunfighter."

Jim stood up. "I wasn't in the saloon. When I got there, Brodey had left. To come here." He took some money out of his pocket and put it on the table. "There was a reward on Brodey's head. Five thousand dollars. I don't need the money. I'd like to give it to you."

The next morning when Janet and the children got up, Jim Boone had gone. "Will he come back, Mom?" Billy asked. Janet looked out of the window across the quiet plains.

"Soon, Billy. Soon."

Carl Taylor

1 Analysing the story: The characters, the development of the action, the setting[1]

a The characters

1. Go through the text and find the characters on the side of the law, and those who are lawless.
2. What are typical characteristics[2] of the people in each group? – Find adjectives in the box below that go with people from one group or the other. Why could some adjectives go with people from both groups?

   brave – friendly – harmless – cruel[3] – peaceful – lonely – happy – rude[4] – impolite – kind – fair – rough[5] – violent – weak – strong – reasonable – tolerant – confident – hardworking – dangerous

3. The characters are not really described in the story. Still, every reader has an idea of what they look like. – How do you imagine the main characters? Perhaps you can draw or paint one of them and explain your picture in a few sentences. If you can't draw well enough just write a short text.

b The development of the action

1. Go through the text and make notes on the development of the action.

The beginning of the story	*The development of the story*	*The end*
Hughes family – have bought land – …	…	…

2. Explain what is typical of a western in the development of this story.

c The setting

What is typical about the setting of this story? Make a list of the different places in the story. How do you imagine them? What is typical of a western?

2 What do you think? *Choose one of the following questions and discuss them in class.*

1. Why does Jim come to the Hughes' family? 2. What are his feelings when he sees Billy with his toy gun? 3. What happens in the saloon after Jim says, "Hello, Brodey"? 4. Why are westerns popular with so many people? 5. What TV series[6] are constructed similarly to westerns? Why? 6. What stories/films do you prefer to westerns? Why?

[1]setting ['setɪŋ] *Schauplatz (einer Erzählung usw.)* [2]characteristic [ˌkærəktə'rɪstɪk] *Merkmal* [3]cruel ['kru:əl] *grausam* [4]rude [ru:d] *unhöflich, grob* [5]rough [rʌf] *grob* [6]series *(sing.* and *pl.)* ['sɪəri:z] *(Sende-)Reihe, Serie*

Reservations

The past

After the Indian Wars were over in 1890, white Americans forced[3] all those Indians who had survived to live on reservations. These were areas of land which the whites decided to "give" to the tribes they had defeated. These reservations were less than 4% of the total land area of the United States, and they were often on infertile[4] land which the whites didn't want.

The Indians couldn't farm much of it and there were few animals which they could hunt. From the beginning the tribes could only survive with financial help and food from the American government.

On the reservations the Indians were under the control of the BIA (Bureau[5] of Indian Affairs). The men in this department[6] were white Americans who often knew or understood little about Indians. They forced the Indians to give up their languages and learn English; they even forced them to give up their Indian ways of life.

The situation today

From a kind of prison the reservations have become homes, places where American Indians can find their identity and keep alive their languages and traditional ways of life. There are over 300 reservations, most of them west of the Mississippi. Some are very small and very poor, with only a few hundred American Indians; others, like the Navajo reservation, cover large areas of land and have large populations. Most share the same problems: unemployment is high; families often rely[7] on welfare cheques from the government to survive; many reservation homes have no electricity, and water sometimes has to be brought from rivers which are often polluted; alcoholism[8] and drug abuse[9] are major social problems.

The US government continues to give financial help, but in recent years it has also encouraged a policy of self-government for the tribes. This has given tribal leaders opportunities[10] to look for different ways of financing their independence and their economies. Some tribes have natural resources[11] under the ground which can be exploited. Some try to attract tourists. Others have found more controversial[12] ways of earning money.

In 1991 the Ojibwa Indians opened a casino on their reservation to attract white Americans. A year later they opened a second casino. The money that the tribe earns from the casinos is used to build houses, hospitals and schools; it is also used to provide work for the unemployed and to finance programmes to help the tribal members who are suffering from alcoholism and drug abuse. Some members of the tribe support this success, but others wonder whether this is really the best way to finance an economy.

☞ Find out …
- what living on a reservation meant to Indians in the past and what it means to them today,
- what the main problems on reservations are,
- how different tribes are trying to finance[1] their independence.

"The end justifies the means"[2] – What would a casino supporter say about this saying? What would someone say who is against the casinos?

[1]finance [faɪ'næns] *finanzieren* [2]the end justifies the means ['dʒʌstɪfaɪ] *der Zweck heiligt die Mittel* [3]force [fɔːs] *zwingen* [4]infertile [ɪn'fɜːtaɪl] *unfruchtbar* [5]Bureau ['bjʊərəʊ] *Amt* [6]department (AE) *Abteilung* [7]rely on [rɪ'laɪ] *abhängig sein von* [8]alcoholism ['ælkəhɒlˌɪzəm] *Mißbrauch* [9]abuse [ə'bjuːs] *Mißbrauch* [10]opportunity [ˌɒpə'tjuːnətɪ] *Gelegenheit* [11]natural resources *(pl.)* [rɪ'zɔːsɪz] *Bodenschätze* [12]controversial [ˌkɒntrə'vɜːʃl] *umstritten*

Nature: the core[1] of Navajo religion

Before you read the text, write down 5-7 words which you think people generally associate with religion.
Compare what different people have written down. Can you find a 'trend' in the words?

Read the text and then write down some words traditional Navajo associate with religion.
What are the similarities/differences between the Navajo ideas and traditional European ideas?
What do you think of the Navajo religion?

Angela's great-grandparents[2] are still alive. They have a hogan and a few sheep. Sometimes Angela goes and helps them. They can hardly speak English, so Angela talks to them in Navajo. Her great-grandparents teach her about the plants; they show her which can be used for medicine and which are good for healing[3] animals. Or they teach her to make blankets and rings. Navajo are very good artists. Angela's great-grandfather is a traditional Indian. He would be happy if there were no roads on the reservation and if they left the coal and gas under the ground.

"In our religion our real mother is the Earth, our real father the Sky. The Earth can get sick – just like you and me. Then it sends warnings. These can be earthquakes or floods[4]. When millions of people come together in cities, in one place, it hurts the Earth. The traffic, the noise, the crowds, they are not good for the Earth and they are not good for people; you get crime, you get illnesses. As people run after money, they forget the Earth, they forget where they come from. They forget that they are nothing; they think they are important. The light of the day, the wind, the rain, the snow, they all talk to us. If we ignore what they say, we ignore our most powerful teachers.

The Navajo drew sand paintings to use in healing the sick and in religious ceremonies. This Navajo sand painting shows Father Sky and Mother Earth, two of the most important Holy[7] People.

"Modern technology is taking us quickly towards a different kind of life. We are using the Earth without thought. We are taking the energy and power out of the Earth – the oil, the gas, the water – it's as if we are taking blood from a human being[5]. If you take too much, it can't survive.

"When you take from the Earth, you must put something back – that something can be as simple as a word: 'Thank you'. We explain to the Earth why we need what we are taking. We try to heal the damage[6] we cause. And how do we know when we are causing damage? Because we can talk to the land. Stand next to the river and look at the water and the fish living in it. Look at the trees in the woods or the sea on the beaches. If we understand the language, we can talk to the animals and the land and they can tell us what is wrong and what we must do – if we look and listen. But when I see how you young people think and behave, I often say that somebody has put a stick in your ears and broken it off. But if you listen to your grandparents or the medicine man, they will open your ears and teach you to talk to the animals, the plants, the trees and the land when it is the proper time."

[1]core [kɔː] *Kern* [2]great-grandparents *Urgroßeltern* [3]heal [hiːl] *heilen* [4]flood [flʌd] *Flutkatastrophe*
[5]human being *Mensch* [6]damage ['dæmɪdʒ] *Schaden* [7]holy ['həʊlɪ] *heilig*

Interpreting[1] and translation practice

Some help before you start: Interpreting is almost always done orally. When you interpret, your partner only wants to know the important information, so it is not necessary to know all the words. (When you practise, however, it is useful to write your texts down so you can compare them.)

Here are some expressions you will need when you interpret:
- **a spoken text (e.g. a conversation):** „Frau/Herr … meint, daß …/möchte wissen, ob/warum/wie …" "Ms/Mrs/Mr … says/thinks …/would like to know if/why/how …"
- **a written text:** „Hier steht …", „Dann heißt es, daß …" "At the beginning of the text it says …","And then it says …"

Translating is almost always a written activity. You have to keep closely to the original and at the same time produce a 'correct' text in the other language. For a good translation you have to know all the words in a text. Whenever you find a new word on these two pages, first try to guess its meaning. If you can't understand it and can't find it in the dictionary at the back of the book, look it up in a proper dictionary.

Unit 1

Here is a short article from "The Dunlap Student Voice" about the Dunlap High prom.
Read the text and interpret it for a friend who can't read English so well.

To buy or not to buy – that is the question

by Sarah Bates

Our country is in a recession. People are losing their jobs all over the country, in Illinois too. Many workers are on strike. This is a big worry to our parents who must feed us, and pay the bills.
What can we do to help? – GET TOGETHER AND PLAN A CHEAPER PROM!
A prom does not need to cost hundreds of dollars. Save money by being creative.
There is no need to go out for an expensive dinner. Girls can rent their dresses, guys can rent their tuxedos. It's wasteful to spend lots of money on a dress you only wear once.
There are also many other things you can do to help. Try to carpool[2] to school and to activities. Gas isn't cheap and carpooling is better for the environment.
When times are hard, it is sometimes necessary to spend less. Think about what our parents are going through. Let's do what we can to save, and still have fun!

SPEAK UP! SPEAK OUT! SPEAK NOW! – SAY WHAT YOU THINK IN THE STUDENT VOICE!

Unit 2

Translate the following text for your school magazine.

Your Own United Nations

Everybody knows about the United Nations and what it does to bring about world peace. But do you know about the Model UN?
In 1968, Paul Sand, a teacher at the American High School in The Hague, organized a Model UN for students. It is now the place where the International Model UN meets and attracts more than 2000 students and teachers. Participants come from more than sixty countries. THIMUN, as The Hague International Model UN is called, is held annually in January and lasts five days. Students become 'UN delegates' and debate everything: human rights, the protection of the environment, conflicts between nations and terrorism.

For more information write to:
The Board of Directors, THIMUN Postbus 84193, 2508 AD, The Hague The Netherlands

(adapted excerpt from: *Current*, May/June 1990)

[1]interpret [ɪn'tɜːprɪt] *dolmetschen* [2]carpool *eine Fahrgemeinschaft bilden*

Unit 3

The following article deals with another large ethnic group in the USA, the Mexican-Americans. *First, interpret it for a friend who can't read English. Then translate it for a German newspaper.*

Will they ever consider themselves American?

Mexican-Americans have strong ties[1] with the culture of the old country.

With a left hook in the final round, Oscar de la Hoya, a 132-pound boxer from Los Angeles, knocked down German world light-weight champion Marco Rudolph, winning the U.S. its only gold medal in boxing at the Barcelona Olympics. De la Hoya ran to his corner to greet his father and told a crowd of well-wishers that the medal was a present for his Mexican mother. He then ran to the center of the ring and began waving two flags – the Stars and Stripes and the green, white and red Mexican flag. "I am an American first," he said, "but Mexican blood runs in my veins."

Mexican-Americans make up just under 40 % of the Los Angeles population and two-thirds of the national Latino population, and many shared de la Hoya's joy. But to some people the celebration was a disturbing sight. What, they asked, did that Mexican flag mean? Are Mexican-Americans not loyal to their country? Are they unwilling to let go of their cultural past? Will they ever consider themselves American? The horrors some predict for an ethnically balkanized L. A. don't worry Al Juarez, a teacher working for the city administration. He believes the Mexican live-and-let-live culture has always had a positive effect on L.A. life.

If Juarez is right, Mexican culture and American citizenship, which made de la Hoya wave two flags in Barcelona, will not divide America, but help bring it together.

(adapted from *Insight*, Sept.28,1992)

Unit 4

Read this text to find out what the I·WÁ·SIL YOUTH PROGRAM is. Then interpret it for someone whose English is not so good.

United Indians of all Tribes Foundation

I · WÁ · SIL YOUTH PROGRAM

Our Philosophy: POSITIVE CHANGE

Through the I·WÁ·SIL YOUTH PROGRAM, Indian and other minority youth can receive a basic education, career-planning assistance, and group and individual counseling. Reintegration into the the public school system will be encouraged. Different kinds of activities at our 'Drop-In Center' are intended to bring down the very high dropout rates between 9th and 12th grade in our high schools.

Our GOALS are: 1 To help Indian and other minority youth, ages 12-18, who no longer regularly attend Seattle public schools, by giving them an education that suits their personality; and 2 to give help to Indian students, grades 6-12, attending a Seattle public school, and who are at risk of strong disciplinary action, so that they can learn to accept the academic and behavioral guidelines of their schools. 3 To reduce the number of minority youth living on the streets of downtown Seattle by guiding them into educational programs and jobs. Education and employment are seen as the keys to independence by many of these young people. 4 To provide medical help on 3 days a week for our youth clients. 5 To provide assistance in case of alcohol and drug addiction. 6 To provide legal system information to youth & parents.

Classroom Hours:	9:00 a.m. to 3:00 p.m. Monday thru Friday
Drop-in Center Hours:	3:00 p.m. to 5:00 p.m. Monday thru Friday
Our address:	102 Prefontaine Place South Seattle, WA 98104 Tel.: (206) 343-3111

* *I·WÁ·SIL means "to change" in an American Indian language.*

[1]tie *Bindung*

Writing practice: formal letters

Read the letter on the right and then find out from the text that follows it what the six parts of a standard formal or business letter are called and how American and British styles are different.

1 Dunlap High School
Students Against Driving Drunk (SADD)
1 High School Drive
Dunlap, IL 63144
October 24, 1994

2 Mr. Ronald Lindsey
Chief[1] of Police
2734 Olive Avenue
Dunlap, IL 63144

3 Dear Mr. Lindsey:

4 The Students Against Driving Drunk (SADD) are organizing a discussion about alcohol abuse[2] on December 2 at 2 p.m. We would like to invite you to join a group of experts to talk about the pain and suffering caused by drunk drivers.

Please let us know as soon as possible if you will be able to come. Thank you.

5 Sincerely yours,

6 *David Wu*

David Wu

1 When you write a formal letter you must give a heading[3]: your address and the date, but not your name. American cities have a ZIP code (the American postcode); British cities have a postcode. In Britain one would write *24 October 1994*.

2 The inside address includes the name of the person or firm you are writing to and the address.

3 The salutation[4] comes after the inside address. If you know the name of the person, start with *Dear Miss/Mrs./Ms./Mr. ...:*. In British English there is no full stop after *Mrs/Ms/Mr*. If you are writing to a firm or group and not to a particular individual, begin with *Dear Sir or Madam:*. British business letters have a comma after the salutation.

4 Begin the body of the letter with a capital letter. In a block style letter, such as the one above, all parts begin at the left margin[5].
Business letters should be short, direct and polite. They should be written in a formal style, so you should not use short forms – write *I am* and *do not*, not *I'm* and *don't*.

5 The standard closing[6] in American business letters is *Sincerely (yours),*. The British use *Yours faithfully,* – if they don't know the person they are writing to – and *Yours sincerely,* – if they know the person.

6 Write your name under the closing. Type[7] your name below your signature[8].

Project The national headquarters[9] of Students Against Driving Drunk (SADD) are in Massachusetts. Write to this organization (P.O. Box 800; Marlboro, MA 01752; USA) and ask for information about its activities.

[1]chief [tʃi:f] *Leiter/in* [2]abuse [ə'bju:s] *Mißbrauch* [3]heading ['hedɪŋ] *Kopf (im Brief)* [4]salutation [ˌsælju:'teɪʃn] *Anrede (im Brief)* [5]margin ['mɑ:dʒɪn] *Rand (einer Seite)* [6]closing *Grußformel (am Briefende)* [7]type *tippen* [8]signature ['sɪgnətʃə] *Unterschrift* [9]headquarters *(pl.)* [ˌhed'kwɔ:təz] *Hauptgeschäftsstelle, Zentrale*

Making notes – developing a network

This Option is an exercise in making and using notes. Before you start, try to find your own answers to these questions:

- When and why do people make notes in real life?
- What should good notes look like?

Now read through the text below once and try to work out what it is about.

One way to prepare a network is to make a list of key words. Take a piece of paper, read through the text again and write down the key words of the text on the left side of your paper. The list of key words on the opposite page will give you an idea of how to do this.
Finally, try to connect the words in the form of a 'network of ideas' as in the model on the opposite page.

Lincoln – a successful failure[1]

Americans think of Abraham Lincoln as one of their greatest presidents. They remember him as the man who preserved[2] the Union[3] in the Civil War and who freed[4] the slaves.

However, Lincoln's future didn't look hopeful when he was born in 1809 into a poor family in Kentucky. Because his family had some legal problems with the land they owned, the Lincolns moved west to Indiana in 1816. "It was a wild region," said Lincoln later, "with many bears and other animals still in the woods." As a young boy, "Abe" helped to clear[5] the family's new land for farming. When his father did not need him, he hired him out to work for neighbours. Lincoln once said that he spent no more than one year in school.
In 1830 the family moved to Illinois. There he had many different jobs. After a time in the army, he became a postmaster[6] and worked as a surveyor[7]. Twice he opened a store with a partner. Both times the store failed[8] and he had to pay back large amounts of money. In the end, however, there was one career that brought him success; he studied law and slowly became a successful lawyer[9].
So now he was what you could call a self-educated[10] and a self-made man.
His main interest, however, was politics. But nothing came easy to him in his political career either. In 1832, he became a candidate[11] for the Illinois state legislature[12], but he was defeated. Two years later he again became a candidate for the legislature, and this time he won. After eight years in state politics, Lincoln wanted a more important position. He believed that he had earned his party's nomination[13] for Congress. In 1843, and again in 1844, the nomination went to other men. In 1846, Lincoln finally received the nomination for Congress – and he was elected. After two years in Washington he returned to his career as a lawyer.
A few years later Lincoln decided to return to politics and to fight against slavery[14]. In 1858, Lincoln tried to win Stephen Douglas's seat in the Senate and challenged him to a number of debates. Douglas was a well-known defender of slavery. Again, Lincoln lost, but the debates made him very popular. The American people began to listen to the man who spoke with such

[1]failure ['feɪljə] *Versager/in; Scheitern, Versagen* [2]preserve [prɪ'zɜːv] *bewahren, erhalten* [3]the Union ['juːnjən] *die USA* [4]free *befreien* [5]clear *(Land) roden* [6]postmaster ['pəʊstmɑːstə] *Postamtsvorsteher/in* [7]surveyor [sə'veɪə] *Landvermesser/in* [8]fail *scheitern* [9]lawyer ['lɔːjə] *Rechtsanwalt/Rechtsanwältin* [10]be a self-educated person *Autodidakt/in sein* [11]candidate ['kændɪdeɪt] [12]state legislature ['ledʒɪsleɪtʃə] *(US) Landtag* [13]nomination [ˌnɒmɪ'neɪʃn] *Nominierung, Aufstellung (von Kandidaten/ Kandidatinnen)* [14]slavery ['sleɪvərɪ] *Sklaverei*

feeling about keeping the nation together and not allowing slavery in any new states.
In 1860 the Republicans chose Lincoln as their candidate for president – and he won the election. And when 11 southern states broke away from the Union and founded a new nation, he said that no state could legally leave.
The hardships[1] and failures of his earlier years, many people think, helped Lincoln to become the kind of leader the nation needed during the Civil War that started half a year later.

key words

one of the greatest presidents:
– preserved Union in Civil War
– freed slaves

poor family:
– worked on farms
– self-educated

moved to Illinois:
many jobs, e.g. postmaster, surveyor

studied law: successful lawyer

main interest politics:
– candidate for legislature
– nomination for Congress
– …

network of ideas

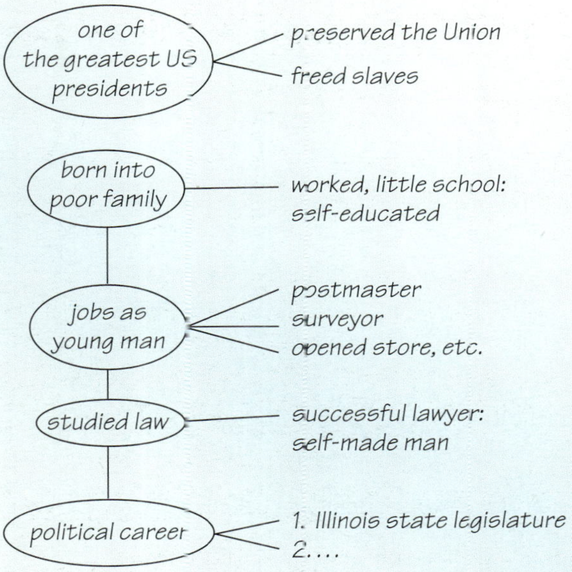

Info box In the tenth class and beyond, you will often be asked to get the information contained in a text down in a short, written form. If you have to make notes and/or develop a network from a written text in a test, then it is especially important that you prepare yourself for what you will have to do:

- Avoid panic by having your writing equipment ready and in order. Don't forget that you will need lots of space for your notes so you will probably need more than one piece of paper.
- Check to see which information you need from the text: Have you been asked for any particular details or aspects of the subject[2]?
- Prepare yourself, before you start reading, by thinking of things you already know about the topic. The title will often help you. Think of what you already know about the subject.

This technique[3] of making notes and developing a network can also be used for listening comprehension. It is best to write down the key words when you are listening to the text a second time and then develop them into a network.

Use your notes and give a short talk on either Lincoln's youth or his political career, contrasting the hardships and failures with his successes.

[1]hardship *Entbehrung* [2]subject *Thema* [3]technique [tek'ni:k] *(Arbeits-)Verfahren, Methode*

Option 16

Using a monolingual[1] dictionary

Do you know what 'chip' means? Well, see if you can understand the word in these sentences:

1. Take the other one – this bowl has got a **chip** in it.
2. Sorry, can I quickly **chip** in? How much is this shirt, please?
3. Some of the Berliners were **chipping** pieces off the Wall and selling them as souvenirs.
4. Fish and **chips** for me, please!
5. Her firm produces **chips** for use in cameras.

Which meanings can you guess from the context or from similar German words? (Careful though: German 'Chips' are not necessarily English 'chips'.) Which words do you have to look up?

- Now use the excerpt from the dictionary and try to find the explanations that fit the 'chips' in the five sentences.
- Have a look at the entries[2] for the two head-words[3] 'chip'. What is the difference? How does the dictionary show this difference?
- What do the numbers (1, 2, 3, …) in each entry tell you?
- Which of the explanations in the dictionary are illustrated? How do you know?
- This dictionary uses **bold**, normal and *italic*[4] print. Say what each type is mainly used for.

What do the Americans call what the British call chips? What do the British call what the Americans call chips? (See the excerpt for help.)

chip¹ /tʃɪp/ *n* **1** thin piece cut or broken off from wood, stone, china, glass, etc: *a chip of wood.* **2** place from which such a piece has been broken: *This mug has a chip in it.* ⇨illus. **3** (*US* **French ˈfry**) (usu *pl*) thin strip of potato fried in deep fat: *a plate of chips* ○ *ˌfish and ˈchips*, ie fish coated in batter, fried and served with chips. ⇨illus at POTATO. **4** (*US*) = CRISP *n.* **5** flat plastic counter²(1) used to represent money, esp in gambling. **6** = MICROCHIP. **7** (also **ˈchip shot**) (esp in golf and football) shot or kick that travels steeply upwards and then lands within a short distance. **8** (idm) **a ˌchip off the old ˈblock** (*infml*) person (esp a man or boy) who is like his father in character. **have a ˈchip on one's shoulder** (*infml*) be bitter, resentful or defiant because one feels that one's past, background, physical appearance, etc, causes other people to be prejudiced against one: *She's got a chip on her shoulder about not having gone to university.* **have had one's ˈchips** (*Brit sl*) be dead, dying or defeated. **when the chips are down** (*infml*) when a crisis point is reached: *When the chips were down he found the courage to carry on.*

□ **ˈchipboard** *n* [U] building material made of compressed wood chips and resin.

CHIPPED CRACKED BROKEN

chip² /tʃɪp/ *v* **(-pp-) 1 (a)** [Tn] break or cut (sth) at the edge or surface: *a badly chipped saucer* ○ *chip a tooth* ○ *He chipped one of my best glasses.* ⇨illus. **(b)** [I] (tend to) break at the edge or surface: *Be careful with these plates — they chip very easily.* ○ *The paint is chipping badly.* **2 (a)** [Tn·pr, Tn·p] ~ **sth from/off sth**; ~ **sth off** break or cut (a small piece) from the edge or surface of sth: *A piece was chipped off the piano when we moved house.* ○ *We chipped the old plaster (away)* (ie removed it in small pieces) *from the wall.* **(b)** [Ipr, Ip] ~ **off (sth)** be broken off in small pieces: *The paint has chipped off where the table touches the wall.* **3** [Tn] shape or carve (sth) by cutting the edge or surface (with an axe, chisel, etc). **4** [Tn esp passive] make (potatoes) into chips (CHIP¹ 3): *chipped potatoes.* **5** [I, Tn] (esp in golf and football, etc) strike or kick (the ball) so that it travels steeply upwards and then lands within a short distance. **6** (phr v) **chip away at sth** continuously break off small pieces from sth: *chipping away at a block of marble with a chisel* ○ (*fig*) *He kept chipping away at the problem until he had solved it.* **chip in (with sth)** (*infml*) **(a)** join in or interrupt a conversation: *She chipped in with some interesting remarks.* **(b)** contribute (money): *If everyone chips ˈin we'll be able to buy her a really nice leaving present.*

▷ **chip·pings** *n* [pl] chips of stone, etc used for making a road surface: *Danger! Loose chippings*, eg as a warning to motorists.

chip·munk /ˈtʃɪpmʌŋk/ *n* small striped squirrel-like N American animal.

From the *Oxford Advanced Learner's Dictionary, 1989*

[1]monolingual [ˌmɒnəˈlɪŋgwəl] *einsprachig* [2]entry [ˈentrɪ] *Eintrag* [3]headword *Stichwort* [4]italic [ɪˈtælɪk] *kursiv*

Dictionary skills

1. As you know, a dictionary uses an alphabetical order. So which word will come after which here?

receiver [rɪ'siːvə] – **reckon** ['rekən] – **rap** [ræp] – **rear** [rɪə] – **receipt** [rɪ'siːt] – **reappear** [ˌriːə'pɪə] – **rearm** [rɪ'ɑːm] – **RAM** [ræm] – **rebellion** [rɪ'beljən] – **recorder** [rɪ'kɔːdə]

Write the words down in their correct order and underline the letter in each word which determines[1] where it belongs.

2. – Why does **chipmunk** come *after* **chippings** in the dictionary excerpt?
– Copy out from the excerpt
a) new words formed on the basis of **chip**
b) phrases and expressions with **chip**.
(The symbol ~, known as a 'tilde'[2], stands for the headword.)

3. You learned above that not every word is listed as a separate headword. Where would you look up the following expressions?

to rain cats and dogs **wavy** **monkey business** **to mess up** **pigheaded** **greenhouse** **chicken-pox**

When you have found out their meaning, you might like to write a story using all seven expressions in any order you like.

4. Combinations of words which regularly go together are called 'collocations'. See if you can find the correct collocation in the sentences on the right. But check in a dictionary, because often the collocations in English are quite different from the ones in German.

a) Since her accident she suffers (at/from/under) bad headaches.
b) Give me the money by Wednesday, please. I'll be away (into/during/in/on) holiday after then.
c) Excuse me, could you please (shoot/make/take/do) a photo of me and my friend in front of the palace?
d) The children didn't know it, but they were in (big/great/huge/large) danger.

Your monolingual dictionary allows you to check spelling, and it explains meanings. But it can help you with much more than that, so it is worth finding out where and how your own dictionary can give you information on
- pronunciation,
- grammar, including irregular forms,
- what preposition a word takes,
- the context you can use a word in,
- alternatives to a word.

Here is a dictionary game you can play. Working in pairs, you look for an interesting-looking word in the dictionary and copy out its meaning (or one of its meanings). Then you make up two false (but likely) definitions of the same word. Finally, everybody writes their word on the board and reads all three definitions. The others must guess the real meaning.

[1]determine [dɪ'tɜːmɪn] *bestimmen* [2]tilde ['tɪldə] *Tilde*

A question of style

- Look at how the three sentences on the right are presented. Then read them and decide which sentence is formal in style, which one is informal and which is neutral[1]. – Explain how you came to your decision.
- Turn to the letter below and the excerpt from a speech at the top of the next page. It is quite clear that both authors intend to convince the reader (or listener) of their point of view: In one text this is done in an extremely formal way, in the other it is done in an informal way. (For both texts you will need a dictionary to look up a number of words.)
  Read the Info box on the next page and then explain, for each text, why the author might have chosen his or her particular style. Try to identify features[2] of each level of style in the two texts.
- Finally, change the text by Clyde Warrior into a more neutral style.

At the beginning the Indians and the white settlers lived together in peace.

Initially[3], neither the Indians nor the white settlers displayed[4] any hostility[5] towards each other.

Hopi Indian Empire
Oraibi, Arizona
March 28, 1949

The President
The White House
Washington, D.C.

To the President:

We, the Hopi Chieftains of the Hopi Pueblos, politely request a word with you.

Acquainted with our traditional form of government and our religious principles; authorized to speak, to act, and to execute our duties for all the common people throughout the land of this Hopi Empire, in accordance with the fundamental principles of life, which were laid down for us by our Great Spirit and by our forefathers, we hereby make known to the government of the United States that the Hopi Empire is still in existence, its traditional path unbroken and its religious order intact and practised, and the Stone Tablets, upon which are written the boundaries of the Hopi Empire, are still in the hands of the Chiefs of Oraibi and Hotevila Pueblos.

What we say is from our hearts. We speak truths that are based upon our tradition and religion. We speak as the first people in this land you call America. And we speak to you, the last people who came here, seeking freedom. And we are speaking to all the American Indian people.

Today, we, the Hopi and the white man, come face to face at the crossroads of our respective lives. At last our paths have crossed, and it was foretold it would be at the most critical time in the history of mankind.

(adapted from: *The Way*)

[1]neutral ['nju:trəl] [2]feature ['fi:tʃə] *Merkmal, Eigenschaft* [3]initially [ɪ'nɪʃlɪ] *anfangs* [4]display [dɪ'spleɪ] *zeigen* [5]hostility [hɒ'stɪlətɪ] *Feindseligkeit*

The following text is from a speech by Clyde Warrior (†1969), one of the most famous Indian leaders:

... I'm fed up with bureaucrats who try to make rules and regulations for programs that are meant to bring progress.
I'm sick and tired of seeing the older generation low rated in the eyes of young people. I could scream when I see young American Indians who accept the horror of American conformity as the only way for Indian progress.
The National Indian Youth Council must introduce some fresh air of new Indianness to this sickroom of stench and conformity. A fresh air of new honesty, a fresh air of new Indian realism, a fresh air of a new Greater Indian America. How about it? Let's raise some hell!

(adapted from: *The Way*)

Info box Luckily for learners, most of English vocabulary and grammar is suitable for nearly all situations. These words and this grammar make up[1] what can be called a **neutral style**. For the learner it is safest to use this style. An **informal style** used in the wrong situation may sound very impolite. A **formal style** in the wrong situation will sound strange, too. It may even make you appear laughable[2]. However, a knowledge of some features of a formal and an informal style will help you to understand people better. It is particularly important for understanding authentic texts you have to deal with in class.
Here are some features of each style:

Formal: words of Greek and Latin origin, abstract[3] nouns; long, complex sentences; passive constructions; author detached[4] from reader; unemotional; written texts (e.g. official reports, business letters)

Informal: use of simple words and expressions whenever possible; short forms (e.g. *don't*); shorter sentences connected by coordinating[5] conjunctions (e.g. *and, but, or*); spoken texts or written texts addressed to people one knows well (e.g. private conversations, personal letters)

Just for fun
Just for fun

On the left you will find a short outline of five different social situations. On the right there is a list of possible words for – well, er, you know. The idea is to choose one or more of the words that would fit the situation. – You will need a monolingual[6] dictionary to do this exercise.

	Would say	Might say	Would not say	
1. At a dance in the best hotel in town: You want to ask one of the waiters. (USA/Britain)	?	?	?	a) toilet b) WC c) bathroom
2. In a pub in Britain: After some drinks you want to ask the lady behind the bar.	?	?	?	d) Gents/Ladies e) loo f) public conveniences
3. In the street in Britain: You want to ask a policeman.	?	?	?	g) restroom
4. At the house of some American friends.	?	?	?	h) john i) bog
5. At the house of a British friend.	?	?	?	h) the ladies'/ men's room

[1]make up *bilden* [2]laughable *lächerlich* [3]abstract ['æbstrækt] [4]detached (from) [dɪ'tætʃt] *distanziert (von)*
[5]coordinating [kəʊ'ɔːdɪneɪtɪŋ] *koordinierend* [6]monolingual [ˌmɒnəʊ'lɪŋgwəl] *einsprachig*

Literary terms and their collocations

action *Handlung*
The ~ takes place in a small town / in 1989.
There is a lot of / hardly any / little ~ in … .
In the course of the story the ~ develops dramatically[1] / … .
The ~ covers the period of a day / two years / … .

author *Autor/in*
The ~ is concerned with[2] … / creates an atmosphere of sadness / … by using … .
The ~*'s* intention is to show us what freedom might mean … .
The ~ wants to make us aware of / make us think about social problems / … .
He/She criticizes / blames / encourages … .
The ~ wants us to change / wants to make us change our attitude towards nature / the weak / … .

character *Person, Figur; Charakter*
A is the main / an important / a minor[3] ~.
B is presented as a friendly / … ~.
The motive for C's behaviour / actions lies in his/her ~.
trait of character *Charakterzug*
Kindness / … is his/her dominant[4] / … ~ ~ ~.
The basic ~*s of* A's ~ are … .

characterize *beschreiben, charakterisieren*
The author ~*s* A implicitly[5] / explicitly.
B *is ~d* as a lazy / an honest / … person.
C *is ~d* by his/her behaviour / by what he/she says / by the narrator's or another character's comments / … .

connotations *Nebenbedeutung(en), Beiklang*
This word / phrase has certain ~ for the reader.
It has ~ of love / warmth / closeness / … .

fable *Fabel*
The animals in the ~ behave as if they were human beings.
In his/her ~, the author criticizes / makes fun of / wants to make us think about … .
The moral of this ~ can be interpreted in different ways.

image *sprachliches Bild*
A guitar / rose / … is the central / dominant / … ~ in the poem / story / … .
The ~ is well-chosen / impressive[6] / powerful / highly suitable / hard to understand / … .
The ~ expresses / reveals[7] / conveys the idea / feeling / meaning / … very well / convincingly / … .
The poet uses the ~ to express / … .
The function of the ~ is to make the reader aware / realize / see … that … .

line *Zeile*
The first / last ~ / *Line* 3 makes it clear / shows that … .
Line 5 focuses on[8] … / attracts the reader's attention / emphasizes[9] / underlines / … .
In the first ~ the author / poet presents the main topic / … .
The central / main theme is introduced / best expressed / hidden / … in ~*s* 15 and 16.
At first glance[10] ~ 2 was unclear / didn't seem to make sense / puzzled me / … .

narrator *Erzähler/in eines narrativen Textes / Prosatextes*
The ~ addresses the reader directly … .
The ~ emphasizes / points out / makes us see … .

novel *Roman* (→ **text, poem, short story**)

play *(Theater-)Stück* (→ **text, poem, short story**)

poem *Gedicht*
The ~ is about / deals with / is concerned with … .
The ~ is easy / hard to understand.
It consists of six lines / stanzas / verses.
It appeals to young people / … .
It arouses[11] people's emotions / pleasant feelings / pity … .
The words "…" in the ~ are related to / associated with winter / … .
Through the ~ the poet makes us aware that … .

poet *Dichter/in* (→ **author**)

poetic[12] *dichterisch, poetisch*
The poet uses end rhyme / special stress patterns[13] / repetition / a certain kind of rhythm[14] / … as a ~ device[15].
The most obvious ~ device in this poem is the use of images / comparisons / … .

[1]dramatic [drə'mætɪk] *dramatisch* [2]be concerned with *sich befassen mit; handeln von* [3]minor ['maɪnə] *Neben(figur, -rolle)* [4]dominant ['---] *dominierend* [5]implicit [-'--] *indirekt* [6]impressive [-'--] *eindrucksvoll, wirkungsvoll* [7]reveal [rɪ'vi:l] *zeigen* [8]focus on *besonders hervorheben,* [9]emphasize ['emfəsaɪz] *betonen* [10]at first glance [glɑ:ns] *auf den ersten Blick* [11]arouse [ə'raʊz] *wecken, erregen* [12]poetic [pəʊ'etɪk] [13]stress pattern *Betonungsschema* [14]rhythm ['rɪðəm] *Rhythmus* [15](poetic) device [dɪ'vaɪs] *(dichterisches) Stilmittel*

point of view *(Erzähl-)Standpunkt, (Erzähl-) Perspektive*
The story is told from the ~ ~ ~ of the narrator / the main character / a third person.
The author presents the events from the main character's / an observer's ~ ~ ~.

reader *Leser/in*
Most ~*s* might like / enjoy the story / poem / play / … because … .
The ~ is puzzled / confused / impressed by the title / ending / unfamiliar images / … .
The ~ must analyse / is forced to read the first line / last stanza / … very closely / several times / … .
The ~ sees things from a different point of view / can identify with the main character / can understand why … .
The ~ is influenced / is expected to get involved / to take sides / … .
The ~ is worried / surprised / deeply moved / misled / … .

repetition *Wiederholung*
The passage / poem / … contains several ~*s*.
The ~ of the word "…" stresses / makes us see … .
The author uses ~ to draw the reader's attention to … .

rhyme *Reim; (sich) reimen*
The ~ scheme[1] of the poem is a-b-a-b / … / (ir)regular.
The ~ scheme contributes / adds to the atmosphere / tone of the poem.
The author makes use of the ~ to emphasize / underline / … that … .
"Move" and "love" *don't* ~.
"Cough" ~*s* with "off".

set: be set in *spielen in, der Schauplatz … ist*
The story *is* ~ *in* a prison camp.
The novel *is* ~ *in* 19th century London.

setting *Schauplatz*
The ~ of this story is (in) a village / … .
The ~ has a symbolic meaning.
The ~ reflects the main character's mood.

short story *Kurzgeschichte*
"…" is typical of / contains the typical elements / shows the typical structure of a ~ ~.
The beginning / exposition[2] of this ~ ~ ends in line X, the actual conflict / the climax is reached in line Y.
The ~ ~ has a surprise / happy / convincing / … ending / is open-ended[3].
In the first paragraph of the ~ ~ the main character / … is introduced / … .
The ~ ~ is set in a prison / … .

speaker (in a poem) *das "Ich" in einem Gedicht* **(→ narrator)**

stanza *Strophe*
The first ~ opens / begins / … with a description[4] of … .
In the second ~ the poet introduces / describes / … .
The first and the last ~*s* are quite simple / similar / totally different / different in structure / tone / … .
The last ~ contains / conveys the message of the poem.

symbol *Symbol*
The bird / … is used as a ~ of freedom / … .
The word "…" is used as a ~ of … .
This ~ stands for … / suggests the idea that … .

symbolic[5] *symbolisch*
The word "…" has ~ qualities / a ~ meaning.
… is ~ of … .

text *Text*
The ~ is an excerpt from / part of / a scene from … / is based on … .
The ~ deals with / is concerned with … .
The ~ is / can be divided into four parts / passages / … .

theme *Thema*
The author treats his/her ~ with humour.
The problem of … is the dominant ~ of the text.

tone *Ton; Stimmung*
The passage has a light / playful / humorous / sad / … ~.
The poet sets/creates a serious / … ~ by using / choosing … .

verse *Strophe* **(→ stanza)**

[1]rhyme scheme [skiːm] *Reimschema* [2]exposition [ˌekspəˈzɪʃn] *Exposition (einführender Teil)*
[3]be open-ended *einen offenen Schluß haben* [4]description [dɪˈskrɪpʃn] *Beschreibung* [5]symbolic [sɪmˈbɒlɪk]

A mixed bag of grammar

Unit 1

Inversion nach *hardly, rarely, never, not only, ...* (Inversion[1] after *hardly, rarely, never, not only, ...*)

Green Pensioner[2] Causes a Stink[3] – 72-year-old pensioner Harry Tucker is so 'green' that his neighbours can't stand it any longer. ***Not only* does he collect** rubbish from his neighbours' dustbins[4], but he also empties[5] it out in his own front garden and divides it up into four piles[6] – glass, tins, paper and vegetable matter[7].

***No sooner* has one pile of rubbish gone** than another begins.

***Not only* does it look** terrible, his neighbours say, but it also smells terrible – ***hardly ever* can they open** their windows.

Im Englischen können folgende Adverbien manchmal am Satzanfang stehen:

hardly (ever) • ***little*** (kaum) • ***rarely*** • ***seldom***[8] (selten) • ***not often*** • ***never (before)*** • ***at no time*** (zu keiner Zeit) • ***only** then/later/...* • ***no sooner ... than*** (kaum ..., da/als ...) • ***nowhere (else)*** • ***in no way*** (auf keinen Fall) • ***not only ..., but also***

In solchen Fällen ändert sich die Wortstellung.

Adverb(iale Bestimmung)	Hilfsverb	Subjekt	(Hilfsverb)	Vollverb	
No sooner	**has**	**one pile**		**gone**	*than* another begins. *(Kaum ..., da beginnt ...)*
Not only	**does**	**it**		**look**	terrible, *but* it *also* smells terrible.
Never	**would**	**I**	**have**	**expected**	someone to have such a strange hobby.

Ex *Here are some of the things the judge said when Harry Tucker appeared in court.*

1. not often – I deal – with a man of your age in this court → *Not often do I deal with a man ... .* 2. never before – I have heard – of a front garden being used as a recycling centre 3. little – you realize – what a nuisance you have been 4. at no time – you talked – to your neighbours 5. rarely – I have known – such interest in the environment 6. in no way – I can excuse – this behaviour

Unit 2

Das deutsche *man* und seine englischen Entsprechungen (German *man* and its English equivalents[9])

Taxi driver: Sorry about the hold-up[10]. People blame us because their journey takes so long. But we do our best. You know what they say: the impossible takes time, miracles[11] take longer.

Passenger: Yes, they'll have to do something about it, the traffic I mean. Thirty years ago, I remember, you could drive straight into London and park your car anywhere. ...

Im Englischen gibt es mehrere Möglichkeiten, das deutsche unpersönliche *man* wiederzugeben. Sieh dir den Dialog noch einmal an: An welchen vier Stellen könnte im Deutschen *man* vorkommen?

Hier sind weitere Beispiele:

If **you**'re in a hurry[12] **you** should take a taxi.	*Wenn man in Eile ist, sollte man ...*
One should not forget to tip the taxi driver.	*Man sollte nicht vergessen, ...*
They're not doing enough to solve London's traffic problems.	*Man tut nicht genug, ...*
Smoking is not allowed in this taxi.	*Man darf in diesem Taxi nicht rauchen.*

[1]inversion [ɪn'vɜːʃn] *Inversion (Wortstellung Hilfsverb – Subjekt)* [2]pensioner ['penʃnə] *Rentner/in* [3]cause a stink *Stunk, Ärger machen* [4]dustbin ['dʌstbɪn] *Mülltonne* [5]empty ['emptɪ] *leeren* [6]pile [paɪl] *Haufen* [7]vegetable matter *pflanzliche Stoffe* [8]seldom ['seldəm] [9]equivalent [ɪ'kwɪvələnt] *Äquivalent, Entsprechung* [10]hold-up *Verzögerung* [11]miracle ['mɪrəkl] *Wunder* [12]in a hurry ['hʌrɪ] *in Eile*

Unit 3

R *used to/would* + Infinitiv (*used to/would* + infinitive)

76-year-old Fred Willis of Castle Combe ***used to*** *have a hobby. But not any longer…*
"**I used to** take my dog Baldrick for a walk every day, on the local golf course. He was very good at finding lost golf balls. So I **used to** bring them home with me and put them in suitcases. When all the suitcases were full, I started putting them in the bath. Now even that's full. So they've all got to go – all 15,692 of them!
"What did I do with them? Nothing. I **used to** be a good golfer when I was younger, but I haven't played for over 20 years."

used to **+ Infinitiv** beschreibt …
- frühere Gewohnheiten → I **used to** take my dog for a walk every day.
- frühere Zustände → I **used to** be a good golfer when I was younger.

Verneinung: ***didn't use to***	– He **didn't use to** play golf when I first met him.	*Er hat (früher) nicht Golf gespielt, …*
Frage: ***Did … use to …?***	– **Did** you **use to** play golf a lot when you were younger?	*Hast du oft Golf gespielt, …?*
Aussprache: ['juːstə]	I **used to** walk to school. / I didn't **use to** walk … / Did you **use to** walk …?	

In Äußerungen über früher regelmäßig wiederholte Handlungen kann auch ***would*** **+ Infinitiv** verwendet werden (oft mit Zeit- und Häufigkeitsangaben wie *always, every day, often, from time to time*):
When I was younger I **would** take my dog for a walk every day.

Ex *Write a few sentences about things that you used to like or do (hobbies, sports, games, food, pop/rock groups, …). – Example:*
I used to like a group called … but now I can't stand them any more.
Alternatively, think of some unpleasant habits that people you know used to have. – Example:
When he was younger, my brother never used to wash his feet – and they smelled!

Unit 4

Die besondere Hervorhebung von Wörtern/Satzteilen (Emphasizing[1] words/parts of the sentence)

Thumbs Down – Police yesterday arrested a hitch-hiker[2] who was standing by the side of the motorway near Bridgwater. The hitch-hiker was wearing high heels[3] and a miniskirt. 'She' turned out to be[4] a 95-kilo male student, John Hobson. He was fined[5] £10 for hitch-hiking on a motorway. Hobson later commented, "**It was my girlfriend who** gave me the idea. She also lent[6] me her miniskirt and high heels. **It was my hairy legs that** made police suspicious[7]. **What surprised me was** their decision to arrest me. I didn't commit a crime[8], did I? Even the police agreed you **do** have a much better chance of getting a lift[9] if you're a girl."

Der Text zeigt dir mehrere Möglichkeiten, einzelne Wörter oder Satzteile besonders hervorzuheben:
- ***It is/was*** **+ (Pro-)Nomen + Relativsatz**
- ***What … is/was …***
- **betontes *do/does/did* + Infinitiv**

Ex *Rewrite the following sentences. Emphasize the underlined words using 'It is/was … + relative clause', 'What … is/was …' or a form of emphatic[10] 'do'.*

1. Well, John <u>looked very attractive</u>. (do) → *Well, John did look very attractive.* 2. Drivers <u>stop to pick up girls</u>. (do) 3. <u>John's attitude</u> made the police angry. (What made …) 4. <u>John's miniskirt</u> didn't make the police suspicious. (It wasn't …) 5. John's girlfriend <u>gets lifts easily</u>. (do) 6. "I mean, <u>there's nothing wrong with pretending that you're a girl</u>." (What I …) 7. The police arrested John <u>on Saturday morning</u>. (It …) 8. <u>The Bridgwater Express</u> reported the story on Sunday. (It …)

[1]emphasize ['emfəsaɪz] *hervorheben* [2]hitch-hiker ['hɪtʃhaɪkə] *Tramper/in* [3]heels *Absätze* [4]she turned out to be … *es stellte sich heraus, daß sie … war* [5]be fined *(ein) Bußgeld bezahlen müssen* [6]lend – lent – lent *(ver)leihen* [7]suspicious [sə'spɪʃəs] *mißtrauisch* [8]commit a crime [kə'mɪt] *ein Verbrechen begehen* [9]get a lift *(von jm.) mitgenommen werden* [10]emphatic [ɪm'fætɪk] *betonend*

Option 20

Linking ideas, linking sentences

Sieh dir die beiden Texte an. Worin unterscheiden sie sich?

1. Mr Brownlow tried to reverse[1] out of the car park. He made an unfortunate mistake. He mixed up first gear[2] with reverse. The car shot forward straight into the wall of the driving test centre. The wall collapsed[3].

2. While trying to reverse out of the car park, Mr Brownlow made an unfortunate mistake. As a result of mixing up first gear with reverse, he caused the car to shoot forward straight into the wall of the driving test centre so that it collapsed.

Um Textzusammenhänge deutlich herauszuarbeiten und stilistisch „geschliffenere" Texte zu produzieren, benutzen wir verschiedene Mittel, um einzelne Sätze – und damit einzelne Gedanken – zu verbinden. Welche Mittel wir wählen, hängt im Englischen wie im Deutschen von einer Reihe von Faktoren ab, z.B.: Sprechen oder schreiben wir? Mit wem kommunizieren wir? Handelt es sich um einen persönlichen Text (etwa um einen privaten Brief oder ein Telefonat) oder um etwas Förmlich-Offizielles (etwa um einen Geschäftsbrief oder einen Zeitungsartikel)?

Die zweite Version des Textes oben stammt aus einem Zeitungsartikel.
Hier sind weitere Auszüge aus diesem Artikel:

FAST FORWARD – Taking a driving test can be a frightening experience. Mr Michael Brownlow (56) of Dunmow in Essex had had 19 driving lessons, **but** he was still understandably nervous **when** he came to take his driving test for the first time.

Having got into the car, Mr Brownlow put on his seatbelt[4] **and** started the engine. **To make him feel less nervous**, the examiner offered Mr Brownlow a sweet.

While attempting to reverse out of the car park, Mr Brownlow made an unfortunate mistake. **As a result of confusing first gear with reverse**, he caused the car to shoot forward straight into the wall of the driving test centre **so that** it collapsed.

Neither Mr Brownlow **nor** the examiner was hurt **but** the car as well as the driving centre were badly damaged.

Examiners take into account[5] the natural nervousness of candidates **whenever possible. Given the circumstances[6] though**, the examiner simply had to fail[7] Mr Brownlow.

In spite of the examiner's decision, Mr Brownlow was optimistic **when** he got out of the car. "I'm determined[8] to get a driving licence," he said. "I won't give up trying just **because of one little setback[9]**."

Versuche einmal, die unterstrichenen Stellen in „normale" Nebensätze *(after he …; while he …; because he …)* umzuwandeln.

Nun sieh dir die fettgedruckten Stellen noch einmal an und versuche, ihnen jeweils eins der folgenden sechs „Etiketten" zuzuordnen.

1. **koordinierende Konjunktionen** verbinden zwei Hauptsätze
2. **subordinierende Konjunktionen** verbinden Haupt- und Nebensatz
3. **Infinitivsätze** „um zu"
4. **Nebensätze ohne Verb** Konjunktion + Adjektiv
5. **Partizipialsätze** (Konjunktion +) Partizip + …
6. **Präpositionalphrasen** Präposition + Nomen/Gerundium

Partizipialsätze anstelle von adverbialen Nebensätzen und Präpositionalphrasen mit einem Gerundium *(as a result of confusing …)* werden vor allem in geschriebenem Englisch verwendet.

[1]reverse [rɪ'vɜːs] *(v.; n.) rückwärts fahren; Rückwärtsgang* [2]gear [gɪə] *Gang* [3]collapse [kə'læps] *einstürzen* [4]put on one's seatbelt ['siːtbelt] *sich anschnallen* [5]take into account [ə'kaʊnt] *berücksichtigen* [6]given the circumstances ['sɜːkəmstənsɪz] *in Anbetracht der Umstände* [7]fail sb. [feɪl] *durchfallen lassen* [8]determined [dɪ'tɜːmɪnd] *fest entschlossen* [9]setback ['setbæk] *Mißerfolg*

Ex 1 Combination competition

a *Look at the following pairs of sentences and try to combine each pair into one sentence. How many different "solutions" can you find for each pair?*

Example: He was an inexperienced driver. He failed the driving test.

→ *As (Since/Because) he was an inexperienced driver,*
→ *As a result of being an inexperienced driver,*
→ *Being an inexperienced driver,*
→ *He was an inexperienced driver, so*
he failed the driving test.

1. He arrived at the test centre. He went inside. *After he had arrived … . / After his arrival … . / …*
2. He wanted to increase his chances of passing. He smiled at the examiner.
3. The examiner noticed that he was nervous. She offered him a sweet.
4. Some drivers are very bad. It is a dangerous job for the examiners.
5. He tried to drive out of the car park. He crashed[1] into the wall.
6. He looked at the examiner's face. He knew he had failed.
7. He had had a lot of lessons. He failed the test.
8. He is an optimist[2]. He will take the test again.

b *Make up three pairs of sentences. Exchange your sentence pairs with a partner. Then combine each pair into one sentence. Try to find as many combinations as possible. – Who found more correct combinations, you or your partner?*

Ex 2 Failed before she started

Read the sentences to find out what happened to Jennifer Lock. Then work with a partner and write a newspaper article, or write down the 'story' as Jennifer might tell it to a friend. Try out different ways of combining sentences in your text. Don't forget that the text should not only be grammatically correct, it should also sound good.
Finally, compare some of the newspaper articles and 'stories'. What are the differences between these two types of text?

Jennifer Lock of Southmead in Bristol was 18 years old.
She was old enough to drive.
She was sure she was a good driver.
She wanted to take her driving test.
She had had three lessons from a driving school.
Her teacher told her she needed a few more.
He said she was not yet ready to take the test.
Ms Lock did not agree.
She thought that three lessons were enough.
She applied[3] to take her test the following week.
She arrived at the test centre.
She was very confident.
She parked the driving school car outside the test centre.
She went inside.
She told the examiner, Brian Skinner, that she was ready.
Mr Skinner told her to wait a moment.
She was five minutes early.
He wanted to finish his coffee.
Ms Lock went outside.
She got into the car.
She waited.
She became impatient.
She wanted the examiner to hurry[4].
She sounded the horn.
The examiner heard the horn.
He came out.
He told Ms Lock that she had failed the test.
It is illegal to sound your horn[5] while parked.
He went back inside.
He finished his coffee.

[1]crash into [kræʃ] *krachen gegen* [2]optimist ['ɒptɪmɪst] [3]apply to take one's test [ə'plaɪ] *einen Fahrprüfungstermin beantragen* [4]hurry ['hʌrɪ] *sich beeilen* [5]sound one's horn [hɔːn] *hupen*

Option **21**

Ways of expressing the future

Im Deutschen verwenden wir meist das Präsens, um über Zukünftiges zu sprechen. Im Englischen gibt es verschiedene Möglichkeiten, beispielsweise das *will-future* oder das *going to-future*. Manchmal ist auch das *present progressive* möglich. In besonderen Fällen kann das *simple present* verwendet werden. Es ist nicht immer einfach, in einer bestimmten Situation die richtige der vier Formen zu wählen. Du wirst allerdings immer verstanden, wenn du das *will-future* oder das *going to-future* benutzt.

R 1

will-future

Next July **I'll be** 18.
I'm sure Tim **will get** the job.
Perhaps Jane **will come** later.
There isn't any milk left. – OK, **I'll get** some.

- um zukünftige Ereignisse vorherzusagen
- um Vermutungen, Hoffnungen, Erwartungen zu äußern; oft mit Ausdrücken wie *I'm sure, I think, I believe, I expect, I hope, I suppose* oder Adverbien wie *perhaps, possibly, probably, surely*
- um spontan auf etwas zu reagieren

going to-future

Sue **is going to study** medicine.
Look at those black clouds. I think **it's going to rain**.

- um auszudrücken, daß jemand vorhat/geplant hat, etwas zu tun
- um auszudrücken, daß etwas mit großer Sicherheit geschehen wird, weil es bereits Anzeichen dafür gibt

Beachte:
In Nebensätzen mit *when, while, before, until, as soon as, as long as* oder *if/unless* steht, auch wenn über Zukünftiges gesprochen wird, weder das *will-future* noch das *going to-future*, sondern das *simple present*:
I'm going to be a doctor when I **grow** up. – I **won't leave** until you **get** here. –
If you **come** later, I **won't see** you.

R 2

present progressive

We**'re flying** to Spain next week.
Another drink? – No thanks, **I'm driving**.

- für etwas, das verabredet oder fest geplant ist; durch eine Zeitangabe oder aus dem Kontext muß deutlich sein, daß es um Zukünftiges geht

⚠ Da häufig zwischen einem Vorhaben und einer festen Verabredung kaum ein Unterschied besteht, kann statt des *present progressive* oft auch das *going to-future* stehen.

simple present

The next tour of the castle **starts** at 2 pm.
The next train **leaves** at 10.

- für etwas, das durch Programme, Fahrpläne u.ä. festgelegt ist *("timetable future")*

Ex 1

Predictions: Horoscopes[1]

Look at the zodiac signs[2]. Choose two of the signs and write next week's horoscope for each of them. Then read the horoscopes you have written to the class and compare them with those written by your classmates. – Look at the two examples for help.

Pisces (20 February - 20 March)
There'll be a lot of extra work for you. But you'll make some extra money.

Aquarius (21 January - 19 February)
You won't be able to keep your promises. A good friend will let you down[3].

[1]horoscope ['hɒrəskəʊp]: Aquarius [ə'kweərɪəs] • Pisces ['paɪsi:z] • Aries ['eəri:z] • Taurus ['tɔ:rəs] • Gemini ['dʒemɪnaɪ]
[2]zodiac sign ['zəʊdɪæk] *Sternzeichen* [3]let sb. down *jn. im Stich lassen, enttäuschen*

Ex 2 **In English, please** *For some of the sentences there isn't just one possible solution.*

1. Bleibt ihr dieses Jahr in den Sommerferien zu Hause? – Nein, wir fahren für vierzehn Tage nach Spanien. 2. Susan hat eine Stelle in einer großen Firma in Liverpool angeboten bekommen. Ich bin sicher, sie wird das Angebot annehmen, obwohl es bedeutet, daß sie von Oxford wegziehen muß. Aber sie wird wahrscheinlich bald neue Freunde in Liverpool finden. 3. Der nächste Zug nach Exeter fährt erst um 14 Uhr. Aber ihr könnt auch den Bus nehmen. Er fährt um 11 Uhr ab. Wenn ihr euch beeilt *(hurry up)*, erreicht *(catch)* ihr ihn noch. Dann seid ihr viel früher in Exeter. 4. Ich rufe dich an, sobald ich nach Hause komme. 5. Es sieht aus, als ob es bald anfängt zu regnen. – Dann brauchen wir den Rasen *(lawn)* heute abend wenigstens nicht zu sprengen. 6. Ich gehe jetzt nach Hause. – Warte, ich komme mit.

3 Die Verlaufsform des Futurs (The future progressive)

I'm sitting at my desk now. This time tomorrow I **won't be sitting** here, **I'll be lying** in the sun. What **will** you **be doing** this time tomorrow?	*Ich sitze gerade an meinem Schreibtisch. Morgen um diese Zeit sitze ich nicht hier, da liege ich in der Sonne. Was machst du morgen um diese Zeit?*

Wenn du ausdrücken möchtest, daß zu einem bestimmten Zeitpunkt oder während eines bestimmten Zeitraums in der Zukunft etwas im Gange (englisch: *in progress*) sein wird, verwendest du das *future progressive*. Es wird mit *will + be + -ing form* gebildet.

4 Das *future perfect* (The future perfect)

I wouldn't buy a new stereo system before April. Prices **will have gone** down by then.	*Ich würde vor April keine neue Stereoanlage kaufen. Bis dahin werden die Preise gesunken sein.*
Will you **have finished** your homework before we have dinner?	*Wirst du deine Hausaufgaben fertig haben, bevor wir Abendbrot essen?*

Das *future perfect* verwendest du, um auszudrücken, daß etwas vor einem bestimmten Zeitpunkt in der Zukunft geschehen sein wird. Das *future perfect* steht oft mit Zeitangaben wie *by Monday, by then, next week, in ten minutes*. Es wird mit *will + have + past participle* gebildet.

Ex 3 *What do you think will have changed in about 25 years? What will you be doing on your 40th birthday? (Your answers needn't be too serious.) – You could start like this:*
I think by 20. . people will have found cheaper ways of flying to the moon, and on my birthday I'll be having a party in outer space[1]. …

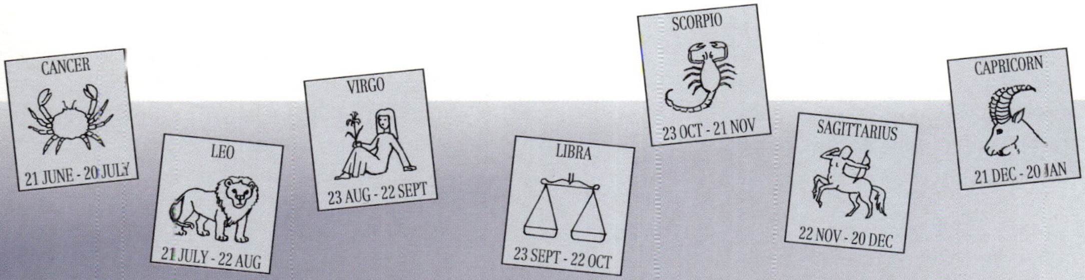

Now find some horoscopes for next week in German magazines or newspapers and compare them with the ones you have written. Tell the class about the differences:
The horoscope I wrote says that people who are Leo/Taurus/… will … . The horoscope I found in … says that they will … .

[1] outer space [ˌaʊtə ˈspeɪs] *Weltraum* Cancer [ˈkænsə] • Leo [ˈliːəʊ] • Virgo [ˈvɜːgəʊ] • Libra [ˈliːbrə] • Scorpio [ˈskɔːpɪəʊ] • Sagittarius [ˌsædʒɪˈteərɪəs] • Capricorn [ˈkæprɪkɔːn]

R The passive

Wie du weißt, wird das Passiv mit einer Form von ***be + past participle*** gebildet. Es kann von allen transitiven Verben (= Verben, die ein **direktes Objekt** nach sich haben) gebildet werden.

1 1. The souvenirs sold in this shop **are made** on the reservation. *(Schild am Verkaufsstand)*

2. Peter Clark: "We **make** all the souvenirs ourselves." *(Auskunft des Verkäufers)*

Das Passiv wird – im Englischen wie im Deutschen – normalerweise verwendet, wenn der/die Handelnde nicht wichtig oder nicht bekannt ist. Das Thema des Passivsatzes (Satz 1) sind die Souvenirs, nicht diejenigen, die die Souvenirs herstellen. Wichtig ist nur, daß die Souvenirs in der Reservation hergestellt worden sind.
Für den Sprecher des Aktivsatzes (Satz 2) sind die Hersteller/innen (wir = wir Navajo) wichtig. Zentrale Aussage ist, daß „wir selbst" die Souvenirs herstellen.

3. The souvenirs were made by a group of Navajo teenagers.

Im Passivsatz 3 sind ebenfalls die *souvenirs* das Thema. Gleichzeitig soll aber ausgesagt werden, wer sie hergestellt hat.
Zur Angabe des/der Handelnden in Passivsätzen wird die Präposition *by* verwendet.

2 **Das Passiv von Verben mit zwei Objekten** (The passive of verbs with two objects)

	subject		*indir. obj.*	*dir. obj.*
active:	They	**gave**	**Angela**	**a job.**
	subject			*dir. obj.*
passive:	**Angela**	**was given**		a job.
	subject			*indir. obj.*
passive:	**A job**	**was given**		to Angela.

Vergleiche:
Angela wurde eine Arbeit gegeben./Man gab Angela eine Arbeit.

Bei Verben mit zwei Objekten *(give sb. sth., show sb. sth., pay sb. sth., promise sb. sth.)* wird meist das indirekte Objekt (Personenobjekt) zum Subjekt des Passivsatzes (**persönliches Passiv**): *Angela was given ... .*

Es kann aber auch das direkte Objekt (Sachobjekt) zum Subjekt werden: *A job was given ... .*

Im Deutschen kann nur das direkte Objekt zum Subjekt des Passivsatzes werden, oder es steht ein Aktivsatz mit *man* oder *jemand.*

Ex 1 *Here are some sentences without subjects, but with two objects. Make two passive sentences from each sentence. Example:*
xxx gave Angela *a job.* a) Angela was given a job. b) *A job* was given to Angela.

1. xxx sent the Navajo a lot of money. 2. xxx offered the Navajo some more land. 3. xxx sent Angela a copy of the article. 4. xxx showed white Americans the reservation. 5. xxx told visitors some Navajo legends . 6. xxx paid the Navajo a lot of money for their stories.

Ex 2 *Complete these questions in the passive. Choose from the verbs in the box.*

ask – give – offer – pay – teach – tell

1. Are the Navajo ... the same rights as other Americans?
2. Is the Navajo language ... in schools?
3. Are visitors ... the truth about the situation of the Navajo today?
4. Is Angela ... a lot of questions by tourists?
5. Are many Navajo students ... places in a high school in Flagstaff?
6. Are the Navajo ... much for the souvenirs they make?

3 **Das Passiv von mehrteiligen Verben** (Verbs + adverb/preposition in the passive)

Auch von mehrteiligen Verben kann ein Passiv gebildet werden. Vergleiche:

	subject		*object*	
active:	The students	**looked up**	some Navajo words.	
	Die Schüler/innen	***schlugen***	*einige Navajo-Wörter*	***nach.***
passive:	Some Navajo words	**were looked up.**		
	Einige Navajo-Wörter	***wurden nachgeschlagen.***		

Weitere Beispiele: *write sth. down, put sth. up, take sth. down, put sth. on, throw sth. away, give sth. up, …*

Eine Reihe von mehrteiligen Verben kann deutschen Schülerinnen und Schülern Probleme bereiten, wenn aus dem Englischen ins Deutsche bzw. aus dem Deutschen ins Englische übersetzt wird. Vergleiche:

All the visitors' questions were talked **about.**	→	***Über alle Fragen der Besucherinnen und Besucher*** *wurde gesprochen.*
In unser Haus *ist eingebrochen worden.*	→	**Our house** has been broken **into.**

Weitere Beispiele: *agree on* (sich einigen auf/über), *speak about* (sprechen über), *look after* (sich kümmern um), *laugh at* (lachen über), …

Ex 3 *See if you can puzzle out a German translation for each of the following sentences.*

1. A programme to preserve the Navajo language has been agreed on.
2. A lot of old Navajo words have been written down.
3. From these words the first Navajo dictionary has been put together.
4. Many Navajo words are unknown to young Navajo and have to be looked up.
5. In language lessons these unknown words are put up in lists on the board.
6. The exact meanings of some of these words are not always agreed on. If that is the case, these words are talked about and analysed by older Navajo.

Ex 4 *Translate the following sentences into English, using passive constructions.*

1. Angela wurde erzogen in dem Glauben an den Wert einer qualifizierten Ausbildung. *(bring up)*
   Angela ***was brought up*** *to believe in the value of a qualified education.*
2. Von zwei Universitäten wurde ihre Bewerbung abgelehnt. *(turn down)*
   Her application … .
3. Es wurde ihr von vielen Lehrerinnen und Lehrern Hilfe angeboten. *(offer)*
   She … .
4. Ihr wurden von vielen Universitäten Informationen zugesandt. *(send)*
   She … .
5. Schließlich wurde ihr ein Platz an der *University of California* versprochen. *(promise)*
   Finally … .

Grammar

Unit 1

Partizipien (Participles)

Wie du weißt, gibt es im Englischen – wie im Deutschen – zwei Arten von Partizipien: das **Partizip Präsens *(present participle)*** und das **Partizip Perfekt *(past participle)***.

G

- Das ***present participle*** endet auf ***-ing***: *relaxing, growing.*
- Das ***past participle*** regelmäßiger Verben endet auf ***-ed***: *polluted, used*; unregelmäßige Verben haben eigene Formen: *taught, broken.*

1 Der adjektivische Gebrauch von Partizipien (The adjectival use of participles)

→ Focus on Grammar, p.9

present participle

A **growing** number of German students would like to take part in school trips abroad.
*Eine **wachsende** Anzahl …*

For most students a school exchange is a **fascinating** experience.
*… eine **faszinierende** Erfahrung.*

past participle

It would certainly be a good thing if more schools offered **organized** trips abroad.
*… **organisierte** Reisen ins Ausland …*

But for many schools the question of money is an **unsolved** problem.
*… ein **ungelöstes** Problem.*

Wie im Deutschen können beide Partizipien wie ein Adjektiv vor einem Nomen stehen.
Häufig bilden Partizipien mit einem anderen Wort ein zusammengesetztes Adjektiv:

• *adjective + participle:*	a **good-looking** singer	*ein/e **gutaussehende/r** Sänger/in*
• *adverb + participle:*	a **well-organized** exchange	*ein **gutorganisierter** Austausch*
• *noun + participle:*	a **time-saving** arrangement	*eine **zeitsparende** Vereinbarung*

→ Word builder's corner, p.17

2 Partizipialsätze anstelle von Relativsätzen (Participle clauses instead of relative clauses)

→ Focus on Grammar, p.9

Partizipialsätze können wie Relativsätze dazu verwendet werden, ein Nomen (oder Pronomen) genauer zu bestimmen.

The students	**taking part in the exchange** who are taking part/who will take part …	will receive more information next week.

Die am Austausch teilnehmenden Schülerinnen und Schüler … .
Die Schülerinnen und Schüler, die am Austausch teilnehmen/teilnehmen werden, … .

Schools	**offering exchange programmes** that offer exchange programmes	are very popular with students.

Austauschprogramme anbietende Schulen … .
Schulen, die Austauschprogramme anbieten, … .

Anders als im Deutschen stehen Partizipialsätze jedoch hinter dem Nomen, auf das sie sich beziehen.
Vergleiche: Schools **offering exchange programmes** …
***Austauschprogramme anbietende** Schulen …*

Beispiele für Partizipialsätze, die ein Pronomen näher bestimmen:

Those	**prepared to help with the organization** who are prepared to help with the organization	should meet at 10 o'clock.

Diejenigen, die bereit sind, bei der Organisation zu helfen, … .

Anybody	**wanting to help** who wants to help	is welcome to join us.

Jede/r, die/der helfen möchte, … .

G

3 Partizipialsätze anstelle von adverbialen Nebensätzen …
(Participle clauses instead of adverbial clauses …)

a … ohne einleitende Konjunktion (… without an introductory conjunction) → Focus on Grammar, p.13

Reading a report about school trips, Anne began to get interested in exchange programmes.
(While/When Anne was reading …) *Als/Während Anne einen Bericht über Schulreisen las, …*

Convinced that other pupils would also like to visit the USA, she decided to get more information.
(Because she was convinced …) *Weil sie überzeugt war, daß …*

Not knowing where to find more information, she asked her English teacher.
(Because she didn't know …) *Weil sie nicht wußte, wo sie weitere Informationen finden könnte, …*

Having written an article for her school magazine, she knew what she was talking about.
(After/Because she had written …) *Nachdem/Weil sie einen Artikel … geschrieben hatte, …*

Partizipialsätze können die gleiche Aufgabe erfüllen wie ein adverbialer Nebensatz. Das im Hauptsatz genannte Subjekt ist in den Beispielsätzen auch Subjekt des Partizipialsatzes (hier: *Anne, she*).
Verneinte Partizipialsätze werden gebildet, indem *not* vor das Partizip gestellt wird.
Am häufigsten sind Partizipialsätze des Grundes *(of reason)* und der Zeit *(of time)*; in vielen Fällen ist allerdings nicht eindeutig zu erkennen, ob der Partizipialsatz Gründe nennt oder zeitliche Informationen gibt (vgl. den letzten Beispielsatz).
Partizipialsätze anstelle von Adverbialsätzen werden vor allem in formellem (besonders in geschriebenem) Englisch verwendet. Sie stehen meist am Satzanfang und werden oft durch ein Komma abgetrennt.

Mit Partizipialsätzen können auch die Begleitumstände einer Handlung beschrieben werden. Im Deutschen verwenden wir dafür meist „und"-Hauptsätze:
Some pupils decided not to take part in the exchange, **explaining** that it would be too expensive.
… und erklärten, daß …

b … eingeleitet durch eine Konjunktion (… introduced by a conjunction) → Focus on Grammar, p.13

Before writing her article for the school magazine, Anne asked some pen-friends for advice.
(Before Anne wrote …) *Bevor Anne ihren Artikel für die Schülerzeitung schrieb, …*

While waiting for their replies, she found some useful information in her English textbook.
(While she was waiting …) *Während sie auf ihre Antworten wartete, …*

When invited to visit an American school, you should remember to be careful with taboo words.
(When you are invited …) *Wenn du eingeladen bist, eine amerikanische Schule zu besuchen, …*

After reading her pen-friends' replies, Anne knew what to write in her article.[1]
(After Anne had read …) *Nachdem Anne die Antworten … gelesen hatte, …*

Although convinced that a trip to the US would be a great experience, she wasn't sure if she'd manage to organize one.
(Although she was convinced …) *Obwohl sie überzeugt war, daß …*

- Partizipialsätze der Zeit werden oft durch folgende Konjunktionen eingeleitet:
  – vor *present participles: after, before, when, while*
  – vor *past participles: when, while.*
  Die Konjunktionen *when* und *while* können in den meisten Fällen weggelassen werden, ohne daß sich die Bedeutung der Sätze verändert.
- Partizipialsätze der Einräumung *(of concession)* werden durch die Konjunktion *(al)though* eingeleitet.

[1] Um Vorzeitigkeit auszudrücken, kannst du statt *After doing* … auch *Having done* … verwenden:
After reading her pen-friends' replies, | Anne knew what to write in her article.
Having read her pen-friends' replies, |

G

c Partizipialsätze mit eigenem Subjekt (Participle clauses with their own subject)

→ Focus on Grammar, p.13

(a) **Having written** an article for the school magazine, **Mr Williams** looked forward to the meeting.
(b) **Class 9b having written** an article for the school magazine, **Mr Williams** looked forward to the meeting.

In Beispiel (a) haben Partizipialsatz und Hauptsatz das gleiche Subjekt *(Mr Williams).* Autor des Artikels ist *Mr Williams.*
In Beispiel (b) haben Partizipialsatz und Hauptsatz verschiedene Subjekte (Partizipialsatz: *class 9b*; Hauptsatz: *Mr Williams*). Autor des Artikels ist *class 9b.*

Weitere Beispiele für Partizipialsätze mit eigenem Subjekt:

The play being over, **we** went home.	*Nachdem das Stück zu Ende war, …*
Jill sat on the sofa, **her face hidden** in her hands.	*… und verbarg das Gesicht in ihren Händen.*

Partizipialsätze mit eigenem Subjekt können durch ***with*** eingeleitet sein:

I can't work **with you making** such a noise.	*…, wenn/weil du solchen Lärm machst.*
With father being unemployed, **we** can't go on holiday.	*Dadurch, daß/Da Vater arbeitslos ist, …*
You can't go to that meeting **with your shoes not cleaned**.	*… mit ungeputzten Schuhen.*

Partizipialsätze mit eigenem Subjekt **ohne einleitendes *with*** findet man eher in formellem oder literarischem Englisch. Sie werden immer durch ein Komma vom Hauptsatz abgetrennt.

Partizipialsätze mit eigenem Subjekt **mit einleitendem *with*** werden auch in der Umgangssprache verwendet. Sie werden nur durch ein Komma abgetrennt, wenn sie vor dem Hauptsatz stehen.

4 Partizipien – besondere Verwendungen (Participles – special uses)

a *have something done (have* + Objekt + Partizip Perfekt) (*have* + object + past participle)

	have	*object*	*past participle*		
You should	**have**	your hair	**cut**.		*Du solltest dir die Haare schneiden lassen.*
Pete	**is having**	his flat	**decorated**.		*Pete läßt gerade seine Wohnung renovieren.*
We	**'ve had**	a garage	**built**.		*Wir haben uns eine Garage bauen lassen.*
Did you	**have**	your car	**washed**	yesterday?	*Hast du gestern dein Auto waschen lassen?*

Du kannst *have something done* verwenden, um auszudrücken, daß jemand etwas (von jemand anderem) machen läßt, d.h. es nicht selbst ausführt.

⚠ ***have something done*** **= etwas tun lassen; veranlassen, daß etwas getan wird**
have done something **= etwas *(selbst)* getan haben**
Vergleiche:

Susan **had** her hair **cut**.	*Susan ließ sich die Haare schneiden.*	(*simple past* von *have sth. cut*)
Susan **had cut** her hair.	*Susan hatte sich die Haare geschnitten.*	(*past perfect* von *cut*)

b Verben der Wahrnehmung + Objekt + Partizip Präsens
(Verbs of perception + object + present participle)

	verb	*object*	*present participle*	
Eve	**saw**	the band	**arriving**.	*Eve sah die Band ankommen.*
She	**heard**	the people	**shouting**.	*Sie hörte die Menschen schreien.*
She	**watched**	them	**rushing** to the stage.	*Sie beobachtete, wie sie zur Bühne stürmten.*
Eve	**felt**	her heart	**beating** wildly.	*Eve spürte, wie/daß ihr Herz wie wild schlug.*

Nach Verben der Wahrnehmung wie ***feel, hear, listen to, notice, see, watch, observe, smell*** kann ein **Objekt + Partizip Präsens** stehen. Im Deutschen steht ein Infinitiv oder ein Nebensatz mit *wie* oder *daß*.

Nach Verben der Wahrnehmung + Objekt kann auch ein Infinitiv stehen. Vergleiche:

verb of perception + object + infinitive
– wenn ein Geschehen vollständig von Anfang bis Ende wahrgenommen wird:
Eve **saw** the band **take** their instruments, **leave** the stage and **get** into their bus.

verb of perception + object + present participle
– wenn ein Geschehen wahrgenommen wird, das noch nicht zu Ende, sondern im Verlauf ist:
Eve **saw** the band slowly **leaving** the stage.

c Verben der Ruhe und Bewegung + Partizip Präsens
(Verbs of rest and movement + present participle)

I can't just **stand** here **waiting**.	*Ich kann nicht einfach hier stehen und warten.*
Mr Cook **remained standing** in the hall.	*Mr Cook blieb in der Halle stehen.*
Some children **came running** towards us.	*Einige Kinder kamen auf uns zugelaufen.*
Then a stone **came flying** through the window.	*Dann kam ein Stein durchs Fenster geflogen.*

Nach Verben der Ruhe wie ***lie, remain*** (bleiben), ***sit, stand*** und nach einigen Verben der Bewegung wie ***come, go*** kann ein **Partizip Präsens** stehen. Beachte die unterschiedliche Wiedergabe im Deutschen.

5 Die *-ing form* – Zusammenfassung (The *-ing form* – summary)

Als ***present participle*** wird die *-ing form* verwendet ...

• zur Bildung der *progressive forms*	The population **is growing** too fast.
• adjektivisch vor einem Nomen	A **growing number** of people ...
• in Partizipialsätzen anstelle von Relativsätzen	The trees **growing in our garden** are very old.
• in Partizipialsätzen anstelle von Adverbialsätzen	**When growing oranges**, you need lots of sun.
• nach Verben der Wahrnehmung + Objekt	It rains so much here that you can almost **watch the grass growing**.
• nach Verben der Ruhe und Bewegung	The dog **lay** there **growing** weaker and weaker.

Als ***gerund*** wird die *-ing form* verwendet ...

• als Subjekt oder Teil eines Subjekts	**Growing up** isn't easy./**Growing plants** is easy.
• als Objekt nach bestimmten Verben	Do you **like growing up** in the country?
• nach Präpositionen	I can walk for miles **without growing** tired.
• nach Adjektiv + Präposition	He was **proud of growing up** in the country.
• nach Nomen + Präposition	The **advantages of growing up** in the country ...
• nach Verb + Präposition	Let's not **talk about growing** old.

G

Grammar 2

Unit 2

Nebensätze (Sub-clauses)

Dein Englisch ist mittlerweile so gut, daß du – sehr wahrscheinlich ganz automatisch – eine Reihe von Nebensätzen verwendest, um dich genauer und geschickter auszudrücken. Damit du Nebensätze noch gezielter einsetzen kannst, bieten dir die folgenden Abschnitte einen systematischen Überblick über …

- **Adverbialsätze**, auch adverbiale Nebensätze genannt *(adverbial clauses)*. Sie haben eine ähnliche Funktion wie adverbiale Bestimmungen:
  adverbialer Nebensatz: **Wherever the senator gave his speech,** people were fascinated.
  adverbiale Bestimmung: **Everywhere on his tour** people were fascinated.
- **Relativsätze** *(relative clauses)*. Sie bestimmen das Nomen näher, auf das sie sich beziehen:
  The senator complained about students **who couldn't say why the Constitution was written**.
  Sie können sich auch auf den ganzen Hauptsatz beziehen:
  Some students couldn't find the US capital on a map, **which is quite surprising**.

> ⚠ Auch in Nebensätzen gilt im Englischen, im Gegensatz zum Deutschen, die Wortstellung ***subject – verb***:
> Wherever **he gave** his speech, … *Wo auch immer **er** seine Rede **hielt**, …*

1 Adverbialsätze (Adverbial clauses)

→ Focus on Grammar, p.22

Adverbiale Nebensätze werden durch eine Konjunktion *(while, when, because, if, so that, …)* eingeleitet. Je nach Wahl der einleitenden Konjunktion beschreibt der Nebensatz zeitliche oder örtliche Umstände, Gründe, Bedingungen, Folgen, … .

Adverbialsätze können **vor** dem Hauptsatz stehen (meist durch ein Komma abgetrennt), **hinter** dem Hauptsatz stehen (in der Regel ohne Komma) oder in den Hauptsatz eingebettet sein:

As soon as the senator had finished his speech, the teachers started to ask questions.
The teachers started to ask questions **as soon as the senator had finished his speech**.
The teachers**, as soon as the senator had finished his speech,** started to ask questions.

a Adverbialsätze der Zeit (Adverbial clauses of time)

We left the meeting **after he had answered our questions**.
…, nachdem er unsere Fragen beantwortet hatte.
We left the meeting **before he had answered our questions**.
…, bevor er unsere Fragen beantwortet hatte.

WEITERE KONJUNKTIONEN:
as als, während • ***as long as*** solange • ***as soon as*** sobald • ***by the time*** bis • ***since*** seit(dem) • ***till/until*** bis • ***when*** als; wenn; wann • ***whenever*** wann (auch) immer; jedesmal, wenn • ***while*** während, solange

b Adverbialsätze des Ortes (Adverbial clauses of place)

Wherever the senator gave his speech, his audience was fascinated.
Überall, wo der Senator seine Rede hielt, … .

KONJUNKTIONEN:
where wo; wohin • ***wherever*** wo (auch) immer; überall, wo; wohin (auch) immer

c Adverbialsätze des Grundes (Adverbial clauses of reason)

The senator was worried **because many teenagers know so little about US history**.
…, weil viele Teenager sehr wenig … wissen.
As/Since students' results have improved, he has hope for the future.
Da die Resultate … sich verbessert haben, … .

KONJUNKTIONEN:
as da, weil • ***since*** da, weil • ***because*** weil

(Sätze mit *as/since* stehen meist **vor**, Sätze mit *because* meist **nach** dem Hauptsatz.)

d Adverbialsätze der Einräumung (Adverbial clauses of concession)

Too many students fail their exams **although our teachers are doing their best**.
..., obwohl unsere Lehrkräfte ihr Bestes geben.

Even if standards have improved, we mustn't think that further reforms are not necessary.
Selbst wenn der Standard sich verbessert hat, ...

KONJUNKTIONEN:
although, though obwohl, obgleich • ***even if, even though*** selbst wenn

e Adverbialsätze des Zwecks (Adverbial clauses of purpose)

We need a better education system **so that our children will be prepared for future challenges**.
..., damit unsere Kinder ... vorbereitet sind.

KONJUNKTIONEN:
so that damit, so daß • ***so*** damit, so daß

f Adverbialsätze der Folge (Adverbial clauses of result)

At 4 o'clock the senator had finished his speech, **so we went back to our hotel**.
..., so daß wir zu unserem Hotel zurückgingen./ ..., daher gingen wir zu unserem Hotel zurück.

KONJUNKTIONEN:
so so daß; daher • ***so that*** so daß; daher

g Bedingungssätze (Adverbial clauses of condition/Conditional clauses)

If we are prepared to learn from the past, our reforms will be successful. (Typ I)
Wenn wir bereit sind, ... zu lernen, ...

If we learned from the past, we might have a chance to improve our future. (Typ II)
Wenn wir aus der Vergangenheit lernten/lernen würden, ...

If we had learned from the past, we would have reacted differently. (Typ III)
Wenn wir aus der Vergangenheit gelernt hätten, ...

KONJUNKTIONEN:
<u>Für Typ I:</u>
if wenn, falls • ***unless*** wenn nicht, außer wenn es sei denn, daß • ***in case (that)*** falls, für den Fall, daß • ***as long as*** sofern, solange

<u>Für Typ II und III:</u>
if wenn, falls

<u>**Bedingungssätze ohne *if***</u>

In formellem Englisch findet man auch Bedingungssätze ohne *if*:

Had we learned from the past, we would have reacted differently.
Wenn wir aus der Vergangenheit gelernt hätten, hätten wir anders reagiert.

Should you ever have the chance of meeting the senator, be sure not to miss it.
Solltest du jemals die Chance haben, den Senator zu treffen, dann verpasse sie nicht.

h Adverbialsätze des Vergleichs (Adverbial clauses of comparison)

Let's all work together now **as Americans have always done in times of crisis**.
..., wie es Amerikanerinnen und Amerikaner in Krisenzeiten immer getan haben.

KONJUNKTION:
as (so) wie

Grammar 2

2 Relativsätze (Relative clauses)

→ Focus on Grammar, p.22

a Bestimmende Relativsätze (Defining relative clauses)

	subject		
(1) The senator is a man	**who**	**enjoys talking to people**.	*…, der gern mit Leuten spricht.*
(2) The senator is a man **(who*)**	**people**	**enjoy talking to**.	*…, mit dem die Leute gern reden.*

Relativpronomen:

who/that – für Personen
which/that – für Dinge, Ideen, usw.
whose – um Besitz oder Zugehörigkeit auszudrücken *(deren, dessen)*

* In formellem Englisch wird für Personen auch *whom* verwendet, wenn das Relativpronomen nicht Subjekt ist.

In Relativsätzen kann entweder das Relativpronomen (Satz 1) oder ein (Pro-)Nomen (Satz 2) Subjekt sein. Wenn das Relativpronomen nicht Subjekt ist, kann es weggelassen werden. Relativsätze ohne Relativpronomen heißen *contact clauses*.
Beachte die Stellung der Präposition in Satz 2.

b Nichtbestimmende Relativsätze (Non-defining relative clauses)

(1) The senator usually gives his speeches with the help of his notes**, which actually are nothing more than a few words and phrases**. — *…, die eigentlich nicht mehr als ein paar Wörter und Satzteile sind.*
(2) Mrs West helps the senator**, who is not very good at organizing things,** to prepare his tour. — *…, der nicht sehr gut darin ist, Dinge zu organisieren.*
(3) The senator wouldn't know what to do without his secretary**, with whom he recently travelled all over the US**. — *…, mit der er kürzlich die gesamte USA bereist hat.*

Diese Hauptsätze wären auch ohne Relativsätze verständlich und eindeutig. Die Relativsätze geben uns lediglich **Zusatzinformationen** zu den Dingen oder Personen, auf die sie sich beziehen (hier: *notes; the senator*). Man nennt sie **nichtbestimmende Relativsätze *(non-defining relative clauses)***. Nichtbestimmende Relativsätze werden durch Kommas vom Hauptsatz abgetrennt.

⚠ – In *non-defining relative clauses* kann das Relativpronomen *that* nicht benutzt werden.
– In *non-defining relative clauses* steht die Präposition meist vor dem Relativpronomen (vgl. Satz 3). In diesem Fall kann für Personen nur das Pronomen *whom* verwendet werden.

Satzbezügliches *which*

Das Relativpronomen *which* (= was) kann sich auf die Aussage eines ganzen Satzes beziehen:

More and more people have begun to think about the education system**, which gives the senator hope for the future**. — *Immer mehr Leute haben angefangen, über das Ausbildungssystem nachzudenken, was dem Senator Hoffnung für die Zukunft macht.*

The senator has decided to repeat his tour next year**, which I think is wonderful**. — *Der Senator hat sich entschieden, nächstes Jahr seine Vortragsreise zu wiederholen, was ich wunderbar finde.*

G

3 Die Wahl der Zeitformen in Nebensätzen (The choice of tenses in sub-clauses)

→ Focus on Grammar, p.23

Du hast in den letzten drei Jahren viel über die Verwendung der Zeiten im Englischen gehört. In Nebensätzen gelten grundsätzlich die gleichen Regeln wie in Hauptsätzen. Das heißt:
Du mußt für jeden Nebensatz entscheiden, welche Verbform für das vorliegende Geschehen oder den erwähnten Zustand die richtige ist. Es ist nicht möglich, die Zeitform des Hauptsatzes blind auf den Nebensatz zu übertragen.
Auf der *Focus on Grammar*-Seite hast du eine Reihe von Hauptsätzen im *simple past* und von *that*-Nebensätzen mit unterschiedlichen Zeitformen gesehen. Die folgende Übersicht zeigt dir wiederum Hauptsätze im *simple past*, allerdings mit einer Reihe unterschiedlicher Nebensätze, an denen die Verwendung der Zeitformen verdeutlicht wird.

The first day our instructor **asked** us when we usually **get up** in the morning.	an activity that takes place regularly *(eine Tätigkeit, die regelmäßig stattfindet)*	**simple present**
We **learned** that Washington **is trying** to improve its image as a tourist city.	an activity that is in progress *(eine Tätigkeit, die im Gange ist)*	**present perfect**
The day after our big party the seminar **ended** early, since we **were** all tired.	a state that was valid in the past *(ein Zustand, der in der Vergangenheit herrschte)*	**simple past**
The president **didn't** start talking until we **were** all **standing** in his office.	an activity that was in progress in the past *(eine Tätigkeit, die in der Vergangenheit im Gange war)*	**past progressive**
Although it **has been** the capital for 200 years, we **found** Washington very modern-looking.	a state that started in the past and continues up to the present *(ein Zustand, der in der Vergangenheit begann und in der Gegenwart noch andauert)*	**present perfect**
We **met** some people who **have been working** for the government for years.	an activity that started in the past and continues up to the present *(eine Tätigkeit, die in der Vergangenheit begann und in der Gegenwart noch andauert)*	**present perfect progressive**
After we **had heard** the senator's speech, we **knew** more about our government.	an activity that took place before a point in the past *(eine Tätigkeit, die vor einem Zeitpunkt in der Vergangenheit stattgefunden hat)*	**past perfect**
We **were** happy that we **were going to see** him again.	a 'future'-activity in the past *(eine Tätigkeit, die von einem vergangenen Zeitpunkt aus betrachtet zukünftig war)*	***going to*-future in the past**
We **were** sad because the course **would** soon **be** over.		***will*-future in the past**

Unit 3

1 Modale Hilfsverben und ihre Ersatzverben (Modal auxiliaries and their substitutes)

→ Focus on Grammar, p.36

G

Modale Hilfsverben und ihre Ersatzverben sind dir bereits bekannt. Du weißt also u.a., daß Modalverben nicht alle Zeiten bilden können.
Die folgende Übersicht zeigt dir anhand einiger Beispiele, welche *modals* bzw. *substitutes* in welcher konkreten Situation benutzt werden.

- **Fähigkeit** (Ability)

Dinkins **was able to win** the election in 1989. — *konnte gewinnen*
There are still many Americans who **can't read**. — *(die) nicht lesen können*

- **Erlaubnis** (Permission)

Today hotels and restaurants **aren't allowed to discriminate** against blacks. — *dürfen nicht diskriminieren*
Every citizen **may vote** in elections. — *darf wählen*

- **Möglichkeit** (Possibility)

One day the United States **could have** a black president. — *könnten/werden vielleicht haben*
The next US president **might not be** white. — *wird vielleicht nicht sein*

- **Zwang oder Notwendigkeit** (Obligation)

The senator says we **must do** more for minorities. — *müssen tun*
Today you **don't have to be** 21 to vote. — *(man) braucht nicht zu sein*

Um das Fehlen von Notwendigkeit auszudrücken, kann man ***don't have to/haven't got to*** oder auch ***needn't***[1] verwenden: You **needn't** be 21 to vote.

> ⚠ Vorsicht: ***mustn't*** drückt ein Verbot aus: You **mustn't** do that. *Das darfst du nicht tun.*

Beachte folgende Besonderheit beim Gebrauch von *must* in indirekter Rede: *must* kannst du auch dann verwenden, wenn das einleitende Verb im *simple past* steht – so als wäre *must* eine *simple past form*:
The senator **said** that he **must/had to** think about the problem.

- **Schlußfolgerungen** (Deductions)

It **must be** very difficult to grow up in the ghetto. — *muß sein*
M.L. King **must have been** an interesting man. — *muß gewesen sein*

- **Vorschläge** (Suggestions)

The president **should be doing** more for minority rights. — *sollte tun*
Congress **should have done** something against discrimination long before 1954. — *hätte tun sollen*

[1] Neben *need* als Modalverb gibt es auch das Vollverb *(to) need to*. Vergleiche:

modales Hilfsverb: You **needn't** be 21 to vote.
Als Hilfsverb wird *need* nur im Präsens verwendet und steht hauptsächlich in verneinten Aussagesätzen, seltener auch in Fragesätzen.

Vollverb: You **don't need to** be 21 to vote.
Als Vollverb steht *need* auch in bejahten Aussagesätzen und kann wie alle Vollverben auch in anderen Zeiten verwendet werden: I **needed to** go to the toilet.

2 Modale Hilfsverben in Schlußfolgerungen (Modals in deductions)

→ Focus on Grammar, p.37

Du weißt nun, daß ***must*** verwendet werden kann, um eine Schlußfolgerung auszudrücken. Diese Seite zeigt dir, daß auch die anderen modalen Hilfsverben für Schlußfolgerungen verwendet werden können, genau wie im Deutschen.
Welches modale Hilfsverb man wählt, hängt davon ab, wie sicher man ist, daß die Schlußfolgerung richtig ist.

G

a Unterschiedliche Grade der Gewißheit (Degrees of certainty)

Hier eine Aufstellung der verschiedenen Modalverben, die für Schlußfolgerungen Verwendung finden, angeordnet nach dem Grad der Gewißheit des Sprechers/der Sprecherin:

ziemlich sicher	You've been working all day – you **must be** very tired.	*mußt sein*
	John **can't have been** at work this morning – he's on holiday.	*kann nicht gewesen sein*
↓ wahrscheinlich	Mary **should be** in Stoke by now – she left London hours ago.	*müßte/dürfte sein*
	John **could be working** today – I think his holidays are over.	*könnte bei der Arbeit sein*
	Mary **may have** time to come and visit us today.	*könnte vielleicht haben*
↓ möglich	John **might** already **have gone**.	*könnte eventuell gegangen sein*

b Zeitbezug (Time reference)

Wie du auf der *Focus on grammar*-Seite 37 gesehen hast, sind die Zeitverhältnisse in Sätzen, die modale Hilfsverben enthalten, nicht so eindeutig wie in „normalen" Sätzen. Vergleiche:

Jill **might not have seen** the film **yesterday**. (Perhaps she didn't see it yesterday.)	*Jill hat den Film gestern vielleicht nicht gesehen.*
Jill **might not have seen** the film **yet**. (Perhaps she hasn't seen it yet.)	*Jill hat den Film vielleicht noch nicht gesehen.*
Jill **might not have seen** the film **by tomorrow**. (Perhaps she won't have seen it by tomorrow.)	*Jill wird den Film bis morgen vielleicht noch nicht gesehen haben.*

Selbst bei unterschiedlichem Zeitbezug werden die gleichen Verbformen verwendet. Deshalb muß man auf die adverbialen Ergänzungen besonders achten, um festzustellen, ob es sich um Vergangenes, Gegenwärtiges oder Zukünftiges handelt.

Wie immer mußt du dir überlegen, ob die Verlaufsform *(progressive form)* angebracht ist oder nicht. Hier sind natürlich die gleichen Faktoren ausschlaggebend wie in allen anderen Sätzen auch:

Jack **must have been playing** tennis **at 2 o'clock**. (I'm certain he was playing tennis at 2 o'clock.)	*Jack muß um 14 Uhr beim Tennisspielen gewesen sein.*
Jack **must have played** tennis **yesterday**. (I'm certain he played tennis yesterday.)	*Jack muß gestern Tennis gespielt haben.*

Grammar 4

Unit 4

Tempora – *simple form* und *progressive form* (Tenses – simple form and progressive form)

→ Focus on Grammar, p.50-51

G

Du hast schon mehrere Male gehört, daß es so etwas wie *activity verbs* und *state verbs* gibt. Beispiele:
- ***activity verbs*** (Tätigkeits- oder Vorgangsverben): *(to) do, (to) work, (to) rain, (to) become, ...*
- ***state verbs*** (Zustandsverben): *(to) be, (to) sound, (to) seem, (to) know, (to) like, (to) hear, ...*

1 **Tätigkeitsverben: *simple form* und *progressive form*** (Activity verbs)

Von *activity verbs* kann man eine *simple form* und eine *progressive form* für alle Zeiten bilden. Die *progressive form* wird verwendet für Handlungen oder Vorgänge, die zu einem bestimmten Zeitpunkt im Verlauf sind, waren oder sein werden.
Du kennst bereits die *progressive form* von *present tense*, *past tense*, *present perfect* und *past perfect*. Auch *will-future* und *going to-future* haben natürlich eine *simple* und eine *progressive form*:

Tomorrow at 2 o'clock he **will be working**.	*wird (gerade) arbeiten/beim Arbeiten sein*
I **am going to be working** when you arrive.	*werde (gerade) arbeiten/beim Arbeiten sein*

Ebenso hat das *'future in the past'* eine *progressive form*:

I knew he **would be working** when his boss came.	*würde (gerade) arbeiten/beim Arbeiten sein*
He thought I **was going to be working** when he arrived.	*würde (gerade) arbeiten/beim Arbeiten sein*

2 **Zustandsverben: nur *simple form*** (State verbs)

Verben, die einen Zustand oder eine Eigenschaft beschreiben, können nur in der *simple form* vorkommen – und das ist eigentlich auch ganz logisch: Zustände und Eigenschaften können nicht im Verlauf *(in progress)* sein. Man kann beispielsweise nicht gerade dabei sein, etwas zu wissen.

She always **knows** the answers to my questions.
I **don't know** where my wife is at the moment.

3 **Tätigkeitsverben – Zustandsverben** (Activity verbs – state verbs)

Du weißt, daß ein Wort verschiedene Bedeutungen haben kann. Es ist daher nicht weiter verwunderlich, daß es Verben gibt, die sowohl *activities* als auch *states* ausdrücken können. Beispielsweise kann *(to) think* ein *state verb* sein und „meinen, halten von" bedeuten, es kann aber auch ein *activity verb* sein und „(nach)denken" heißen. Nur als *activity verb* kann es in der *progressive form* erscheinen. Vergleiche:

What **does** the ranger **think** about the inscription?	Zustand → *state verb*
What **is** he **thinking** about at this moment?	Vorgang → *activity verb*

4 **Tempora und Texte** (Tenses and texts)

In den letzten Jahren hast du die unterschiedlichsten Texte im Englischunterricht geschrieben. Drei Textsorten kommen in der Schule, aber auch in der wirklichen Welt, besonders häufig vor:
a) Man muß oft Situationen/„Bilder" beschreiben. *(**descriptive texts**)*
b) Man muß oft von Ereignissen oder Vorgängen erzählen. *(**narrative texts**)*
c) Man muß sich mit einem Thema inhaltlich-argumentativ auseinandersetzen. *(**argumentative texts**)*

G

a Beschreibende Texte (Descriptive texts)

Dear Diary: I**'m looking** out of my window onto the street at the moment, where an accident **has** just **happened**. Several people **are standing** around an ambulance. A little boy **has been hit** by a car and now he**'s lying** in the street. He**'s not moving**. A doctor **has been examining** him for several minutes. I **hope** he **isn't hurt** seriously and that he**'ll** even **be riding** his bike again tomorrow. And I **hope** people **will drive** slower down our street in the future.

Ein deskriptiver („beschreibender") Text kann nicht nur ein Bild (vgl. Text 1 auf S. 50), einen Gegenstand oder eine Person beschreiben, sondern auch, wie in einer Momentaufnahme, eine Szene aus einem Geschehen – wie eine Art „Schnappschuß" aus dem Leben. In solchen deskriptiven Texten benötigt man häufig das *present progressive*, da Handlungen und Vorgänge dargestellt werden, die gerade im Verlauf sind. (Die einzigen *simple forms* im Beispiel oben sind *state verbs*.)
Das typischste Vergangenheitstempus ist das *present perfect*, da die vergangenen Ereignisse in ihrer Auswirkung auf die Gegenwart beschrieben werden: *A little boy* ***has been hit*** *by a car and now he's lying on the street.*
Für mögliche zukünftige Entwicklungen verwendet man die verschiedenen *future forms*.

b Erzählende Texte (Narrative texts)

On my way home yesterday I **hit** a little boy on his bike. I **had worked** hard all day and **was** a bit tired. I **prayed** that he **would be** OK. While the doctor **was examining** him, the boy suddenly **stood up** and **got back** onto his bike. What luck! Most of us **drive** too fast …

In narrativen („erzählenden") Texten wird eine Geschichte erzählt. Weil es meist um abgeschlossene aufeinander folgende Vorgänge in der Vergangenheit geht, benötigt man in erster Linie das *simple past*.
Wenn man schildern möchte, was zu einem bestimmten Zeitpunkt gerade vor sich ging, benutzt man das *past progressive: While the doctor* ***was examining*** *him … .*
Um auf Ereignisse oder Zustände Bezug zu nehmen, die noch weiter in der Vergangenheit oder in der Zukunft liegen, verwendet man das *past perfect* bzw. das *'future in the past'*.
Das *simple present* steht nur in Aussagen, die allgemeingültig sind.

c Argumentative Texte (Argumentative texts)

It **is** a simple fact that most people **drive** too fast down our street. There **have been** two accidents in the last two years. The last one **happened** only yesterday. What we **need** now **are** pedestrian crossings and a lower speed limit. When traffic **is** slower there **are** fewer accidents. Now some people **are** finally **becoming** aware of the danger so perhaps some action **will be taken**. If we **don't do** something soon, somebody **is going to be killed**.

In einem argumentativen Text versucht man meistens, die Leserinnen und Leser von seinen eigenen Vorstellungen zu überzeugen; man legt seine Meinung dar, begründet sie und versucht, sie als allgemeingültig darzustellen – daher verwendet man oft das *simple present*.
Um seine Meinung zu begründen, gibt man oft Beispiele aus der Vergangenheit. Daher trifft man in argumentativen Texten auch auf die verschiedenen Vergangenheitstempora.
Außerdem ist es in solchen Texten notwendig, Vorhersagen über künftige Entwicklungen zu machen. Dafür nimmt man die verschiedenen *future forms*.
In argumentativen Texten findet man also eine größere Mischung von Zeit- und Verbformen als in beschreibenden bzw. erzählenden Texten.

Vocabulary

Das folgende Wörterverzeichnis *(Vocabulary)* enthält die neuen Wörter des Buches in der Reihenfolge ihres Vorkommens. **Eingerückte Wörter** sollen mit dem vorausgehenden Wort mitgelernt werden, obwohl sie nicht an der betreffenden Stelle der *Unit* vorkommen.
Fett gedruckte Wörter (z. B. „**literature**") gehören zum „produktiven" Wortschatz – du sollst sie beim eigenen Sprechen und Schreiben verwenden können. **Normal gedruckte Wörter** (z. B. „airline") gehören zum „rezeptiven" Wortschatz – du sollst sie verstehen, wenn du sie hörst oder liest.
Mit einem ° versehene Wörter (z. B. „°panel") gehören zum sogenannten „Situationswortschatz". Es sind Wörter, die zum Thema einer bestimmten *Unit* gehören, aber in nachfolgenden *Units* nicht als bekannt vorausgesetzt werden.
Eigennamen (einschließlich **Ländernamen** und davon abgeleiteter Adjektive) und **grammatische Fachausdrücke** werden nicht im *Vocabulary* aufgeführt. Sie stehen gesammelt auf den Seiten 202/203 bzw. 204/205.
Nicht aufgeführt sind englische Wörter wie *clown, computer, film star, quizmaster, restaurant*, die du ohne weiteres verstehst. Alle diese Wörter findest du aber mit Angabe ihrer Aussprache in der alphabetischen Wortliste (S. 169 ff.).

~ – Die **Tilde** (~) in der dritten Spalte steht anstelle des Eintrags in der ersten Spalte. Pro Tilde muß ein Wort eingesetzt werden. (Beispiel: (to) **provide** sth. **(for** sb.) – The company *~s* lunch *for* its employees.)

▸◂ – Dieses Symbol in der dritten Spalte weist dich auf ein bekanntes Wort mit **gegensätzlicher Bedeutung** hin. (Beispiel: **outgoing** – kontaktfreudig, extravertiert – ▸◂ **shy**)

Betonungszeichen: ' = Hauptbetonung, ˌ = Nebenbetonung
(Beispiel: **physical punishment** [ˌfɪzɪkl 'pʌnɪʃmənt] – Hauptbetonung: ['pʌnɪʃmənt], Nebenbetonung: [ˌfɪzɪkl])

Abkürzungen:
p. = page Ex = Exercise
sb. = somebody sth. = something
jd. = jemand jm. = jemandem jn. = jemanden js. = jemandes
sing. = singular pl. = plural
adj. = adjective adv. = adverb conj. = conjunction n. = noun prep. = preposition v. = verb
infml. = informal (umgangssprachlich, informell) fml. = formal (formell)
AE = American English BE = British English

Introduction

p. 7	**literature** ['lɪtrətʃə]	Literatur	novels, short stories, poems, plays, etc. Toni Morrison won the Nobel ['nəʊbel] prize for ~.
	°panel ['pænl]	*etwa:* Bildtafel	
	first of all ['fɜːst‿əv‿ˌɔːl]	als erstes, zu (aller)erst	Today there is a test on the past perfect. *First ~ ~*, please put your English books away.
	(to) come into sb.'s mind	jm. einfallen, in den Sinn kommen	I'm going to show you some pictures now. Look at them and tell me what *~s into your ~*.

Unit 1: American high schools

p. 8	airline ['eəlaɪn]	Fluggesellschaft	I'm flying to Boston. – What ~ are you flying with?
	guidance counselor ['gaɪdəns ˌkaʊnsələ] (AE)	*Schulberater/in an einer High School, berät Schüler/innen bei persönlichen und schulischen Problemen und bei der Berufswahl*	If you need some advice about career planning, go and talk to your ~ ~.
	principal ['prɪnsəpl] (AE)	Schulleiter/in, Direktor/in	In the US, headteachers are called *~s*.
	°soft drink [ˌsɒft 'drɪŋk] (AE)	*Oberbegriff für süße, kohlensäurehaltige Getränke wie Cola u.ä.*	
	(to) **provide** sth. **(for** sb.) [prə'vaɪd]	(jm.) etwas zur Verfügung stellen, (jm.) etwas bereitstellen	to give or supply something (to somebody) The company *~s* lunch *for* its employees.
	couple ['kʌpl]	(Ehe-)Paar	two people who are married, living together, etc.; two people who are together at some place

(p. 8)	auto mechanics *(sing.)* ['ɔ:təʊ mɪˌkænɪks] (AE)	Kfz-Technik	Jane likes to repair cars. She wants to take a course in ~ ~ next term.
	(to) **regret** [rɪ'gret], **-tt-**	bedauern, bereuen	to wish that one had not done something ⚠ *Wir bedauern, Ihnen mitteilen zu müssen, daß … = We regret to tell you that …* (fml.)
	°cheerleader ['tʃɪəli:də]	*jd., der die Zuschauer bei Sportveranstaltungen zum Beifall anfeuert*	
	try-out ['traɪaʊt] (AE)	Probe(vorstellung) *(bei einer Mannschaft usw.)*	a test to see if somebody is good enough to become a member of a band, a football team, etc.
	editor ['edɪtə]	Redakteur/in; Herausgeber/in	Ms Brown is responsible for all the articles on the sports page. She is our sports ~.
	coward ['kaʊəd]	Feigling	I'm afraid of going to the doctor. I'm a real ~.
	no matter what/ how/… ['mætə]	egal, was/wie/…	Don't buy anything, *no ~ what* the shop assistant tells you.

Focus on GRAMMAR

p. 9	highlight ['haɪlaɪt]	Höhepunkt	the best or most interesting part of something You can see the game's *~s* on TV again tonight.
	°place of interest [ˌpleɪs‿əv‿'ɪntrəst]	Sehenswürdigkeit	

Stress in compounds and noun phrases

Changing the stress can change the meaning. Compare:

the 'German ˌteacher	der Deutschlehrer/die Deutschlehrerin
the ˌGerman 'teacher	der deutsche Lehrer/die deutsche Lehrerin

Here are some more examples:

the 'bluefish	der Blaubarsch	**the 'visitors' book**	das Gästebuch
the ˌblue 'fish	der blaue Fisch	**the ˌvisitors' 'book**	das Buch der Gäste
the 'darkroom	die Dunkelkammer	**the 'White House**	das Weiße Haus
the ˌdark 'room	das dunkle Zimmer	**the ˌwhite 'house**	das weiße Haus
a 'greenhouse	ein Gewächshaus	**'Yellowstone**	Yellowstone*(park)*
a ˌgreen 'house	ein grünes Haus	**a ˌyellow 'stone**	ein gelber Stein

	incomplete [ˌɪnkəm'pli:t]	unvollständig, unvollendet, unfertig	not having all its parts ⧓ complete
	(to) **run** sth. [rʌn]	etwas leiten, führen, verwalten	Could you please tell me who your boss is? – That's Ms Adams. She ~s this organization.
	construction [kən'strʌkʃn]	Konstruktion *(eines Satzes)*	noun from "(to) construct" Find the sentences that contain participle *~s*.
p. 10	(to) **establish** [ɪ'stæblɪʃ]	herstellen *(Kontakt, Beziehung)*; gründen	The EU *has ~ed* good relations with Canada. The firm is over 100 years old. It *was ~ed* in 1893.
	°sophomore ['sɒfəmɔ:]	(US) *Schüler/in der 10. Klasse; Student/in im 2. Studienjahr*	
	°junior ['dʒu:njə]	(US) *Schüler/in der 11. Klasse; Student/in im 3. Studienjahr*	
	(to) be drunk [drʌŋk]	betrunken sein	After three bottles of beer, he *was* too ~ to drive home.
	(to) hit sb./sth. [hɪt], -tt-, – hit – hit	jn./etwas anfahren	The car ~ the dog, but it was not seriously injured.
	(to) **handle** ['hændl]	umgehen mit, fertig werden mit	I have a lot of problems, and I don't know how I'm going to ~ them all at once.

V

Unit 1

(p. 10)	**drug** [drʌg]	Droge, Rauschgift; Medikament	Heroin ['herəʊɪn] and cocaine [kəʊ'keɪn] are hard ~*s*. He has to take ~*s* for his heart problem. ⚠ *(to) be on drugs* = high sein; (regelmäßig) Drogen oder Medikamente nehmen *drugstore* (AE) = **1.** Apotheke; **2.** Drogerie
	inner city [ˌɪnə 'sɪtɪ]	innerstädtisches Wohngebiet *(mit sozialen und wirtschaftlichen Problemen)*	In the US, minority groups often live in the ~ *city*. Crime in the US is not just an ~*-city* problem.
	real [rɪəl] (AE, infml.)	sehr, äußerst	It's *real* cloudy. = Colloquial [kə'ləʊkwɪəl] *(umgangssprachlich)* for: It's very/really cloudy.
	Afro- ['æfrəʊ]	afro-, Afro-	*Afro*-American music is popular around the world.
	chemistry ['kemɪstrɪ]	Chemie	Marie Curie won the Nobel prize for ~ in 1911.
	°snail mail ['sneɪl meɪl] (slang)	Briefpost *(wörtlich: Schneckenpost)*	
p. 11	°freshman ['freʃmən]	(US) *Schüler/in der 9. Klasse; Student/in im 1. Studienjahr*	
	elementary school [ˌelɪ'mentərɪ sku:l]	(US) *(meist sechsjährige)* Grundschule	a school usually for the first six years of education
	schedule [BE: 'ʃedju:l; AE: 'skedʒu:l]	Zeitplan; AE *auch:* Stundenplan	a plan of work that must be done, for example ⚠ BE: *timetable*
	°requirement [rɪ'kwaɪəmənt] (AE)	Pflichtfach	
	°elective [ɪ'lektɪv] (AE)	Wahlfach	
	°shop [ʃɒp] (AE)	Werkunterricht	
	application *(meist sing.)* [ˌæplɪ'keɪʃn]	Anwendung	Does the scientist's work have any practical ~?
	extra-curricular activity [ˌekstrəkə'rɪkjʊlə]	außerunterrichtliche Aktivität, Arbeitsgemeinschaft	Clubs and sports are *extra-~ ~ies*. They take place after school.
	throughout [θru:'aʊt]	während des/der; überall in	It rained ~ the day. = It rained the whole day. ~ the land, the house, etc. = in every part of the land, the house, etc.
	association [əˌsəʊsɪ'eɪʃn]	Verband, Vereinigung; Assoziation	Sarah works for an ~ which helps deaf people. This school doesn't have pleasant ~s for me. I failed in maths.

Some sports at American high schools

baseball ['beɪsbɔ:l]	Baseball	°lacrosse [lə'krɒs]	Lacrosse *(Spiel, bei dem ein Ball mit Schlägern in ein Tor geschleudert wird)*
basketball	Basketball	soccer ['sɒkə]	Fußball
°cross country [ˌkrɒs 'kʌntrɪ]	Querfeldein*(lauf)*	track and field [ˌtræk‿ənd 'fi:ld]	Leichtathletik
°field hockey ['hɒkɪ]	Hockey	volleyball	Volleyball
football	Football	wrestling ['reslɪŋ]	Ringen
°golf [gɒlf]	Golf		
gymnastics	Turnen		

Focus on WORDS

p. 12	appearance *(meist sing.)* [ə'pɪərəns]	Aussehen, (äußere) Erscheinung; Auftreten, Erscheinen	noun from "(to) appear" the way that somebody or something looks; the arrival of somebody or something
	outgoing [ˌaʊt'gəʊɪŋ]	kontaktfreudig, extravertiert	▸◂ shy Julia is a very ~ ['---] girl. She doesn't mind talking to strangers. – I wish I was so [ˌ-'--].
	casual ['kæʒʊəl]	*(Person)* lässig, locker, gelassen; *(Situation, Kleidung usw.)* zwanglos, locker	▸◂ formal He seemed very ~ when he asked her to dance. Should I wear a tie to dinner? – No, it's a ~ affair.
	slim [slɪm]	schlank, dünn	thin, but not too thin ▸◂ fat

(p. 12)	gorgeous ['gɔːdʒəs]	hinreißend, prächtig	very beautiful
	(to) be familiar to sb. [fə'mɪlɪə]	jm. bekannt sein	to be well-known to somebody
	trait (of character) ['treɪt, BE *auch:* treɪ]	(Charakter-)Eigenschaft, (Wesens-)Zug	She is very honest. I think that is her most important ~.
	self-conscious [ˌself'kɒnʃəs]	unsicher, gehemmt	When I first got glasses, I was very *self-~*. ⧓ self-confident
	spoiled [spɔɪld]	verwöhnt, verzogen	As a child he got everything. That's why he is so ~.
	(to) spoil [spɔɪl] – spoilt/spoiled – spoilt/spoiled	*(Kinder)* verziehen; *(Personen)* verwöhnen; *(Landschaft, Stimmung usw.)* ruinieren, verderben	They give their son whatever he wants. They *are* really *~ing* him. The service in the hotel was excellent. We really enjoyed *being ~ed*. Birgit was robbed in Florida. That *~ed* her holiday.
	(to) **paint** [peɪnt]	malen; (an)streichen, lackieren	That is a beautiful picture. *Did* you ~ it? I'm moving, but I have to ~ my new flat first.
	paint [peɪnt]	Farbe *(zum Malen)*, Lack	noun from "(to) paint"
	painting ['peɪntɪŋ]	Gemälde	Mona Lisa is a ~ by Leonardo da Vinci.
	(to) **be fond of** sb./sth. [fɒnd]	jn./etwas mögen, gern haben	to like sb. very much, especially when you have known them for a long time; to like sth., especially sth. that you have liked for a long time

Focus on GRAMMAR

p. 13	It's up to you.	Es hängt von dir ab. Das überlasse ich dir.	Should we go to an Italian or a Chinese restaurant? – I don't care. *It's ~ to you.*
	(to) **mention** ['menʃn]	erwähnen	to say or write sth. about sb. or sth. Frank dropped French. – Yes, he *had ~ed* that to me.
	(to) **consider** [kən'sɪdə]	halten für, betrachten als	I'*d* always *~ed* Martha (to be) an outgoing person, but, in fact, she's a bit shy.

(to) consider

The teachers **consider** the editors of *Student Voice* (to be) well-informed students.	Die Lehrer **halten** die Redakteure von *Student Voice* **für** gut informierte Schüler/innen.
The editors **are considering** some changes in the layout.	Die Redakteure **ziehen** einige Veränderungen im Layout **in Erwägung**.
David **is considering** writing an article about the activities of SADD.	David **denkt darüber nach**, ob er einen Artikel über die Aktivitäten von SADD schreiben soll.
The *Student Voice* editors try to **take** the interests of their readers **into consideration**.	Die Redakteure von *Student Voice* bemühen sich, die Interessen ihrer Leserinnen und Leser zu **berücksichtigen**.

	reusable [riː'juːzəbl]	wiederverwendbar, wiederverwertbar	Something you can use again is ~.
	°styrofoam ['staɪrəfəʊm] (AE)	Styropor	
	(to) get rid of sb./sth. [ˌget 'rɪd‿əv]	jn./etwas loswerden	to become free of somebody or something. Our TV is so old. Let's *get ~ of* it and buy a new one.
1 Ex 1	notice-board ['nəʊtɪsbɔːd] (*meist* BE)	Schwarzes Brett, Anschlagtafel	The German Club put a note on the ~-~ to say when the next meeting is.
	°senior ['siːnɪə]	(US) *Schüler/in der 12. Klasse; Student/in im 4. Studienjahr*	
	(to) sunbathe ['sʌnbeɪð]	sonnenbaden	to sit or lie in the sun in order to make your skin go brown
2	absolutely ['æbsəluːtlɪ]	absolut, unbedingt	completely, totally
	unfit [ʌn'fɪt]	ungeeignet	My boss said I was totally ~ for the new office job.
	amusement [ə'mjuːzmənt]	Unterhaltung, Vergnügen	Our holiday camp offers young people a wide variety of *~s*.

Unit 1

Just for fun

p. 14	°eagle ['i:gl]	Adler	
	°stuck [stʌk]	festgeklemmt, festgeklebt	
	°centipede ['sentɪpi:d]	Tausendfüßler	
1 Ex 3	manuscript ['mænjʊskrɪpt]	Manuskript	The editor corrected all the spelling mistakes in the author's ~.
	violent ['vaɪələnt]	gewalttätig, brutal; heftig	adjective from "violence" Most people are afraid of ~ criminals. Some students have a ~ dislike of homework. ▸◂ calm, gentle, peaceful
	(to) **increase** [ɪn'kri:s]	zunehmen, ansteigen; erhöhen	Violent crime *~d* by 4% last year. The government plans to ~ the tax on petrol.
	(to) **ignore** sb./sth. [ɪg'nɔ:]	jn./etwas ignorieren, nicht beachten	to pay no attention to somebody/something Bill *~d* the doctor's advice and continued to smoke.
	(to) **pretend** [prɪ'tend]	so tun, als ob; vortäuschen	When I mentioned her name he *~ed* he knew her. I don't think Ann is asleep, I think she*'s ~ing*.
	physical punishment *(sing.)* [ˌfɪzɪkl 'pʌnɪʃmənt]	Körperstrafe, Prügelstrafe	Teachers are no longer allowed to hit their pupils – today ~ ~ is illegal in schools.
5	°telegraph ['telɪgrɑ:f]	Telegraf	
	°Morse code [ˌmɔ:s 'kəʊd]	Morsealphabet	
	professional *(adj.; n.)* [prə'feʃnəl]	Berufs-, professionell, Fach-; Berufssportler/in, Profi	Tennis is her full-time job. She is a ~ tennis player. a person who plays a sport for money; a person who does her/his work with skill
	°dot [dɒt]	Morsepunkt	
	°dash [dæʃ]	Morsestrich	
6	(to) modernize ['mɒdənaɪz]	modernisieren	to make more modern The subway system is very old. The city should ~ it.
	(to) **observe** [əb'zɜ:v]	beobachten, zusehen	to watch carefully

Verbs and nouns

(to) **amuse** [ə'mju:z]	(sich) amüsieren, unterhalten	(to) **edit** ['edɪt]	redigieren; herausgeben
amusement	Unterhaltung, Vergnügen	**editor**	Redakteur/in; Herausgeber/in
(to) **appear**	erscheinen, auftauchen; scheinen	(to) **observe**	beobachten, zusehen
appearance *(meist sing.)*	Aussehen, (äußere) Erscheinung; Auftreten, Erscheinen	**observation** [ˌɒbzə'veɪʃn]	Beobachtung
(to) **construct**	bauen, konstruieren	(to) **paint**	malen; (an)streichen, lackieren
construction	Konstruktion	**painting**	Gemälde
(to) **continue** (with)	fortfahren (mit), fortsetzen	(to) **reduce** [rɪ'dju:s]	verringern, reduzieren
continuation [kənˌtɪnjʊ'eɪʃn]	Fortsetzung, Fortdauer	**reduction** [rɪ'dʌkʃn]	Verringerung, Reduzierung
(to) **declare** [dɪ'kleə]	erklären, verkünden	(to) **rob**	berauben, ausrauben
declaration [ˌdeklə'reɪʃn]	Erklärung	**robbery** ['rɒbərɪ]	Raub(überfall)
		(to) **understand**	verstehen, begreifen
		understanding	Verständnis

(to) make a mess [mes]	Unordnung/Dreck machen	The kitchen is really dirty now. I didn't think cooking a Chinese meal would *make* such *a* ~.
separate ['seprət]	einzeln, getrennt	England and Scotland are two ~ countries. ⚠ *Aussprache:* (to) separate ['sepəreɪt] – separate ['seprət]

p. 17

Verbs + *to*-infinitive

Barry **decided** to do his homework later.
She **expects** to finish the article tomorrow.

Karen **wants** to go shopping on Saturday.
We **aren't allowed** to talk during tests.

Nach diesen Verben steht der ***to*-Infinitiv**:

agree	zustimmen	**decide**	sich entscheiden, beschließen
arrange	vereinbaren	**expect**	erwarten
choose	beschließen	**hope**	hoffen
learn	lernen	**refuse**	sich weigern
offer	anbieten	**try**	versuchen
plan	planen, vorhaben	**want**	wollen
promise	versprechen	**would like**	gern *(tun/sein)* wollen
seem	*(zu sein/tun)* scheinen	**would love**	sehr gern *(tun/sein)* wollen

Der *to*-Infinitiv steht außerdem immer in Verbindung mit den modalen Ersatzverben:

be able to do	tun können	**have** to do	tun müssen
be allowed to do	tun dürfen		

Verbs + *-ing* Form

My sister **enjoys** watching soap operas.
Have you **finished** tidying up your room?

The children **didn't mind** playing in the rain.
I don't **miss** playing tennis.

Nach diesen Verben steht die ***-ing form***:

avoid	vermeiden	**like***	gern tun, mögen
begin*	anfangen	**love***	sehr gern tun
continue*	weitermachen (mit)	**mind**	etwas dagegen haben
dislike	nicht mögen, nicht gern tun	**miss**	vermissen, versäumen
enjoy	sehr gern tun, genießen	**practise**	üben
finish	beenden, aufhören (mit)	**prefer***	lieber tun, vorziehen
give up	aufgeben, aufhören (mit)	**quit**	aufhören (mit)
go on	weitermachen (mit)	**risk**	wagen, riskieren
hate*	sehr ungern tun	**start***	anfangen
imagine	sich *(etwas)* vorstellen	**stop**	aufhören (mit)
keep (on)	weiter tun, weiter…	**suggest**	vorschlagen

Nach den Verben, die mit einem * gekennzeichnet sind, kann bei gleicher Bedeutung auch der *to*-Infinitiv stehen:

It **started** **raining**. / **to rain**.

Beachte, daß die *-ing form* nach einigen Verben auch ein „eigenes Subjekt" haben kann:

I don't **like** | **Peter** / **him** **using** my car. — *Ich mag (es) nicht, daß Peter mein Auto benutzt.*

In formellem Englisch wird auch der *s*-Genitiv bzw. ein *possessive adjective* verwendet:

I don't **like** | **Peter's** / **his** **using** my car.

battery ['bætrɪ]	Batterie	I need two new *~ies* for my personal stereo.

1 Text Waiting

p. 18

(to) **speculate (about, on)** ['spekjʊleɪt]	spekulieren (über)	Although nobody knows what went on at the meeting, the papers *are ~ing about* what was said.
What's going through her mind? [maɪnd]	Was geht ihr durch den Kopf? Woran denkt sie?	Do you know *what* just *went through my ~?* = Do you know what I just thought?
as far as I'm concerned [kən'sɜːnd]	meiner Meinung nach, was mich betrifft	You can keep your stupid book *as far as I'm ~*. ⚠ *Betonung:* You should stress the word "I'm".
bow tie [ˌbəʊ 'taɪ]	(Frack-)Schleife, Fliege	

V

Unit 1

p. 19	(to) fill up [ˌfɪl‿ˈʌp]	(sich) füllen, vollfüllen	to become or make something completely full
	thankful [ˈθæŋkfəl]	dankbar	After a week of rain we were ~ when it stopped.
	schoolyard [ˈsku:ljɑ:d]	Schulhof	an area of land next to the school buildings where pupils can play between lessons
	(to) **ask** sb. **out** [ˌɑ:sk‿ˈaʊt]	jn. einladen *(ins Kino, zum Essen usw.)*	Pat likes Carl, but she's too shy to ~ him *out*.
	pity (for) [ˈpɪtɪ]	Mitleid, Mitgefühl (mit)	Thousands of people are dying. Have you no ~? ⚠ *(to) feel pity for sb.* = mit jm. Mitleid haben
	Cheer up! [ˌtʃɪər‿ˈʌp]	Kopf hoch! Laß den Kopf nicht hängen!	You look so sad today. *Cheer ~!* Today is Friday and there is no school tomorrow.
	(to) cheer sb. up	jn. aufmuntern, aufheitern	to make somebody happier
	°on the house	auf Kosten des Hauses	
	(to) **empty** [ˈemptɪ]	(sich) (ent)leeren	▸◂ (to) fill
	°skating-rink [ˈskeɪtɪŋrɪŋk]	Schlittschuhbahn; Rollschuhbahn	
	(to) dress up [ˌdres‿ˈʌp]	sich feinmachen; sich verkleiden	It's a formal dinner, so we'll have to *dress* ~. For the party I'm going to *dress* ~ as a pirate.
	°lipstick [ˈlɪpstɪk]	Lippenstift	
	°passion [ˈpæʃn]	Leidenschaft	
	tragic [ˈtrædʒɪk]	tragisch	At the end of the film the hero died. It was ~.
	playfully [ˈpleɪfəlɪ]	neckisch, schelmisch	
	That's news to me. [nju:z]	Das ist mir neu.	There is an English test tomorrow. – *That's ~ to me.*
	news *(sing.)*	Neuigkeit(en)	Have you heard the ~? We're getting a new teacher. ⚠ *news* = **1.** Nachricht(en); **2.** Neuigkeit(en)
	(to) be in one's right mind (infml.)	bei (klarem) Verstand sein	Have you heard the news? Kevin wants to swim across the Channel. – He can't *be in his ~ ~*.

Phrases with "mind"

I'm using your personal stereo. **Do you mind**?	… **Hast du etwas dagegen (einzuwenden)**?
Where are you going on holiday? – To Ireland. I've finally **made up my mind**.	… – Nach Irland. Ich habe **mich** endlich **entschieden**.
He gave all his money to charity. Do you think he's still **in his right mind**?	… Glaubst du, daß er noch **bei (klarem) Verstand** ist?
Have you thought about doing your homework? – Yes, that thought **has gone through my mind**.	… Ja. Der Gedanke **ist mir** (schon) **durch den Kopf gegangen**.
Is your decision final? – Yes, nothing can **change my mind**.	… – Ja. Nichts kann **meine Meinung** (noch) **ändern**.
This is not a quiz. Just say what **comes into your mind**.	… Sag einfach, was **dir** (gerade) **einfällt**.
I forgot to bring your CD. – **Never mind**.	… – **Macht nichts**.
After I lost my job I was in a terrible **state of mind**.	… in einer schlimmen **(geistigen) Verfassung**.

	thoughtful [ˈθɔ:tfəl]	rücksichtsvoll, aufmerksam; nachdenklich	Thank you for your kind card. That was very ~ of you. She looked ~ for a moment. Then she began to write.
	(to) **deserve** [dɪˈzɜ:v]	verdienen, Anspruch haben auf	After learning so many new words you ~ a break.
	similarity (to) [ˌsɪməˈlærətɪ]	Ähnlichkeit (mit)	noun from "similar"
p. 20	**narrator** [nəˈreɪtə]	Erzähler/in	person who tells a story, especially in a book ⚠ *act<u>or</u>, doct<u>or</u>, edit<u>or</u>, narrat<u>or</u>, sail<u>or</u>*
	graph [grɑ:f]	(Kurven-)Diagramm, graphische Darstellung	The ~ shows how the world population has grown since 1900.
	emotion [ɪˈməʊʃn]	Gefühl, Emotion	a strong feeling such as love, fear, hate, etc.
	oral [ˈɔ:rəl]	mündlich	▸◂ written Everyone passed the ~ part of the test.
	portrait [ˈpɔ:trət]	Porträt, Bild	a picture, painting or photograph of somebody; a description of somebody or something in words

(p. 20.)	storyline ['stɔːrɪlaɪn]	Handlung *(einer Erzählung)*	the plot [plɒt] of a story
	point of view [ˌpɔɪnt‿əv 'vjuː]	(Erzähl-)Standpunkt, (Erzähl-)Perspektive	perspective [pə'spektɪv] from which the topics, characters and events in a text are presented; an opinion, a way of looking at a situation
	°(to) appeal to [ə'piːl]	ansprechen, gefallen	
	taste [teɪst]	Geschmack	noun from "(to) taste" I like Steven's new sofa. – Yes, he has very good ~.

The last dance of the year

p. 20	°apart from [ə'pɑːt]	außer, abgesehen von	°committee [kə'mɪtɪ]	Ausschuß, Komitee
	°academic [ˌækə'demɪk]	*hier:* schulisch	°fundraiser ['fʌndreɪzə]	Spendenaktion, Aktivität zum Geldsammeln
	°practical ['præktɪkl]	praktisch		
	°prom [prɒm]	(US) *Schüler-/Studentenball*	°usher ['ʌʃə]	Platzanweiser/in
			°coronation [ˌkɒrə'neɪʃn]	Krönung
	°tuxedo [tʌk'siːdəʊ] (AE)	Smoking	°donut ['dəʊnʌt] (AE)	Berliner (Pfannkuchen)

Unit 2: Washington, D.C.

p. 21	°logo ['ləʊgəʊ]	Logo, Emblem	
	°foundation [faʊn'deɪʃn]	Stiftung	
	(to) be based in … [beɪst]	seinen (Firmen-)Sitz in … haben	Where is Pam working now? – In Paris. She*'s been ~ in* Paris for a year now.
	(to) **govern** ['gʌvən]	herrschen über, regieren	In Africa poverty *~s* the lives of many people. The US *is ~ed* by a president.
	°(to) mean to do sth. [miːn]	vorhaben, etwas zu tun	
	°governor ['gʌvənə]	*hier:* Herrscher/in	
	°(to) arm oneself with sth. [ɑːm]	sich mit etwas wappnen, rüsten	
	headquarters *(pl.)* [ˌhed'kwɔːtəz]	Zentrale, Hauptgeschäftsstelle; Hauptquartier	the place from which an organization is controlled Where are the firm's ~? – In New York, I believe. The president flew to army ~ to talk to his generals.

Washington sights and institutions

the White House ['waɪt haʊs] das Weiße Haus *(offizielle Residenz des Präsidenten/der Präsidentin der USA)*

the Oval Office [ˌəʊvl‿'ɒfɪs] „das ovale Büro" *(Amtszimmer des Präsidenten/der Präsidentin im Weißen Haus)*

Congress ['kɒŋgres] der Kongreß *(Parlament, bestehend aus Senat und Repräsentantenhaus)*

the House of Representatives [ˌreprɪ'zentətɪvz], (infml.:) **the House** das Repräsentantenhaus

the Senate ['senɪt] der Senat

Capitol Hill [ˌkæpɪtl 'hɪl], (infml.:) **the Hill** „der Kapitolsberg" *(Kongreßgebäude)*

the Pentagon ['pentəgɒn] „das Fünfeck" *(Sitz des US-Verteidigungsministeriums)*

the Supreme Court [sʊˌpriːm 'kɔːt] *der Oberste Gerichtshof in den USA*

the FBI [ˌef biː 'aɪ] **(Federal Bureau of Investigation)** [ˌfedrəl ˌbjʊərəʊ əv‿ɪnˌvestɪ'geɪʃn] *US-Bundeskriminalamt*

the Washington Monument [ˌwɒʃɪŋtən 'mɒnjʊmənt] *170 m hoher Obelisk zu Ehren George Washingtons (1732-1799)*

the Lincoln Memorial [ˌlɪŋkən mə'mɔːrɪəl] *Gedenkstätte zu Ehren Abraham Lincolns (1809-1865)*

Arlington National Cemetery [ˌɑːlɪŋtən ˌnæʃnəl 'semətrɪ] *Nationalfriedhof der USA (mit dem Grab des Unbekannten Soldaten)*

the Vietnam Veterans Memorial [viːetˌnæm ˌvetərənz mə'mɔːrɪəl] *Gedenkstätte für die im Vietnamkrieg (1964-1975) gefallenen oder vermißten amerikanischen Soldaten*

the Smithsonian Institution [smɪθˌsəʊnɪən‿ˌɪnstɪ'tjuːʃn] *Forschungseinrichtung mit Museen, Bibliotheken und Observatorium*

the (National) Mall [mɔːl] *parkähnliche Promenade zwischen Capitol und Lincoln Memorial*

Unit 2

(p. 21)	military ['mɪlɪtərɪ]	militärisch, Militär-	adjective used to talk about soldiers, armies or war
	magnificent [mæg'nɪfɪsənt]	prächtig, herrlich	wonderful, gorgeous The view from the top of the building is truly ~. ⧓ bad, ordinary
	yard [jɑ:d]	Yard *(= ca. 91,4 cm)*	

Length [leŋθ] = Länge(nmaße)

1 inch (in.) [ɪntʃ]	= 2.540 cm
1 foot (ft.) (= 12 inches)	= 0.305 m
1 yard (yd.) (= 3 feet)	= 0.914 m
1 mile (m.) (= 1,760 yards)	= 1.609 km

Focus on GRAMMAR

p. 22	senator ['senətə]	Senator/in	a member of the Senate Each state sends two *~s* to the US Senate.
	talk (about, on) [tɔ:k]	Vortrag, Rede (über)	The MP's ~ *on* the economy was broadcast on TV. ⚠ *eine Rede halten = (to) give a talk*
	°conference ['kɒnfrəns]	*hier: (Lehrer- usw.)* Verband	
	reform [rɪ'fɔ:m]	Reform	a change in something in order to make it better
	participant (in) [pɑ:'tɪsɪpənt]	Teilnehmer/in (an)	a person who takes part in an activity How many *~s in* the course were there?
	democracy [dɪ'mɒkrəsɪ]	Demokratie	a system of government in which the people choose the government by voting ⚠ *Aussprache:* democratic [ˌdemə'krætɪk] democracy [dɪ'mɒkrəsɪ]
	at one time or another	irgendwann (einmal)	All my friends have used this product *at one ~ or ~*.
	constitution [ˌkɒnstɪ'tju:ʃn]	Verfassung	the (system of) laws of a country Most democracies have a written ~.
	(to) fail to do sth. [feɪl]	etwas nicht tun (können); versäumen, etwas zu tun	A new government could not be formed because the party leaders *~ed to* agree on major political issues.
	(to) meet [mi:t] – met [met] – met	*(Anforderungen usw.)* gerecht werden, entsprechen	We saw the film, but it failed to ~ our expectations. ⚠ *(to) meet* = **1.** sich treffen; *(jn.)* treffen; *(jn.)* kennenlernen; **2.** *(Anforderungen usw.)* gerecht werden, entsprechen
	basic ['beɪsɪk]	grundlegend, Grund-	For this course you need a ~ knowledge of physics.
	(to) water sth. down [ˌwɔ:tə 'daʊn]	etwas verwässern, abschwächen	to change a report, a statement, etc. so that it is weaker
	speech (on, about) [spi:tʃ]	Vortrag, Rede (über)	a formal talk given to a (large) group of people ⚠ *eine Rede halten = (to) give/make a speech*
p. 23	**objective** [əb'dʒektɪv]	objektiv	not influenced by personal feelings, based on facts
	seminar (on) ['semɪnɑ:]	Seminar (über)	a class at a university, college, etc. in which a group of students discuss or study sth. with a teacher
	thrilled [θrɪld]	begeistert	pleased and excited about something ⧓ bored
	educational [ˌedjʊ'keɪʃnəl]	pädagogisch; Lehr-, Bildungs-	adjective from "education"
	(to) be valid ['vælɪd]	gültig sein	They were not allowed to get on the plane because their passports *were* no longer ~.
p. 24	section ['sekʃn]	Teil, Ausschnitt	This ~ of the book examines the US political system.
	layout ['leɪaʊt]	Anordnung, Anlage; Layout	For the architect the ~ of the rooms was important. Have you noticed that the magazine has a new ~?
	(to) **reflect** [rɪ'flekt]	(wider)spiegeln; reflektieren	Her choice of cars *~ed* her social position. White cars ~ light better than black cars.
	(to) **connect (to, with)** [kə'nekt]	verbinden (mit)	to link This highway *~s* Dunlap *with* Chicago.
	recent ['ri:snt]	jüngste(r, s), neueste(r, s)	having happened or been done a short time ago Surveys show that ~ political reforms are popular. ⧓ old
	(to) **be involved (in)** [ɪn'vɒlvd]	etwas zu tun haben (mit), beteiligt sein (an)	Some people think that he *is ~ in* criminal activities.

(p. 24)	(to) **get involved (in)**	verwickelt, hineingezogen werden (in); sich engagieren (bei), beteiligen (an)	We *got ~ in* a fight with our neighbours about the president's talk. Do you think that churches should *get* more *~ in* politics?
	duty ['dju:tɪ]	Pflicht	(legal) obligation, task that you have to do
p. 25	**gas** [gæs]	Gas	Helium ['hi:lɪəm] is a ~.
	rate [reɪt]	*(Wachstums-, Inflations- usw.)*Rate	Washington has the highest murder ~ in the nation. ⚠ *exchange rate* = Wechselkurs

Focus on WORDS

p. 26	**chancellor** ['tʃɑ:nsələ]	Kanzler/in	Adenauer was ~ from 1949 to 1963. ⚠ (in GB:) *the Chancellor* (short for "the Chancellor of the Exchequer" [ɪks'tʃekə]) = der/die Finanzminister/in
	(to) **represent** [ˌreprɪ'zent]	vertreten, repräsentieren; darstellen	In democracies elected politicians ~ the interests of their voters in parliament. Phonetic [fə'netɪk] symbols ~ sounds.
	(to) **elect** sb. (sth.) [ɪ'lekt]	jn. (zu etwas) wählen	to choose somebody for a position by voting Abraham Lincoln *was ~ed* president in 1860. ⚠ *(to) choose sth.* = etwas auswählen *(to) elect sb. sth.* = jn. zu etwas wählen *(to) vote for* = jn. wählen, jm. seine Stimme geben, (ab)stimmen für
	House of Commons ['kɒmənz]	(GB) das britische Unterhaus	In Britain, MPs are elected to the *House of ~* for five years.
	House of Lords [lɔ:dz]	(GB) das britische Oberhaus	The *House of ~* is a separate and less powerful part of the British parliament.
	(to) abolish [ə'bɒlɪʃ]	abschaffen; *(ein Gesetz)* aufheben	Some students would like to ~ all tests. This law is unfair and parliament should ~ it.
	capitalism ['kæpɪtəlɪzəm]	Kapitalismus	economic system in which businesses are owned by individuals who want to make a profit
	communism ['kɒmjʊnɪzəm]	Kommunismus	▸◂ capitalism Eastern European ~ did not survive the 1980s.

Political parties

In the US there are two large political parties, the **Democratic Party** and the **Republican** [rɪ'pʌblɪkən] **Party**. Since the Civil War (1861-1865) all the presidents have been either **Democrats** ['deməkræts] or **Republicans**.

In den USA gibt es zwei große politische Parteien, die **Demokratische Partei** und die **Republikanische Partei**. Seit dem Bürgerkrieg (1861-1865) waren alle Präsidenten entweder **Demokraten** oder **Republikaner**.

⚠ In some other countries there are also parties that call themselves "Republicans". However, that does not mean that these parties have similar ideas to the Republican Party in the US.

Since World War II all prime ministers in Britain have belonged either to the **Conservative** [kən'sɜ:vətɪv] **Party** or to the **Labour** ['leɪbə] **Party**. The **Liberals** ['lɪbrəlz] and the **Social Democratic Party** formed a new party in 1988, the **Liberal Democrats**.

Seit dem 2. Weltkrieg gehörten alle Premierminister in Großbritannien entweder zur **Konservativen Partei** oder zur **Labour Party** *(wörtl.: „Arbeitspartei")*. Die **Liberalen** und die **Sozialdemokratische Partei** gründeten 1988 eine neue Partei, die **Liberaldemokraten**.

In democracies voters can generally vote for parties with **conservative**, **liberal**, **socialist** ['səʊʃəlɪst] or **communist** ['kɒmjʊnɪst] tendencies.

In Demokratien können Wähler im allgemeinen Parteien mit **konservativen**, **liberalen**, **sozialistischen** oder **kommunistischen** Tendenzen wählen.

dictatorship [dɪk'teɪtəʃɪp]	Diktatur	▸◂ democracy government by a leader who has total power
equality [ɪ'kwɒlətɪ]	Gleichheit	The senator supports ~ between the sexes.
opposition (to) [ˌɒpə'zɪʃn]	Opposition, Widerstand (gegen)	The plan to increase taxes is unpopular. In fact, *~ to* the government's plan is growing every day. ⚠ (in GB:) *the Opposition* = die Opposition(spartei/en)

(p. 26)	monarchy ['mɒnəkɪ]	Monarchie	state ruled by a king or queen
	minister ['mɪnɪstə]	Minister/in	Last night I dreamt that the ~ of education was going to get rid of final exams.

Ministerien und Minister/innen in Großbritannien und den USA

GB	US	
ministry ['mɪnɪstrɪ], **department**	**department, ministry**	Ministerium
secretary of state ['sekrətrɪ], **minister**	**secretary** [AE: 'sekrəteri:]	Minister/in
– **Foreign (and Commonwealth) Office**	– **Department of State/State Department**	– Außenministerium
• **Foreign Secretary**	• **Secretary of State**	• Außenminister/in
– **Home Office**	– **Department of the Interior** [ɪn'tɪərɪə]	– Innenministerium
• **Home Secretary**	• **Secretary of the Interior**	• Innenminister/in
– **Department of Employment**	– **Department of Labor** ['leɪbə]	– Arbeitsministerium
• **Employment Secretary**	• **Secretary of Labor**	• Arbeitsminister/in
– **Treasury** ['treʒərɪ]	– **Department of the Treasury/ Treasury Department**	– Finanzministerium
• **Chancellor of the Exchequer** [ɪks'tʃekə]	• **Secretary of the Treasury**	• Finanzminister/in
– **Department of Trade and Industry**	– **Department of Commerce/ Commerce Department**	– Wirtschaftsministerium
• **Trade (and Industry) Secretary**	• **Secretary of Commerce** ['kɒmɜ:s]	• Wirtschaftsminister/in
– **Ministry of Defence** [dɪ'fens]	– **Department of Defense/ Defense Department**	– Verteidigungsministerium
• **Defence Secretary**	• **Secretary of Defense**	• Verteidigungsminister/in

⚠ Wenn man über Minister/innen **anderer Länder** spricht, benutzt man „foreign minister", „minister of the interior", „minister of finance", „minister of commerce", „defence minister" usw.
Example: The European foreign ministers met in Brussels last week.

V

	candidate (for) ['kændɪdeɪt]	Kandidat/in (für)	We have three very good *~s for* the job.
	coalition [ˌkəʊə'lɪʃn]	Koalition	the joining of two or more political parties to form a government, for example
	(to) reform [rɪ'fɔ:m]	reformieren	verb from "reform"
	brilliant ['brɪljənt]	brillant, genial	Newton was a ~ scientist. ⧓ ordinary, simple, stupid
2 Ex 1	**summary** ['sʌmərɪ]	Zusammenfassung	After you have read the story write a short ~.
	°item ['aɪtəm]	*hier:* Titel *(Bücher usw.)*	
	librarian ['laɪbreərɪən]	Bibliothekar/in	If you can't find a book in the library, ask the ~.
2	°jumbled ['dʒʌmbld]	durcheinandergewürfelt	
	whereas [weər'æz]	wohingegen, während	in contrast, while Sue likes Chinese food, ~ Mike likes Italian food.
3	in time	rechtzeitig	She got to the airport just *in ~* to catch her flight and she managed to arrive at the meeting on time. ⚠ *on time* = pünktlich, zur angegebenen Zeit
4	far-reaching [ˌfɑ:'ri:tʃɪŋ]	weitreichend, folgenschwer	having, or going to have, a great influence on a lot of other things
	(to) **raise** [reɪz]	erhöhen; (hoch)heben	to increase something; to lift something ⚠ *(to) raise a question* = eine Frage aufwerfen, vorbringen
	gasoline ['gæsəli:n] (AE)	Benzin	BE petrol = AE gasoline, gas

2 Ex 5

Verbal expressions in English – adverbs in German

You already know many verbal expressions like the following which are translated as adverbs in German:

Senator Dawson **seems to** speak to Close Up students almost every year./It **seems** (that) he speaks to Close Up students almost every year.	Senator Dawson spricht **anscheinend** fast jedes Jahr mit Close Up-Schülern und Schülerinnen.
He **enjoys** talking to the students.	Er redet **gern** mit den Schülern und Schülerinnen.

Here are some more examples:

He **is said to be** a very good speaker.	Er ist **angeblich** ein sehr guter Redner.
Do you **happen to** know what the senator will talk about?	Weißt du **zufällig**, worüber der Senator sprechen wird?
He **is likely to** talk about how we can improve our schools.	Er wird **wahrscheinlich** darüber sprechen, wie wir unsere Schulen verbessern können.
Our teachers **are certain to** inform us if he can't come on Friday.	Unsere Lehrer/innen werden uns **bestimmt** informieren, falls er am Freitag nicht kommen kann.

6	space [speɪs]	Weltraum; Raum, Platz	the area outside the Earth's atmosphere; an area that is empty or not used
	moon [muːn]	Mond	Neil Armstrong was the first man to walk on the ~.
	(to) **touch** [tʌtʃ]	berühren, anfassen	to put your hand or fingers on sb./sth., for example *Don't ~* the plate – it's very hot.
	rock [rɒk] (AE)	Stein	The astronauts brought back ~*s* from the moon. ⚠ *rock* = **1.** Fels(en); **2.** (AE) Stein

Words Words Words

p. 30	common ['kɒmən]	häufig, weitverbreitet	"Meyer" is a very ~ name in Germany. ▸◂ rare, unusual
	(to) predict [prɪ'dɪkt]	voraussagen, vorhersagen	to say what will happen in the future (because you have special knowledge)
	exclusively [ɪk'skluːsɪvlɪ]	ausschließlich	I seem to be spending my free time almost ~ in front of the TV. I suppose I should get active.

2 Text How will you vote, Senator?

p. 31	**aid** [eɪd]	Hilfe, Unterstützung	help, support Many developing countries need more ~. ⚠ *foreign aid* = Entwicklungshilfe
	weapon ['wepən]	Waffe	thing designed or used to hurt or kill people
	(to) retrain [riː'treɪn]	umschulen	After he lost his job he *was ~ed*. Now he is a cook.
	(to) **train** [treɪn]	ausbilden, schulen; trainieren	to learn the skills you need for a particular job Tracy is in the gym. She ~*s* five days a week.
	(to) **attend** [ə'tend]	besuchen, teilnehmen an *(Kurs, Schule usw.)*	to go to (a place) My family ~*s* church regularly. ⚠ *jn. besuchen = (to) visit sb.*
	luckily ['lʌkɪlɪ]	glücklicherweise, zum Glück	adverb from "lucky"
	close [kləʊs]	knapp *(Sieg, Ergebnis)*	The election was very ~, but our candidate won. ⚠ *Aussprache:* close [kləʊs] – (to) close [kləʊz]
	indeed [ɪn'diːd]	in der Tat, tatsächlich	Isn't that a strange story? – Yes, ~.
	°(to) lobby sb./for sth. ['lɒbɪ]	*(auf Politiker)* Einfluß nehmen/etwas durchzusetzen versuchen *(Antrag, Gesetz)*	
	inn [ɪn]	Gasthaus, kleines Hotel	a word often used in the names of pubs or small hotels, especially old ones
	industrialist [ɪn'dʌstrɪəlɪst]	Industrielle(r)	owner or manager of a large industrial company
	campaign [kæm'peɪn]	Wahlkampf; (Werbe-) Kampagne	He was elected because he had a good (election) ~. Please support our ~ against nuclear weapons.

V

Unit 2

p. 32	**Congratulations (on** sth.)! *(pl.)* [kən,grætʃʊ'leɪʃnz]	Herzlichen Glückwunsch (zu etwas)!	You won the election? *C~*! *C~ on* passing your exam! ⚠ *(to) offer sb. one's congratulations* (fml.) = jm. gratulieren, jn. beglückwünschen ⚠ *Herzlichen Glückwunsch zum Geburtstag!* = *Happy birthday!*
	(to) **congratulate** sb. **(on** sth.) [kən'grætʃʊleɪt]	jm. (zu etwas) gratulieren	We *~d* her *on* winning first prize.
	foreign policy [,fɒrən 'pɒləsɪ]	Außenpolitik	The State Department is responsible for defining America's *foreign ~*.
	contract ['kɒntrækt]	Vertrag	He was given a two-year ~ by the New York Giants.
	(to) adapt (to) [ə'dæpt]	(sich) anpassen (an)	Klaus could not ~ *to* the hot climate in Arizona.
	(to) restructure [,riː'strʌktʃə]	umstrukturieren	To ~ a business, for example, means to reorganize it. In times of economic crisis many firms *are ~ed*.
	(to) shut down [,ʃʌt 'daʊn] – shut – shut	zumachen, schließen *(Fabrik usw.)*	Business was so bad that the small bakery had to ~ *down*.
	(to) **remain** [rɪ'meɪn]	bleiben; übrigbleiben	to stay in the same place or condition, to not change; to be left after other people or things have gone
p. 33	unbearable [ʌn'beərəbl]	unerträglich	Today must be the hottest day of the year. – Yes, the heat is ~.
	(to) proceed [prə'siːd] (fml.)	vorgehen, verfahren; fortfahren	How should the government ~ in this case? After a short break we *~ed* with our work.
	(to) **praise (for)** [preɪz]	loben (für, wegen)	Ms Walker *~d* her students *for* their good work.

Verbs and nouns with the same form

(to) **aid** sb.	jm. helfen	(to) **progress** ⚠ [prəʊ'gres]	vorankommen, Fortschritte machen
aid	Hilfe, Unterstützung	**progress** ⚠ ['prəʊgres]	Fortschritt(e)
(to) **boycott** ['--]	boykottieren	(to) **reform**	reformieren
boycott	Boykott	**reform**	Reform
(to) **experience**	erfahren, erleben	(to) **reward**	belohnen
experience	Erfahrung, Erlebnis	**reward**	Belohnung, Finderlohn
(to) **hate**	hassen, gar nicht mögen	(to) **schedule**	anberaumen *(Sitzung)*, planen
hate	Haß	**schedule**	Zeitplan; AE *auch:* Stundenplan
(to) **increase** ⚠ [ɪn'kriːs]	zunehmen, ansteigen; erhöhen	(to) **talk** (about)	reden, sprechen (über)
increase (in) ⚠ ['ɪŋkriːs]	Zunahme, Anstieg (von); Erhöhung	**talk** (about, on)	Vortrag, Rede (über)
(to) **paint**	malen; (an)streichen	(to) **taste**	1. schmecken; 2. probieren, kosten
paint	Farbe *(zum Malen)*, Lack	**taste**	Geschmack
(to) **permit** ⚠ [pə'mɪt]	erlauben, gestatten	(to) **worry**	sich Sorgen machen
permit ⚠ ['pɜːmɪt]	Genehmigung(sschein), *(schriftliche)* Erlaubnis	**worry**	Sorge; Unruhe
(to) **praise** (for)	loben (für, wegen)		
praise	Lob		

	(to) **criticize (for)** ['krɪtɪsaɪz]	kritisieren (wegen)	to say what is bad or wrong with sb. or sth. ⧓ (to) praise (for) ⚠ *critical* ['krɪtɪkl] – *(to) criticize* ['krɪtɪsaɪz]

The birth of a capital

p. 33	°none (of) [nʌn]	keine(r, s) (von)
	°bank [bæŋk]	Ufer *(eines Flusses)*
	°branch [brɑːntʃ]	Zweig

Unit 3: Blacks in the USA

Song: Free at last

p. 34	°(al)mighty [ɔːl'maɪtɪ]	(all)mächtig	
	°yonder ['jɒndə]	dort drüben	
	graveyard ['greɪvjɑːd]	Friedhof	an area of land where dead people are buried
	°walk [wɔːk]	(Wander-)Weg	
	fair [feə]	heiter, schön *(Wetter)*	After a week of rain, we will have ~ weather today. ⚠ *fair* = **1.** gerecht, fair; **2.** heiter, schön *(Wetter)*

I have a dream

p. 35	°brotherhood ['brʌðəhʊd]	Brüderlichkeit	
	(to) **judge (by/from)** [dʒʌdʒ]	beurteilen (nach)	People *are* often *~d by* their appearance.
	content ['kɒntent]	Gehalt, Inhalt *(einer Rede, eines Buches usw.)*	The politician gave a long speech about violence in society. However, not everyone in her party agreed with the ~ of her speech.
	contents *(pl.)*	Inhalt *(von Behältnissen, Räumen usw.)*	At the airport the ~ of my suitcase were examined. ⚠ *table of contents* = Inhaltsverzeichnis
	°molehill ['məʊlhɪl]	Maulwurfshügel	
	(to) join hands [dʒɔɪn 'hændz]	sich die Hände reichen	to hold each other's hands Hundreds *joined* ~ to form a chain across the bridge.

Terms used in the US to refer to blacks and members of other minorities

In the 1960s the slogan "black is beautiful" became popular in the black community. It expressed a new pride[1] in black identity, history and culture. Since then ***black*** – a noun and an adjective – is the term that is used most often when referring to a person of African origin in the United States (and in Britain). It is also the term used by the black community itself.

Today, many Americans, both black and white, also use the term ***African American*** *(n.; adj.)* when referring to black Americans.

The term ***people of color*** is used in formal situations to refer to members or groups of non-European origin (e.g. black people, Asians, Native Americans). Some people think that this term should be used – and not 'minority' or 'minorities' – because these groups are not in the minority in many parts of America.

[1] [praɪd] Stolz

In 1940, the **African American** author Richard Wright wrote a novel about a 19-year-old **black** in Chicago who kills a white woman.	1940 schrieb der **afroamerikanische** Autor Richard Wright einen Roman über einen 19jährigen **Schwarzen** in Chicago, der eine weiße Frau tötet.
The book became a bestseller, the first written by an **African American**.	Das Buch wurde ein Bestseller – der erste von einem **Afroamerikaner**.
In the following years other **black** writers also wrote books attacking racism.	In den folgenden Jahren schrieben andere **schwarze** Schriftsteller Bücher, die … .
A well-known writer in the *Times* wrote that most authors today deal mainly with the white middle class. They should also be dealing with the problems of the poor and **people of color**.	… Diese Schriftsteller sollten sich auch mit den Problemen der Armen und der **farbigen Minderheiten/der Farbigen** befassen.

⚠ The term *Negro*, pl. *Negroes* ['niːgrəʊ] should be avoided except in special, historical contexts like 'negro spiritual'.

Historical timeline

p. 34	°servant ['sɜːvənt]	Diener/in	
	tobacco [tə'bækəʊ]	Tabak	Europeans have been smoking ~ for centuries.
	slavery ['sleɪvərɪ]	Sklaverei	condition of being a slave By the early 1800s, the northern states had ended ~.

Unit 3

(p. 34)	°the Union ['ju:njən]	*1. historische Bezeichnung für die USA; 2. die Nordstaaten (im Bürgerkrieg)*	
	basis ['beɪsɪs], *pl.* **bases** ['beɪsi:z]	Grundlage, Basis	They say love is the ~ of a good marriage. She works for us on a part-time ~.
	(to) **free** [fri:]	befreien	In 1863 President Lincoln ~*d* the slaves in the South.
	official *(adj.; n.)* [ə'fɪʃl]	offiziell, amtlich; Beamte(r), Beamtin	We'll get the ~ election results tomorrow. A government ~ talked with the reporters.
	facilities *(pl.)* [fə'sɪlətɪz]	Einrichtung(en)	The school has excellent sports ~. It has its own swimming-pool, tennis courts and a large gym.
	equal ['i:kwəl]	gleich	the same in size, amount, number, etc. Women are demanding ~ pay for ~ work.

Adjectives and nouns

angry	wütend	**equal** ⚠ ['i:kwəl]	gleich
anger (at) ['æŋgə]	Ärger, Wut (über)	**equality** ⚠ [ɪ'kwɒlətɪ]	Gleichheit
biological [ˌbaɪə'lɒdʒɪkl]	biologisch	**responsible** (for)	verantwortlich (für)
biology	Biologie	**responsibility** (for) [rɪˌspɒnsə'bɪlətɪ]	Verantwortung, Verantwortlichkeit (für)
democratic ⚠ [ˌdemə'krætɪk]	demokratisch	**similar**	ähnlich
democracy ⚠ [dɪ'mɒkrəsɪ]	Demokratie	**similarity** (to)	Ähnlichkeit (mit)
economic ⚠ [ˌi:kə'nɒmɪk]	(volks)wirtschaftlich	**skilled** (in, at) [skɪld]	ausgebildet, erfahren Fach-; geschickt (in)
economy ⚠ [ɪ'kɒnəmɪ]	(Volks-)Wirtschaft	**skill**	Fähigkeit, Fertigkeit; Geschick(lichkeit)
educational	pädagogisch; Lehr-, Bildungs-	**tragic**	tragisch
education	(Schul-, Aus-)Bildung; Erziehung	**tragedy**	Tragödie, Katastrophe
emotional [ɪ'məʊʃnəl]	gefühlsmäßig, emotional	**violent**	gewalttätig, brutal; heftig
emotion	Gefühl, Emotion	**violence**	Gewalt, Gewalttätigkeit

p. 35	(to) desegregate [ˌdi:'segrɪgeɪt]	die Rassentrennung aufheben an	In the US, laws were passed in the fifties to ~ public facilities.
	segregation [ˌsegrɪ'geɪʃn]	Rassentrennung	A system of ~ was introduced in America in 1896. Blacks were sent to different schools from whites. ▸◂ integration
	climax ['klaɪmæks]	Höhepunkt	the most important and exciting part of a film, etc.
	movement ['mu:vmənt]	Bewegung	Do you support the ~ to stop the killing of whales? Julie's back hurts so much that every ~ is painful.
	mayor [meə]	Bürgermeister/in	sb. who has been elected to lead and represent a city
	(to) assassinate [ə'sæsɪneɪt]	*(aus politischen Gründen)* ermorden	President John F. Kennedy *was ~d* in Dallas on November 22, 1963.
	riot ['raɪət]	Aufruhr, Aufstand	The crowd was angry. The police were afraid of a ~.
	governor ['gʌvənə]	(US) Gouverneur/in *(eines US-Bundesstaates)*	a person who governs a US state
	novelist ['nɒvəlɪst]	Romanschriftsteller/in	a person who writes novels

Focus on GRAMMAR

p. 36	substitute ['sʌbstɪtju:t]	(Stell-)Vertreter/in, Ersatz	Their dog was a ~ for the children they did not have. Foreign aid is important, but it is no ~ for economic development.
	goal [gəʊl]	Ziel; Tor *(im Sport)*	I want to survive this class. That's my ~ for the year. Roberto scored two ~*s* in today's football match.

V

(p. 36)	deduction [dɪ'dʌkʃn]	(Schluß-)Folgerung, Deduktion	something one works out from the facts that one already knows
	(to) deduce (from) [dɪ'djuːs]	folgern, schließen (aus)	verb from "deduction" I *~d from* his name that he was French.
	appendix [ə'pendɪks], *pl.* appendices [ə'pendɪsiːz]	Anhang *(eines Buches)*	section at the end of a book that gives extra information
	mistrust [ˌmɪs'trʌst]	Mißtrauen	*M~* between countries can lead to war.
p. 37	certainty ['sɜːtəntɪ]	Sicherheit, Gewißheit	No one can say with any ~ if the candidate will win.
	spy [spaɪ]	Spion/in	Mata Hari was executed in 1917 for being a ~.
	officer ['ɒfɪsə]	Offizier/in	a person who gives orders to others in the army
	at the latest [ət ðə 'leɪtɪst]	spätestens	Our flight leaves at 7.30. We'll have to be at the airport by 6.30 ~ *the* ~.
	(to) reread [ˌriː'riːd]	erneut (durch)lesen	to read something again
	scale [skeɪl]	Skala	On a ~ of one to ten, how good was the concert?
	identical [aɪ'dentɪkl]	identisch, gleich	exactly the same
	professional [prə'feʃnəl]	Berufstätige/r *(in akademischen, angesehenen Berufen)*	person who works as a doctor, architect, etc. ⚠ *professional* = **1.** Berufstätige(r) *(in akademischen, angesehenen Berufen)*; **2.** Berufs-, professionell, Fach-; **3.** Profi
p. 38	caption ['kæpʃn]	Bildunterschrift; Überschrift *(eines Artikels)*	words that are written above or below a picture to explain what it is about; title of an article in a magazine, etc.
	lawyer ['lɔːjə]	Rechtsanwalt/Rechtsanwältin	somebody who helps people with legal problems
	(to) make ends meet [ˌ- - '-]	*(finanziell)* über die Runden kommen	Ron's parents have little money. They have trouble *making* ~ ~.
	trap [træp]	Falle	We caught all the mice with some new *~s*.
	aged [eɪdʒd]	im Alter von, -jährig	Men ~ 45 and over should have their hearts checked.
p. 39	(to) **get/be used to** sth./**doing** sth. [ˌget/ˌbiː 'juːstə]	sich an etwas gewöhnen/an etwas gewöhnt sein	Rebecca soon *got ~ to* driving on the left side of the road in the UK.

used to + Infinitiv/(to) get/be used to + -ing form

In the South blacks **used to have** to sit in the back of buses.	Im Süden **mußten** Schwarze **früher** in Bussen (immer) hinten sitzen.
Many blacks couldn't **get used to sitting** in the back. In 1955 they started a bus boycott.	Viele Schwarze konnten **sich** nicht **daran gewöhnen**, hinten **zu sitzen**. …
Some blacks believe that many whites **are** still not **used to seeing** successful blacks.	Manche Schwarze glauben, daß viele Weiße sich noch immer nicht **daran gewöhnt haben**, erfolgreiche Schwarze **zu sehen**.
⚠ I used to do it.	Ich habe es früher immer getan.
I'm used to doing it./I'll get used to doing it.	Ich bin daran gewöhnt, es zu tun./Ich werde mich daran gewöhnen, es zu tun.

	annoying [ə'nɔɪɪŋ]	ärgerlich, lästig	He always corrects me. It's so ~.
	insult ['ɪnsʌlt]	Beleidigung	Joe shouted *~s* at Jim. He called him stupid and lazy.
	(to) face sb./sth. [feɪs]	sich jm/einer Sache gegenübersehen, jm./einer Sache (mutig) ins Auge sehen	The dying man bravely *~d* death. ⚠ *let's face it* (infml.) = machen wir uns doch nichts vor
	(to) **make it** (infml.)	es schaffen, Erfolg haben	The train leaves at 3.37. You*'ll ~ it* if you hurry. Cathy *will* never *~ it* as a singer. She has no talent.
	yet *(conj.)* [jet]	doch, dennoch	They are very poor and ~ they're happy.
	(to) **live on** sth.	von etwas leben, sich von etwas ernähren	Unemployed people don't have much money to ~ *on*.
	welfare *(sing.)* ['welfeə] (AE)	Sozialhilfe	money paid by the government to people who are poor, ill or unemployed ⚠ *(to) be on welfare* = Sozialhilfe beziehen

V

(p. 39)	°poverty line ['pɒvətɪ laɪn]	Armutsgrenze	
	(to) worry oneself sick (about sb./sth.)	vor Sorge (um jn./etwas) krank werden	to worry a lot (about somebody or something)

either

Either can be used …

– as an adverb. When one negative statement follows another, you can put *either* at the end of the second one:

I don't like maths and I don't like history **either**.	… und Geschichte mag ich **auch nicht**.
I wasn't tired. – No, I wasn't **either**.	… Nein, ich **auch nicht**.

– as a pronoun which describes a choice. It is often followed by *of* + noun phrase:

Would you like **either of** the shirts? – No, I don't like **either** (**of** them).	Möchtest du eins der **beiden** Hemden? – Nein, mir gefallen **beide** nicht./…keins (von **beiden**).

– in front of a singular countable noun *(zählbares Nomen)*:

She didn't like **either** suggestion.	Sie mochte **beide** Vorschläge nicht.

Either … or is used to express an alternative:

His birthday is **either** today **or** tomorrow.	Er hat **entweder** heute **oder** morgen Geburtstag.

	°gulf [gʌlf]	Kluft	
	talented ['tæləntɪd]	talentiert, begabt	brilliant She plays the piano well. – Yes, she's a ~ musician.
	qualification *(usually pl.)* [ˌkwɒlɪfɪ'keɪʃn]	Qualifikation; Zeugnis	Paul didn't get the job as he didn't have the right ~*s*. I haven't got any ~*s* in German Literature.
	well-off [ˌwel'ɒf]	wohlhabend	▸◂ poor
	(to) contribute (to) [kən'trɪbjuːt]	beitragen, beisteuern (zu)	The high price of land ~ *to* the high rents.
	(to) head [hed]	anführen, leiten, *(einer Organisation)* vorstehen	Do you know who the president of this firm is? – Yes, it is ~*ed* by Pam Bond.

V

Focus on WORDS

p. 40	frustrated [frʌ'streɪtɪd]	frustriert, enttäuscht	angry, e.g. because you cannot have or do what you want
	satisfaction [ˌsætɪs'fækʃn]	Befriedigung; Zufriedenheit	Bob really enjoys learning Spanish. It gives him a lot of ~.
	affection (for sb./sth.) [ə'fekʃn]	Zuneigung (zu jm./etwas)	feeling of loving or liking (somebody/something) Her mother never showed her much ~.
	joy [dʒɔɪ]	Freude	feeling of great happiness
	anxiety [æŋ'zaɪətɪ]	Angst, Sorge	the feeling you have when you worry
	rage [reɪdʒ]	Wut, Zorn, Rage	violent or great anger ▸◂ joy, pleasure
	thermometer [θə'mɒmɪtə]	Thermometer	instrument that shows how hot or cold something is
	(to) **be concerned about** [kən'sɜːnd]	besorgt sein um, sich Sorgen machen um	to be worried about
	(to) **be scared (of** sb./sth.) [skeəd]	Angst haben (vor jm./etwas)	to be afraid (of somebody or something)
3 Ex 1	°racial pioneer [ˌreɪʃl ˌpaɪə'nɪə]	„Rassenpionier"	
	income ['ɪnkʌm]	Einkommen	the money you receive for your work, for example
	(to) **achieve** [ə'tʃiːv]	*(ein Ziel)* erreichen; leisten, zustande bringen	What are your aims in life? What do you hope to ~? What a terrible day. I ~*d* only half of what I had planned to do.
2	extreme [ɪk'striːm]	extrem	very great degree or intensity [ɪn'tensətɪ] ▸◂ average, common, ordinary
3	power ['paʊə]	Vollmacht, Befugnis	The law gives the police special ~*s*. ⚠ *power* = **1.** Macht; **2.** Vollmacht, Befugnis

3 Ex 4

German *sollen*

If you want to know what blacks wanted to achieve in the 60s you **should** read King's speech from August 1963. (…, **solltest** du [eigentlich] Kings Rede … lesen.)

Every student **ought to** read it. (… **sollte** sie [eigentlich] lesen.)

I have a copy of the speech at home. **Shall I** bring it tomorrow? (… **Soll ich** sie … mitbringen?)

The speech **was intended to** convince Americans that civil rights laws were needed. (Die Rede **sollte** … überzeugen, daß … .)

It **was meant to** be the climax of the protest march to Washington, D.C. (Sie **sollte** der Höhepunkt … sein.)

Today, blacks wonder how much longer they **are supposed**[1] **to** wait until King's dream becomes reality. (…, wie lange sie noch warten **sollen,** bis … .)

[1] [sə'pəʊst]

King's speech in Washington **is said to** have been the climax of the Civil Rights Movement. (… **soll** [angeblich] der Höhepunkt … gewesen sein./Es heißt bzw. man sagt, daß … .)

Before he gave his speech, King **is supposed to** have been very nervous. (… **soll** King [angeblich] sehr nervös gewesen sein./Es heißt bzw. man sagt, daß … .)

King **is believed to** have been the most important black leader of his time. (King **soll** [angeblich] … gewesen sein./Es heißt bzw. man sagt, daß … .)

King **was reported to** have been very happy when he received the Nobel Peace Prize in 1964. (King **soll** [angeblich] sehr glücklich gewesen sein als … ./Es heißt bzw. man sagt, daß … .)

Mit *ought to* und *should* kannst du jemanden auffordern, etwas zu tun. Mit *shall I/we …?* kannst du fragen, ob etwas getan werden sollte, wenn du dir nicht ganz sicher bist, ob es auch nötig oder erwünscht ist.
Mit *be intended to, be meant to* und *be supposed to* kannst du ausdrücken, daß jemand anders wünscht, daß etwas geschieht bzw. erreicht wird.

Mit *be said to, be supposed to, be believed to* und *be reported to* kannst du zum Ausdruck bringen, daß du das wiedergibst, was jemand anders gesagt oder geschrieben hat, ohne zu wissen, ob das auch wirklich wahr ist.

consequence ['kɒnsɪkwəns]	Folge, Konsequenz	result or effect of something else Not studying for the test had extreme *~s*.
(to) take sth. for granted ['grɑːntɪd]	etwas als selbstverständlich betrachten	to show too little attention to something In the developed world we ~ clean water *for* ~.
°magic carpet ['mædʒɪk]	fliegender Teppich *(wörtl.: „Zauberteppich")*	
(to) act [ækt]	sich verhalten, benehmen	She hated his insults, but she *~ed* as if they didn't hurt her feelings.
6 °(US) marshal ['mɑːʃl]	(US) Polizeichef/in	

3 Text **Two ways to 16th Street**

p. 45

breeze [briːz]	Brise, leichter Wind	light wind
(to) **drown** [draʊn]	*hier: (Stimme)* übertönen; ertrinken; ertränken	Her joy *was ~ed* in a sea of tears. The child fell into the river and *~ed*. The farmer *~ed* the cats.
someplace ['sʌmpleɪs] (AE, infml.)	irgendwo(hin)	somewhere If you want to smoke, please sit ~ else.
package (of) ['pækɪdʒ]	Päckchen, Paket	something packed in a box or in paper There was a ~ for me at the post office.
(to) cruise the streets [kruːz]	in den Straßen herumfahren, spazierenfahren	to drive around – usually quite slowly – in a car without any particular place to go

V

V

Unit 3/4

(p. 45)	**wealthy** ['welθɪ]	wohlhabend, reich	rich ⧓ poor
	wealth [welθ]	Wohlstand, Reichtum	Which do you value most: ~ or health? ⧓ poverty
	°ain't [eɪnt] (nonstandard)	*umgangssprachlich für:* am not, aren't, isn't, haven't, hasn't	
p. 46	**in between** [ˌɪn bɪ'twiːn]	zwischendurch, dazwischen	The film ends at 6.00 and the concert starts at 8.00, so we could have a meal *in ~*. In our neighbourhood we have mainly semi-detached houses with a few detached houses *in ~*.
	°big bucks [bɪg 'bʌks] (AE, infml.)	'ne Menge Kohle, reichlich Moneten	
	air conditioning *(sing.)* ['eə kənˌdɪʃnɪŋ]	Klimaanlage	Because the summers in the US are usually very hot, most new cars come with ~ ~.
	flashlight ['flæʃlaɪt] (AE)	Taschenlampe	the AE word for BE "torch"
	shocked [ʃɒkt]	schockiert	When I told my mother I had failed, she looked ~.
	amazed (at, by) [ə'meɪzd]	erstaunt, verblüfft (über)	very surprised I was ~ *at* how well Heike speaks English now.
	(to) frighten sb./sth. away ['fraɪtn]	jn. verscheuchen, abschrecken	Walk quietly so that you *don't* ~ the animals *away*.
	(to) **change into jeans/…**	sich (umziehen und) Jeans/… anziehen	For the party Richard *~d into* another pair of trousers.
	jail [dʒeɪl]	Gefängnis	prison
	if you can help it	wenn du es vermeiden kannst	= if you can avoid it Don't come later than 6.00 *if you can ~ it*.
p. 47	**passage** ['pæsɪdʒ]	Passage, Textstelle	short section from a book, speech, piece of music, etc. In his speech he quoted a ~ from the Bible.
	(in)stability [(ˌɪn)stə'bɪlətɪ]	(In-)Stabilität	Since the end of the cold war, political *in~* in some areas of the world has increased.
	force ['fɔːs]	Kraft; Zwang	The *~s* of nature cannot be controlled. The police had to use ~ when they arrested the man.
	(to) **struggle (with** sb./sth., **for** sth.) ['strʌgl]	kämpfen (mit jm./etwas, um etwas)	The police officer *~ed with* the robber. The two leaders *are ~ing for* power.
	sentence ['sentəns]	(Gerichts-)Urteil	Heather received a ~ of 5 years for the crime.

The history of the blues

p. 47	°rhythm and blues [ˌrɪðem‿ən 'bluːz]	Rhythm and Blues *(Musikrichtung)*	
	°traditional [trə'dɪʃnəl]	traditionell	

Unit 4 American Indians

p. 48	saying ['seɪɪŋ]	Sprichwort, Redensart	a well-known phrase that gives advice about sth. There is a ~ that "man shall not live by bread alone".
	(to) **contradict** [ˌkɒntrə'dɪkt]	widersprechen	to say that sth. someone says is wrong or not true The fight started when he *~ed* what she had said. ⧓ (to) agree
	snake [sneɪk]	Schlange	a long thin animal without legs
	(to) **color** (AE)/**colour** (BE) ['kʌlə]	färben	to put colours on something The little boy *~ed* the picture blue.
	turkey ['tɜːkɪ]	Truthahn, Truthenne	In Britain and the US, many people eat ~ at Christmas.
	°buck deer [ˌbʌk 'dɪə]	Rehbock	

(p. 48)	by this time	unterdessen, zu diesem Zeitpunkt	*By this* ~, 1989, it was too late to stop the protesters who were demanding democracy.
	(to) **feel sorry for** sb./sth.	jn./etwas bedauern; etwas bereuen	Judy broke her leg last week. I really *feel ~ for* her. I still *feel ~ for* what I said to him. It was not nice.

(to) regret/regret/(to) be sorry/(to) feel sorry

If you don't visit the White House when you're in Washington, D.C., you**'ll** always **regret** it.	…, **wirst** du es immer **bereuen**.
She **has** often **regretted** quitting her job.	Sie **hat** es oft **bereut**, daß … .
He **regretted** that he had hurt her so much.	Er **bereute**, daß er sie so verletzt hatte.
We **regret** to inform you that someone else has been chosen for the job. (fml.)	Wir **bedauern**, Ihnen mitteilen zu müssen, daß … .
We accept your decision to leave the company with great **regret**. (fml.)	Wir akzeptieren Ihre Entscheidung, die Firma zu verlassen, mit großem **Bedauern**.
That was a stupid thing to say. **I'm sorry**.	… Es **tut mir leid**.
I **was sorry** to hear about your grandmother's death.	Es **tat mir leid** zu hören, daß deine Großmutter gestorben ist.
I **feel** so **sorry for** children whose parents don't have any time for them.	Ich **bedauere** Kinder sehr, deren Eltern keine Zeit für sie haben.
He **felt sorry for** what he had done.	Er **bereute**, was er getan hatte.

	(to) stretch [stretʃ]	*hier:* schlängeln; sich erstrecken	The queue *~ed* around the whole building.
	°bow [bəʊ]	Bogen	
	°arrow ['ærəʊ]	Pfeil	
	°It thrashed its tail all around. [θræʃ]	Sie schlug mit dem Schwanz um sich.	
	(to) hang around [hæŋ] – hung [hʌŋ] – hung (infml.)	herumlungern	to stay in or near a place not doing very much A lot of kids don't know what to do with their time, so they just ~ *around* and do nothing.
	reservation [ˌrezə'veɪʃn]	(Indianer-)Reservation, Reservat	an area of land where American Indians live
	alcoholic [ˌælkə'hɒlɪk] *(n.; adj.)*	Alkoholiker/in; alkoholisch	An ~ is a person who drinks too much. In this restaurant we don't serve ~ drinks.
	°superstitious [ˌsuːpə'stɪʃəs]	abergläubisch	
	ceremony ['serəmənɪ]	Zeremonie, Feier	a formal public or religious event
p. 49	**frog** [frɒg]	Frosch	a small animal with long back legs that lives near water
	pond [pɒnd]	Teich	a small lake
	harmony ['hɑːmənɪ]	Harmonie, Einklang	Newspapers say there is little ~ in the government. ▸◂ conflict
	civilized ['sɪvəlaɪzd]	zivilisiert	Our aim should be to help create a more ~ world.
	vice-(president) [ˌvaɪs 'prezɪdənt]	Vize-(Präsident/in)	In the US, if the president is assassinated the ~-president becomes the next president.
	°maize [meɪz]	Mais	
	version ['vɜːʃn]	Fassung *(eines Textes)*; Version *(eines Berichts)*	In our English class today we compared different *~s* of the same poem. Many did not believe the official ~ of the accident.
	(to) **publish** ['pʌblɪʃ]	veröffentlichen	Melville's novel "Moby Dick" *was ~ed* in 1851.

Focus on GRAMMAR

p. 50	°ranger ['reɪndʒə]	(US) Förster/in, Wächter/in *(in einem Nationalpark)*	
	°inscription [ɪn'skrɪpʃn]	Inschrift	
	narrative ['nærətɪv]	erzählend, narrativ	A ~ text tells a story.
	descriptive [dɪ'skrɪptɪv]	beschreibend, darstellend, deskriptiv	giving a picture in words I don't like novels that have long ~ passages.
	argumentative [ˌɑːgjʊ'mentətɪv]	argumentativ	An ~ text discusses an issue.

Unit 4

(p. 50)	°marker ['mɑːkə]	Hinweisschild	
	senseless ['sensləs]	sinnlos	having no meaning or purpose ▸◂ meaningful, reasonable, sensible
	mood [muːd]	*hier:* Botschaft; Stimmung	the way that you feel at a particular time Rachel is in a bad ~. Her boyfriend didn't phone.
	(to) get (sth.) across (to sb.) [ə'krɒs]	(jm.) (etwas) verständlich machen, (etwas) herüberbringen	(cause sth.) to be communicated (to sb.) or understood (by sb.) The candidate failed to *get* his ideas ~ *to* the voters.
	(to) kneel [niːl] – knelt [nelt]/kneeled – knelt/kneeled	knien	In some religions people ~ when they pray. ⚠ *(to) kneel down* = niederknien
	°chisel ['tʃɪzl]	Meißel	
	°mallet ['mælɪt]	Holzhammer	
	native ['neɪtɪv]	eingeboren, einheimisch	The Indians are America's ~ population. ⚠ *(to) be a native German* = gebürtiger Deutscher/gebürtige Deutsche sein ⚠ *native speaker* = Muttersprachler/in
	miserable ['mɪzərəbl]	erbärmlich, jämmerlich, gräßlich	Many Indians live on reservations in ~ conditions. ▸◂ comfortable, good
	confrontation [ˌkɒnfrʌn'teɪʃn]	Konfrontation	a fight or an argument The ~ between east and west is over.
p. 51	(to) **approach** [ə'prəʊtʃ]	anpacken *(Aufgabe, Problem)*; sich nähern	to begin to deal with sth.; to come nearer to sb./sth. This is a difficult problem. How should we ~ it? The queen's car slowly *~ed* Parliament.
	(to) have a look at sb./sth.	sich jn./etwas ansehen, einen Blick auf jn./etwas werfen	to look at somebody or something *Have a ~ at* the picture on page 48 and then describe it.
p. 52	(to) be located [ləʊ'keɪtɪd]	sich befinden	Much of California's computer industry *is* ~ in the Bay Area.
	(to) cover ['kʌvə]	sich erstrecken über *(eine Fläche, Zeitspanne)*	Forests ~ more than 50% of the land in this region. ⚠ *(to) cover* = **1.** bedecken, zudecken; **2.** sich erstrecken über *(eine Fläche, Zeitspanne)*
	setting ['setɪŋ]	Schauplatz	the place where the action of a film or a book takes place
	countless ['kaʊntləs]	unzählig, zahllos	very many
	self-government [ˌself'gʌvnmənt]	Selbstverwaltung	After World War II many colonies demanded ~-~.

Collective nouns

Our family always **spends** Christmas in the country.	Unsere Familie (als Gruppe) … .
The family usually **arrive** throughout the morning of Christmas Eve.	Die Familie (die einzelnen Mitglieder der Familie) … .
The team **has** won all **its** games so far.	Die Mannschaft (als Gruppe) … .
The team **were** talking about **their** next game.	Die Mannschaft (die einzelnen Mitglieder) … .

A collective noun *(Sammelbezeichnung, Kollektivum)* names a group of people, animals or things. Most collective nouns can take a singular or plural verb. It takes a singular verb when the speaker thinks of the group as a single unit; it takes a plural verb when the speaker is thinking of the individual members of the group. If you refer back to a collective noun, you choose a singular pronoun if the verb is singular, and a plural pronoun if the verb is plural.
Here is a list of some common collective nouns: *army, band, class, club, company, couple, crowd, family, government, group, majority, minority, party, team.*

⚠ In AE collective nouns nearly always take singular verbs. In BE plural verbs are generally preferred.
The collective nouns *people, police* and *cattle* always take plural verbs.

	traditionally [trə'dɪʃnəlɪ]	traditionell(erweise), üblicherweise	Employees who have worked for our company for 25 years ~ get a gold watch.

(p. 52)	traditional	traditionell	Here country people sometimes wear their ~ clothes. ⧓ new, modern, unusual
	scattered ['skætəd]	verstreut; vereinzelt *(Regenschauer)*	My friends live ~ all over the world. The weather forecast says we'll have ~ showers today.
	°hogan ['həʊgən]	*traditionelle achtseitige Behausung der Navajo-Indianer*	
	(to) face (east) [feɪs]	nach (Osten) gehen, liegen *(Haus usw.)*	My room is very dark because it ~*s* north.
p. 53	tribal ['traɪbl]	Stammes-	adjective from "tribe"
	amount [ə'maʊnt]	Menge	Germany still has large ~*s* of coal. ⚠ *amount* = **1.** Betrag, Summe; **2.** Menge
	natural gas [ˌnætʃrəl 'gæs]	Erdgas	Do you use electricity or ~ ~ for cooking?
	(to) **exploit** [ɪk'splɔɪt]	ausbeuten; verwerten	to use sth. or to treat sb. unfairly or selfishly; to develop sth. or make better use of sth.
	°arts and crafts [ˌɑːts_ən 'krɑːfts]	Kunsthandwerk	
	extra ['ekstrə]	zusätzlich, Extra-	more than what is usual, expected or necessary
	presentation [ˌprezən'teɪʃn]	Präsentation, Darbietung	noun from "(to) present"
	imaginary [ɪ'mædʒɪnərɪ]	(frei) erfunden; eingebildet	existing only in the imagination; not real ⧓ real, true

Focus on WORDS

p. 54	**value** ['væljuː]	Wert; Nutzen	the amount of money sth. is worth; the usefulness of sth.
	(to) **value** sb./sth.	jn./etwas (hoch-) schätzen, achten	to think sb. or sth. is very important and worth a lot. I *don't* always ~ my brother's advice.
	(to) attach importance to sth. [ə'tætʃ]	etwas Bedeutung beimessen	Bill ~*es* great ~ *to* what other people say.
	fancy ['fænsɪ]	schick *(Auto, Laden)*; raffiniert *(Gerät)*; ausgefallen *(Design)*	⧓ basic, cheap, ordinary, simple. I drive a ~ car, eat in ~ restaurants, have a ~ stereo system and own a ~ house. What more do I need?

Stressed *do/does/did*

You can use *do/does/did* in positive statements for special emphasis[1]. The infinitive comes after *do/does/did*. *Do* can also come at the beginning of an imperative sentence, for emphasis.

[1] ['emfəsɪs] Betonung, Hervorhebung

I don't attach great importance to fancy clothes, but I **do** think it is sometimes important to be well-dressed.	Ich lege keinen großen Wert auf schicke Kleidung, aber ich glaube, daß es manchmal wichtig ist, gut angezogen zu sein.
My father often disagrees with my political ideas. However, he **does** respect them.	… Allerdings respektiert er sie.
Although she was not very interested in languages, she **did** learn German and French.	…, hat sie dennoch Deutsch und Französisch gelernt.
Do have another piece of cake.	Nimm dir doch noch ein Stück Kuchen!
Do call me if you need any help.	Ruf mich bitte an, falls du (irgendwelche) Hilfe brauchst!

item ['aɪtəm]	Punkt *(in einer Liste)*, Ding, Sache	Larry bought only two ~*s* at the grocery store: a bottle of milk and a magazine.
individuality [ˌɪndɪvɪdʒʊ'ælətɪ]	Individualität	the qualities that make sb./sth. different from other people/things
the elements *(pl.)* ['elɪmənts] (fml.)	Naturkräfte, Elemente	forces of nature, the weather. Do you think we will ever be able to control *the* ~?
element	Element	What a story! It has all the ~*s* of a soap opera. Iron and gold, for example, are ~*s*.

Unit 4

(p. 54)	material [mə'tɪərɪəl]	materiell	adjective from "material" Peggy attaches a lot of importance to ~ things.
	status ['steɪtəs]	(gesellschaftliche) Stellung, Rang, Status	The government has just published a new report on the ~ of children in society.
	personality [ˌpɜːsə'nælətɪ]	Persönlichkeit	You should judge someone by their ~ and not by how they look.
	extended family [ɪkˌstendɪd 'fæmlɪ]	Großfamilie	a family not only of parents and children, but also in which grandparents, aunts, uncles, etc. live

"Families"

extended family	= Großfamilie
nuclear family [ˌnjuːklɪə 'fæmlɪ]	= Kleinfamilie
one-parent family/ single-parent family	= Familie mit alleinerziehendem Elternteil

	(to) extend	verlängern; sich ausdehnen, erstrecken	They are going to ~ the road as far as Brentwood. How far does the wall ~?
	elderly ['eldəlɪ]	ältere(r, s)	She is very active for an ~ woman.
	achievement [ə'tʃiːvmənt]	Leistung, Errungenschaft	Cindy won the chess competition. – That's quite an ~ for a ten-year-old.
	punctual ['pʌŋktʃʊəl]	pünktlich	Trains here are not very ~. ▸◂ late
4 Ex 1	stereotype ['sterɪətaɪp]	Stereotyp, Klischee	a particular idea about a type of person or thing, which is often not true in reality
	(to) associate (with) [ə'səʊʃɪeɪt]	assoziieren, (gedanklich) verbinden (mit)	Fast food restaurants *are* usually *~d with* the US.
	°the plains (= the Great Plains) *(pl.)* [pleɪnz]	die *(nordamerikanische)* Prärie	
	ancestor ['ænsestə]	Vorfahr(e)/Vorfahrin	My *~s* settled in America in the 19th century.
	(to) **force** sb. **to do** sth. [fɔːs]	jn. zwingen, etwas zu tun	to make sb. do sth. that they do not want to do The robber *~d* me *to* give him my money.
	public ['pʌblɪk]	Öffentlichkeit	people in general The ~ is/are in favour of the new laws. ⚠ *public* = **1.** Öffentlichkeit; **2.** öffentlich
	fortunately ['fɔːtʃənətlɪ]	zum Glück, glücklicherweise	Yesterday we had a picnic. *F~* it didn't rain.
	proposal [prə'pəʊzl]	(Heirats-)Antrag; Vorschlag	Some movie stars get marriage *~s* in the mail. We've been arguing about the government's ~ to build a new motorway.
	romantic [rəʊ'mæntɪk]	romantisch	Simon is so ~. He just bought me a fancy new dress. ▸◂ practical, realistic, unromantic
2	°hyphenated American ['haɪfəneɪtɪd]	*Amerikaner/in schottischer usw. Abstammung*	
	descendant [dɪ'sendənt]	Nachfahr/Nachfahrin	person whose family goes back to a certain ancestor
	(to) **fascinate** ['fæsɪneɪt]	faszinieren	to attract or interest somebody very much My teacher loves English grammar. It *~s* her.
	explorer [ɪk'splɔːrə]	Forschungsreisende(r)	Captain James Cook was a famous British ~.
3	chief [tʃiːf]	(Indianer-)Häuptling	the leader of a group of people, especially of a tribe ⚠ *Herr Behm ist mein Chef. = Mr Behm is my boss.*
	(to) **practise** ['præktɪs]	ausüben *(Beruf, Religion)*	Many came to America to be able to ~ their religion. ⚠ *practise* = **1.** üben, trainieren; **2.** ausüben *(Beruf, Religion)*
	°monk [mʌŋk]	Mönch	
	°saint [seɪnt]	Sankt, Heilige(r)	
	(to) **float** [fləʊt]	*(auf dem Wasser)* schwimmen, treiben	Wood *~s* in water, stones don't. ▸◂ (to) sink
	(to) **prove** sth. **(to** sb.) [pruːv]	(jm.) etwas beweisen	to show (sb.) that something is true I'm a prince. – Can you ~ it *to* me?

(4 Ex 3)	°justice ['dʒʌstɪs] (AE)	Richter/in *(am obersten Gerichtshof)*	
	(to) fear [fɪə]	befürchten	After the test he *~ed* the worst.
	at the cost of sth.	auf Kosten von etwas	She saved his life, but only *at the ~ of* her own life.
	gender ['dʒendə]	*(grammatisches)* Geschlecht; Genus	Differences of race and ~ are not important here. In German the choice of article depends on the ~ of the noun.
	medium-size [ˌmiːdɪəm'saɪz]	mittelgroß	Do you want a large or a small drink? – Can I have a ~-~ coke?

Words Words Words

p. 58	(to) **damage** ['dæmɪdʒ]	beschädigen	Last week's storm ~d several houses in our town.
	thief [θiːf], *pl.* **thieves** [θiːvz]	Dieb/in	a person who steals something ⚠ For most words ending in 'f' or 'fe', you form the plural by adding '-s': chief – chiefs For a small group of words ending in 'f' or 'fe', you change the 'f' to a 'v' and add '-s' or '-es': knife – knives, half – halves, -self – -selves, shelf – shelves, thief – thieves, wife – wives
	from abroad	aus dem Ausland	Where is your guest from? – He's *from ~*, from Italy.
	TV set	Fernsehgerät	Where is the TV programme? – On top of the *TV ~*.
	knight [naɪt]	Ritter; Springer *(Schachfigur)*	a soldier who rode on a horse and fought long ago; a chess piece (often looks like the head of a horse)

4 Text **A question of identity**

p. 59	(to) arise [ə'raɪz] – arose [ə'rəʊz] – arisen [ə'rɪzn]	auftreten, entstehen	to appear If any problems ~, please call me.
	(to) **apply (to** sb. **for** sth.) [ə'plaɪ]	sich (bei jm. um etwas) bewerben; (bei jm. etwas) beantragen	to make a formal request (to sb. for sth.) I *had ~ed for* 15 jobs before I was offered one. I've lost my passport. I have to *~ for* a new one.
	(to) **do terribly/ well/…**	furchtbar/gut/… abschneiden	How was the test? – Very hard. I'm afraid I*'ve done ~*.

Phrases with "do" and "make"

(to) **do business** (with)	Geschäfte machen (mit)	(to) **make a choice**	eine Wahl treffen
(to) **do a class in**	einen Kurs besuchen in	(to) **make one's own clothes**	seine Kleidung selbst nähen
(to) **do an exercise**	eine Übung machen	(to) **make coffee/soup**	Kaffee/Suppe kochen
(to) **do** sb. **a favour**	jm. einen Gefallen tun	(to) **make a comment** (about/on)	einen Kommentar abgeben, eine Bemerkung machen (über/zu)
(to) **do one's homework**	seine Hausaufgaben machen	(to) **make a decision**	eine Entscheidung treffen
(to) **do the housework/ dishes**	die Hausarbeit machen/abwaschen	(to) **make ends meet**	(finanziell) über die Runden kommen
(to) **do a good job**	gute Arbeit leisten	(to) **make a film**	einen Film drehen
(to) **do 70 mph**	70 Meilen pro Stunde fahren	(to) **make friends** (with)	Freunde finden; sich anfreunden (mit)
(to) **do a lot of reading/ walking**	viel lesen/spazierengehen	(to) **make it** (infml.)	es schaffen, Erfolg haben
(to) **do the shopping**	einkaufen (gehen), Einkäufe machen	(to) **make money**	Geld verdienen
(to) **do a test** (meist BE)	einen Test/eine Arbeit schreiben	(to) **make notes**	(sich) Notizen machen
(to) **do a translation**	eine Übersetzung machen	(to) **make a phone call**	telefonieren
(to) **do well at school**	gut sein in der Schule	(to) **make a speech**	eine Rede halten
		(to) **make sense**	(einen) Sinn ergeben, Sinn machen
		(to) **make sure**	sicherstellen, sichergehen; dafür sorgen
		(to) **make trouble**	Ärger machen

(to) make into	verwandeln in, machen zu	The old train station *was made ~* a museum last year.

V

Unit 4

(p. 59)	**none (of)** [nʌn]	keine(r, s) (von)	Where is the butter? – There's ~ (= no butter) left. ⚠ *Pronunciation:* none [nʌn] of us non-stop [nɒn]
	(to) **afford (to do** sth.) [ə'fɔːd]	(es) sich leisten (können, etwas zu tun)	to have enough money or time to be able to do sth. I lost my job, so I can't ~ *to* buy a new car. ⚠ 'Afford' is almost always used with 'can', 'could' or 'be able'.
p. 60	(to) **be homesick (for)** ['həʊmsɪk]	Heimweh haben (nach)	to feel unhappy when you are away from home
	warmth [wɔːmθ]	Wärme	In winter these plants need a lot of ~. ▸◂ cold
	(to) **compete (against/ with** sb. **for** sth.) [kəm'piːt]	(gegen jn./mit jm. um etwas) konkurrieren, kämpfen	Several companies *are ~ing with* each other *for* the contract to build the new bridge.

Verbs and nouns

(to) **achieve**	(ein Ziel) erreichen; leisten, zustande bringen	(to) **disagree** (with)	anderer Meinung sein (als), nicht übereinstimmen (mit)
achievement	Leistung, Errungenschaft	**disagreement** [dɪsə'griːmənt]	Uneinigkeit; Meinungsverschiedenheit
(to) **apologize**	sich entschuldigen	(to) **exploit**	ausbeuten; verwerten
apology [ə'pɒlədʒɪ]	Entschuldigung	**exploitation** [ˌeksplɔɪ'teɪʃn]	Ausbeutung, Ausnutzung; Nutzung
(to) **associate** (with)	assozieren, (gedanklich) verbinden mit	(to) **explore** [ɪk'splɔː]	erforschen
association	Assoziation; Verband, Vereinigung	**explorer**	Forschungsreisende(r)
(to) **compete** (against/ with) ⚠ [kəm'piːt]	konkurrieren, kämpfen (gegen/mit)	(to) **move**	(um)ziehen; (sich) bewegen
competition ⚠ [ˌkɒmpə'tɪʃn]	Wettbewerb, Wettkampf; Konkurrenz	**movement**	Bewegung
(to) **contradict**	widersprechen	(to) **present**	darlegen, präsentieren
contradiction [ˌkɒntrə'dɪkʃn]	Widerspruch; Gegensatz	**presentation**	Präsentation, Darbietung
(to) **contribute** (to) ⚠ [kən'trɪbjuːt]	beitragen, beisteuern (zu)	(to) **prove**	beweisen
contribution (to) ⚠ [ˌkɒntrɪ'bjuːʃn]	Beitrag (zu)	**proof**	Beweis(e), Nachweis(e)
(to) **deduce** (from)	folgern, schließen (aus)	(to) **publish**	veröffentlichen
deduction	(Schluß-)Folgerung, Deduktion	**publication** [ˌpʌblɪ'keɪʃn]	Veröffentlichung, Publikation
		(to) **rule**	regieren, herrschen über
		ruler	Herrscher/in; Lineal

intelligent [ɪn'telɪdʒənt]	intelligent, klug	Sarah learns very quickly and easily. She must be a very ~ young girl. ▸◂ stupid
(to) **let** sb. **down** [let] **– let – let**	jn. im Stich lassen, enttäuschen	My friends promised to help me on Saturday. But they *let* me ~. They didn't come.
(to) throw oneself into one's work	sich in die Arbeit stürzen	After the death of her husband she *threw* herself *into* her ~.
(to) drive/fly/go/… by	vorbeifahren/-fliegen/ -gehen/…	During the test I didn't notice how quickly the time *went* ~.
(to) **blow** [bləʊ] – **blew** [bluː] – **blown** [bləʊn]	blasen, wehen	The wind *is ~ing* hard today.
(to) acquire [ə'kwaɪə]	erwerben	to get or obtain ▸◂ (to) give up, (to) lose

p. 61	partly ['pɑːtlɪ]	teilweise, zum Teil	Fred goes to the disco ~ because he likes the music and ~ because he likes to meet his friends there.
	(to) **change**	wechseln *(die Schule, Geld usw.)*	Grandma ~*d* churches because she didn't like the new priest.

(to) change/change

Berlin **has changed** a lot since my last visit.	Berlin **hat sich** seit meinem letzten Besuch sehr **verändert**.
The witch **changed** the prince **into** a frog.	Die Hexe **verwandelte** den Prinzen **in** einen Frosch.
After work I usually **change into** more comfortable clothes.	Nach der Arbeit **ziehe** ich mir meist bequemere Kleidung **an**.
Do you still want to buy this shirt? – No, **I've changed** my **mind**.	… – Nein, ich **habe** meine **Meinung geändert**.
She is rich and famous, but I wouldn't want to **change places with** her.	Sie ist reich und berühmt, aber ich würde **mit** ihr nicht **tauschen** wollen.
We must **change** (trains) at Crewe.	In Crewe müssen wir **umsteigen**.
The government thinks **changes** in the school system are necessary.	Die Regierung glaubt, daß **Veränderungen** im Schulsystem notwendig sind.
Could you **change** this ten dollar bill? – I'm sorry, I don't have any **change**.	Könntest du mir den 10-Dollarschein **wechseln**? – Tut mir leid, ich habe kein **Kleingeld**.

	°lonesome ['ləʊnsəm] *(meist* AE)	einsam, verlassen	
	gay [geɪ]	fröhlich, lustig *(veraltet)*; Schwuler; schwul	*here:* happy a homosexual [ˌhəʊməʊ'sekʃʊəl] person, especially a man *G~* organizations are fighting to end discrimination.
	shabby ['ʃæbɪ]	schäbig	Peter looks so ~ in his old clothes.
	room [ruːm]	Platz	My flat is too small, there isn't enough ~ for my things. ⚠ *room* = **1.** Zimmer, Raum; **2.** Platz

Canyon de Chelly

p. 61	°Bluecoat ['bluːkəʊt] (AE)	*jd., der eine blaue Uniform trägt*	
	°transcontinental [ˌtrænzkɒntɪ'nentl]	transkontinental	
	°track [træk]	(Eisenbahn-)Schiene	
	°revolt [rɪ'vəʊlt]	Aufstand, Revolte	

V

Unit 5: The world of literature

Dreams and dreaming

p. 63	(to) **address** [ə'dres]	sprechen zu, eine Ansprache halten vor	a formal way to say "to speak to" Mr Clinton ~*ed* a farmers' meeting.

Talking to groups of people

The governor **addressed** the mayors' conference in St. Louis.	Der Gouverneur **sprach zu** den Bürgermeistern auf der Konferenz in St. Louis.
The senator **gave a talk on** public education to the teacher's organization.	Der Senator **hielt einen Vortrag** vor der Lehrerorganisation **über** das Schulsystem.
The president **made an** important **speech about** America's foreign policy.	Der Präsident **hielt eine** wichtige **Rede über** Amerikas Außenpolitik.
The vice-president **spoke to** reporters about her trip to Europe.	Die Vize-Präsidentin **sprach mit** Reportern über ihre Reise nach Europa.
Prof. Mittelman **talked about** Langston Hughes' poems.	Prof. Mittelman **sprach über** die Gedichte von Langston Hughes.

Unit 5

(p. 63)	concrete(ly) ['kɒŋkriːt, -lɪ]	konkret	Can I have your ~ proposals for a class trip by tomorrow?
	repetition [ˌrepə'tɪʃn]	Wiederholung	noun from "(to) repeat"
	stanza ['stænzə]	Strophe *(eines Gedichtes)*	a verse of a poem Anke, please read the first ~ of the poem aloud.
	spirit ['spɪrɪt]	Geist, Sinn	After our first win the team ~ improved. ⚠ *Geist, Gespenst* = ghost
	image ['ɪmɪdʒ]	*(sprachliches)* Bild, bildlicher Ausdruck	In the poem, the ~ of the dying rose makes the reader think about the relationship between beauty and death.
p. 64	**moral** ['mɒrəl]	Moral, Lehre	a lesson in the right way to behave that can be learned from a story or from something that happens
	fable ['feɪbl]	Fabel	a story that has a moral and that often has animals as characters Have you read Aesop's ['iːsɒp] ~*s*?
	°moth [mɒθ]	Nachtfalter, Motte	

"Big" numbers

1,000,000	=	one million	eine Million
1,000,000,000	=	one billion (10^9) ['bɪljən]	eine Milliarde
1,000,000,000,000	=	one trillion (10^{12}) ['trɪljən]	eine Billion
1,000,000,000,000,000	=	one quadrillion (10^{15}) [kwɒ'drɪljən]	eine Trillion

⚠ Formerly in BE one billion was 1,000,000,000,000 (one million million) and one trillion was 1,000,000,000,000,000,000 (one million million million).

	(to) **get away (from)**	entkommen, entwischen (aus); weg-, fortkommen (von)	to succeed in escaping or leaving The criminals *got ~ from* the police. Today I can't ~ ~ *from* work until 8.
	(to) **characterize** ['kærəktəraɪz]	charakterisieren, beschreiben	to describe somebody's behaviour and attitudes The novelist ~*s* her hero as intelligent and brave.
	(to) lose touch (with)	den Kontakt verlieren (zu)	to no longer have contact Over the years I'*ve lost ~ with* my school friends.
p. 70	series (*sing.* and *pl.*) ['sɪəriːz]	Reihe; (Fernseh-)Serie	We had a ~ of bank robberies in our town last year. Many American TV ~ are popular around the world.
	(to) **commit, -tt-** [kə'mɪt]	*(ein Verbrechen, Selbstmord)* begehen	to do something bad or illegal Mr West ~*ted* a series of murders. ⚠ Double "t": admitted – committed – regretted
	relevance (to) ['reləvəns]	Bedeutung, Relevanz (für)	The teacher did not understand the ~ of the pupil's comments.
	(to) **confront (with)** [kən'frʌnt]	konfrontieren (mit)	In the test the students *were ~ed with* grammatical terms they did not know.
	explicit(ly) [ɪk'splɪsɪt, -lɪ]	ausdrücklich, explizit	clearly and fully expressed The teacher ~*ly* warned the pupils not to go on the ice. ▸◂ indirect(ly)
	(to) infer (from), -rr- [ɪn'fɜː] (fml.)	(er)schließen, folgern (aus), ableiten (von)	to deduce As a result of some of his statements, I could ~ a lot about his private life. ⚠ Double "r": inferred – preferred – referred
	motive ['məʊtɪv]	Motiv, Beweggrund	a reason for doing something Financial problems were the ~ for the crime.
	theme [θiːm]	Thema, Leitgedanke	topic or central idea of a talk, book, text, etc.
p. 71	axe (BE)/ax (AE) [æks]	Axt, Beil	a tool for cutting down trees, for example
	°(to) forge [fɔːdʒ]	schmieden; fälschen	
p. 72	mass (of) [mæs]	Masse, Menge (von); Massen-	a large number or amount There were ~ protests against the war. *M~es of* people marched in the streets.
	°count [kaʊnt]	Graf	
p. 73	packet ['pækɪt]	Päckchen	package

(p. 73)	°printing press ['prɪntɪŋ pres]	Druckerpresse	
	medium ['mi:dɪəm], *pl. usually* media	*(künstlerisches)* Medium	Television is a good ~ for advertising. The artist chose the ~ of oil for her painting.

Playing with language

p. 74	(to) **point** sth. **out (to** sb.)	(jn.) auf etwas hinweisen	The guide *~ed out* all the important sights *to* us. Our teacher *~ed out* that there are several versions of the poem.
p. 75	applause [ə'plɔ:z]	Applaus, Beifall	The guest speaker received a round of ~.
	°Fellow citizens, … [ˌfeləʊ 'sɪtɪzənz]	Liebe Mitbürgerinnen, liebe Mitbürger, …	
	humorous ['hju:mərəs]	humorvoll, lustig	funny ▸◂ serious
	tone [təʊn]	Stimmung, Atmosphäre; Ton, Klang	general character of a book, for example; the quality or character of a sound Most of her novels have a humorous ~. This piano has an excellent ~.
	°outer space [ˌaʊtə 'speɪs]	Weltraum	
	concerning [kən'sɜ:nɪŋ]	bezüglich	about He doesn't answer questions ~ his private affairs.
	definite(ly) ['defənət, 'defənətlɪ]	sicher(lich), bestimmt	certain(ly), sure(ly) Nobody runs as fast as Sue. She'll *~ly* win the race. ⚠ *Do you want to take a break now? – Definitely!* (infml.) = *Yes/Certainly.*

Intensifying[1] adverbs (Verstärkende Adverbien)

You're **absolutely** right.	Du hast völlig recht.	I **quite** agree with you.	Ich stimme völlig mit Dir überein.
She's **completely** normal.	Sie ist ganz normal.		
I'm **deeply** concerned.	Ich bin tief besorgt.	I'm **really** happy.	Ich bin richtig froh.
That's **definitely** correct.	Das ist auf jeden Fall richtig.	I'm **terribly** sorry.	Es tut mir schrecklich leid.
It's **entirely** different.	Es ist ganz anders.	She's **totally** blind.	Sie ist völlig blind.
It's **extremely** hot.	Es ist extrem heiß.		
He's **highly** critical.	Er ist sehr kritisch.		

[1] [ɪn'tensɪfaɪɪŋ]

at first glance [glɑ:ns]	auf den ersten Blick	when seen or examined for the first time *At ~ ~* I thought the test was going to be easy. But it wasn't.
(to) **disturb** [dɪ'stɜ:b]	stören	If he's asleep, please *don't* ~ him.
°inverted commas *(pl.)* [ɪnˌvɜ:tɪd 'kɒməz] (BE)	Anführungszeichen, Gänsefüßchen	
shape [ʃeɪp]	*(äußere)* Form	Here are pieces of wood in different sizes and *~s*
(to) adjust (to) [ə'dʒʌst]	(sich) anpassen (an), (sich) gewöhnen (an)	The steel industry *is ~ing to* international competition.

Verbs with a preposition I

The plants in this region have had to **adapt to** extreme temperatures.	Die Pflanzen in dieser Region mußten sich **an** extreme Temperaturen **anpassen**.
After the holidays it takes time to **adjust to** school again.	Nach den Ferien dauert es, bis man sich **an** die Schule wieder **gewöhnt** hat.
I've **applied to** several companies in the area **for** a part-time job.	Ich habe mich **bei** mehreren Firmen in der Gegend **um** einen Teilzeitjob **beworben**.
Wine is often **associated with** France.	Wein wird oft **mit** Frankreich **assoziiert**.
Several new players are **competing against** each other **for** a position in the team.	Einige neue Spieler **konkurrieren gegen**einander **um** einen Platz in der Mannschaft.
The coach **congratulated** her team **on** the win.	Die Trainerin **gratulierte** ihrer Mannschaft **zum** Sieg.

(p. 75)

Verbs with a preposition II

She **contributed** greatly **to** our success.	Sie hat wesentlich **zu** unserem Erfolg **beigetragen**.
The teacher **criticized** the students **for** being lazy.	Der Lehrer **kritisierte** die Schüler **wegen** ihrer Faulheit.
The police **deduced from** the evidence that he could not have committed the crime.	Die Polizei **schloß aus** den Beweisen, daß er das Verbrechen nicht hätte begehen können.
In this company you don't usually **get away from** work until late.	In dieser Firma **kommt** man normalerweise erst spät **von** der Arbeit **weg**.
We do not **judge** our employees **by** their appearance.	Wir **beurteilen** unsere Angestellten nicht **nach** ihrem Aussehen.
We were **praised for** our hard work.	Wir wurden **für** unsere harte Arbeit **gelobt**.
The newspaper **speculated about** the future of the president.	Die Zeitung **spekulierte über** die Zukunft des Präsidenten.
The two parties are **struggling for** power.	Die zwei Parteien **kämpfen um** die Macht.
He **wastes** a lot of money **on** fancy cars.	Er **verschwendet** viel Geld **für** schicke Autos.

middle ['mɪdl]	mittlere(r, s)	Do you see the three cars? Ours is the ~ one.
°extraterrestrial [ˌekstrətə'restrɪəl]	Außerirdische(r); außerirdisch	

Writing your own literature

p. 76	°saga ['sɑːgə]	Geschichte; Heldenepos; Saga	
	°clerihew ['klerɪhjuː]	*vierzeiliger humoristischer Vers*	
	characteristic [ˌkærəktə'rɪstɪk]	(typisches) Merkmal; charakteristisch	"What did the man look like?" asked the policeman. "Did he have any special ~*s*?" Those churches are ~ of the region.

V

The End Fredric Brown

Professor Jones had worked on the problem of time for many years.
"But at last I've found the answer," he said to his daughter. "This machine can take us into the past."
He pushed a button[1] on the machine.
"This ought to make time go backwards."
"Backwards go time make to ought this."
Machine the on button a pushed he.
"Past the into us take can machine this." Daughter his to said he, "Answer the found I've last at but."
Years many for time of problem the on worked had Jones Professor

Brown Fredric *End The*

[1]button ['bʌtn] Knopf

Das *Dictionary* enthält den Wortschatz der Bände C1 bis C4. In der Regel wird nur die Schreibweise und Aussprache des britischen Englisch angegeben.
Wörter, die als Fußnote auf der Seite ihres Vorkommens erklärt werden, sind nicht im Dictionary enthalten.

A

a [ə] ein(e); **five lessons a week** fünf Stunden pro Woche
abandon [ə'bændən] verlassen, im Stich lassen
ability [ə'bɪlətɪ] Fähigkeit
able ['eɪbl]**: be able to** können, fähig sein zu
abolish [ə'bɒlɪʃ] abschaffen; *(ein Gesetz)* aufheben
about [ə'baʊt] **1.** ungefähr, etwa; **2.** wegen, bezüglich; um; über; **What about ...?** Wie wäre es mit ...? Was ist mit ...? **The book is about ...** Das Buch handelt von ...; **write about** schreiben über; **3. be about to do sth.** kurz davor sein, etwas zu tun
above [ə'bʌv] **1.** *(adv.)* oben; **2.** *(prep.)* über, oberhalb (von)
abroad [ə'brɔːd] im/ins Ausland; **from abroad** aus dem Ausland
absent ['æbsənt]**: be absent** fehlen, abwesend sein
absolutely ['æbsəluːtlɪ] absolut, unbedingt
absorb [əb'sɔːb] absorbieren, aufnehmen
accent ['æksənt] Akzent
accept [ək'sept] akzeptieren, annehmen
accident ['æksɪdənt] Unfall
accommodation *(sing.)* [əˌkɒmə'deɪʃn] Unterkunft
according to [ə'kɔːdɪŋ] nach, laut, zufolge
accountant [ə'kaʊntənt] Buchhalter/in
ache [eɪk] schmerzen, weh tun; **earache** ['ɪəreɪk] Ohrenschmerzen; **headache** ['hedeɪk] Kopfschmerzen, Kopfweh; **stomach ache** ['stʌmək_eɪk] Bauchschmerzen, Magenschmerzen
achieve [ə'tʃiːv] *(ein Ziel)* erreichen; leisten, zustande bringen; **achievement** [ə'tʃiːvmənt] Leistung, Errungenschaft
acid rain [ˌæsɪd 'reɪn] saurer Regen
acquire [ə'kwaɪə] erwerben
across [ə'krɒs] (quer) über, durch; **get across** verständlich machen, herüberbringen
act [ækt] spielen, aufführen; sich verhalten, benehmen; **act as ...** die Rolle des/der ... übernehmen
action ['ækʃn] Handlung, Tat; **take action** etwas unternehmen
active ['æktɪv] aktiv, rege
activity [æk'tɪvətɪ] Betätigung, Aktivität, Tätigkeit
actor ['æktə] Schauspieler/in
actually ['æktʃʊəlɪ] wirklich, tatsächlich, in der Tat; eigentlich
AD [ˌeɪ'diː] *(from Latin "anno Domini")* n. Chr.
adapt (to) [ə'dæpt] (sich) anpassen (an); **adapted from** adaptiert von, eine Bearbeitung von
add (to) [æd] hinzufügen (zu)
additional [ə'dɪʃənl] zusätzliche(r, s), weitere(r, s); **additionally** [ə'dɪʃnəlɪ] zusätzlich, außerdem
additive ['ædətɪv] Zusatz(stoff)
address [ə'dres] **1.** Adresse, Anschrift; **2.** sprechen zu, eine Ansprache halten vor
adjust (to) [ə'dʒʌst] (sich) anpassen (an), (sich) gewöhnen (an)
administration [ədˌmɪnɪ'streɪʃn] Verwaltung
admire [əd'maɪə] bewundern
admit [əd'mɪt] zugeben
adult ['ædʌlt] Erwachsene(r)
advantage [əd'vɑːntɪdʒ] Vorteil
adventure [əd'ventʃə] Abenteuer
advertise sth. ['ædvətaɪz] Reklame machen, werben für etwas; **advertisement** [əd'vɜːtɪzmənt], (infml. *auch:*) **advert** ['ædvɜːt] (BE)**, ad** [æd] Anzeige, Annonce, Reklame
advice *(sing.)* [əd'vaɪs] Rat, Ratschlag; Ratschläge; **Take my advice.** Hör(t) auf meinen Rat.
advise [əd'vaɪz] (be)raten; **advise sb. (not) to do sth.** jm. raten, etwas (nicht) zu tun; **advise sb. against doing sth.** jm. davon abraten, etwas zu tun; **adviser** Berater/in
aerobics [eə'rəʊbɪks] Aerobic
affair [ə'feə] Angelegenheit, Sache
affect [ə'fekt] betreffen, sich auswirken auf; beeinträchtigen
affection (for) [ə'fekʃn] Zuneigung (zu)
afford [ə'fɔːd] sich leisten
afraid [ə'freɪd]**: be afraid (of)** Angst haben (vor); **I'm afraid** leider, ich fürchte
African American [ˌæfrɪkən ə'merɪkən] (AE) **1.** afroamerikanisch; **2.** Afroamerikaner/in
Afro- ['æfrəʊ] afro-, Afro-
after ['ɑːftə] **1.** *(prep.)* nach *(zeitlich)*; **after lunch** nach dem Mittagessen; **day after day** Tag für Tag; **2.** *(conj.)* nachdem; **3.** hinter ... her; **look after** sich kümmern um
afternoon [ˌɑːftə'nuːn] Nachmittag; **Good afternoon.** Guten Tag. *(nachmittags)*; **in the afternoon(s)** am Nachmittag, nachmittags; **this afternoon** heute nachmittag
again [ə'gen] wieder, noch einmal; **once again** noch einmal
against [ə'genst] gegen
age [eɪdʒ] Alter; **at the age of** im Alter von; **aged** im Alter von, -jährig
ago [ə'gəʊ]**: a year ago** vor einem Jahr; **long ago** [ˌlɒŋ_ə'gəʊ] vor langer Zeit; **not long ago** vor kurzem
agree [ə'griː] **1.** übereinstimmen, zustimmen; **2.** sich einigen, sich einig werden/sein; **agree on** vereinbaren
aggressive (towards) [ə'gresɪv] aggressiv (gegenüber)
aid [eɪd] Hilfe, Unterstützung; **aid sb.** jm. helfen
aim [eɪm] **1.** Ziel; **2. aim (at)** zielen (auf); *(Waffe usw.)* richten (auf)
air [eə] Luft; **air-conditioning** *(sing.)* ['eəkənˌdɪʃnɪŋ] Klimaanlage; **airline** ['eəlaɪn] Fluggesellschaft; **airmail** ['eəmeɪl] Luftpost; **airport** ['eəpɔːt] Flughafen
alarm [ə'lɑːm] Alarm; Alarmanlage
alcohol ['ælkəhɒl] Alkohol; **alcoholic** [ˌælkə'hɒlɪk] **1.** Alkoholiker/in; **2.** alkoholisch
A-level (exam) ['eɪˌlevl] (BE) *etwa:* Abitur
algebra ['ældʒɪbrə] Algebra
alive [ə'laɪv] lebendig, am Leben; **keep alive** am Leben (er)halten
all [ɔːl] alle; **all day** den ganzen Tag; **all over the bungalow** im ganzen Bungalow verteilt, überall im Bungalow; **all (the) year** das ganze Jahr über; **Are you all right?** Geht es dir/Ihnen (noch) gut? **That's all right.** Schon gut. Nichts zu danken. **not ... at all** überhaupt nicht

D

allow [ə'laʊ] erlauben; **be allowed to** [ə'laʊd] dürfen
almost ['ɔ:lməʊst] fast, beinahe
alone [ə'ləʊn] allein; **leave sb. alone** jn. in Ruhe lassen
along [ə'lɒŋ] entlang, *(eine Straße)* hinunter; **get along (with)** auskommen (mit), sich verstehen (mit)
aloud *(adv.)* [ə'laʊd] laut *(= hörbar)*
alphabet ['ælfəbet] Alphabet
already [ɔ:l'redɪ] schon, bereits
also ['ɔ:lsəʊ] auch
alternative [ɔ:l'tɜ:nətɪv] **1.** Alternative; **2.** Alternativ-; **alternatively** [ɔ:l'tɜ:nətɪvlɪ] andererseits, als Alternative
although [ɔ:l'ðəʊ] obwohl
altogether [ˌɔ:ltə'geðə] insgesamt
always ['ɔ:lweɪz] immer
am [æm]**: I am** ich bin
... am [ˌeɪ_'em] *(from Latin "ante meridiem")* ... Uhr morgens *(zwischen 0 und 12 h)*
AM [ˌeɪ_'em] Mittelwelle*(nsender)*
amazed (at, by) [ə'meɪzd] erstaunt, verblüfft (über)
ambulance ['æmbjələns] Krankenwagen
American [ə'merɪkən] **1.** amerikanisch; **2.** Amerikaner/in
among [ə'mʌŋ] (mitten) unter, zwischen *(mehreren Personen oder Dingen)*
amount [ə'maʊnt] Betrag, Summe; Menge
amuse [ə'mju:z] (sich) amüsieren, unterhalten; **amusement** [ə'mju:zmənt] Unterhaltung, Vergnügen
an [ən] ein(e)
analyse ['ænəlaɪz] analysieren, untersuchen
ancestor ['ænsestə] Vorfahr(e)/Vorfahrin
and [ænd, ənd, ən] und; **both ... and ...** sowohl ... als auch ...
anger (at) ['æŋgə] Ärger, Wut (über)
Anglo-Saxon [ˌæŋgləʊ'sæksn] **1.** angelsächsisch; **2.** Angelsachse/Angelsächsin
angry (with) ['æŋgrɪ] wütend, böse (auf)
animal ['ænɪməl] Tier
annoyed [ə'nɔɪd] verärgert; **annoying** [ə'nɔɪɪŋ] ärgerlich, lästig
anorak ['ænəræk] Anorak
another [ə'nʌðə] ein(e) andere(r, s); noch ein(e)
answer ['ɑ:nsə] **1.** antworten, beantworten; **answer the phone** ans Telefon gehen;
2. answer (to) Antwort (auf);
answering machine ['ɑ:nsərɪŋ məˌʃi:n] Anrufbeantworter
anti-(British) ['æntɪ] anti(britisch)
anxiety [æŋ'zaɪətɪ] Angst, Sorge
any ['enɪ] (irgend)welche(r, s); jede(r, s) (beliebige); **any?** irgendwelche? **not ... any** kein(e); **not (...) any more** nicht mehr, kein(e, n) ... mehr
anybody/anyone ['enɪbɒdɪ/'enɪwʌn] (irgend) jemand; jede(r) beliebige; **anybody?** (irgend) jemand? **not ... anybody** niemand
anything ['enɪθɪŋ] (irgend) etwas; **anything?** (irgend) etwas? **not ... anything** nichts
anyway ['enɪweɪ] außerdem; wie dem auch sei; sowieso; trotzdem
anywhere ['enɪweə] irgendwo, irgendwohin; **anywhere?** irgendwo? irgendwohin? **not ... anywhere** nirgendwo; nirgendwohin
apartment [ə'pɑ:tmənt] *(meist* AE) Wohnung; **apartment house** (AE) Mietshaus, Wohnblock
apologize (to sb. for sth.) [ə'pɒlədʒaɪz] sich (bei jm. für etwas) entschuldigen; **apology** [ə'pɒlədʒɪ] Entschuldigung
apostrophe [ə'pɒstrəfɪ] Apostroph
appear [ə'pɪə] **1.** erscheinen, auftauchen; **2.** scheinen; **appearance** [ə'pɪərəns] Aussehen, (äußere) Erscheinung; Auftreten, Erscheinen
appendix [ə'pendɪks], *pl.* **appendices** [ə'pendɪsi:z] Anhang *(eines Buches)*
appetite (for) ['æpɪtaɪt] Appetit (auf)
applause [ə'plɔ:z] Applaus, Beifall
apple ['æpl] Apfel
application *(meist sing.)* [ˌæplɪ'keɪʃn] Anwendung
apply (to sb. for sth.) [ə'plaɪ] sich (bei jm. um etwas) bewerben; (bei jm. etwas) beantragen
appointment [ə'pɔɪntmənt] Termin
approach [ə'prəʊtʃ] **1.** anpacken *(Aufgabe, Problem)*; **2.** sich nähern
April ['eɪprəl] April
architect ['ɑ:kɪtekt] Architekt/in
are [ɑ:]**: you are** du bist/ihr seid/Sie sind; **they are** sie sind
area ['eərɪə] **1.** Gebiet, Gegend; **2.** Fläche
argue (about) ['ɑ:gju:] (sich) streiten (über, wegen); **argument** ['ɑ:gjʊmənt] **1.** Streit, Auseinandersetzung; **2.** Argument; **argumentative** [ˌɑ:gjʊ'mentətɪv] argumentativ
arise [ə'raɪz] auftreten, entstehen
arm [ɑ:m] Arm
army ['ɑ:mɪ] Armee, Heer
around [ə'raʊnd] um ... (herum); in ... umher, durch
arrange [ə'reɪndʒ] **1.** (an)ordnen; **2.** vereinbaren, arrangieren; **arrangement** [ə'reɪndʒmənt] Vereinbarung, Abmachung
arrest [ə'rest] verhaften, festnehmen
arrival [ə'raɪvl] Ankunft; **arrive** [ə'raɪv] ankommen, eintreffen
arrogant ['ærəgənt] arrogant, überheblich
art [ɑ:t] (bildende) Kunst; **artist** ['ɑ:tɪst] Künstler/in
article ['ɑ:tɪkl] Artikel
as [æz, əz] **1.** als, während; **2.** weil, da; **3.** wie; **as big as** so groß wie; **as far as** bis (nach/zu); **as if** als ob; **as long as** sofern, solange; **as soon as** sobald; **as well as** und auch, ebenso wie; **just as tired** genauso müde
Asian ['eɪʃn, 'eɪʒn] **1.** asiatisch; **2.** Asiate/Asiatin
ask [ɑ:sk] fragen; **ask a question** eine Frage stellen; **ask for** bitten um; **ask sb. out** jn. einladen *(ins Kino, zum Essen usw.)*; **ask sb. to do sth.** jn. bitten, etwas zu tun; **ask the way** nach dem Weg fragen
asleep [ə'sli:p]**: be asleep** schlafen; **fall asleep** einschlafen
aspect ['æspekt] Aspekt, Gesichtspunkt
aspirin ['æsprɪn] Aspirin
assassinate [ə'sæsɪneɪt] *(aus politischen Gründen)* ermorden
assembly [ə'semblɪ] Schulversammlung mit Andacht
assistant [ə'sɪstənt] Assistent/in; **shop assistant** Verkäufer/in
associate (with) [ə'səʊʃɪeɪt] assoziieren, (gedanklich) verbinden (mit); **association** [əˌsəʊsɪ'eɪʃn] Verband, Vereinigung; Assoziation
astronaut ['æstrənɔ:t] Astronaut/in
at [æt, ət] bei, an; **at a holiday park** in einem Ferienpark; **at Easter** zu/an Ostern; **at first** zuerst, am Anfang; **at home** zu Hause, daheim; **at last** schließlich, endlich; **at least** wenigstens, zumindest; mindestens; **at lunchtime** mittags, in der Mittagspause; **at midnight** um Mitternacht; **at night** nachts, in der Nacht, am (späten) Abend; **at number 5** im Haus Nr. 5; **at once** (so)gleich, sofort; **at platform 6** am Bahnsteig 6, auf Gleis 6; **at school** in der Schule; **at 7 o'clock** um 7 Uhr/19 Uhr; **at that time** damals, zu jener Zeit; **at the end of** am Ende von;

D

at the house am/beim Haus; **at the moment** im Augenblick, gerade; **at the weekend** (BE) am Wochenende; **good at** gut in, geschickt in; **not ... at all** überhaupt nicht
athletic [æθ'letɪk] athletisch; **athletics** *(sing.)* **1.** (BE) Leichtathletik; **2.** (AE) Sport
atmosphere ['ætməsfɪə] Atmosphäre
attach importance to sth. [ə'tætʃ] etwas Bedeutung beimessen
attack [ə'tæk] **1.** Angriff; **2.** angreifen
attend [ə'tend] besuchen, teilnehmen an *(Kurs, Schule usw.)*
attention [ə'tenʃn]**: pay attention (to)** aufmerksam sein, aufpassen (auf)
attitude (towards) ['ætɪtju:d] Haltung, Einstellung (gegenüber, zu)
attract [ə'trækt] anziehen, anlocken; **attraction** [ə'trækʃn] Attraktion; **attractive** [ə'træktɪv] attraktiv, reizvoll
audio-visual [ˌɔ:dɪəʊ'vɪʒʊəl] audiovisuell
August ['ɔ:gəst] August
aunt [ɑ:nt] Tante
Australian [ɒ'streɪlɪən] **1.** australisch; **2.** Australier/in
authentic [ɔ:'θentɪk] authentisch, echt
author ['ɔ:θə] Autor/in
auto(mobile) ['ɔ:təʊ, 'ɔ:təməʊbi:l] (AE) Auto(mobil); **auto mechanics** *(sing.)* ['ɔ:təʊ mɪˌkænɪks] (AE) Kfz-Technik
autumn ['ɔ:təm] Herbst
avenue ['ævənju:] Boulevard, Allee
average ['ævərɪdʒ] **1.** Durchschnitt; **2.** durchschnittlich, Durchschnitts-
avoid [ə'vɔɪd] vermeiden
awake [ə'weɪk]**: be awake** wach sein
aware [ə'weə]**: be/become aware of** sich bewußt sein/werden, merken
away [ə'weɪ] weg, fort; **break away (from)** [ˌbreɪk_ə'weɪ] sich lösen, trennen (von); sich losreißen (von)
axe (BE)/**ax** (AE) [æks] Axt, Beil

B

baby ['beɪbɪ] Baby, Säugling
back [bæk] **1.** zurück; **go back to** zurückgehen auf, zurückreichen bis; **2.** hinterer Teil, Rückseite; Rücken; **back door** Hintertür; **background** ['bækgraʊnd] Hintergrund; Herkunft; **backwards** ['bækwədz] rückwärts; nach hinten
bad [bæd] schlecht, schlimm; unartig; **bad at** schlecht/ungeschickt in
badminton ['bædmɪntən] Badminton, Federball
bag [bæg] Tasche, Beutel, Tüte
baked beans [ˌbeɪkt 'bi:nz] gebackene Bohnen *(in Tomatensoße)*
baker ['beɪkə] Bäcker/in; **bakery** ['beɪkərɪ] Bäckerei
balcony ['bælkənɪ] Balkon
ball [bɔ:l] Ball; **ball-point pen** (AE) Kugelschreiber
banana [bə'nɑ:nə] Banane
band [bænd] Band, (Musik-)Gruppe
bank [bæŋk] Bank, Sparkasse; **bottle bank** (BE) Altglascontainer
bar [bɑ:] **1.** *(Schokoladen-, Müsli-)* Riegel; **2.** Bar
bark [bɑ:k] bellen
baseball ['beɪsbɔ:l] Baseball
based: be based in ... [beɪst] den (Firmen-)Sitz in ... haben **be based on** basieren auf
basic ['beɪsɪk] grundlegend, Grund-
basis ['beɪsɪs] *pl.* **bases** ['beɪsi:z] Grundlage, Basis
basket ['bɑ:skɪt] Korb; **basketball** ['bɑ:skɪtbɔ:l] Basketball
bath [bɑ:θ] Bad; **baths** (Schwimm-)Bad; **have a bath** baden, ein Bad nehmen; **bathroom** Bad(ezimmer)
battery ['bætrɪ] Batterie
battle ['bætl] Schlacht, Kampf
bay [beɪ] Bucht
BC [ˌbi:'si:] **(before Christ)** v. Chr.
be [bi:] sein; **Be careful.** [ˌbi: 'keəfəl] Seien Sie/Sei/Seid vorsichtig!
beach [bi:tʃ] Strand
bean [bi:n] Bohne
bear [beə] Bär
beat [bi:t] schlagen
beautiful ['bju:təfəl] (wunder-)schön; **beauty** ['bju:tɪ] Schönheit
because [bɪ'kɒz] weil; **because of** wegen
become [bɪ'kʌm] werden
bed [bed] Bett; **in bed** im Bett; **bedroom** ['bedru:m] Schlafzimmer
beer [bɪə] Bier
before [bɪ'fɔ:] **1.** *(prep.)* vor *(zeitlich, Reihenfolge)*; **2.** *(conj.)* bevor, ehe; **3.** schon einmal, zuvor
begin [bɪ'gɪn] anfangen, beginnen; **beginner** Anfänger/in, Neuling; **beginning** Anfang, Beginn
behave [bɪ'heɪv] sich benehmen, sich verhalten; **behaviour (towards)** [bɪ'heɪvjə] Verhalten, Benehmen (gegenüber)
behind [bɪ'haɪnd] hinter; **from behind** von hinten; **leave behind** zurücklassen
believe (in) [bɪ'li:v] glauben (an); **be believed to be** (angeblich sein) sollen
bell [bel] Glocke, Klingel
belong to [bɪ'lɒŋ] gehören (zu)
below [bɪ'ləʊ] **1.** *(adv.)* unten; **2.** *(prep.)* unter(halb von)
best [best]**: (the) best** (der/die/das) beste; am besten
bestseller [ˌbest'selə] Bestseller
better ['betə] besser
between [bɪ'twi:n] zwischen; **in between** zwischendurch, dazwischen
beyond [bɪ'jɒnd] über ... hinaus, jenseits von
Bible ['baɪbl] Bibel
big [bɪg] groß; **the Big Apple** *umgangssprachliche Bezeichnung für „New York"*
bike [baɪk] (Fahr-)Rad; **ride a bike** radfahren; **bike path** Radweg
bill [bɪl] **1.** Rechnung; **2.** (AE) (Geld-)Schein
billion ['bɪljən] Milliarde(n)
bingo ['bɪŋgəʊ] Bingo *(Glücksspiel mit Zahlen)*
biography [baɪ'ɒgrəfɪ] Biographie
biology [baɪ'ɒlədʒɪ] Biologie; **biological** [ˌbaɪə'lɒdʒɪkl] biologisch; **bio-technology** [ˌbaɪəʊtek'nɒlədʒɪ] Biotechnologie, Biotechnik
bird [bɜ:d] Vogel; **birdseed** ['bɜ:dsi:d] Vogelfutter
biro ['baɪrəʊ] (BE) Kugelschreiber
birth [bɜ:θ] Geburt; **date of birth** Geburtsdatum; **birthday** Geburtstag; **birthplace** Geburtsort
biscuit ['bɪskɪt] (BE) Keks, Plätzchen
bit [bɪt]**: a bit** ein bißchen, etwas
bite [baɪt] **1.** beißen; **2.** Biß; Bissen, Happen
bitter ['bɪtə] bitter, verbittert; **bitterness** Bitterkeit
black [blæk] **1.** schwarz; **2.** Schwarze(r); **blacken** schwärzen
blame sb. (for sth.) [bleɪm] jn. Vorwürfe machen (wegen etwas); jm. die Schuld geben (an etwas); **Who is to blame?** Wer hat schuld?
blank [blæŋk] (Text-)Lücke
blanket ['blæŋkɪt] (Woll-)Decke
blind [blaɪnd] blind
block of flats [ˌblɒk_əv 'flæts] (BE) (Miets-)Haus, Wohnblock
blouse [blaʊz] Bluse

D

blow [bləʊ] blasen, wehen
blue [blu:] blau
blues [blu:z] Blues
board [bɔ:d] (Wand-)Tafel; Brett
boat [bəʊt] Boot, Schiff
body ['bɒdɪ] Körper; **care of the body** Körperpflege; **part of the body** Körperteil
bold print [ˌbəʊld 'prɪnt] fette Schrift, Fettdruck
bomb [bɒm] **1.** Bombe; **2.** bombardieren; **bomber** ['bɒmə] Bombenleger/in
bone [bəʊn] Knochen
book [bʊk] **1.** Buch; Heft; **bookshop** Buchhandlung; **2.** buchen, reservieren
booth [bu:θ]**: (tele)phone booth** (AE) Telefonzelle
border ['bɔ:də] Grenze
bored [bɔ:d] gelangweilt; **boring** ['bɔ:rɪŋ] langweilig
born [bɔ:n]**: I was born …** Ich bin … geboren
borrow ['bɒrəʊ] (sich) borgen, (sich) ausleihen
boss [bɒs] Chef/in, Vorgesetzte(r)
both [bəʊθ] beide, beides; **both … and …** sowohl … als auch …
bottle ['bɒtl] Flasche; **returnable bottle** Mehrwegflasche, Pfandflasche; **bottle bank** (BE) Altglascontainer
bottom ['bɒtəm] unteres Ende
bow tie [ˌbəʊ 'taɪ] Fliege, (Frack-)Schleife
bowl [bəʊl] Schüssel, Schale
bowling ['bəʊlɪŋ] Bowling
box [bɒks] Kiste, Karton; **box of matches** ['mætʃɪz] Streichholzschachtel; **letter box** (BE) Briefkasten; **(tele)phone box** (BE) Telefonzelle
Boxing Day ['bɒksɪŋ deɪ] (BE) zweiter Weihnachtsfeiertag (26.12.)
boy [bɔɪ] Junge; **boyfriend** ['bɔɪfrend] (fester) Freund
boycott ['bɔɪkɒt] **1.** Boykott; **2.** boykottieren
bracket ['brækɪt] Klammer *(Satzzeichen)*
brain [breɪn] Gehirn
brave [breɪv] tapfer, mutig
bread [bred] Brot; **bread roll** Brötchen
break [breɪk] **1.** *(etwas)* zerbrechen; brechen; **break away (from)** sich lösen, trennen (von); sich losreißen (von); **2. break (with)** Bruch (mit); **3. break-in** ['breɪk‿ɪn] Einbruch; **break in** einbrechen; **4.** Pause; **take a break** eine Pause machen
breakfast ['brekfəst] Frühstück; **have breakfast** frühstücken; **for breakfast** zum Frühstück
breathe (in/out) [bri:ð] (ein-/aus-)atmen
breeze [bri:z] Brise, leichter Wind
bridge [brɪdʒ] Brücke
bright [braɪt] hell, leuchtend
brilliant ['brɪljənt] toll, klasse; brillant, genial
bring [brɪŋ] bringen; **bring up children** Kinder großziehen, Kinder erziehen
Britain, Great Britain ['brɪtn] Großbritannien; **British** ['brɪtɪʃ] **1.** britisch; **2.** Brite/Britin
broadcast ['brɔ:dkɑ:st] *(Radio-/Fernsehsendung)* senden, ausstrahlen; übertragen
brochure ['brəʊʃə] Broschüre, Prospekt
brother ['brʌðə] Bruder
brown [braʊn] braun
brush [brʌʃ] **1.** (Haar-)Bürste; **2. brush one's teeth** (sich) die Zähne putzen
bubble ['bʌbl] *(Luft-, Seifen-, Sprech-)*Blase
budgie ['bʌdʒɪ] Wellensittich
build [bɪld] bauen; **builder** Bauarbeiter/in; Bauunternehmer/in; **building** Gebäude
bully ['bʊlɪ] **1.** schikanieren, tyrannisieren; **2.** *jd., der Schwächere schikaniert*
bungalow ['bʌŋgələʊ] Bungalow, einstöckiges Haus
burn [bɜ:n] **1.** (ver)brennen; **2.** anbrennen
bury ['berɪ] begraben
bus [bʌs] (Auto-)Bus; **on the bus** im Bus; **bus stop** Bushaltestelle
bush [bʊʃ] Busch
business ['bɪznɪs] Unternehmen, Geschäft; Geschäftswelt; **do business with** Geschäfte machen mit
busy ['bɪzɪ] **1.** beschäftigt; **2.** belebt, verkehrsreich; hektisch
but [bʌt, bət] aber; **not only … but (also) …** nicht nur … sondern (auch) …
butcher ['bʊtʃə] Metzger/in, Fleischer/in; **butcher's** Metzgerei, Metzgerladen, Fleischerei
butter ['bʌtə] Butter
buy [baɪ] kaufen
by [baɪ] **1.** von, durch; **by air/sea** auf dem Luft-/Seeweg; **by bike/car/bus/…** mit dem Fahrrad/Auto/Bus/…; **by the river** am Fluß; **2.** bis (zu); **by the year 2010** bis zum Jahr 2010; im Jahr 2010; **by the time** bis; **by this time** unterdessen, zu diesem Zeitpunkt; **3. drive/fly/go/… by** vorbeifahren/-fliegen/-gehen
Bye. [baɪ] Tschüs!

C

c (= circa) ['sɜ:kə] ca. (= circa)
cab [kæb] Taxi
cable ['keɪbl] Kabel
café ['kæfeɪ] kleines Restaurant; Café; Imbißstube; **cafeteria** [ˌkæfə'tɪərɪə] Selbstbedienungsrestaurant, Cafeteria
cake [keɪk] Kuchen, Torte
calendar ['kæləndə] Kalender
call [kɔ:l] **1.** Anruf; **2.** rufen; nennen; anrufen; **be called** heißen; **call sb. names** Schimpfwörter zu jm. sagen
calm [kɑ:m] ruhig, ausgeglichen; **calm down** (sich) beruhigen
camcorder ['kæmˌkɔ:də] Camcorder *(Videokamera mit eingebauter Abspielfunktion)*
camera ['kæmrə] Fotoapparat, Kamera
camp [kæmp] **1.** (Zelt-)Lager; **2.** zelten, campen; **campground** ['kæmpgraʊnd] (AE)**/campsite** ['kæmpsaɪt] (BE) Zeltplatz, Campingplatz
campaign [kæm'peɪn] **1.** Wahlkampf; **2.** (Werbe-)Kampagne
can [kæn, kən] können, dürfen; **can't** [kɑ:nt] **(= cannot** ['kænɒt]**)** nicht können, nicht dürfen
can [kæn] *(meist* AE) Dose, Büchse
candidate (for) ['kændɪdeɪt] Kandidat/in (für)
canoeing [kə'nu:ɪŋ] Kanufahren
canyon ['kænjən] Cañon
cap [kæp] (Schirm-)Mütze, Kappe
capital ['kæpɪtl] **1.** Großbuchstabe; Groß-; **2.** Hauptstadt
capitalism ['kæpɪtəlɪzəm] Kapitalismus
captain ['kæptɪn] Kapitän/in; Mannschaftsführer/in
caption ['kæpʃn] Bildunterschrift; Überschrift *(eines Artikels)*
capture ['kæptʃə] erobern, einnehmen; gefangennehmen
car [kɑ:] Auto; **car park** (BE) (großer) Parkplatz, Parkhaus
caravan ['kærəvæn] (BE) Wohnwagen

D

carbon dioxide [ˌkɑːbən daɪ'ɒksaɪd] Kohlendioxyd
card [kɑːd] (Spiel-, Post-)Karte; **credit card** ['kredɪt kɑːd] Kreditkarte
care (about) [keə] **1.** sich kümmern (um); wichtig nehmen; **They don't care.** Das ist ihnen egal. **2. care of the body** Körperpflege
career [kə'rɪə] Beruf, Karriere; (berufliche) Laufbahn
carefree ['keəfriː] sorgenfrei, sorglos; **careful** ['keəfəl] **1.** vorsichtig; **2.** sorgfältig; **careless 1.** unvorsichtig; **2.** nachlässig, unachtsam
carpenter ['kɑːpəntə] Tischler/in, Schreiner/in
carpet ['kɑːpɪt] Teppich
carrot ['kærət] Möhre, Karotte, Mohrrübe
carry ['kærɪ] tragen; befördern; **carry sth. out** etwas durchführen, ausführen
cartoon [kɑː'tuːn] Cartoon; Zeichentrickfilm
case [keɪs] Fall; **in case** falls, für den Fall, daß
cash [kæʃ] Bargeld; (infml. *auch:*) Geld
cassette [kə'set] Kassette; **cassette-recorder** Kassettenrecorder
castle ['kɑːsl] Burg; Schloß
casual ['kæʒʊəl] *(Person)* lässig, locker, gelassen; *(Situation, Kleidung usw.)* zwanglos, locker
cat [kæt] Katze
catalogue ['kætəlɒg] Katalog
catch [kætʃ] fangen; erwischen
cathedral [kə'θiːdrəl] Kathedrale, Dom
Catholic ['kæθlɪk] **1.** Katholik/in; **2.** katholisch
cattle *(pl.)* ['kætl] Rindvieh, Rinder
cause [kɔːz] **1.** verursachen; **2.** Ursache; **a good cause** ein guter Zweck
cave [keɪv] Höhle
CD [ˌsiː'diː], **compact disc** [ˌkɒmpækt 'dɪsk] CD
ceiling ['siːlɪŋ] (Zimmer-)Decke
celebrate ['seləbreɪt] feiern; **celebration** [ˌselə'breɪʃn] (Gedenk-)Feier
cellar ['selə] Keller
Celtic ['keltɪk] Keltisch, keltisch
cent (¢) [sent] Cent *(US-Münze)*
centimetre ['sentɪmiːtə] Zentimeter
central ['sentrəl] Zentral-, Mittel-
centre ['sentə] Zentrum, Mitte
century ['sentʃərɪ] Jahrhundert
ceremony ['serəmənɪ] Zeremonie, Feier
certain ['sɜːtn] **1.** bestimmte(r, s); **2.** sicher, gewiß; **certainty** ['sɜːtəntɪ] Sicherheit, Gewißheit
chain [tʃeɪn] Kette
chair [tʃeə] Stuhl
challenge ['tʃælɪndʒ] **1.** herausfordern; **2. challenge (to)** Herausforderung (für)
champion ['tʃæmpɪən] Meister/in, Sieger/in
chance [tʃɑːns] Chance, Gelegenheit; **take a chance** ein Risiko eingehen; es darauf ankommen lassen
chancellor ['tʃɑːnsələ] **1.** Kanzler/in; **2.** (BE) Finanzminister/in
change [tʃeɪndʒ] **1.** wechseln *(die Schule, Geld usw.)*; **2.** (sich) verändern; **change (into)** verändern, umwandeln (in); **change into jeans/...** sich (umziehen und) Jeans/... anziehen; **change one's mind** seine Meinung ändern; **change places (with)** die Plätze tauschen (mit) *(auch im übertragenen Sinn)*; **3.** umsteigen; **4.** (Ver-)Änderung, Wechsel; **5.** Wechselgeld
channel ['tʃænl] Kanal; (Fernseh-) Kanal
character ['kærəktə] Charakter, Wesen; **characteristic** [ˌkærəktə'rɪstɪk] (typisches) Merkmal; charakteristisch **characterize** ['kærəktəraɪz] charakterisieren, beschreiben
charge [tʃɑːdʒ] **1.** *(Geld)* in Rechnung stellen, berechnen, verlangen; **2.** Gebühr
charity ['tʃærətɪ] wohltätige Einrichtung
chart [tʃɑːt] Tabelle, Schaubild, Diagramm
cheap [tʃiːp] billig, preiswert
check [tʃek] (über)prüfen, kontrollieren
check [tʃek] (AE) **1.** Rechnung; **2. check (for)** Scheck (über *eine Summe*)
check-in ['tʃek_ɪn] Einchecken; Abfertigung; **check in** [ˌtʃek_'ɪn] sich anmelden, eintragen *(Hotel)*; einchecken *(Flughafen)*
cheer [tʃɪə] jubeln, Beifall spenden; **cheering** ['tʃɪərɪŋ] Jubel, Beifall; **cheer sb. up** [ˌtʃɪər_'ʌp] jn. aufmuntern, aufheitern; **Cheer up!** Kopf hoch! Laß den Kopf nicht hängen!
chemical ['kemɪkl] Chemikalie; **chemist** ['kemɪst] (BE) Apotheker/in; Drogist/in; **chemist's** (BE) Apotheke; Drogerie; **chemistry** ['kemɪstrɪ] Chemie
cheque (for) [tʃek] (BE) Scheck (über *eine Summe*)
chess [tʃes] Schach
chest [tʃest] Brust(korb)
chestnut ['tʃesnʌt] Kastanienbaum; Kastanie
chicken ['tʃɪkən] Huhn; (Brat-) Hähnchen
chief [tʃiːf] (Indianer-)Häuptling
child [tʃaɪld], *pl.* **children** ['tʃɪldrən] Kind
chimney ['tʃɪmnɪ] Schornstein
Chinese [tʃaɪ'niːz] **1.** Chinesisch, chinesisch; **2.** Chinese/Chinesin
chips *(pl.)* [tʃɪps] (BE) Pommes frites
chocolate ['tʃɒklət] Schokolade
choice (of) [tʃɔɪs] (Aus-)Wahl (an); **make a choice** eine Wahl treffen
choir ['kwaɪə] Chor
choose [tʃuːz] (aus)wählen, aussuchen
Christ [kraɪst] Christus; **Christian** ['krɪstʃən] **1.** Christ/in; **2.** christlich; **Christian name** (BE) Vorname; **Christianity** [ˌkrɪstɪ'ænətɪ] das Christentum, die Christenheit
Christmas ['krɪsməs] Weihnachten; **Christmas Day** der erste Weihnachtsfeiertag (25.12.); **Christmas Eve** [ˌkrɪsməs_'iːv] Heiligabend (24.12.); **the Christmas holidays** die Weihnachtsfeiertage; BE *auch:* die Weihnachtsferien; **Father Christmas** (BE) der Weihnachtsmann
church [tʃɜːtʃ] Kirche
cinema ['sɪnəmə] (*meist* BE) Kino
circle ['sɜːkl] Kreis
citizen ['sɪtɪzən] (Staats-)Bürger/in, Staatsangehörige(r)
city ['sɪtɪ] Stadt, Großstadt
civil: civil rights *(pl.)* [ˌsɪvl 'raɪts] Bürgerrechte; **civil war** [ˌsɪvl 'wɔː] Bürgerkrieg
civilize ['sɪvəlaɪz] zivilisieren; **civilized** zivilisiert
claim [kleɪm] behaupten
class [klɑːs] **1.** Klasse; **2.** (BE) Klasse(nstufe); **classmate** ['klɑːsmeɪt] Klassenkamerad/in, Mitschüler/in; **classroom** Klassenzimmer; **classless** klassenlos *(Gesellschaft)*; **working class** Arbeiterklasse; **3.** (AE) (Unterrichts-)Stunde; **4.** (AE) (Schul-)Fach
classical ['klæsɪkl] klassisch
clause [klɔːz] (Teil-, Glied-)Satz
clean [kliːn] **1.** sauber; **2.** saubermachen, reinigen
clear [klɪə] klar, deutlich; **clearly** eindeutig, klar

D

clever ['klevə] klug, schlau; **cleverness** Klugheit, Schlauheit
cliché ['kli:ʃeɪ] Klischee, Gemeinplatz
client ['klaɪənt] Klient/in
cliff [klɪf] Klippe, Fels
climate ['klaɪmət] Klima
climax ['klaɪmæks] Höhepunkt
climb [klaɪm] klettern, steigen; **climber** ['klaɪmə] Bergsteiger/in
clock [klɒk] (Wand-, Stand-)Uhr
close [kləʊz] schließen, zumachen; **closed** [kləʊzd] geschlossen, zu
close [kləʊs] **1.** genau, gründlich; **2.** knapp *(Sieg, Ergebnis)*; **3. close (to)** nahe (bei/an); **closely** *(adv.)* eng
cloth [klɒθ] Stoff; Tuch, Lappen
clothes *(pl.)* [kləʊðz, kləʊz] Kleidung(sstücke)
cloud [klaʊd] Wolke; **cloudless** wolkenlos, klar; **cloudy** bewölkt
clown [klaʊn] Clown
club [klʌb] Klub; Verein
clue [klu:] Hinweis, Anhaltspunkt
coach [kəʊtʃ] **1.** (Reise-)Bus; **2.** Trainer/in
coal [kəʊl] Kohle
coalition [ˌkəʊə'lɪʃn] Koalition
coast [kəʊst] Küste; **on the coast** an der Küste
coat [kəʊt] Mantel
cocktail ['kɒkteɪl] Cocktail
coffee ['kɒfɪ] Kaffee; **make coffee** Kaffee kochen
coin [kɔɪn] Münze
coke [kəʊk] Cola
cold [kəʊld] **1.** kalt; **be/feel cold** frieren; **2.** Kälte; **3.** Erkältung; **I've got a cold.** Ich bin erkältet.
collage [kɒ'lɑ:ʒ] Collage
colleague ['kɒli:g] Kollege, Kollegin
collect [kə'lekt] **1.** sammeln; einsammeln; **collection** [kə'lekʃn] Sammlung; **2.** abholen
college ['kɒlɪdʒ] Fach-, Hochschule
collocation [ˌkɒlə'keɪʃn] Kollokation *(Wörter, die oft zusammen vorkommen)*
colon ['kəʊlən] Doppelpunkt; **semicolon** [ˌsemɪ'kəʊlən] Semikolon
colonial [kə'ləʊnɪəl] kolonial, Kolonial-; **colonist** ['kɒlənɪst] Kolonist/in, Siedler/in; **colony** ['kɒlənɪ] Kolonie
colour ['kʌlə] **1.** Farbe; **2.** färben
column ['kɒləm] Spalte *(auf Buchseite usw.)*
comb [kəʊm] **1.** Kamm; **2.** kämmen
combination [ˌkɒmbɪ'neɪʃn] Kombination, Zusammenstellung; **combine (with)** [kəm'baɪn] kombinieren, verbinden (mit)

come [kʌm] kommen; **come across** stoßen auf, treffen auf; **come in** hereinkommen; **Come on!** Los! Komm schon! **come true** Wirklichkeit werden, wahr werden
comfortable ['kʌmftəbl] bequem, behaglich
comic ['kɒmɪk] Comic-Heft
comma ['kɒmə] Komma
comment (about/on) ['kɒment] **1.** Kommentar, Bemerkung (über/zu); **2. comment (on)** kommentieren, sich äußern (zu)
commercial [kə'mɜ:ʃl] Werbespot, (Radio-, Fernseh-)Werbung
commit [kə'mɪt] *(ein Verbrechen, Selbstmord)* begehen
common ['kɒmən] häufig, weitverbreitet; **have sth. in common** etwas miteinander gemein haben
communicate (with) [kə'mju:nɪkeɪt] kommunizieren (mit), sich verständigen (mit); **communication** [kəˌmju:nɪ'keɪʃn] Kommunikation; **communications** *(pl.)* Nachrichtentechnik, Telekommunikation
communism ['kɒmjʊnɪzəm] Kommunismus; **communist** ['kɒmjʊnɪst] **1.** Kommunist/in; **2.** kommunistisch
community [kə'mju:nətɪ] Kommune, Gemeinde; Gemeinschaft
commute [kə'mju:t] pendeln *(zwischen Wohnung und Arbeitsplatz)*
company ['kʌmpənɪ] **1.** Gesellschaft, Begleitung; **2.** Firma
compare (to/with) [kəm'peə] vergleichen (mit); **compare (with)** sich vergleichen lassen (mit); **compared to** verglichen mit, im Vergleich zu; **comparison** [kəm'pærɪsn] **1.** Vergleich; **2.** Steigerung
compete (against/with/for) [kəm'pi:t] konkurrieren, kämpfen (gegen/mit/um); **competition** [ˌkɒmpə'tɪʃn] **1.** Wettkampf, Wettbewerb; **2.** Konkurrenz
complain [kəm'pleɪn] sich beschweren, sich beklagen; **complaint** Beschwerde
complete [kəm'pli:t] **1.** vervollständigen, ergänzen; beenden; **2.** vollkommen; vollständig; **completely** völlig
comprehensive school [ˌkɒmprɪ'hensɪv] (BE) Gesamtschule
computer [kəm'pju:tə] Computer, Rechner; **computer science** [kəmˌpju:tə 'saɪəns] Informatik
concerned [kən'sɜ:nd]**: as far as I'm concerned** meiner Meinung nach, was mich betrifft; **be concerned about** besorgt sein um, sich Sorgen machen um; **concerning** [kən'sɜ:nɪŋ] bezüglich
concert ['kɒnsət] Konzert
concrete(ly) ['kɒnkri:t, -lɪ] konkret
condition [kən'dɪʃn] **1.** Zustand; **2.** Bedingung, Voraussetzung
conference ['kɒnfrəns] Konferenz
confident ['kɒnfɪdənt] selbstbewußt; zuversichtlich
conflict ['kɒnflɪkt] **1.** Konflikt, Auseinandersetzung; **2. conflict (with)** [kən'flɪkt] sich widersprechen; im Widerspruch stehen (zu)
confront (with) [kən'frʌnt] konfrontieren (mit); **confrontation** [ˌkɒnfrʌn'teɪʃn] Konfrontation
confused [kən'fju:zd] verwirrt, durcheinander; wirr, konfus; **confusing** [kən'fju:zɪŋ] verwirrend
congestion [kən'dʒestʃn]**: traffic congestion** *(sing.)* Verkehrsstau(s), verstopfte Straßen
congratulate [kən'grætʃʊleɪt] gratulieren, beglückwünschen; **congratulations (on)** *(pl.)* [kənˌgrætʃʊ'leɪʃnz] Herzlichen Glückwunsch (zu)! **offer sb. one's congratulations** (fml.) jm. gratulieren, jn. beglückwünschen
Congress ['kɒŋgres] (US-)Parlament
connect (to/with) [kə'nekt] verbinden (mit); **connection** [kə'nekʃn] Verbindung
conquer ['kɒŋkə] erobern; besiegen
consequence ['kɒnsɪkwəns] Folge, Konsequenz; **consequently** ['kɒnsɪkwəntlɪ] folglich, infolgedessen, daher
conservation [ˌkɒnsə'veɪʃn] Naturschutz, Umweltschutz; **conserve** [kən'sɜ:v] erhalten, bewahren
conservative [kən'sɜ:vətɪv] **1.** Konservative(r); **2.** konservativ
consider [kən'sɪdə] **1.** in Betracht, in Erwägung ziehen; **2.** sich überlegen, nachdenken über; **3.** halten für, betrachten als; **take sth. into consideration** [kənˌsɪdə'reɪʃn] etwas in Erwägung ziehen, etwas bedenken
consist of [kən'sɪst] bestehen aus
constitution [ˌkɒnstɪ'tju:ʃn] Verfassung
construct [kən'strʌkt] bauen, konstruieren; **construction** [kən'strʌkʃn] Konstruktion
consumer [kən'sju:mə] Verbraucher/in, Konsument/in
contact ['kɒntækt] **1.** Kontakt, Verbindung; **2.** Kontakt aufnehmen mit, sich in Verbindung setzen mit
contain [kən'teɪn] enthalten

D

content ['kɒntent] Gehalt, Inhalt *(einer Rede, eines Buches usw.)*; **contents** *(pl.)* Inhalt *(von Behältnissen, Räumen usw.)*
context ['kɒntekst] Kontext, Zusammenhang
continent ['kɒntɪnənt] Kontinent
continuation [kənˌtɪnjʊ'əɪʃn] Fortsetzung, Fortdauer; **continue (with)** [kən'tɪnjuː] fortfahren (mit), fortsetzen; **continuously** [kən'tɪnjʊəslɪ] ununterbrochen, ständig
contract ['kɒntrækt] Vertrag
contradict [ˌkɒntrə'dɪkt] widersprechen; **contradiction** [ˌkɒntrə'dɪkʃn] Widerspruch; Gegensatz
contrast **1.** ['kɒntrɑːst] Kontrast, Gegensatz; **2.** [kən'trɑːst] kontrastieren, gegenüberstellen
contribute (to) [kən'trɪbjuːt] beitragen, beisteuern (zu); **contribution (to)** [ˌkɒntrɪ'bjuːʃn] Beitrag (zu)
control [kən'trəʊl] **1.** Kontrolle; **2.** unter Kontrolle halten, beherrschen; kontrollieren, steuern
conversation [ˌkɒnvə'seɪʃn] Gespräch, Unterhaltung
convey (to) [kən'veɪ] übermitteln (an) *(Nachricht, Botschaft)*
convince [kən'vɪns] überzeugen
cook [kʊk] **1.** kochen, zubereiten; **2.** Koch, Köchin; **cooker** (BE) Herd; **cookery** ['kʊkərɪ] Kochen
cool [kuːl] kühl
copier ['kɔpɪə] Fotokopierer
copy ['kɒpɪ] **1.** Kopie, Abschrift; **2.** kopieren; abschreiben
corn [kɔːn] Getreide, Korn; AE *auch:* Mais
corner ['kɔːnə] Ecke
cornflakes *(pl.)* ['kɔːnfleɪks] Cornflakes
Cornish ['kɔːnɪʃ] kornisch, aus/in Cornwall
correct [kə'rekt] **1.** richtig, korrekt; **2.** berichtigen, korrigieren
cost [kɒst] **1.** *(Geld)* kosten; **2.** *(sing.)* Kosten; Preis; **at the cost of** auf Kosten von
costume ['kɒstjuːm] Kostüm, Tracht
cotton ['kɒtn] Baumwolle
cough [kɒf] Husten
could [kʊd] **1.** konnte(n); **2.** könnte(n)
counselor (AE)/**counsellor** (BE) ['kaʊnsələ] Berater/in; **guidance counselor** ['gaɪdəns ˌkaʊnsələ] (AE) *Schulberater/in an einer High School, berät Schüler/innen bei persönlichen und schulischen Prblemen und bei der Berufswahl*
count [kaʊnt] zählen; **countless** ['kaʊntləs] unzählig, zahllos
country ['kʌntrɪ] Land; **in the country** auf dem Land; **countryside** Landschaft, (ländliche) Gegend
county ['kaʊntɪ] Grafschaft, Verwaltungsbezirk
couple ['kʌpl] (Ehe-)Paar; **a couple of** (infml.) ein paar
course [kɔːs] Kurs, Lehrgang; **course work** *projektähnlicher Unterricht*; **of course** [əv 'kɔːs] natürlich, selbstverständlich
court [kɔːt] **1.** Spielfeld, Platz; **2.** Gericht(shof), Gerichtssaal; **take sb. to court** jn. vor Gericht bringen, verklagen
cousin ['kʌzn] Vetter, Kusine
cover ['kʌvə] **1.** bedecken, zudecken; **2.** sich erstrecken über *(eine Fläche, Zeitspanne)*; **be covered with/in** bedeckt sein mit
cow [kaʊ] Kuh; **cowboy** ['kaʊbɔɪ] Cowboy
coward ['kaʊəd] Feigling
crazy ['kreɪzɪ] verrückt; **drive sb. crazy** (infml.) jn. zur Verzweiflung treiben, jn. verrückt machen
cream [kriːm] **1.** Sahne; **2.** Creme
create [krɪ'eɪt] schaffen; **creative** [krɪ'eɪtɪv] schöpferisch, kreativ; **creative writing** [krɪˌeɪtɪv 'raɪtɪŋ] schöpferisches Schreiben
credit card ['kredɪt kɑːd] Kreditkarte
crew [kruː] Besatzung, Mannschaft
cricket ['krɪkɪt] Kricket *(englisches Schlagballspiel)*
crime [kraɪm] Verbrechen; **criminal** ['krɪmɪnl] **1.** Verbrecher/in, Kriminelle(r); **2.** kriminell
crisis ['kraɪsɪs], *pl.* **crises** ['kraɪsiːz] Krise
crisps [krɪsps] (BE) Kartoffelchips
critical (of) ['krɪtɪkl] kritisch (gegenüber); **criticize (for)** ['krɪtɪsaɪz] kritisieren (wegen)
cross [krɒs] überqueren; kreuzen; **crossing** Überfahrt; **pedestrian crossing** [pəˌdestrɪən 'krɒsɪŋ] (BE) Fußgängerüberweg; **crossroads** *(sing.)* ['krɒsrəʊdz] (BE) (Straßen-)Kreuzung
crowd [kraʊd] (Menschen-)Menge; **crowded** ['kraʊdɪd] überfüllt
cruise [kruːz]: **cruise the streets** in den Straßen herumfahren, spazierenfahren
cry [kraɪ] **1.** weinen; **2.** rufen, schreien; **3.** Schrei
cultural ['kʌltʃrəl] kulturell, Kultur-; **culture** ['kʌltʃə] Kultur
cup [kʌp] Tasse; **a cup of tea** eine Tasse Tee
cupboard ['kʌbəd] Schrank
curious ['kjʊərɪəs] neugierig
currency ['kʌrənsɪ] Währung
curry ['kʌrɪ] *scharfes, mit Curry gewürztes Gericht*
curtain ['kɜːtn] Vorhang, Gardine
custom ['kʌstəm] Brauch, Sitte
customer ['kʌstəmə] Kunde/Kundin
cut [kʌt] **1.** Schnitt; Schnittwunde; **2. cut (off)** (etwas ab)schneiden; **cut down** *(Bäume)* fällen
cycle ['saɪkl] radfahren

D

Dad/dad [dæd] Vati, Papa
daily ['deɪlɪ] täglich
damage ['dæmɪdʒ] beschädigen
dance [dɑːns] **1.** tanzen; **2.** Tanz; Ball; **dancer** Tänzer/in
danger ['deɪndʒə] Gefahr; **dangerous** ['deɪndʒərəs] gefährlich
dark [dɑːk] dunkel; **darkness** ['dɑːknəs] Dunkelheit
darts [dɑːts] *britisches Pfeilwurfspiel*
dash [dæʃ] Gedankenstrich
date [deɪt] Datum; **date of birth** Geburtsdatum
daughter ['dɔːtə] Tochter
day [deɪ] Tag; **all day** den ganzen Tag; **day after day** Tag für Tag; **one day** eines Tages; **these days** heutzutage; **in those days** damals, in jenen Tagen; **day care** ['deɪ keə] Kinder(tages)betreuung, Alten(tages)betreuung
dead [ded] tot; **deadly** Tod-, tödlich; **death** [deθ] Tod
deaf [def] taub, gehörlos; **deafen** taub machen
deal with [diːəl] sich befassen mit; handeln von
Dear …, [dɪə] Liebe(r) …, **Dear Sir or Madam, …** Sehr geehrte Damen und Herren, …;
death [deθ] Tod
debate (on, about) [dɪ'beɪt] **1.** Debatte (über); **2. debate (sth.)** (über etwas) debattieren, diskutieren
December [dɪ'sembə] Dezember
decide [dɪ'saɪd] (sich) entscheiden, beschließen; **decide on** sich entscheiden für; **decision** [dɪ'sɪʒn] Entscheidung, Entschluß;

D

make/take a decision eine Entscheidung treffen, fällen
declaration [ˌdeklə'reɪʃn] Erklärung; **declare** [dɪ'kleə] erklären, verkünden
decorate ['dekəreɪt] renovieren *(tapezieren, streichen usw.)*
deduce (from) [dɪ'dju:s] folgern, schließen (aus); **deduction** [dɪ'dʌkʃn] (Schluß-)Folgerung, Deduktion
deep [di:p] tief; **deepen** vertiefen, tiefer machen
defeat [dɪ'fi:t] besiegen
defend [dɪ'fend] verteidigen
define [dɪ'faɪn] definieren, festlegen; **defining** definierend, bestimmend; **definition** [ˌdefə'nɪʃn] Definition
definite(ly) ['dəfənət, -lɪ] sicherlich, bestimmt
degree [dɪ'gri:] Grad
deliver [dɪ'lɪvə] **1.** liefern; **2.** *(Zeitungen)* austragen, zustellen
demand [dɪ'mɑ:nd] **1.** verlangen, fordern; erfordern; **2. demand (for)** Forderung (nach)
democracy [dɪ'mɒkrəsɪ] Demokratie; **democrat** ['deməkræt] Demokrat/in; **democratic** [ˌdemə'krætɪk] demokratisch; **democratically** [ˌdemə'krætɪklɪ] demokratisch
deny [dɪ'naɪ] (ab)leugnen, bestreiten, dementieren
depart (from) [dɪ'pɑ:t] abfahren, abreisen (von, aus); **departure** [dɪ'pɑ:tʃə] Abfahrt, Abreise
department store [dɪ'pɑ:tmənt stɔ:] Kaufhaus
departure [dɪ'pɑ:tʃə] Abfahrt, Abreise
depend on [dɪ'pend] abhängig sein von, abhängen von
derelict ['derəlɪkt] verlassen und verfallen, heruntergekommen
descendant [dɪ'sendənt] Nachfahr/Nachfahrin
describe [dɪ'skraɪb] beschreiben; **descriptive** [dɪ'skrɪptɪv] beschreibend, darstellend, deskriptiv
desegregate [ˌdi:'segrɪgeɪt] die Rassentrennung aufheben an
desert ['dezət] Wüste
deserve [dɪ'zɜ:v] verdienen, Anspruch haben auf
design [dɪ'zaɪn] **1.** Design, Konstruktion, Entwurf; **2.** entwerfen, konstruieren
desk [desk] Schreibtisch, Schülertisch; **desk-top publishing** [ˌdesktɒp 'pʌblɪʃɪŋ], **DTP** [ˌdi:ti:'pi:] DTP *(Erstellung und Gestaltung von Druckschriften mittels Computer)*
destination [ˌdestɪ'neɪʃn] (Fahrt-)Ziel, Bestimmungsort
destroy [dɪ'strɔɪ] zerstören, vernichten
detached [dɪ'tætʃt]**: detached house** (BE) freistehendes Haus; **semi-detached house** ['semɪdɪˌtætʃt 'haʊs] (BE) Doppelhaushälfte
detail ['di:teɪl] Einzelheit, Detail
develop [dɪ'veləp] (sich) entwickeln; aufbauen; **developing country** [dɪ'veləpɪŋ ˌkʌntrɪ] Entwicklungsland; **development** [dɪ'veləpmənt] Entwicklung; Aufbau, Ausbau
devil ['devl] Teufel
diagram ['daɪəgræm] Diagramm, Schaubild
dial ['daɪəl] wählen *(beim Telefonieren)*
dialect ['daɪəlekt] Dialekt, Mundart
dialogue ['daɪəlɒg] Dialog
diary ['daɪərɪ] **1.** Tagebuch; **2.** Notizbuch, Taschenkalender
dictatorship [dɪk'teɪtəʃɪp] Diktatur
dictionary ['dɪkʃənrɪ] Wörterbuch
die (of) [daɪ] sterben (an)
diesel ['di:zl] Diesel(motor/-kraftstoff)
diet ['daɪət] Ernährung, Eßgewohnheit; Diät; **be on a diet** eine Diät machen
difference ['dɪfrəns] Unterschied; **different (from)** ['dɪfrənt] anders (als); verschieden, andere(r, s)
difficult ['dɪfɪkəlt] schwierig; **difficulty** ['dɪfɪkəltɪ] Schwierigkeit
dilemma [dɪ'lemə] Dilemma
dime [daɪm] (AE) Zehncentmünze
diner ['daɪnə] (AE) (kleines, billiges) Restaurant
dining-room ['daɪnɪŋ ru:m] Eßzimmer
dinner ['dɪnə] Mittag-, Abendessen
direct [dɪ'rekt, daɪ'rekt] direkt, unmittelbar
direction [dɪ'rekʃn, daɪ'rekʃn] Richtung
dirt [dɜ:t] Schmutz, Dreck; **dirty** schmutzig, dreckig
disabled [dɪs'eɪbld] behindert
disadvantage [ˌdɪsəd'vɑ:ntɪdʒ] Nachteil
disagree (with) [ˌdɪsə'gri:] anderer Meinung sein (als), nicht übereinstimmen (mit); **disagreement** [ˌdɪsə'gri:mənt] Uneinigkeit; Meinungsverschiedenheit
disappear [ˌdɪsə'pɪə] verschwinden
disappoint [ˌdɪsə'pɔɪnt] enttäuschen; **disappointed** enttäuscht; **disappointment** Enttäuschung
disaster [dɪ'zɑ:stə] Katastrophe, Desaster
disco ['dɪskəʊ] Disko(thek)
discontinue [ˌdɪskən'tɪnju:] abbrechen, einstellen, nicht weiterführen
discover [dɪ'skʌvə] entdecken; **discovery** [dɪ'skʌvərɪ] Entdeckung
discriminate against [dɪ'skrɪmɪneɪt] diskriminieren, benachteiligen; **discrimination (against)** [dɪˌskrɪmɪ'neɪʃn] Diskriminierung, Benachteiligung (von)
discuss sth. [dɪ'skʌs] etwas besprechen, über etwas diskutieren; **discussion** [dɪ'skʌʃn] Diskussion, Besprechung
dishes ['dɪʃɪz]**: wash the dishes** (das Geschirr) spülen, abwaschen
dishonest [dɪs'ɒnɪst] unehrlich
disk [dɪsk] Diskette
dislike [dɪs'laɪk] **1.** nicht gern haben, nicht mögen; **2. dislike (of, for)** Abneigung (gegen)
display [dɪ'spleɪ]**: wall display** Wandzeitung, Wandbild
disposal [dɪ'spəʊzl] (Müll-)Entsorgung, Beseitigung; **dispose of sth.** [dɪ'spəʊz] etwas beseitigen
distance ['dɪstəns] Entfernung, Strecke
district ['dɪstrɪkt] Gebiet, Bezirk
disturb [dɪ'stɜ:b] stören
divide (into) [dɪ'vaɪd] (auf)teilen (in)
divorced [dɪ'vɔ:st] geschieden; **get divorced** sich scheiden lassen
DIY [ˌdi:‿aɪ'waɪ] (BE)**, Do it yourself** Heimwerken
do [du:] tun, machen; **do terribly/well/...** furchtbar/gut/... abschneiden
doctor ['dɒktə] Arzt/Ärztin
document ['dɒkjʊmənt] Dokument, Unterlage; Urkunde; **documentary** [ˌdɒkjʊ'mentərɪ] Dokumentarfilm, Dokumentarbericht
dog [dɒg] Hund
dollar ($) ['dɒlə] Dollar
door [dɔ:] Tür; **back door** Hintertür; **front door** Haustür
double ['dʌbl] Doppel-; doppelt
doubt [daʊt] Zweifel
down [daʊn] hinunter, herunter; **down there** da unten; **put down** **1.** aufschreiben, eintragen; **2.** hinlegen, abstellen; **shut down** zumachen, schließen *(Fabrik usw.)*; **upside down** [ˌʌpsaɪd 'daʊn] verkehrt herum, auf dem Kopf; **downstairs** [ˌdaʊn'steəz] unten (im

D

Haus); nach unten, (die Treppe) hinunter; **downtown** (AE) [ˌdaʊn'taʊn] (in der/die) Innenstadt

dozen ['dʌzn] Dutzend

Dr = Doctor ['dɒktə] Dr. = Doktor

drama ['drɑːmə] Drama, Schauspiel(kunst)

draw [drɔː] **1.** zeichnen; **2.** ziehen

dream [driːm] **1.** Traum; **2.** träumen; **dreamer** Träumer/in

dress [dres] **1.** Kleid; **2.** (sich) anziehen, (sich) kleiden; **dress up** sich feinmachen; sich verkleiden; **dressed** angezogen; **get dressed** sich anziehen

drink [drɪŋk] **1.** trinken; **2.** Getränk; **drinkable** trinkbar; **drinking-water** Trinkwasser

drive [draɪv] **1.** *(ein Auto, einen Bus)* fahren; **2.** (Auto-, Bus-)Fahrt; **drive sb. crazy** (infml.) jn. zur Verzweiflung treiben, jn. verrückt machen; **drive-in restaurant** ['draɪvɪn 'restərɒnt] (*meist* AE) *Schnellimbiß, wo Kunden im Auto bedient werden*; **driver** Fahrer/in; **driving licence** (BE)**/driver's license** (AE) ['laɪsəns] Führerschein

drop [drɒp] **1.** fallen lassen; **2.** *(Schulfach)* abwählen, abgeben; **3.** weglassen, auslassen

drown [draʊn] ertrinken; ertränken; *(Stimme)* übertönen

drug [drʌg] **1.** Droge, Rauschgift; **2.** Medikament; **be on drugs** high sein; (regelmäßig) Drogen oder Medikamente nehmen; **drugstore** (AE) **1.** Apotheke; **2.** Drogerie

drummer ['drʌmə] Schlagzeuger/in

drunk [drʌŋk]**: be drunk** betrunken sein

dry [draɪ] **1.** trocken; **2.** (ab)trocknen

due [djuː]**: be due (back)** (zurück)erwartet werden

dump [dʌmp] *(Müll, Schutt usw.)* abladen, auskippen, wegwerfen

during *(prep.)* ['djʊərɪŋ] während

duty ['djuːtɪ] Pflicht

E

each [iːtʃ] jede(r, s) einzelne; **each other** einander, sich (gegenseitig)

ear [ɪə] Ohr; **earache** ['ɪəreɪk] Ohrenschmerzen

early ['ɜːlɪ] früh; zu früh

earn [ɜːn] *(Geld)* verdienen

earth [ɜːθ] Erde; **on earth** auf der Erde; **earthquake** ['ɜːθkweɪk] Erdbeben

east [iːst] **1.** Osten; **2.** nach Osten; **3. east (of)** östlich (von); **eastern** ['iːstən] Ost-, östlich

Easter ['iːstə] Ostern; **at Easter** zu/an Ostern

easy ['iːzɪ] einfach, leicht

eat [iːt] essen

economic [ˌiːkə'nɒmɪk] (volks)wirtschaftlich, ökonomisch; **economics** *(sing.)* [ˌiːkə'nɒmɪks] Volkswirtschaftslehre; **economy** [ɪ'kɒnəmɪ] (Volks-)Wirtschaft

edit ['edɪt] redigieren; herausgeben; **editor** ['edɪtə] Redakteur/in; Herausgeber/in

educate ['edjʊkeɪt] (aus)bilden, schulen; erziehen; **education** [ˌedjʊ'keɪʃn] (Schul-, Aus-)Bildung; Erziehung; **public education** (AE) staatliches Bildungs-/Schulsystem; staatliche Bildung; **educational** pädagogisch; Lehr-, Bildungs-

effect [ɪ'fekt] (Aus-)Wirkung

efficient [ɪ'fɪʃnt] effizient, wirtschaftlich; leistungsfähig, tüchtig

e.g. [ˌiː'dʒiː] *(from Latin "exempli gratia")* z.B. (= zum Beispiel)

egg [eg] Ei

either ... or ... ['aɪðə / 'iːðə ... ɔː] entweder ... oder ...; **not . . either** auch nicht; auch kein

elderly ['eldəlɪ] ältere(r, s)

elect sb. (sth.) [ɪ'lekt] jn. (zu etwas) wählen; **election** [ɪ'lekʃn] *(politische)* Wahl; **general election** (GB) Parlamentswahl(en)

electrical [ɪ'lektrɪkl] elektrisch, Elektro-; **electricity** [ɪˌlek'trɪsətɪ] Strom, Elektrizität

electronic [ɪˌlek'trɒnɪk] elektronisch; **electronics** *(sing.)* Elektronik

element ['elɪmənt] Element; **the elements** *(pl.)* (fml.) Naturkräfte, Elemente

elementary school [ˌelɪ'mentərɪ skuːl] (US) *(meist sechsjährige) Grundschule in den USA*

elephant ['elɪfənt] Elefant

else [els]**: anybody/anything/anywhere else?** sonst (noch) jemand/ etwas/(irgend)wo? **somebody/something/somewhere else** jemand anderes/etwas anderes/ woanders; **who/what/where/why/... else?** wer/was/wo/warum/... sonst (noch)?

embarrassing [ɪm'bærəsɪŋ] peinlich, beschämend

emigrate ['emɪgreɪt] auswandern, emigrieren

emotion [ɪ'məʊʃn] Gefühl, Emotion; **emotional** [ɪ'məʊʃnəl] gefühlsmäßig, emotional

emperor ['empərə] Kaiser; **empress** ['emprəs] Kaiserin

empire ['empaɪə] Reich

employ [ɪm'plɔɪ] beschäftigen, anstellen; **employable** [ɪm'plɔɪəbl] als Arbeitskraft geeignet, vermittelbar; **employee** [ɪm'plɔɪiː] Arbeitnehmer/in, Angestellte(r); **employer** Arbeitgeber/in; **employment** Beschäftigung; Arbeit

empress ['emprəs] Kaiserin

emptiness ['emptɪnəs] Leere; **empty** ['emptɪ] leer; (sich) (ent)leeren

encourage [ɪn'kʌrɪdʒ] ermutigen, Mut machen; **encouraging** ermutigend

encyclopedia [ɪnˌsaɪklə'piːdɪə] Enzyklopädie, Lexikon

end [end] **1.** Ende; **at the end (of)** am Ende (von); **in the end** schließlich, am Ende, zum Schluß; **endless** endlos; **2. end (in)** enden (auf, mit); beenden; **ending** Ende, (Ab-)Schluß; Endung

enemy ['enəmɪ] Feind/in

energy ['enədʒɪ] Energie; Ausdauer

engine ['endʒɪn] Motor, Maschine

England ['ɪŋglənd] England; **English** ['ɪŋglɪʃ] **1.** Englisch; englisch; **2.** Engländer/in; **Englishman/Englishwoman** Engländer/in

enjoy [ɪn'dʒɔɪ] genießen; **enjoy doing sth.** etwas gern tun; **enjoy oneself** viel Spaß haben, sich amüsieren; **enjoyable** [ɪn'dʒɔɪəbl] unterhaltsam, nett

enough [ɪ'nʌf] genug

ensemble [ɒn'sɒmbl] Ensemble

enter ['entə] hineingehen (in), eintreten (in), betreten; **entrance (to)** ['entrəns] Eingang (zu); **entrance fee** ['entrəns fiː] Eintritt(sgeld)

enterprise ['entəpraɪz] Unternehmung; Unternehmen

entertain [ˌentə'teɪn] unterhalten; **entertaining** unterhaltsam; **entertainment** Unterhaltung, Entertainment

enthusiastic(ally) [ɪnˌθjuːzɪ'æstɪk(lɪ)] begeistert, enthusiastisch

entirely [ɪn'taɪəlɪ] völlig, ganz

entrance (to) ['entrəns] Eingang (zu); **entrance fee** ['entrəns fiː] Eintritt(sgeld)

envelope ['envələʊp] Briefumschlag

D

environment [ɪn'vaɪrənmənt] Umwelt; **environment-friendly** umweltfreundlich; **environmental** [ɪnˌvaɪrən'mentl] Umwelt-
equal ['i:kwəl] gleich; **equality** [ɪ'kwɒlətɪ] Gleichheit
equipment [ɪ'kwɪpmənt] Ausrüstung
escape (from) [ɪ'skeɪp] entkommen, fliehen (aus)
especially [ɪ'speʃlɪ] besonders, insbesondere
essay ['eseɪ] Aufsatz, Essay
establish [ɪ'stæblɪʃ] herstellen *(Kontakt, Beziehung)*; gründen
etc. (= et cetera, etcetera) [et'setrə] usw.
ethnic ['eθnɪk] ethnisch; Volks-
European [ˌjʊərə'pi:ən] **1.** Europäer/in; **2.** europäisch; **European Community (EC)** [kə'mju:nətɪ] Europäische Gemeinschaft (EG); **European Union (EU)** ['ju:njən] Europäische Union (EU)
even ['i:vn] sogar, selbst; **not even** nicht einmal; **even if** selbst wenn; **even though** selbst wenn; obwohl
evening ['i:vnɪŋ] Abend; **in the evening(s)** am Abend, abends; **on the first evening** am ersten Abend; **this evening** heute abend
event [ɪ'vent] Ereignis
ever ['evə] je, jemals, schon mal; **for ever, forever** [fər'evə] für immer; **not ever** niemals; **the worst fight ever** der härteste Kampf, den es je/bis jetzt gegeben hat
every ['evrɪ] jede(r, s); **for every 100 metres** pro 100 Meter
everybody ['evrɪbɒdɪ] jede(r), alle
everything ['evrɪθɪŋ] alles
everywhere ['evrɪweə] überall
evidence (of) *(sing.)* ['evɪdəns] Beweis(e), Anzeichen (für)
exact [ɪg'zækt] genau; **exactly** genau
exam [ɪg'zæm] Prüfung, Examen; **do/take an exam** eine Prüfung machen
examine [ɪg'zæmɪn] untersuchen
example [ɪg'zɑ:mpl] Beispiel; **for example (e.g.)** zum Beispiel (z.B.)
excellent ['eksələnt] ausgezeichnet, hervorragend
except [ɪk'sept] außer, bis auf; **except for** bis auf, abgesehen von; **exception** [ɪk'sepʃn] Ausnahme
excerpt ['eksɜ:pt] (Text-)Auszug, Exzerpt
exchange [ɪks'tʃeɪndʒ] **1.** Austausch, Umtausch; **2.** (aus)tauschen; **exchange for** umtauschen, eintauschen gegen

excited (about) [ɪk'saɪtɪd] aufgeregt, freudig erregt (wegen); **exciting** aufregend, spannend; **excitement** Aufregung
exclamation mark [ˌekskləˈmeɪʃn mɑ:k] Ausrufezeichen
exclusively [ɪk'sklu:sɪvlɪ] ausschließlich
excuse 1. [ɪk'skju:s] Entschuldigung; Ausrede;
2. Excuse me. [ɪk'skju:z mi:] Entschuldigung. Darf ich Sie mal stören?
execute ['eksɪkju:t] hinrichten; **execution** [ˌeksɪ'kju:ʃn] Hinrichtung
exercise ['eksəsaɪz] Übung
existing [ɪg'zɪstɪŋ] existierend, bestehend
expect [ɪk'spekt] erwarten; annehmen; **expectation** [ˌekspek'teɪʃn] Erwartung
expensive [ɪk'spensɪv] teuer
experience [ɪk'spɪərɪəns] **1.** Erfahrung, Erlebnis; **2.** erfahren, erleben; **be experienced (in)** erfahren sein (in); Erfahrung haben (mit)
expert ['ekspɜ:t] Fachmann/Fachfrau, Experte/Expertin
explain [ɪk'spleɪn] erklären, erläutern; **explanation** [ˌeksplə'neɪʃn] Erklärung, Erläuterung
explicit(ly) [ɪk'splɪsɪt, -lɪ] ausdrücklich, explizit
explode [ɪk'spləʊd] **1.** explodieren; **2.** zur Explosion bringen; **3.** *(Theorie)* widerlegen; **explosion** [ɪk'spləʊʒn] Explosion, Knall
exploit [ɪk'splɔɪt] ausbeuten; verwerten; **exploitation** [ˌeksplɔɪ'teɪʃn] Ausbeutung, Ausnutzung; Nutzung
explore [ɪk'splɔ:] erforschen; **explorer** [ɪk'splɔ:rə] Forschungsreisende(r)
export 1. ['ekspɔ:t] Ausfuhr, Export; **2.** [ɪk'spɔ:t] ausführen, exportieren
express [ɪk'spres] ausdrücken, äußern; **expression** [ɪk'spreʃn] Ausdruck
extend [ɪk'stend] verlängern; sich ausdehnen, erstrecken; **extended family** Großfamilie
extinct [ɪk'stɪŋkt] ausgestorben
extra ['ekstrə] zusätzlich, Extra-; **extra-curricular activity** [ˌekstrəkə'rɪkjʊlə] außerunterrichtliche Aktivität, Arbeitsgemeinschaft

extraordinary [ɪk'strɔ:dnərɪ] außergewöhnlich, ungewöhnlich
extreme [ɪk'stri:m] extrem; **extremely** äußerst; **extremist** [ɪk'stri:mɪst] **1.** Extremist/in; **2.** extremistisch
eye [aɪ] Auge

F

fable ['feɪbl] Fabel
face [feɪs] Gesicht; **face sb./sth.** sich jm./einer Sache gegenübersehen, jm./einer Sache (mutig) ins Auge sehen; **face (east)** nach (Osten) gehen, liegen *(Haus usw.)*; **let's face it** (infml.) machen wir uns doch nichts vor
facilities *(pl.)* [fə'sɪlətɪz] Einrichtung(en)
fact [fækt] Tatsache; **in fact** eigentlich, genau gesagt; in Wirklichkeit
factory ['fæktrɪ] Fabrik
fail to do sth. [feɪl] etwas nicht tun (können); versäumen, etwas zu tun; **fail (an exam)** (eine Prüfung) nicht bestehen, durchfallen
fair [feə] **1.** gerecht, fair; **2.** heiter, schön *(Wetter)*; **fairness** Gerechtigkeit, Fairneß
faithfully ['feɪθfəlɪ]**: Yours faithfully, ...** Mit freundlichen Grüßen ...; Hochachtungsvoll ...
fall [fɔ:l] (hin)fallen; **fall asleep** einschlafen; **fall in love with sb.** sich in jn. verlieben; **fall over** umfallen, hinfallen
fall [fɔ:l] (AE) Herbst
false [fɒls, fɔ:ls] falsch, unecht
familiar [fə'mɪlɪə]**: be familiar to sb.** jm. bekannt sein
family ['fæmlɪ] Familie; **one-parent family/single-parent family** Familie mit alleinerziehendem Elternteil
famous ['feɪməs] berühmt
fan [fæn] Fan, begeisterte(r) Anhänger/in
fancy ['fænsɪ] schick *(Auto, Laden)*; raffiniert *(Gerät)*; ausgefallen *(Design)*
fantastic [fæn'tæstɪk] fantastisch
far [fɑ:] weit; **far-reaching** [ˌfɑ:'ri:tʃɪŋ] folgenschwer, weitreichend; **as far as I'm concerned** [kən'sɜ:nd] meiner Meinung nach, was mich betrifft; **so far** bis jetzt, bisher
fare [feə] Fahrgeld, Fahrpreis

farm [fɑːm] **1.** Bauernhof, Farm; **2.** *(Land)* bewirtschaften, bebauen; Landwirtschaft betreiben; **farmer** Bauer/Bäuerin; Farmer/in; **farming** Landwirtschaft

farther ['fɑːðə] weiter (entfernt)

fascinate ['fæsɪneɪt] faszinieren; **fascinated** ['fæsəneɪtɪd] fasziniert, begeistert; **fascinating** faszinierend, fesselnd

fashion ['fæʃn] Mode

fast [fɑːst] schnell; **fast-food restaurant** ['fɑːst,fuːd 'restərɒnt] Schnellrestaurant, Schnellimbiß

fat [fæt] **1.** Fett; **2.** dick, fett

father ['fɑːðə] Vater; **Father Christmas** [,fɑːðə 'krɪsməs] (BE) der Weihnachtsmann

fault [fɒlt, fɔːlt] Schuld, Fehler

favour ['feɪvə]: **in favour of** zugunsten (von); **in sb.'s favour** zu js. Gunsten

favourite ['feɪvrət] Lieblings-

fax [fæks] **1.** Telefax; Telefaxgerät; **2.** fernkopieren, faxen

fear (of) [fɪə] **1.** Angst, Furcht (vor); **2. fear** befürchten

February ['februərɪ] Februar

fed up [,fed_'ʌp]: **be/get fed up (with)** die Nase voll haben (von), etwas satt haben

federal ['fedərəl] Bundes-; **federal holiday** [,fedərəl 'hɒlədeɪ] (AE) Feiertag *(, an dem alle Bundesbehörden geschlossen sind)*

fee [fiː] Gebühr, Beitrag; **entrance fee** ['entrəns fiː] Eintritt(sgeld)

feed [fiːd] füttern

feel [fiːl] **1.** fühlen, sich fühlen; empfinden, meinen; **2.** befühlen, abtasten; **feel sorry for (sb./sth.)** (jn./etwas) bedauern; (etwas) bereuen; **I feel sick.** Mir ist schlecht/übel. **feeling** ['fiːlɪŋ] Gefühl

felt-tip ['felttɪp] Filzstift

female ['fiːmeɪl] **1.** weibliche Person; **2.** weiblich

fence [fens] Zaun

ferry ['ferɪ] Fähre

fertilize ['fɜːtəlaɪz] düngen; befruchten; **fertilizer** Dünger, Düngemittel

festival ['festɪvl] Fest, Festival

fetch [fetʃ] holen

few [fjuː] wenige; **a few** ein paar, einige; **in the past few years** in den vergangenen/letzten Jahren

fiction ['fɪkʃn] Prosa, Belletristik; Fiktion

field [fiːəld] Feld, Wiese; (Sport-) Platz

fight [faɪt] **1.** Kampf; **2.** (be)kämpfen; sich streiten; **fighter** Kämpfer/in

figure ['fɪgə] **1.** Zahl, Ziffer; **2.** Figur, Gestalt

fill [fɪl] füllen; **fill in 1.** einsetzen; **2.** ausfüllen *(Formular)*; **fill up** (sich) füllen, vollfüllen

film [fɪlm] Film; **filmstar** Filmstar

final ['faɪnəl] letzte(r, s); endgültige(r, s); **finally** ['faɪnəlɪ] schließlich, endlich

financial [faɪ'nænʃl] finanziell

find [faɪnd] finden; **Find out about ...** Erkundige dich über ...

fine [faɪn] gut, fein, schön; **She's fine.** Ihr geht's gut. Es geht ihr gut.

finger ['fɪŋgə] Finger

finish ['fɪnɪʃ] (be)enden; aufhören (mit)

fire ['faɪə] Feuer, Brand; **fireworks** *(pl.)* Feuerwerk(skörper)

firm [fɜːm] Firma

first [fɜːst] **1.** erste(r, s); **first name** Vorname; **2.** zuerst, zunächst; **first of all** als erstes, zu(aller)erst; **at first** zuerst, am Anfang; **firstly** erstens

fish, *pl.* **fish** [fɪʃ] Fisch; **fishing** Fischerei; **go fishing** angeln gehen, fischen gehen

fit [fɪt] **1.** gesund, fit; **2.** passen; **fitness** ['fɪtnəs] Fitneß

fitter ['fɪtə] Maschinenschlosser/in, Mechaniker/in

flag [flæg] Fahne, Flagge

flame [fleɪm] Flamme

flashlight ['flæʃlaɪt] (AE) Taschenlampe

flat [flæt] **1.** flach, eben; **flatten** flach machen, ebnen; **2.** (BE) (Miet-) Wohnung; **block of flats** (BE) (Miets-)Haus, Wohnblock

flight [flaɪt] Flug

float [fləʊt] *(auf dem Wasser)* schwimmen, treiben

floor [flɔː] (Fuß-)Boden

flour ['flaʊə] Mehl

flower ['flaʊə] **1.** Blume; Blüte; **2.** blühen

flu [fluː]: **I've got the flu.** Ich habe (die) Grippe.

fly [flaɪ] fliegen

FM [,ef_'em] UKW*(-Sender)*

fog [fɒg] Nebel; **foggy** neblig

folk song ['fəʊk sɒŋ] Volkslied; Folksong

follow ['fɒləʊ] folgen; verfolgen; **following** folgend

fond [fɒnd]: **be fond of** mögen, gern haben

food [fuːd] Essen, Nahrung; Lebensmittel; Futter

fool [fuːl] Narr/Närrin, Dummkopf; **make a fool of sb.** jn. lächerlich machen

foot [fʊt], *pl.* **feet** [fiːt] **1.** Fuß; **2.** *Längenmaß (= 30,48 cm)*; **football** ['fʊtbɔːl] **1.** (BE) Fußball; **2.** (AE) amerikanischer Fußball; **footstep** ['fʊtstep] (Fuß-)Schritt

for [fɔː, fə] für; **for a long time** lange (Zeit); **for an hour** eine Stunde (lang); seit einer Stunde; **for breakfast/lunch/...** zum Frühstück/ Mittagessen/...; **for ever, forever** [fər'evə] für immer; **for example (e.g.)** zum Beispiel (z.B.)

force ['fɔːs] **1.** Kraft; Zwang; **2.** zwingen

forecast ['fɔːkɑːst] Vorhersage, Voraussage

foreign ['fɒrən] ausländisch, fremd; **foreigner** Ausländer/in; **foreign policy** [,fɒrən 'pɒləsɪ] Außenpolitik

forest ['fɒrɪst] Wald, Forst

forever, for ever [fər'evə] für immer

forget [fə'get] vergessen

fork [fɔːk] Gabel

form [fɔːm] **1.** (BE) Klasse, Jahrgang; **2.** Form; **form of transport** [,fɔːm_əv 'trænspɔːt] Verkehrsmittel; **3.** (sich) bilden, formen; **formation** [fɔː'meɪʃn] Bildung, Formung

formal ['fɔːml] formell, förmlich

former ['fɔːmə] frühere(r, s), ehemalige(r, s); **formerly** früher

fortunately ['fɔːtʃənətlɪ] zum Glück, glücklicherweise

forum ['fɔːrəm] Forum

forward(s) ['fɔːwəd(z)] vorwärts, nach vorn; **look forward to sth./ doing sth.** sich auf etwas freuen/ sich darauf freuen, etwas zu tun

found [faʊnd] gründen

fountain ['faʊntɪn] Springbrunnen

free [friː] **1.** befreien; **2.** frei, Frei-; **3.** kostenlos; **freedom** ['friːdəm] Freiheit

French [frentʃ] **1.** Französisch, französisch; **2.** Franzose/ Französin; **French fries** [,frentʃ 'fraɪz] *(meist* AE) Pommes frites

fresh [freʃ] frisch

Friday ['fraɪdɪ, 'fraɪdeɪ] Freitag

fridge [frɪdʒ] Kühlschrank

friend [frend] Freund/in; **make friends (with)** Freunde finden; sich anfreunden (mit); **friendliness** Freundlichkeit; **friendly** freundlich, nett

D

frighten away ['fraɪtn] verscheuchen, abschrecken; **be frightened (of)** Angst haben (vor)
frog [frɒg] Frosch
from [frɒm, frəm] von, aus; **from now on** von jetzt an, ab jetzt; **from then on** von da an; **from … to** von … bis; **from what I've seen** nach dem zu urteilen, was ich gesehen habe; **where … from?** woher?
front [frʌnt]**: front door** [ˌfrʌnt 'dɔ:] Haustür; **in front of** vor; **the front** die Vorderseite; vorn
frontier ['frʌntɪə] Grenze
frown [fraʊn] die Stirn runzeln
fruit [fru:t] Obst, Früchte; Frucht
frustrated [frʌ'streɪtɪd] frustriert, enttäuscht
full [fʊl] voll; **full stop** [ˌfʊl 'stɒp] (BE) Punkt *(Satzzeichen)*; **full-time** [ˌfʊl'taɪm] Vollzeit-, ganztags
fun [fʌn] Spaß; **they're fun** sie sind lustig; es macht Spaß mit ihnen; **funny** ['fʌnɪ] lustig, komisch
function ['fʌŋkʃn] **1.** Funktion; **2.** funktionieren, fungieren
furniture *(sing.)* ['fɜ:nɪtʃə] Möbel; **piece of furniture** Möbelstück
further ['fɜ:ðə] **1.** weiter; **2.** weitere(r, s), noch; **furthermore** [ˌfɜ:ðə'mɔ:] ferner, außerdem, darüber hinaus
future ['fju:tʃə] Zukunft

G

gallery ['gælərɪ] Galerie
game [geɪm] Spiel; **game show** Spielshow *(im Fernsehen)*; **games** (BE) Mannschaftsspiele und Leichtathletik *(in der Regel im Freien)*
gang [gæŋ] Bande
garage ['gærɑ:dʒ] Garage
garden ['gɑ:dn] Garten
gas [gæs] **1.** Gas; **2.** (AE) Benzin; **gasoline** (AE) ['gæsəli:n] Benzin; **gas station** (AE) Tankstelle; **natural gas** [ˌnætʃərəl 'gæs] Erdgas
gate [geɪt] Tor, Pforte
gay [geɪ] **1.** Schwuler, **2.** schwul; **3.** *(veraltet)* fröhlich, lustig
GCSE [ˌdʒi:si:_es_'i:] (GB) *etwa:* mittlere Reife
gender ['dʒendə] *(grammatisches)* Geschlecht; Genus
general ['dʒenrəl] **1.** General/in; **2.** allgemein, generell; **general election** [ˌdʒenrəl_ɪ'lekʃn] (GB) Parlamentswahl(en); **in general** im allgemeinen; **generalize** ['dʒenrəlaɪz] verallgemeinern; **generally** im allgemeinen
generation [ˌdʒenə'reɪʃn] Generation
genetic [dʒə'netɪk] genetisch
gentle ['dʒentl] zart, sanft, behutsam
geography [dʒɪ'ɒgrəfɪ] Geographie
German ['dʒɜ:mən] **1.** deutsch, Deutsch; **2.** Deutsche(r); **Germany** ['dʒɜ:mənɪ] Deutschland
get [get] **1.** bekommen; **2.** besorgen, (ab)holen; **3. get angry/tired/cold/…** ärgerlich/müde/kalt/… werden; **4. get (to)** (hin)kommen, gelangen (zu/nach); **get across** verständlich machen, herüberbringen; **get along (with)** auskommen (mit), sich verstehen (mit); **get an idea (of)** einen Eindruck/eine Vorstellung bekommen (von); sich einen Eindruck verschaffen (von); **get away from** entkommen, entwischen (aus); weg-, fortkommen (von); **get changed** sich umziehen; **get divorced** sich scheiden lassen; **get in(to) a car/get on a bus/train/plane** in ein Auto/einenBus/Zug/ein Flugzeug (ein)steigen; **get married** heiraten; **get off a bus/train/plane/get out of a car** aus einem Bus/Zug/Flugzeug/ Auto aussteigen; **Get out (of here).** Raus (hier)! **get rid of** loswerden; **get together** zusammenkommen, sich treffen; **get to know** kennenlernen; erfahren; **get up** aufstehen
ghetto ['getəʊ] G(h)etto
ghost [gəʊst] Geist, Gespenst
giant ['dʒaɪənt] **1.** Riese; **2.** riesig, Riesen-
girl [gɜ:l] Mädchen; **girlfriend** ['gɜ:lfrend] (feste) Freundin
give [gɪv] geben; schenken; **give (sth.) up** (etwas) aufgeben
glad [glæd] froh
gladiator ['glædɪeɪtə] Gladiator/in
glance [glɑ:ns]**: at first glance** auf den ersten Blick
glass [glɑ:s] Glas
glasses *(pl.)* ['glɑ:sɪz] (eine) Brille
global ['gləʊbl] global, weltumspannend, Welt-; **global warming** [ˌgləʊbl 'wɔ:mɪŋ] Erwärmung der Erdatmosphäre
glove [glʌv] Handschuh
glue [glu:] kleben
go [gəʊ] **1.** gehen, fahren; **2. go blind/red/hard/…** blind/rot/hart/… werden; **go fishing** angeln gehen, fischen gehen; **go for a ride** herumfahren, eine Spazierfahrt machen; **go for a walk** spazierengehen; **go on** im Gange sein, vorgehen; **go on (doing sth.)** etwas weiter tun, weiter-; **go to work** arbeiten gehen; **go up** steigen, in die Höhe gehen; **They are going to do it.** Sie werden es tun. Sie haben vor, es zu tun.
goal [gəʊl] Ziel; Tor *(im Sport)*
God, god [gɒd] Gott
gold [gəʊld] Gold; **golden** ['gəʊldn] golden; Gold-; **goldfish,** *pl.* **goldfish** ['gəʊldfɪʃ] Goldfisch
golf [gɒlf] Golf
good [gʊd] gut; **good at** gut in, geschickt in; **good-looking** [ˌgʊd'lʊkɪŋ] gutaussehend; **Good afternoon.** Guten Tag. *(nachmittags)*; **Good morning.** Guten Morgen. Guten Tag. *(vormittags)*; **Goodbye.** [ˌgʊd'baɪ] Auf Wiedersehen. Tschüs.
goods *(pl.)* [gʊdz] Güter, Waren
gorgeous ['gɔ:dʒəs] hinreißend, prächtig
got [gɒt]**: have got** haben, besitzen; **have got to** *(tun)* müssen
gotten ['gɒtn] (AE) *Partizip Perfekt von „to get"* (= BE „got")
govern ['gʌvən] regieren, herrschen über; **government** ['gʌvnmənt] Regierung; **governor** ['gʌvənə] (US) Gouverneur/in *(eines US-Bundesstaates)*
grade [greɪd] **1.** (Zeugnis-)Note, Zensur; **2.** (AE) Klasse(nstufe)
graduate ['grædʒʊət] Hochschulabsolvent/in, Akademiker/in; AE *auch:* Schulabgänger/in
graffiti *(sing.)* [grə'fi:ti:] Graffiti
gram [græm] Gramm
grammar ['græmə] Grammatik
Gran [græn] (infml.) Oma
grand-: granddaughter ['grændɔ:tə] Enkelin; **grandfather** ['grænfɑ:ðə] Großvater; **Grandma** ['grænmɑ:] (infml.) Oma; **grandmother** ['grænmʌðə] Großmutter; **grandparents** ['grænpeərənts] Großeltern; **grandson** ['grænsʌn] Enkel
Grandad ['grændæd] (infml.) Opa
granted ['grɑ:ntɪd]**: take sth. for granted** etwas als selbstverständlich betrachten
grass [grɑ:s] Gras
grateful ['greɪtfəl]**: be grateful (to sb.)** (jm.) dankbar sein
grave [greɪv] Grab; **graveyard** ['greɪvjɑ:d] Friedhof

D

great [greɪt] **1.** groß, beträchtlich; **2.** großartig, super, klasse; **3.** bedeutend, berühmt; **Great Britain** [ˌgreɪt 'brɪtn] Großbritannien
greed [gri:d] Habgier
green [gri:n] grün; **greenhouse effect** ['gri:nhaʊs_ɪˌfekt] Treibhauseffekt
greet [gri:t] (be)grüßen
grey [greɪ] grau
grill [grɪl] grillen
grin [grɪn] **1.** Grinsen; **2. grin (at)** (an)grinsen
grizzly bear ['grɪzlɪ ˌbeə] Grizzly(bär)
grocery store ['grəʊsərɪ stɔ:] Lebensmittelladen
ground [graʊnd] (Erd-)Boden
group [gru:p] Gruppe
grow [grəʊ] **1.** wachsen; **2.** anbauen, anpflanzen; **3. grow old/easier/...** alt/einfacher/... werden; **4. grow up** aufwachsen, erwachsen werden; **growth** [grəʊθ] Wachstum
guard dog ['gɑ:d dɒg] Wachhund
guess [ges] (er)raten
guest [gest] Gast; **guest house** ['gest haʊs] Pension
guidance counselor ['gaɪdəns ˌkaʊnsələ] (AE) *Schulberater/in an einer High School, berät Schülerinnen und Schüler bei persönlichen und schulischen Problemen und bei der Berufswahl*
guide [gaɪd] **1.** (Fremden-)Führer/in; **2.** führen, leiten; **guidebook** ['gaɪdbʊk] Reiseführer, Stadtführer; **guided tour (of)** [ˌgaɪdɪd 'tʊə] Führung (durch); **go on a guided tour** eine Führung mitmachen
guitar [gɪ'tɑ:] Gitarre
gun [gʌn] Schußwaffe
guy [gaɪ] (infml.) Typ, Kerl; **you guys** ['ju: ˌgaɪz] (AE, infml.) ihr Leute *(schließt auch Mädchen/Frauen ein)*
gym [dʒɪm] Sport-, Turnhalle; **gymnastics** [dʒɪm'næstɪks] Gymnastik, Turnen

H

habit ['hæbɪt] (An-)Gewohnheit
hair *(sing.)* [heə] Haar, Haare; **haircut** ['heəkʌt] Haarschnitt; **hairstyle** ['heəstaɪl] Frisur
half [hɑ:f], *pl.* **halves** [hɑ:vz] Hälfte; **one and a half** eineinhalb, anderthalb; **half a ...** ein(e) halbe(r, s) ...; **half past eight** [ˌhɑ:f pɑ:st_'eɪt] halb neun (8.30/20.30); **half the ...** der/die/das halbe ...
hall [hɔ:l] Saal, Halle; Flur, Diele
Hallo. [hə'ləʊ] (Guten) Tag. Hallo. **Say hallo to ... .** Grüß(t) ... (von mir).
hamburger ['hæmbɜ:gə] Hamburger
hammer ['hæmə] **1.** Hammer; **2. hammer a nail into the wall** einen Nagel in die Wand schlagen
hamster ['hæmstə] Hamster
hand [hænd] **1.** Hand; **2. hand out** austeilen, verteilen; **hand sb. sth.** jm. etwas (über)geben
handle ['hændl] umgehen mit, fertig werden mit
handsome ['hænsəm] gutaussehend *(bezogen auf Männer/Jungen)*
hang [hæŋ] **(hung – hung)** (auf)hängen *(Bilder, Wäsche)*; **hang around** (infml.) herumlungern
hang [hæŋ] **(hanged – hanged)** (er)hängen
happen (to) ['hæpən] geschehen, passieren (mit)
happiness ['hæpɪnəs] Zufriedenheit, Glück; **happy** ['hæpɪ] glücklich, froh
harbour ['hɑ:bə] Hafen
hard *(adj.; adv.)* [hɑ:d] hart, schwer; **harden** ['hɑ:dn] härten; hart werden; **hard-working** [ˌhɑ:d'wɜ:kɪŋ] fleißig, hart arbeitend; **hardly** kaum
harmful ['hɑ:mfəl] (gesundheits-)schädlich; **harmless** ['hɑ:mləs] harmlos; unschädlich
harmony ['hɑ:mənɪ] Harmonie, Einklang
hat [hæt] Hut
hate [heɪt] hassen, gar nicht mögen; **hate doing sth.** etwas sehr ungern tun
have [hæv] haben; **have a bath** baden, ein Bad nehmen; **have a coke/a hamburger** eine Cola trinken/einen Hamburger essen; **have a look at** sich ansehen, einen Blick werfen auf; **have a party** eine Party feiern; **have a race** ein Rennen veranstalten; **have breakfast/tea/...** frühstücken/Abendbrot/... essen; **have got** haben, besitzen; **have got to** *(tun)* müssen; **have sth. done** etwas *(von jm.)* tun/machen lassen; **have to** *(tun)* müssen
he [hi:] er
head [hed] **1.** Kopf; **headache** ['hedeɪk] Kopfschmerz(en); **headline** ['hedlaɪn] Schlagzeile; **headphones** *(pl.)* ['hedfəʊnz] Kopfhörer; **headquarters** (pl.) [ˌhed'kwɔ:təz] Zentrale, Hauptgeschäftsstelle; Hauptquartier; **headteacher** [ˌhed'ti:tʃə] (BE) Schuldirektor/in; **2.** anführen, leiten, *(einer Organisation)* vorstehen
health [helθ] Gesundheit; **healthy** gesund
hear [hɪə] hören; **hear of** hören von
heart [hɑ:t] Herz
heat [hi:t] Hitze; **heating** Heizung
heavy ['hevɪ] schwer
hectare ['hekteə] Hektar *(=10.000 qm)*
height [haɪt] Höhe, Größe
helicopter ['helɪkɒptə] Hubschrauber; **heliport** ['helɪpɔ:t] Hubschrauberlandeplatz, Heliport
Hello. [he'ləʊ] Hallo. (Guten) Tag.
help (with) [help] **1.** Hilfe (bei); **2.** helfen (bei); **I can't/couldn't help going there.** Ich muß/mußte dort einfach hingehen. **if you can help it** wenn du es vermeiden kannst; **helper** Helfer/in; **helpful** ['helpfəl] hilfsbereit; hilfreich, nützlich; **helpless** ['helpləs] hilflos
her [hɜ:, hə] **1.** sie, ihr; **2.** *(poss. adj.)* ihr(e); **hers** *(poss. pron.)* ihre(r, s); **herself** [hɜ:'self] sich (selbst)
here [hɪə] hier
hero, *pl.* **heroes** ['hɪərəʊ] Held/in
hide (from) [haɪd] (sich) verstecken (vor)
high [haɪ] hoch; **high-class** (sozial) hochgestellt; erstklassig; **high school** (AE) Oberschule; **high tech** [ˌhaɪ 'tek] High-Tech (Spitzentechnologie); **highly** ['haɪlɪ] höchst, sehr, hoch-; **highway** (AE) Autobahn
highlight ['haɪlaɪt] Höhepunkt
hill [hɪl] Hügel, Berg
him [hɪm] ihn, ihm; **himself** [hɪm'self] sich (selbst)
hire ['haɪə] *(meist* BE) *(Auto, Boot usw.)* mieten, leihen *(gegen Gebühr)*
his [hɪz] **1.** *(poss. adj.)* sein(e); **2.** *(poss. pron.)* seine(r, s)
Hispanic [hɪ'spænɪk] **1.** Hispano-Amerikaner/in; **2.** hispanisch
historical [hɪ'stɒrɪkl] historisch; **history** ['hɪstrɪ] Geschichte
hit [hɪt] **1.** Hit; **2.** schlagen, treffen; **hit sb./sth.** jn./etwas anfahren; **hit the water** aufs Wasser aufschlagen
hobby ['hɒbɪ] Hobby, Freizeitbeschäftigung

D

hockey ['hɒkɪ] Hockey
hold [həʊld] **1.** (fest)halten; **2.** *(eine Veranstaltung)* abhalten; **hold a job** eine Arbeit haben; eine Stellung bekleiden; **hold out one's hand to sb.** jm. die Hand entgegenstrecken; **hold up** hochhalten
hole [həʊl] Loch
holiday ['hɒlədeɪ] **1.** Feiertag; **2.** (BE) Urlaub, Ferien; **on holiday** in Urlaub; **be/go on holiday** Urlaub machen; **holiday home** Ferienwohnung
home [həʊm] **1.** Heim, Zuhause; **2.** nach Hause, heim; **at home** zu Hause, daheim; **holiday home** Ferienwohnung; **home economics** [ˌhəʊm_iːkə'nɒmɪks] Hauswirtschaft(slehre); **home-made** [ˌhəʊm'meɪd] selbstgemacht; **home town** ['həʊm taʊn] Heimatstadt; **homeless** obdachlos; **homelessness** Obdachlosigkeit; **be homesick (for)** ['həʊmsɪk] Heimweh haben (nach); **homework** *(sing.)* ['həʊmwɜːk] Hausaufgaben
honest ['ɒnɪst] ehrlich
hooligan ['huːlɪgən] Hooligan *(Randalierer/in, besonders bei Massenveranstaltungen)*
hope [həʊp] **1.** Hoffnung; **2. hope for** hoffen auf; **I hope so** ich hoffe es; hoffentlich; **hopeful** hoffnungsvoll, optimistisch; **hopeless** hoffnungslos
horizon [hə'raɪzn] Horizont
horrified ['hɒrɪfaɪd] entsetzt
horse [hɔːs] Pferd
hospital ['hɒspɪtl] Krankenhaus; **in hospital** im Krankenhaus
host [həʊst] Gastgeber/in
hostel: youth hostel ['juːθ hɒstl] Jugendherberge
hot [hɒt] **1.** heiß; warm *(Mahlzeit, Wasser)*; **2.** scharf (gewürzt)
hotel [həʊ'tel] Hotel
hour ['aʊə] Stunde
house [haʊs] Haus; **household** ['haʊshəʊld] Haushalt; **housework** ['haʊswɜːk] Haus(halts)arbeit
how [haʊ] wie; **How are you?** Wie geht es dir? **How do you like …?** Wie gefällt dir …? Wie findest du …? **How many?** Wie viele? **How much?** Wieviel? **How much is/are …?** Was kostet/kosten …?
however [haʊ'evə] **1.** jedoch, aber; **2.** wie (auch) immer
huge [hjuːdʒ] sehr groß, riesig
human ['hjuːmən] menschlich
humour ['hjuːmə]**: a sense of humour** [ˌsens_əv 'hjuːmə] (Sinn für) Humor; **humorous** ['hjuːmərəs] humorvoll, lustig
hunger ['hʌŋgə] Hunger; **hungry** ['hʌŋgrɪ] hungrig; **I'm hungry.** Ich habe Hunger.
hunt [hʌnt] jagen; **hunter** Jäger/in
hurt [hɜːt] verletzen, weh tun
husband ['hʌzbənd] (Ehe-)Mann
hyphen ['haɪfn] Bindestrich

I

I [aɪ] ich
ice [aɪs] Eis; **ice-cream** [ˌaɪs'kriːm] (Speise-)Eis; **ice-cream parlor** ['pɑːlə] (AE) Eisdiele; **icy** eisig, vereist
idea [aɪ'dɪə] Idee, Einfall; Vorstellung; **no idea** (infml.) keine Ahnung
ideal [aɪ'dɪəl] **1.** ideal, vollkommen; **2.** Ideal(vorstellung); **idealistic** [aɪˌdɪə'lɪstɪk] idealistisch
identical [aɪ'dentɪkl] identisch, gleich
identify [aɪ'dentɪfaɪ] (sich) identifizieren
identity [aɪ'dentətɪ] Identität
i.e. [ˌaɪ_'iː] *(from Latin "id est")* **(= that is)** d.h. (= das heißt)
if [ɪf] **1.** ob; **as if** als ob; **2.** wenn, falls; **even if** selbst wenn
ignorance ['ɪgnərəns] Unwissenheit, Unkenntnis, Ignoranz; **ignorant** **1.** unwissend, ungebildet; **2.** ungehobelt, unhöflich
ignore [ɪg'nɔː] ignorieren, nicht beachten
ill [ɪl]**: be ill** krank sein; **illness** Krankheit
illegal [ɪ'liːgl] ungesetzlich, illegal
illustrate ['ɪləstreɪt] illustrieren, veranschaulichen; **illustration** [ˌɪlə'streɪʃn] Bild, Abbildung, Illustration
image ['ɪmɪdʒ] *(sprachliches)* Bild, bildlicher Ausdruck
imaginary [ɪ'mædʒɪnərɪ] (frei) erfunden; eingebildet; **imagination** [ɪˌmædʒɪ'neɪʃn] Phantasie, Einbildung(skraft); **imagine** [ɪ'mædʒɪn] sich *(gedanklich)* vorstellen
immigrant ['ɪmɪgrənt] Einwanderer/Einwanderin; **immigrate** ['ɪmɪgreɪt] einwandern, immigrieren; **immigration** [ˌɪmɪ'greɪʃn] Einwanderung, Immigration
impatience [ɪm'peɪʃns] Ungeduld; **impatient** [ɪm'peɪʃnt] ungeduldig
imperfect [ɪm'pɜːfɪkt] unvollkommen
impersonal [ɪm'pɜːsnəl] unpersönlich
impolite [ˌɪmpə'laɪt] unhöflich; **impoliteness** Unhöflichkeit
import **1.** ['ɪmpɔːt] Import, Einfuhr; **2.** [ɪm'pɔːt] importieren, einführen
importance [ɪm'pɔːtns] Wichtigkeit; **important** [ɪm'pɔːtnt] wichtig
impossible [ɪm'pɒsəbl] unmöglich
impression [ɪm'preʃn] Eindruck
improbable [ɪm'prɒbəbl] unwahrscheinlich
improve [ɪm'pruːv] besser machen/werden, (sich) (ver)bessern
impulse buyer ['ɪmpʌls ˌbaɪə] „Spontankäufer/in"
in [ɪn] in; **one in ten** jede(r, s) zehnte, eine(r, s) von zehn; **in case** falls, für den Fall, daß; **in English** auf englisch; **in fifty years (from now)** in fünfzig Jahren; **in front of** vor; **in order to** um zu; **in such a way (that)** so, dergestalt (, daß); **in the country** auf dem Land; **in the morning(s)/afternoon(s)/evening(s)** am Morgen/Nachmittag/Abend; morgens/nachmittags/abends; **in the picture** auf dem Bild, auf dem Foto; **in the sky** am Himmel; **in the world** auf der (ganzen) Welt; **in this weather** bei diesem Wetter
inch [ɪntʃ] *Längenmaß (= 2,54 cm)*
incident ['ɪnsɪdənt] Ereignis, Vorfall
include [ɪn'kluːd] beinhalten, (mit) einschließen, enthalten
income ['ɪnkʌm] Einkommen
incomplete [ˌɪnkəm'pliːt] unvollständig, unvollendet, unfertig
increase **1.** [ɪn'kriːs] zunehmen, ansteigen; erhöhen; **2. increase (in)** ['ɪŋkriːs] Zunahme, Anstieg (von); Erhöhung
indeed [ɪn'diːd] in der Tat, tatsächlich
independence (from) [ˌɪndɪ'pendəns] Unabhängigkeit (von); **independent (of)** [ˌɪndɪ'pendənt] unabhängig (von)
Indian ['ɪndɪən] **1.** Inder/in; indisch; **2.** Indianer/in; indianisch
indirect [ˌɪndɪ'rekt, ˌɪndaɪ'rekt] indirekt
individual [ˌɪndɪ'vɪdʒʊəl] **1.** Individuum, Einzelne(r); **2.** individuell, Einzel-;

D

individuality [ˌɪndɪvɪdʒʊ'ælətɪ] Individualität, Einzigartigkeit *(der Persönlichkeit)*

indoors [ˌɪn'dɔːz] (nach) drinnen, im Haus

industrial [ɪn'dʌstrɪəl] industriell; Industrie-; **industrialist** [ɪn'dʌstrɪəlɪst] Industrielle(r); **industry** ['ɪndəstrɪ] Industrie, Industriezweig

infer (from) [ɪn'fɜː] (fml.) (er)schließen, folgern (aus), ableiten (von)

influence ['ɪnflʊəns] **1.** Einfluß; **2.** beeinflussen

inform [ɪn'fɔːm] informieren, benachrichtigen; **informer** [ɪn'fɔːmə] Informant/in, Spitzel; **information** *(sing.)* [ˌɪnfə'meɪʃn] Information(en); Auskunft, Auskünfte

informal [ɪn'fɔːml] informell, nicht förmlich

inhuman [ɪn'hjuːmən] unmenschlich, inhuman

injured ['ɪndʒəd] verletzt

inn [ɪn] Gasthaus, kleines Hotel

inner city [ˌɪnə 'sɪtɪ] innerstädtisches Wohngebiet *(mit sozialen und wirtschaftlichen Problemen)*

innocent ['ɪnəsənt] unschuldig

inside [ˌɪn'saɪd] **1.** *(prep.)* innerhalb (von); **2.** *(adv.)* (nach) drinnen

instability [ˌɪnstə'bɪlətɪ] Instabilität

install [ɪn'stɔːl] installieren, einrichten, einbauen

instead [ɪn'sted] statt dessen; **instead of** (an)statt, an Stelle von

instinct ['ɪnstɪŋkt] Instinkt

institution [ˌɪnstɪ'tjuːʃn] Institution

instruction [ɪn'strʌkʃn] Anweisung, Anleitung; **instructor** [ɪn'strʌktə] Ausbilder/in, Lehrer/in

instrument ['ɪnstrəmənt] Instrument

insult ['ɪnsʌlt] Beleidigung

integration [ˌɪntɪ'greɪʃn] Integration

intelligent [ɪn'telɪdʒənt] intelligent, klug

intend to do [ɪn'tend] zu tun beabsichtigen; **be intended to be** sein sollen; **intention** [ɪn'tenʃn] Absicht, Intention

interest (in) ['ɪntrəst] **1.** Interesse (an); **2.** interessieren (für); **interested (in)** interessiert (an); **interesting** interessant

international [ˌɪntə'næʃnəl] international

interrupt [ˌɪntə'rʌpt] unterbrechen

intersection [ˌɪntə'sekʃn] *(meist* AE) (Straßen-)Kreuzung

interview ['ɪntəvjuː] **1.** Interview; **2.** befragen, interviewen; **interviewer** ['ɪntəvjuːə] Interviewer/in

into ['ɪntuː, 'ɪntʊ, 'ɪntə] in (... hinein)

intolerance (towards) *(sing.)* [ɪn'tɒlərəns] Intoleranz (gegenüber); **intolerant (of)** intolerant (gegenüber)

introduce [ˌɪntrə'djuːs] einführen; vorstellen, bekanntmachen; **introduction** [ˌɪntrə'dʌkʃn] Einführung, Einleitung; **introductory** [ˌɪntrə'dʌktərɪ] einleitend, Einführungs-

invade [ɪn'veɪd] einmarschieren in, einfallen in

invent [ɪn'vent] erfinden; **invention** [ɪn'venʃn] Erfindung; **inventor** [ɪn'ventə] Erfinder/in

invest (in) [ɪn'vest] anlegen, investieren (in)

invitation [ˌɪnvɪ'teɪʃn] Einladung; **invite** [ɪn'vaɪt] *(Gäste)* einladen

involved [ɪn'vɒlvd]**: be involved (in)** etwas zu tun haben (mit), beteiligt sein (an); **get involved (in)** verwickelt, hineingezogen werden (in); sich engagieren (bei), beteiligen (an)

Irish ['aɪrɪʃ] irisch, Irisch

iron ['aɪən] Eisen

irregular [ɪ'regjʊlə] unregelmäßig

irresponsible [ˌɪrɪ'spɒnsəbl] unverantwortlich, verantwortungslos

island ['aɪlənd] Insel

issue ['ɪʃuː] Sachverhalt, Angelegenheit, (Streit-)Frage

it [ɪt] es; *(bei Sachen und Tieren auch:)* er, sie; **its** **1.** *(poss. adj.)* sein(e), ihr(e); **2.** *(poss. pron.)* seine(r, s), ihre(r, s); **itself** [ɪt'self] sich (selbst)

Italian [ɪ'tæljən] **1.** Italienisch, italienisch; **2.** Italiener/in

item ['aɪtəm] Punkt *(in einer Liste)*, Ding, Sache

J

jacket ['dʒækɪt] Jacke, Jackett, Sakko

jam: traffic jam ['træfɪk dʒæm] (Verkehrs-)Stau

January ['dʒænjʊərɪ] Januar

jazz [dʒæz] Jazz(musik)

jealous (of) ['dʒeləs] eifersüchtig (auf); neidisch (auf)

jeans *(pl.)* [dʒiːnz] Jeans

job [dʒɒb] **1.** Arbeit(sstelle), Beruf; **2.** Aufgabe; **hold a job** eine Arbeit haben; eine Stellung bekleiden

join [dʒɔɪn] **1.** beitreten, eintreten in *(einen Klub usw.)*; **2.** sich anschließen, mitkommen; **join hands** sich die Hände reichen; **join in (sth./doing sth.)** mitmachen (bei etwas), sich beteiligen (an etwas)

joke [dʒəʊk] **1.** Witz, Scherz; **2.** scherzen, witzeln

journey ['dʒɜːnɪ] Reise, Fahrt

joy [dʒɔɪ] Freude

judge [dʒʌdʒ] **1.** Richter/in; **2. judge (by/from)** beurteilen (nach)

judo ['dʒuːdəʊ] Judo

juice [dʒuːs] Saft; **juicy** saftig

July [dʒuː'laɪ] Juli

jump [dʒʌmp] springen

June [dʒuːn] Juni

junior high school ['dʒuːnɪə] (US) *die ersten drei Jahre der High School*; **juniors** ['dʒuːnjəz] (BE) Junioren(mannschaft)

just [dʒʌst, dʒəst] **1.** bloß, nur; **2.** einfach; **3.** gerade (jetzt); **just about** (infml.) fast, so gut wie; **just as tired** genauso müde; **just as well** genausogut; **just like** genau wie; **just over a pound** knapp über ein Pfund; **just round the corner** gleich um die Ecke

K

keen [kiːn]**: be keen on** (BE, infml.) sehr mögen; **be keen on doing sth.** (BE, infml.) etwas sehr gern/unbedingt tun wollen

keep [kiːp] **1.** behalten; **2.** halten *(Tiere)*; **3.** aufbewahren; **keep a diary** Tagebuch führen; **keep a promise** ein Versprechen halten; **keep alive** am Leben (er)halten; **keep an eye on sb./sth.** auf jn./etwas aufpassen; **keep (on) doing sth.** etwas weiter tun, weiter-; **keep sb. off sth.** jn. von etwas fernhalten; **keep sb. out** jn. draußen halten; **keep the peace** den Frieden bewahren, erhalten

ketchup ['ketʃəp] Ketchup

key [kiː] Schlüssel; **key word** Schlüsselwort

kick [kɪk] **1.** Tritt; **2.** treten, kicken

kid [kɪd] (infml.) Kind; Jugendliche(r)

kidney ['kɪdnɪ] Niere; **kidney machine** Dialyseapparat zur Blutwäsche, künstliche Niere

kill [kɪl] töten

kilo ['kiːləʊ] Kilo(gramm)

kilometre (km) ['kɪləmiːtə] Kilometer (km)
kind [kaɪnd] **1.** freundlich, gütig, nett; **2. kind (of)** Art
king [kɪŋ] König; **kingdom** ['kɪŋdəm] Königreich
kiss [kɪs] **1.** Kuß; **2.** küssen
kitchen ['kɪtʃn] Küche
kiwi ['kiːwiː] Kiwi
knee [niː] Knie; **kneel** [niːl] knien; **kneel down** niederknien
knife [naɪf], *pl.* **knives** [naɪvz] Messer
knight [naɪt] Ritter; Springer *(Schachfigur)*
knock (on) [nɒk] klopfen (gegen/an); **knock sb. down** jn. an-, überfahren; jn. umstoßen, niederschlagen
know [nəʊ] wissen; kennen; **get to know** kennenlernen; erfahren; **you know** weißt du, nämlich; **knowledge** *(sing.)* ['nɒlɪdʒ] Kenntnis(se), Wissen; **known** [nəʊn] bekannt

L

label ['leɪbl] Etikett
ladder ['lædə] Leiter
lady ['leɪdɪ] Dame
lake [leɪk] (Binnen-)See
lamp [læmp] Lampe
land [lænd] **1.** Land, Grund und Boden; **2.** landen, anlegen; **landowner** ['lændəʊnə] Grundbesitzer/in; **landscape** ['lændskeɪp] Landschaft, Landschaftsbild
language ['læŋgwɪdʒ] Sprache
large [lɑːdʒ] groß, umfangreich
last [lɑːst] **1.** (an-, fort)dauern; **2.** (aus)reichen; **3.** letzte(r, s); **4.** vorige(r, s); **last night** gestern abend; letzte Nacht; **at last** schließlich, endlich
late [leɪt] **1.** spät; **2. late (for)** zu spät, verspätet (für/zu); **lately** ['leɪtlɪ] in letzter Zeit; **latest** ['leɪtɪst] letzte(r, s), neueste(r, s); **at the latest** spätestens; **later on** später; **sooner or later** früher oder später
Latin ['lætɪn] Latein, lateinisch
laugh (at) [lɑːf] lachen (über); *(jn.)* auslachen; **laughter** *(sing.)* ['lɑːftə] Lachen, Gelächter
law [lɔː] Gesetz; **lawyer** ['lɔːjə] Rechtsanwalt/Rechtsanwältin; **pass a law** ein Gesetz verabschieden
layout ['leɪaʊt] Anordnung, Anlage; Layout
laziness ['leɪzɪnəs] Faulheit; **lazy** faul, träge; **lazybones** *(sing.)* ['leɪzɪbəʊnz] (infml.) Faulpelz
lead (to) [liːd] führen, leiten (zu/nach); **leader** ['liːdə] Leiter/in, (An-)Führer/in
lean [liːn] (sich) (an)lehnen
learn [lɜːn] lernen; **learner** Lerner/in
least [liːst] am wenigsten; **least of all** am allerwenigsten; **at least** wenigstens, zumindest; mindestens
leather ['leðə] Leder
leave [liːv] **1.** verlassen; **2.** weggehen, abfahren; **3.** (zurück)lassen, liegen/stehen lassen; **leave behind** zurücklassen; **leave out** auslassen, nicht berücksichtigen; **leave sb. alone** jn. in Ruhe lassen; **leave school** (BE) von der Schule abgehen
left [left] linke(r, s), nach links; **on the left** links, auf der linken Seite
leg [leg] Bein
legal ['liːgl] **1.** gesetzlich, legal; **2.** juristisch, rechtlich; **legalize** ['liːgəlaɪz] legalisieren
legend ['ledʒənd] Legende, Sage
leisure time ['leʒə taɪm] Freizeit
lemonade [ˌleməˈneɪd] Limonade
less [les] weniger
lesson ['lesn] (*meist* BE) (Unterrichts-)Stunde; **lessons** Unterricht
let [let] (zu)lassen; **Let's ... = Let us ...** Laß(t) uns .../Lassen Sie uns ...; **let sb. do sth.** jn. etwas tun lassen; zulassen, daß jd. etwas tut; **let sb. down** jn. im Stich lassen, enttäuschen
letter ['letə] **1.** Buchstabe; **2.** Brief; **letter box** (BE) Briefkasten
level ['levl] Niveau, Stufe
liberal ['lɪbrəl] **1.** Liberale(r); **2.** liberal
library ['laɪbrərɪ] Bücherei, Bibliothek; **librarian** [laɪ'breərɪən] Bibliothekar/in
licence (BE)**/license** (AE) ['laɪsəns]**: driving licence** (BE)**/driver's license** (AE) Führerschein
lie [laɪ] liegen
lie [laɪ] **1.** Lüge; **2. lie (to)** (an-, be-)lügen
life [laɪf], *pl.* **lives** [laɪvz] (das) Leben; **lifetime** Leben(szeit)
lift [lɪft] (hoch)heben
light [laɪt] **1.** leicht; **2.** Licht, Lampe; **traffic lights** *(pl.)* ['træfɪk laɪts] (Verkehrs-)Ampel
like [laɪk] **1.** (ähnlich) wie; **like this** so, auf diese Weise; folgendermaßen; **What is ... like?** Wie ist ...? **2.** *(conj.)* (infml.) als ob; wie; **3.** (gern) mögen, gern haben; **like doing sth.** etwas gern tun; **How do you like ...?** Wie gefällt dir ...? Wie findest du ...? **I'd like = I would like** ich möchte (gern), ich hätte gern
likely ['laɪklɪ] wahrscheinlich; **most likely** höchstwahrscheinlich; **be likely to do** wahrscheinlich tun
limit: speed limit ['spiːd ˌlɪmɪt] Geschwindigkeitsbeschränkung
line [laɪn] **1.** Zeile; **2.** Linie; **3.** (Telefon-)Leitung
link [lɪŋk] **1.** Verbindung, Beziehung; **2.** (sich) verbinden, verknüpfen; **linking** ['lɪŋkɪŋ] verbindend, verknüpfend
liquid: washing liquid ['wɒʃɪŋ ˌlɪkwɪd] (BE) flüssiges Waschmittel
list [lɪst] **1.** Liste, Verzeichnis; **2.** auflisten, aufführen, aufzählen
listen (to sb./sth.) ['lɪsn] (jm.) zuhören; (sich etwas) anhören; horchen; **listener** Zuhörer/in
literature ['lɪtrətʃə] Literatur
litre (BE)**/liter** (AE) ['liːtə] Liter
little ['lɪtl] klein; **(a) little** (ein) wenig
live [lɪv] leben, wohnen; **live on sth.** von etwas leben, sich von etwas ernähren; **living-room** ['lɪvɪŋ ruːm] Wohnzimmer
live [laɪv] live, direkt; **lively** ['laɪvlɪ] lebhaft;
load [ləʊd] (auf-, ein-, be)laden
local ['ləʊkl] örtlich, Lokal-, am Ort
located [ləʊ'keɪtɪd]**: be located** sich befinden
loneliness ['ləʊnlɪnəs] Einsamkeit; **lonely** ['ləʊnlɪ] einsam, verlassen
long [lɒŋ] lang; **as long as** sofern, solange; **no longer** nicht mehr, nicht länger
look [lʊk] **1.** aussehen; **look (at)** (an)sehen, (an)schauen; **look after** sich kümmern um; **look for** suchen; **look forward to** sich freuen auf; **look up** *(ein Wort)* nachschlagen; **2.** Blick; **have a look at** sich ansehen; einen Blick werfen auf;
lorry ['lɒrɪ] (BE) Lastwagen, LKW
lose [luːz] verlieren; **lose one's way** sich verirren, sich verlaufen; **lose touch (with)** den Kontakt verlieren (zu); **loser** Verlierer/in; **lost** [lɒst] verloren
lot [lɒt]**: a lot (of)/lots (of)** viele, viel; **like sth. a lot** etwas sehr mögen

D

lot [lɒt]**: parking lot** (AE) (großer) Parkplatz

loud [laʊd] laut

lovable ['lʌvəbl] liebenswert

love [lʌv] **1.** lieben, sehr mögen, sehr gern haben; **love doing sth.** etwas sehr gern tun; **lovable** liebenswert; **2.** Liebe; **fall in love with sb.** sich in jn. verlieben.
Love, … Viele liebe Grüße von …; **love** mein Lieber/meine Liebe *(informelle Anrede)*

lovely ['lʌvlɪ] schön, herrlich, hübsch

low [ləʊ] niedrig

luck [lʌk] Glück; **luckily** ['lʌkɪlɪ] glücklicherweise, zum Glück; **Good luck.** Viel Glück! **be lucky** Glück haben; **lucky boy/girl/…** Glückspilz

luggage ['lʌgɪdʒ] Gepäck

lunch [lʌntʃ] Mittagessen; **for lunch** zum Mittagessen; **lunch hour** ['lʌntʃ‿ˌaʊə] Mittagspause; **lunchtime** Mittagspause; **at lunchtime** mittags, in der Mittagspause

M

machine [mə'ʃi:n] Maschine, Apparat, Gerät; **machinery** *(sing.)* [mə'ʃi:nərɪ] Maschinerie, Maschinen

Madam, madam ['mædəm] meine Dame *(höfliche Anrede)*

magazine [ˌmægə'zi:n] Zeitschrift

magician [mə'dʒɪʃn] Zauberer/Zauberin

magnificent [mæg'nɪfɪsənt] prächtig, herrlich

mail [meɪl] *(meist* AE) **1.** *(Brief)* abschicken, einwerfen; *(Paket)* aufgeben; **2.** Post(sendungen); **airmail** ['eəmeɪl] Luftpost; **electronic mailbox** [ˌɪlektrɒnɪk 'meɪlbɒks] elektronischer Briefkasten, Mailbox

main [meɪn] Haupt-; **mainly** hauptsächlich

major ['meɪdʒə] bedeutende(r, s), größere(r, s); **majority** [mə'dʒɒrətɪ] Mehrheit

make [meɪk] machen, zubereiten; bilden; **make coffee/soup** Kaffee/Suppe kochen; **make ends meet** *(finanziell)* über die Runden kommen; **make friends (with)** Freunde finden; sich anfreunden (mit); **make into** verwandeln in, machen zu; **make it** (infml.) es schaffen, Erfolg haben; **make a mess** Unordnung/Dreck machen; **make sb. do sth.** jn. veranlassen/zwingen, etwas zu tun; **make sense** (einen) Sinn ergeben, Sinn machen; **make sth. sth.** etwas zu etwas machen; **make sure** sicherstellen, sichergehen; dafür sorgen *(, daß)*; **make up** sich ausdenken

male [meɪl] **1.** männliche Person; **2.** männlich

man [mæn], *pl.* **men** [men] Mann; **man-made** [ˌmæn'meɪd] künstlich

manage to do sth. ['mænɪdʒ] es schaffen, etwas zu tun; **manager** ['mænɪdʒə] Geschäftsführer/in

manuscript ['mænjʊskrɪpt] Manuskript

many ['menɪ] viele; **How many?** Wie viele?

map [mæp] Stadtplan, Landkarte

march [mɑ:tʃ] **1.** Marsch; Demonstration; **2.** marschieren

March [mɑ:tʃ] März

mark [mɑ:k] Note, Zensur

market ['mɑ:kɪt] Markt

marriage (to) ['mærɪdʒ] Ehe (mit); Heirat; **marry** ['mærɪ] heiraten; **married** verheiratet; **get married** heiraten

mass (of) [mæs] Masse, Menge (von); Massen-

massacre ['mæsəkə] Massaker, Blutbad

match [mætʃ] **1.** Spiel, Wettkampf; **2.** Streichholz; **box of matches** Streichholzschachtel; **3.** passen zu; zusammenpassen

mate [meɪt] (BE, infml.) Kumpel

material [mə'tɪərɪəl] **1.** Material; **2.** materiell

math [mæθ] (AE)/**maths** [mæθs] (BE) Mathe(matik)

matter ['mætə]**: It doesn't matter.** Das macht nichts. **no matter how/what/…** egal, wie/was/…; **What's the matter?** Was ist los?

may [meɪ] dürfen; **it may be** es kann sein, es ist vielleicht

May [meɪ] Mai

maybe ['meɪbɪ] vielleicht

mayor [meə] Bürgermeister/in

me [mi:] mich, mir; **it wasn't me** ich war es nicht

meal [mi:l] Mahlzeit, Essen

mean [mi:n] **1.** bedeuten; **2.** meinen (= sagen wollen); **meaning** ['mi:nɪŋ] Bedeutung; **be meant to be** [ment] sein sollen

meat [mi:t] Fleisch

mechanics [mɪ'kænɪks]**: auto mechanics** *(sing.)* (AE) Kfz-Technik

media ['mi:dɪə]**: the media** *(pl.)* die Medien; **medium** ['mi:dɪəm], *pl. usually* **media** *(künstlerisches)* Medium

medium-size [ˌmi:dɪəm'saɪz] mittelgroß

medical ['medɪkl] medizinisch, Medizin-; ärztlich; **medicine** ['medsn] Medizin, Arznei

meet [mi:t] **1.** sich treffen; *(jn.)* treffen; *(jn.)* kennenlernen; **2.** *(Anforderungen usw.)* gerecht werden, entsprechen; **meeting** ['mi:tɪŋ] Besprechung; Treffen, Versammlung

melt [melt] schmelzen

member (of) ['membə] Mitglied (von, in); **Member of Parliament** [ˌmembər‿əv 'pɑ:ləmənt] (GB) Mitglied des Unterhauses

memorial [mɪ'mɔ:rɪəl] **1.** Denkmal, Gedenkstätte; **2.** Gedenk-

memory ['memərɪ] Gedächtnis

mention ['menʃn] erwähnen

menu ['menju:] Speisekarte

merry: Merry Christmas! [ˌmerɪ 'krɪsməs] Fröhliche Weihnachten!

mess *(sing.)* [mes] Durcheinander, Unordnung, Dreck

message ['mesɪdʒ] Nachricht, Botschaft; **messenger** ['mesɪndʒə] Bote/Botin

metal ['metl] Metall

metre ['mi:tə] Meter

metropolitan area [ˌmetrə'pɒlɪtn] städtischer Großraum, Ballungsraum

microphone ['maɪkrəfəʊn] Mikrophon

middle ['mɪdl] **1.** Mitte; **2.** mittlere(r, s)

midnight ['mɪdnaɪt] Mitternacht; **at midnight** um Mitternacht

might [maɪt] könnte(n) vielleicht; **they might go out …** sie gehen vielleicht (manchmal) aus …

mile [maɪl] Meile *(= ca. 1,6 km)*; **miles per hour (mph)** [ˌmaɪlz pər‿'aʊə] Meilen pro Stunde

military ['mɪlɪtərɪ] militärisch, Militär-

milk [mɪlk] Milch; **milkshake** [ˌmɪlk'ʃeɪk] *Milchmixgetränk*

million ['mɪlɪən] Million(en)

mind [maɪnd] **1.** etwas einzuwenden haben gegen; **Never mind.** [ˌnevə 'maɪnd] Macht nichts. Egal. **2. change one's mind** seine Meinung ändern; **come into sb.'s mind** jm. einfallen, in den Sinn kommen; **go through her/his mind** ihr/ihm durch den Kopf

schießen; **in one's right mind** (infml.) bei (klarem) Verstand; **make up one's mind** sich entscheiden; **state of mind** (geistige) Verfassung, (Gemüts-)Zustand; **What's going through her mind?** Was geht ihr durch den Kopf? Woran denkt sie?
mine [maɪn] *(poss. pron.)* meine(r, s)
mine [maɪn] Bergwerk; **miner** Bergarbeiter/in
mini- ['mɪnɪ] Mini-, Klein-; **minibus** ['mɪnɪbʌs] Kleinbus
minister ['mɪnɪstə] Minister/in
minority [maɪ'nɒrətɪ] Minderheit
minute ['mɪnɪt] Minute; **a ten-minute walk** zehn Minuten zu Fuß; **in a minute** gleich, sofort; **Wait a minute!** Einen Augenblick! Moment mal!
mirror ['mɪrə] Spiegel
misbehave [ˌmɪsbɪ'heɪv] sich schlecht benehmen
miserable ['mɪzərəbl] erbärmlich, jämmerlich, gräßlich
misinform [ˌmɪsɪn'fɔːm] falsch informieren
mislead [ˌmɪs'liːd] irreführen
misplaced [ˌmɪs'pleɪst] unangebracht, deplaziert, fehl am Platz
Miss [mɪs] Fräulein/Frau ... *(unverheiratet)*
miss [mɪs] **1.** verpassen, verfehlen; **2.** vermissen; **missing** fehlend; **be missing** fehlen
mission ['mɪʃn] Mission(sstation)
misspell [ˌmɪs'spel] falsch schreiben
mistake [mɪ'steɪk] Fehler, Irrtum
mistreat [ˌmɪs'triːt] mißhandeln, schlecht behandeln
mistrust [ˌmɪs'trʌst] Mißtrauen
misunderstand [ˌmɪsʌndə'stænd] mißverstehen; **misunderstanding** [ˌmɪsʌndə'stændɪŋ] Mißverständnis
misuse [ˌmɪs'juːz] mißbrauchen, zweckentfremden
mix [mɪks] (miteinander) verkehren, auskommen; (sich) mischen; **mix up** verwechseln, durcheinanderbringen; **mixed** gemischt; **mixed bag** „bunte Mischung"; **mixture** ['mɪkstʃə] Mischung
model ['mɒdl] Modell
modem ['məʊdem] Modem
modern ['mɒdn] modern; **modernize** ['mɒdənaɪz] modernisieren
modify ['mɒdɪfaɪ] **1.** *(Verb, Adjektiv usw.)* näher bestimmen; **2.** modifizieren, abwandeln
mom [BE: mɒm, AE: mɑːm] (AE) Mutti, Mama
moment ['məʊmənt]**: at the moment** im Augenblick, gerade, zur Zeit
monarchy ['mɒnəkɪ] Monarchie
Monday ['mʌndɪ, 'mʌndeɪ] Montag
money ['mʌnɪ] Geld
monitor ['mɒnɪtə] Bildschirm, Monitor
monkey ['mʌŋkɪ] Affe
monster ['mɒnstə] Monster, Ungeheuer
month [mʌnθ] Monat; **monthly** monatlich
monument ['mɒnjʊmənt] Denkmal
mood [muːd] Stimmung
moon [muːn] Mond
moped ['məʊped] Moped
moral ['mɒrəl] Moral, Lehre
more [mɔː] mehr; weitere; **more than** mehr als; **once more** noch einmal; **one more** noch ein(e); **some more** noch einige, noch etwas; **more interesting** interessanter
morning ['mɔːnɪŋ] Morgen, Vormittag; **Good morning.** Guten Morgen. Guten Tag. *(vormittags)*; **in the morning(s)** am Morgen, morgens; **on Monday morning** am Montag morgen; **this morning** heute morgen
most [məʊst] **1.** (der/die/das) meiste, die meisten; **2.** am meisten; **most of all** am allermeisten; **most of the time** die meiste Zeit; **(the) most famous** (der/die/das) berühmteste; am berühmtesten; **most likely** höchstwahrscheinlich; **mostly** meist(ens), größtenteils
mother ['mʌðə] Mutter
motivate ['məʊtɪveɪt] motivieren
motive ['məʊtɪv] Motiv, Beweggrund
motorbike ['məʊtəbaɪk] (BE) Motorrad; **motorway** ['məʊtəweɪ] (BE) Autobahn
motto ['mɒtəʊ] Motto, Wahlspruch
mountain ['maʊntɪn] Berg
mouse [maʊs], *pl.* **mice** [maɪs] Maus
mouth [maʊθ] **1.** Mund; **2.** (Fluß-) Mündung
move [muːv] **1.** (um)ziehen; **2.** (sich) bewegen; **movement** ['muːvmənt] Bewegung; **moving** ['muːvɪŋ] bewegend
movie ['muːvɪ] *(meist* AE) Film; **movie theater/movies** (AE) Kino
MP [ˌem'piː]**, Member of Parliament** [ˌmembər_əv 'pɑːləmənt] (GB) Mitglied des Unterhauses
Mr ['mɪstə] Herr ...
Mrs ['mɪsɪz] Frau ... *(verheiratet)*
Ms [məz] Frau ... *(verheiratet oder unverheiratet)*
much [mʌtʃ] viel; **How much?** Wieviel? **How much is/are ...?** Was kostet/kosten ...? **like/love/... very much** sehr mögen/lieben/...
mud [mʌd] Schlamm, Matsch
muddled ['mʌdld] durcheinander(gebracht)
muesli ['mjuːzlɪ] Müsli
mug [mʌg] Becher, Krug
Mum/mum [mʌm] (BE) Mutti, Mama
murder ['mɜːdə] **1.** Mord; **2.** (er)morden; **murderer** Mörder/in
museum [mjuː'ziːəm] Museum
music ['mjuːzɪk] Musik; **musical** ['mjuːzɪkl] Musical; **musician** [mjuː'zɪʃn] Musiker/in
must [mʌst] müssen; **mustn't** nicht dürfen
mustard ['mʌstəd] Senf
my [maɪ] *(poss. adj.)* mein(e); **myself** [maɪ'self] mir, mich (selbst)
mystery ['mɪstrɪ] Geheimnis, Rätsel

N

nail [neɪl] Nagel; **hammer a nail into the wall** einen Nagel in die Wand schlagen
name [neɪm] **1.** Name; **Christian name** ['krɪstʃən neɪm] Vorname; **first name** Vorname; **What's your name?** Wie heißt du? Wie heißen Sie? **What's in a name?** Was bedeutet schon ein Name? Namen sind Schall und Rauch. **call sb. names** Schimpfwörter zu jm. sagen; **2.** (be-, er)nennen
narrative ['nærətɪv] erzählend, narrativ; **narrator** [nə'reɪtə] Erzähler/in
narrow ['nærəʊ] eng, schmal
nasty ['nɑːstɪ] gemein, gehässig
nation ['neɪʃn] Nation, Volk; **national** ['næʃnəl] national; **national paper** überregionale Zeitung; **nationality** [ˌnæʃə'nælətɪ] Staatsangehörigkeit, Nationalität; **nationalize** ['næʃnəlaɪz] verstaatlichen
native ['neɪtɪv] eingeboren, einheimisch; **Native American** [ˌneɪtɪv_ə'merɪkən] amerik. Ureinwohner/in; **be a native German** gebürtiger Deutscher/ gebürtige Deutsche sein; **native speaker** Muttersprachler/in

D

natural ['nætʃrəl] natürlich, Natur-; **natural gas** [ˌnætʃrəl 'gæs] Erdgas; **nature** ['neɪtʃə] Natur
near [nɪə] **1.** in der Nähe, nahe; **nearest** nächstgelegene(r, s); **nearly** fast, beinahe; **2. near/near to** *(prep.)* in der Nähe (von), nahe (bei)
necessarily [ˌnesə'serəlɪ] unbedingt, notwendigerweise; **necessary** ['nesəsərɪ] notwendig, nötig
neck [nek] Hals
need [ni:d] brauchen, benötigen; **needn't** nicht brauchen, nicht müssen
neighbour ['neɪbə] Nachbar/in; **neighbourhood** ['neɪbəhʊd] Nachbarschaft
neither ... nor ... ['naɪðə / 'ni:ðə ... nɔ:] weder ... noch ...
nervous ['nɜ:vəs] nervös, aufgeregt, ängstlich; **nervousness** Nervosität
nest [nest] Nest
network ['netwɜ:k] Netz(werk)
never ['nevə] nie, niemals; **Never mind.** [ˌnevə 'maɪnd] Macht nichts. Egal.
new [nju:] neu; **New Year's Day** [ˌnju: jɪəz 'deɪ] Neujahr(stag); **New Year's Eve** [ˌnju: jɪəz_'i:v] Silvester; **newcomer** ['nju:kʌmə] Neuling; **news** *(sing.)* [nju:z] **1.** Nachricht(en); **2.** Neuigkeit(en); **That's news to me.** Das ist mir neu. **newsagent** ['nju:zeɪdʒənt] (BE) Zeitungshändler/in; **newsagent's** (BE) Zeitungsladen; **newspaper** Zeitung; **newsstand** ['nju:zstænd] Zeitungskiosk, Zeitungsstand
next [nekst] **1.** nächste(r, s) *(zeitlich, Reihenfolge)*; **2.** *(adv.)* als nächstes; das nächste Mal; **3. next to** *(prep.)* (direkt) neben; **next door** nebenan
nice [naɪs] schön, nett
nickel [nɪkl] (AE) Fünfcentmünze
night [naɪt] Nacht, (später) Abend; **at night** nachts, in der Nacht, am (späten) Abend
no [nəʊ] **1.** nein; **2.** kein, keine; **no longer** nicht mehr, nicht länger; **no one** niemand
No. (= number) Nr. (= Nummer)
nobody/no one ['nəʊbədɪ/'nəʊ wʌn] niemand
nod [nɒd] nicken
noise [nɔɪz] Lärm, Geräusch; **noisy** ['nɔɪzɪ] laut, lärmend; **noiselessly** ['nɔɪzləslɪ] geräuschlos
non- [nɒn] nicht-; Nicht-; **non-fiction** [ˌnɒn'fɪkʃn] Sachbücher; **non-profitmaking** [ˌnɒn'prɒfɪtmeɪkɪŋ] gemeinnützig; **non-returnable** [ˌnɒnrɪ'tɜ:nəbl] Einweg-*(Flasche)*; ohne Pfand, nicht wiederverwendbar; **non-stop** [ˌnɒn'stɒp] ununterbrochen, non-stop; **non-violent** [ˌnɒn'vaɪələnt] gewaltlos
none (of) [nʌn] keine(r, s) (von)
nonsense ['nɒnsəns] Unsinn
nor: neither ... nor ... ['naɪðə / 'ni:ðə ... nɔ:] weder ... noch ...
normal ['nɔ:məl] normal; **normally** ['nɔ:məlɪ] normalerweise
north [nɔ:θ] **1.** Norden; **2.** nach Norden; **3. north (of)** nördlich (von); **northern** ['nɔ:ðən] Nord-, nördlich
nose [nəʊz] Nase
not [nɒt] nicht; **not ... at all** überhaupt nicht; **not ... either** auch nicht; auch kein; **not even** nicht einmal; **not ever** niemals; **not ... until** nicht vor/erst um; nicht ... bevor; **not ... yet** noch nicht
note [nəʊt] **1.** (BE) (Geld-)Schein, Banknote; **2.** Notiz; Entschuldigungsschreiben; **notepaper** ['nəʊtpeɪpə] Briefpapier
nothing ['nʌθɪŋ] nichts
notice ['nəʊtɪs] (be)merken; **notice-board** ['nəʊtɪsbɔ:d] *(meist* BE) Schwarzes Brett
novel ['nɒvl] Roman; **novelist** ['nɒvəlɪst] Romanschriftsteller/in
November [nəʊ'vembə] November
now [naʊ] nun, jetzt; **from now on** von jetzt an, ab jetzt
nowhere ['nəʊweə] nirgendwo; nirgendwohin
nuclear: nuclear family [ˌnju:klɪə 'fæmlɪ] Kleinfamilie; **nuclear power** [ˌnju:klɪə 'paʊə] Kernkraft
nuisance ['nju:sns]: **it's a nuisance** es ist lästig, es ist ärgerlich
number ['nʌmbə] Zahl, Nummer; **a number of** mehrere
nurse [nɜ:s] Krankenpfleger/in, Krankenschwester

O

oak [əʊk] Eiche
object ['ɒbdʒɪkt] Gegenstand, Objekt
objective [əb'dʒektɪv] objektiv
obligation [ˌɒblɪ'geɪʃn] Verpflichtung, Pflicht
observation [ˌɒbzə'veɪʃn] Beobachtung; **observe** [əʊ'zɜ:v] beobachten, zusehen
obtain [əb'teɪn] (fml.) erlangen, erhalten
obvious ['ɒbvɪəs] offensichtlich
ocean ['əʊʃn] Ozean
o'clock [ə'klɒk]: **7 o'clock** 7 Uhr/ 19 Uhr
October [ɒk'təʊbə] Oktober
odd one out [ˌɒd wʌn_'aʊt] „Fremdkörper" (= Welches Wort paßt hier nicht?)
of [ɒv, əv] von; **a cup of tea** eine Tasse Tee; **of course** natürlich, selbstverständlich; **out of ...** ['aʊt_əv] aus ... hinaus; **There were five of them.** Sie waren zu fünft.
off [ɒf] **1.** aus, ausgeschaltet; **2.** (von ...) herunter
offer ['ɒfə] **1.** Angebot; **special offer** [ˌspeʃl_'ɒfə] Sonderangebot; **2.** (an)bieten
office ['ɒfɪs] Büro
officer ['ɒfɪsə] Offizier/in; **(police) officer** (Polizei-)Beamter/Beamtin, Polizist/in
official [ə'fɪʃl] 1. offiziell, amtlich; 2. Beamte(r), Beamtin
often ['ɒfn] oft
oil [ɔɪl] Öl
OK. = Okay. [əʊ'keɪ] Gut. In Ordnung.
old [əʊld] alt
on [ɒn] **1.** auf; **2.** an, eingeschaltet; **on holiday** in Urlaub; **on Monday (morning)** am Montag (morgen); **on Mondays** montags; **on the bus/ train/plane** im Bus/Zug/Flugzeug; **on the coast** an der Küste; **on the first evening** am ersten Abend; **on the radio/on TV** im Radio/im Fernsehen; **on the (tele)phone** am Telefon; **on the Thames** an der Themse; **on time** pünktlich; **go on** weitermachen; **walk/drive/... on** weitergehen/weiterfahren/...; **from now on** von jetzt an, ab jetzt; **from then on** von da an
once [wʌns] **1.** einst, (früher) einmal; **2.** einmal; **at once** sofort, gleich; gleichzeitig; **once more/once again** noch einmal
one [wʌn] man; **oneself** [wʌn'self] sich (selbst); **no one** niemand; **one day** eines Tages; **the Mexican ones** die mexikanischen; **which one** welche(r, s); **one-sided** [ˌwʌn'saɪdɪd] einseitig
only ['əʊnlɪ] nur, bloß; erst; **not only ... but (also)** nicht nur ... sondern (auch); **the only ...** der/die/das einzige ...
onto ['ɒntʊ, 'ɒntə] auf (... hinauf)
open ['əʊpən] **1.** offen, geöffnet; **2.** öffnen, aufmachen; sich öffnen; eröffnen
operation [ˌɒpə'reɪʃn] Operation *(auch medizinisch)*, Unternehmung

D

operator ['ɒpəreɪtə] Vermittlung; Telefonist/in
opinion [ə'pɪnjən] Meinung; **in my opinion** meiner Meinung nach
opposite ['ɒpəzɪt] **1.** gegenüber (von); **2.** Gegenteil
opposition (to) [ˌɒpə'zɪʃn] Opposition, Widerstand (gegen)
or [ɔː] oder; **either … or …** ['aɪðə / 'iːðə … ɔː] entweder … oder …
oral ['ɔːrəl] mündlich
orange ['ɒrɪndʒ] **1.** orangefarben; **2.** Apfelsine, Orange
order ['ɔːdə] **1.** Reihenfolge; Ordnung, Anordnung; **2.** Bestellung, Auftrag, Order; **3.** Befehl; **4.** bestellen; **5. order sb. to do sth.** jm. befehlen/jn. auffordern, etwas zu tun; **6. in order to** um zu
ordinary ['ɔːdnərɪ, 'ɔːdɪnərɪ] gewöhnlich, normal
organization [ˌɔːgənaɪ'zeɪʃn] Organisation; **organize** ['ɔːgənaɪz] organisieren; aufbauen; **organizer** Organisator/in, Veranstalter/in
origin ['ɒrɪdʒɪn] Ursprung; Abstammung; **original** [ə'rɪdʒnəl] **1.** Original; **2.** ursprünglich, Original-
other ['ʌðə]**: (the) other** (der/die/das) andere; die anderen; **each other** [ˌiːtʃ‿'ʌðə] einander, sich (gegenseitig)
ought to [ɔːt] sollte(n), müßte(n) eigentlich
our ['aʊə, ɑː] *(poss. adj.)* unser(e); **ours** ['aʊəz] *(poss. pron.)* unsere(r, s); **ourselves** [aʊə'selvz] uns (selbst)
out here/there [aʊt] hier/da draußen; **out (of …)** aus (… hinaus), aus (… heraus); **ask sb. out** jn. einladen *(ins Kino, zum Essen usw.)*
outdoors [ˌaʊt'dɔːz] (nach) draußen, im Freien
outgoing [ˌaʊt'gəʊɪŋ] kontaktfreudig, extravertiert
outing ['aʊtɪŋ] Ausflug
outline ['aʊtlaɪn] Entwurf, Grundriß
outside [ˌaʊt'saɪd] **1.** *(prep.)* außerhalb (von); **2.** *(adv.)* (nach) draußen
outskirts *(pl.)* ['aʊtskɜːts] Außenbezirke, Stadtrand; **on the outskirts** am Stadtrand
outspoken [ˌaʊt'spəʊkən] *(Person)* offen(herzig), direkt; *(Äußerung)* unverblümt
oven ['ʌvn] Backofen
over ['əʊvə] über; **all over the bungalow** im ganzen Bungalow verteilt, überall im Bungalow; **be over** zu Ende sein, vorüber sein; **over the years** im Lauf der Jahre; **over there** da/dort drüben; **fall over** hin-, umfallen
overhead projector [ˌəʊvəhed prə'dʒektə] **(OHP)** Tageslichtprojektor
overnight [ˌəʊvə'naɪt] über Nacht
overreact [ˌəʊvərɪ'ækt] überreagieren
overuse [ˌəʊvə'juːs] übermäßiger Gebrauch
own [əʊn]**: my/your/… own** mein(e)/dein(e)/… eigene(r, s); **on one's own** allein, selbständig
own [əʊn] besitzen; **owner** ['əʊnə] Besitzer/in
ozone layer ['əʊzəʊn ˌleɪə] Ozonschicht

P

pack [pæk] (ein)packen
package (of) ['pækɪdʒ] Päckchen, Paket
packet ['pækɪt] Päckchen
page [peɪdʒ] (Buch-/Heft-)Seite
pain [peɪn] Schmerz(en)
paint [peɪnt] **1.** Farbe *(zum Malen)*, Lack; **2.** malen; (an)streichen, lackieren; **painter** Maler/in; Anstreicher/in; **painting** Gemälde
pair (of) [peə] Paar
pajamas *(pl.)* [pə'dʒɑːməz] (AE) Schlafanzug
Pakistani [ˌpɑːkɪ'stɑːnɪ] **1.** Pakistaner/in, Pakistani; **2.** pakistanisch
palace ['pæləs] Palast
panic ['pænɪk] Panik
panther ['pænθə] Panther
paper ['peɪpə] **1.** Papier; **2.** Zeitung; **national paper** überregionale Zeitung
parade [pə'reɪd] Parade, Umzug
paragraph ['pærəgrɑːf] Absatz, Abschnitt
Pardon? ['pɑːdn] Wie bitte?
parentheses [pə'renθəsiːz] (*meist* AE) Klammern *(Satzzeichen)*
parent ['peərənt] Elternteil; **parents** Eltern; **one-parent family/single-parent family** Familie mit alleinerziehendem Elternteil
park [pɑːk] **1.** Park; **2.** parken; **car park** (BE)**/parking lot** (AE) (großer) Parkplatz
parliament ['pɑːləmənt] Parlament
part [pɑːt] **1.** Teil; **part of the body** Körperteil; **part of town** Stadtteil, Stadtviertel; **part-time** [ˌpɑːt'taɪm] Teilzeit-, halbtags; **partly** teilweise, zum Teil; **2.** Rolle *(in einem Theaterstück, Film usw.)*; **take part (in)** teilnehmen (an), mitmachen (bei)
participant (in) [pɑː'tɪsɪpənt] Teilnehmer/in (an)
particular [pə'tɪkjʊlə] bestimmte(r, s), spezielle(r, s)
partner ['pɑːtnə] Partner/in
party ['pɑːtɪ] **1.** Party, Feier; **have a party** eine Party feiern; **2.** Partei
pass [pɑːs] **1.** vergehen, vorübergehen *(Zeit)*; **pass by** vorbeigehen, vorüberziehen; **2.** *(eine Prüfung)* bestehen; **3.** *(ein Gesetz)* verabschieden; **4. pass sth.** etwas (herüber)reichen; **pass the ball** den Ball abspielen
passage ['pæsɪdʒ] Passage, Textstelle
passenger ['pæsɪndʒə] Passagier/in; Mitfahrer/in
passport ['pɑːspɔːt] (Reise-)Paß
past [pɑːst] **1.** Vergangenheit; **2.** vergangen; **in the past few years** in den vergangenen/letzten Jahren; **3.** *(prep.)* vorbei, vorüber (an); **quarter past eight** [ˌkwɔːtə pɑːst‿'eɪt] Viertel nach acht (8.15/20.15)
pasta ['pæstə] Teigwaren, Nudeln
patent ['peɪtnt] patentieren (lassen)
path [pɑːθ]**,** *pl.* **paths** [pɑːðz] Weg, Pfad; **bike path** Radweg
patience ['peɪʃns] Geduld; **patient** ['peɪʃnt] **1.** geduldig; **2.** Patient/in
pause [pɔːz] innehalten, eine Pause machen
pavement ['peɪvmənt] (BE) Gehweg
pay [peɪ] **1.** Bezahlung; Lohn, Löhne; **pay phone** Münztelefon; **2. pay (for)** bezahlen; **pay attention (to)** aufmerksam sein, aufpassen (auf)
P.E. [ˌpiː‿'iː] **(Physical Education)** [ˌfɪzɪkl‿edjʊ'keɪʃn] Turnen, Sport(unterricht) *(in der Regel in der Halle)*
pea [piː] Erbse
peace [piːs] Friede(n); **peaceful** ['piːsfəl] friedlich
pedestrian [pə'destrɪən] Fußgänger/in; **pedestrian crossing** [pəˌdestrɪən 'krɒsɪŋ] (BE) Fußgängerüberweg
pen [pen] Füller; **ball-point pen** (AE) Kugelschreiber; **pen-friend** Brieffreund/in
pence [pens] Pence *(Mehrzahl von BE „penny“)*
pencil ['pensl] Bleistift; **pencil-case** Federmappe, Federtasche

penny ['penɪ] **1.** (BE) *kleinste britische Münze*; **2.** (AE) Eincentmünze
pension ['penʃn] Altersrente, Pension
people ['pi:pl] (die) Leute, (die) Menschen; **people of color** (AE) *Amerikaner/innen bzw. Menschen nicht-europäischer Herkunft*
per [pɜ:, pə] pro; **per cent (%)** [pə'sent] Prozent; **miles per hour (mph)** ['maɪlz pər_'aʊə] Meilen pro Stunde
perfect ['pɜ:fɪkt] vollkommen, perfekt
perform [pə'fɔ:m] aufführen
perhaps [pə'hæps] vielleicht
period ['pɪərɪəd] **1.** Epoche; Zeitspanne, Phase; **2.** (AE) Punkt *(Satzzeichen)*
permission [pə'mɪʃn] Erlaubnis, Genehmigung
permit **1.** ['pɜ:mɪt] Genehmigung(sschein), *(schriftliche)* Erlaubnis; **2.** [pə'mɪt] erlauben, gestatten
persecute ['pɜ:sɪkju:t] verfolgen *(aus politischen oder religiösen Gründen)*
person ['pɜ:sn] Person; **personal** ['pɜ:snəl] persönlich; **personal stereo** „Walkman"; **personality** [,pɜ:sə'nælətɪ] Persönlichkeit
pet [pet] Haustier
petrol ['petrəl] (BE) Benzin; **petrol station** (BE) Tankstelle
phone [fəʊn] **1.** anrufen; **2.** Telefon; **answer the phone** ans Telefon gehen; **on the phone** am Telefon; **pay phone** Münztelefon; **(tele)phone box** (BE)/**(tele)phone booth** [bu:θ] (AE) Telefonzelle
photo (of) ['fəʊtəʊ] Foto (von); **photograph** ['fəʊtəgrɑ:f] Fotografie, (Licht-)Bild; **photographer** [fə'tɒgrəfə] Fotograf/in; **take photos** Fotos machen
phrase [freɪz] (Rede-)Wendung, Ausdruck; **phrasebook** ['freɪzbʊk] Sprachführer
physical ['fɪzɪkl]: **Physical Education** [,fɪzɪkl_ edjʊ'keɪʃn] **(P.E.)** Turnen, Sport(unterricht) *(in der Regel in der Halle)*; **physical punishment** *(sing.)* [,fɪzɪkl 'pʌnɪʃmənt] Körperstrafe, Prügelstrafe; **physical therapist** [,fɪzɪkl 'θerəpɪst] (AE)/ **physiotherapist** [,fɪzɪəʊ'θerəpɪst] (BE) Physiotherapeut/in, Krankengymnast/in
physics *(sing.)* ['fɪzɪks] Physik
physiotherapist [,fɪzɪəʊ'θerəpɪst] (BE) Physiotherapeut/in, Krankengymnast/in
piano [pɪ'ænəʊ] Klavier

pick up [,pɪk_'ʌp] **1.** abholen, mitnehmen *(mit dem Auto)*; **2.** *(vom Boden)* aufheben
picnic ['pɪknɪk] Picknick; **have a picnic** ein Picknick machen
picture (of) ['pɪktʃə] Bild, Foto (von); **in the picture** auf dem Bild/Foto
pie [paɪ] **1.** (Obst-)Kuchen; **2.** (Fleisch-)Pastete
piece (of) [pi:s] Stück; **piece of furniture** Möbelstück
pink [pɪŋk] rosa, pink
pirate ['paɪrət] Pirat/in, Seeräuber/in
pity (for) ['pɪtɪ] Mitleid, Mitgefühl (mit); **feel pity for sb.** mit jm. Mitleid haben; **What a pity!** Wie schade!
pizza ['pi:tsə] Pizza
place [pleɪs] Ort, Platz, Stelle; **take place** stattfinden
plan [plæn] **1.** Plan; **2.** planen
plane [pleɪn] Flugzeug; **on the plane** im Flugzeug
planet ['plænɪt] Planet
plant [plɑ:nt] **1.** Pflanze; **2.** (ein-)pflanzen
plastic ['plæstɪk] Plastik, Kunststoff; Plastik-
plate [pleɪt] Teller
platform ['plætfɔ:m] **1.** Bahnsteig, Gleis; **2.** Plattform
play [pleɪ] **1.** spielen; **play the piano** Klavier spielen; **playfully** ['pleɪfəlɪ] neckisch, schelmisch; **player** Spieler/in; **2.** Schauspiel, (Theater-)Stück
pleasant ['pleznt] angenehm
please [pli:z] bitte *(in Fragen und Aufforderungen)*; **(Yes,) please.** Danke, gern. **be pleased (with)** zufrieden sein (mit), sich freuen (über)
pleasure ['pleʒə] Vergnügen, Freude; **It's been a pleasure meeting you.** Es hat mich gefreut, Sie/Dich/Euch kennenzulernen.
pliers *(pl.)* ['plaɪəz] Zange
plural ['plʊərəl] Plural, Mehrzahl
plus [plʌs] plus
... pm [,pi:_'em] *(from Latin "post meridiem")* ... Uhr nachmittags oder abends *(zwischen 12 und 24 h)*
pocket ['pɒkɪt] Tasche *(an einem Kleidungsstück)*; **pocket-money** (BE) Taschengeld
poem ['pəʊɪm] Gedicht; **poet** ['pəʊɪt] Dichter/in
point [pɔɪnt] **1.** Punkt; **point of view** [,pɔɪnt_əv 'vju:] (Erzähl-)Standpunkt, (Erzähl-)Perspektive; **2. point (at, to)** zeigen, deuten (auf); **point out** hinweisen auf

poison ['pɔɪzn] **1.** vergiften; **2.** Gift
police [pə'li:s] Polizei; **police officer** [pə'li:s_,ɒfɪsə] Polizeibeamter/Polizeibeamtin, Polizist/in; **police station** Polizeiwache, Polizeirevier
policy ['pɒləsɪ] Verfahren(sweise), Politik; **foreign policy** [,fɒrən 'pɒləsɪ] Außenpolitik
polite [pə'laɪt] höflich; **politeness** [pə'laɪtnəs] Höflichkeit
political [pə'lɪtɪkl] politisch; **politician** [,pɒlə'tɪʃn] Politiker/in; **politics** *(sing.)* ['pɒlətɪks] Politik
pollute [pə'lu:t] *(die Umwelt)* verschmutzen; **pollution** [pə'lu:ʃn] (Umwelt-)Verschmutzung
pond [pɒnd] Teich
poor [pɔ:, pʊə] arm
pop music ['pɒp mju:zɪk] Popmusik
popular (with) ['pɒpjʊlə] beliebt (bei); **popularly** ['pɒpjʊləlɪ] allgemein, landläufig
population [,pɒpjʊ'leɪʃn] Bevölkerung, Einwohner(zahl)
port [pɔ:t] Hafen(stadt)
portrait ['pɔ:trət] Porträt, Bild
position [pə'zɪʃn] Position, Lage, Stellung
possible ['pɒsəbl] möglich; **possibility** [,pɒsə'bɪlətɪ] Möglichkeit; **possibly** ['pɒsəblɪ] vielleicht, möglicherweise; **They couldn't possibly help.** Sie konnten unmöglich helfen.
post [pəʊst] **1.** (BE) *(Brief)* abschicken, einwerfen; *(Paket)* aufgeben; **2.** (BE) Post(sendungen); **post office** Post(amt); **postcard (of)** Postkarte, Ansichtskarte (von *einer Gegend usw.*); **postcode** (BE) Postleitzahl
post-(industrial) post(industriell)
poster ['pəʊstə] Poster
pot [pɒt] Kanne; Topf
potato [pə'teɪtəʊ], *pl.* **potatoes** Kartoffel
pottery ['pɒtərɪ] Töpfern
pound [paʊnd] **1. (£)** Pfund *(britische Währung)*; **2.** Pfund *(454 g)*
poverty ['pɒvətɪ] Armut
power ['paʊə] Macht; Vollmacht, Befugnis; **powerful** stark; mächtig, gewaltig; **powerless** machtlos, kraftlos
practice ['præktɪs] Übung, Training; **practise** ['præktɪs] üben, trainieren; ausüben *(Beruf, Religion)*
praise [preɪz] **1.** loben; **2.** Lob
pray [preɪ] beten
precise [prɪ'saɪs] präzise, genau

predict [prɪ'dɪkt] voraussagen, vorhersagen; **prediction** [prɪ'dɪkʃn] Voraussage, Vorhersage
prefer (to) [prɪ'fɜ:] lieber haben (als), *(etwas einer anderen Sache)* vorziehen; **preference (for)** ['prefrəns] Vorliebe (für)
prefix ['pri:fɪks] Vorsilbe, Präfix
prejudice (against) ['predʒʊdɪs] Vorurteil, Voreingenommenheit (gegen, gegenüber); **prejudiced (against)** voreingenommen (gegen)
preparation [ˌprepə'reɪʃn] Vorbereitung; **prepare** [prɪ'peə] vorbereiten, zubereiten; **be prepared (to do sth.)** bereit sein (, etwas zu tun)
pre-question ['pri:ˌkwestʃn] vorgeschaltete, vorangestellte Frage
present **1.** ['preznt] Gegenwart; **2.** ['preznt] aktuell, gegenwärtig; **present-day** [ˌpreznt'deɪ] heutig; **3.** ['preznt] Geschenk; **4. present (to)** [prɪ'zent] darlegen, präsentieren; **presentation** [ˌprezən'teɪʃn] Präsentation, Darbietung
preserve [prɪ'zɜ:v] erhalten, bewahren
president ['prezɪdənt] Präsident/in
pressure ['preʃə] Druck, Zwang
pretend [prɪ'tend] so tun, als ob; vortäuschen
pretty ['prɪtɪ] hübsch
prevent [prɪ'vent] verhindern; **prevent sb. from doing sth.** jn. daran hindern, etwas zu tun; jn. davon abhalten, etwas zu tun
price [praɪs] (Kauf-)Preis
priest [pri:st] Priester/in
primary school ['praɪmərɪ sku:l] Grundschule
prime minister [ˌpraɪm 'mɪnɪstə] Premierminister/in, Ministerpräsident/in
prince [prɪns] Prinz; **princess** [prɪn'ses] Prinzessin
principal ['prɪnsəpl] (AE) Schulleiter/in, Direktor/in
print: bold print [bəʊld 'prɪnt] fette Schrift, Fettdruck; **print media** Printmedien *(= Zeitungen, Zeitschriften, Bücher)*; **printer** Drucker
prison ['prɪzn] Gefängnis
private ['praɪvət] privat; persönlich
privilege ['prɪvəlɪdʒ] Ehre, Privileg
prize [praɪz] (Sieger-)Preis, Gewinn
pro-(British) [prəʊ] pro(britisch)
probable ['prɒbəbl] wahrscheinlich; **probability** [ˌprɒbə'bɪlətɪ] Wahrscheinlichkeit; **probably** ['prɒbəblɪ] wahrscheinlich
problem ['prɒbləm] Problem
proceed [prə'si:d] vorgehen, verfahren; fortfahren
produce **1.** *(sing.)* ['prɒdju:s] *(landwirtschaftliche)* Erzeugnisse; **2.** [prə'dju:s] produzieren, herstellen, erzeugen; **product** ['prɒdʌkt] Produkt, Erzeugnis; **production** [prə'dʌkʃn] Produktion, Herstellung
professional [prə'feʃnəl] **1.** Berufs-, professionell, Fach-; **2.** Berufssportler/in, Profi; **3.** Berufstätige/r *(in akademischen, angesehenen Berufen)*
professor [prə'fesə] Professor/in
profile ['prəʊfaɪl] **1.** Kurzbiographie, Kurzporträt; **2.** Profil
profit ['prɒfɪt] **1.** Gewinn, Profit; **2.** profitieren, Gewinn machen
program ['prəʊgræm] **1.** (Computer-)Programm; **2.** (AE) Programm; (Radio-, Fernseh-)Sendung; **3.** programmieren *(Computer)*; **programmer** Programmierer/in
programme ['prəʊgræm] (BE) **1.** Programm; (Radio-, Fernseh-) Sendung; **2.** programmieren *(Videorecorder u.ä.)*
progress *(sing.)* ['prəʊgres] **1.** Fortschritt(e); **be in progress** im Gange sein; **2. progress** [prəʊ'gres] vorankommen, Fortschritte machen
project ['prɒdʒekt] Projekt; Aufgabe
promise ['prɒmɪs] **1.** versprechen; **2.** Versprechen; **keep a promise** ein Versprechen halten
prompt [prɒmpt] Stichwort, Anregung
pronounce [prə'naʊns] aussprechen; **pronunciation** [prəˌnʌnsɪ'eɪʃn] Aussprache
proof [pru:f] Beweis(e), Nachweis(e)
propaganda [ˌprɒpə'gændə] Propaganda
proper ['prɒpə] richtig, passend, geeignet; **properly** ['prɒpəlɪ] richtig, ordentlich, sachgemäß
proposal [prə'pəʊzl] (Heirats-) Antrag; Vorschlag
protect [prə'tekt] (be)schützen; **protection (against)** [prə'tekʃn] Schutz (vor)
protest **1.** ['prəʊtest] Protest, Widerspruch; **2. protest (against, about)** [prə'test] protestieren (gegen)
Protestant ['prɒtɪstənt] **1.** Protestant/in; **2.** protestantisch, evangelisch
proud (of) [praʊd] stolz (auf)
prove [pru:v] beweisen
provide sth. (for sb) [prə'vaɪd] (jm.) etwas zur Verfügung stellen, (jm.) etwas bereitstellen
province ['prɒvɪns] Provinz
provoke [prə'vəʊk] provozieren
P.S. [ˌpi:‿'es] *(from Latin "post scriptum")* P.S. *(Nachtrag zu einem Brief)*
psychology [saɪ'kɒlədʒɪ] Psychologie
pub [pʌb] (*meist* BE) Kneipe, Lokal
public ['pʌblɪk] **1.** Öffentlichkeit; **2.** öffentlich; **public education** [ˌpʌblɪk‿ˌedjʊ'keɪʃn] staatliches Bildungs-/Schulsystem; staatliche Bildung
publication [ˌpʌblɪ'keɪʃn] Veröffentlichung, Publikation; **publish** ['pʌblɪʃ] veröffentlichen
pudding ['pʊdɪŋ] (BE) Nachtisch, Süßspeise; **for pudding** zum Nachtisch
pull (out) [ˌpʊl‿'aʊt] (heraus)ziehen; **pull down** abreißen, niederreißen
pullover ['pʊləʊvə] Pullover
punctual ['pʌŋktʃʊəl] pünktlich
punctuation [ˌpʌŋktʃʊ'eɪʃn] Zeichensetzung, Interpunktion; **punctuation marks** [ˌpʌŋktʃʊ'eɪʃn mɑ:ks] Satzzeichen
puncture ['pʌŋktʃə] (BE) Reifenpanne
punish ['pʌnɪʃ] (be)strafen; **punishment** ['pʌnɪʃmənt] Strafe, Bestrafung; **physical punishment** *(sing.)* [ˌfɪzɪkl 'pʌnɪʃmənt] Körperstrafe, Prügelstrafe
pupil ['pju:pl] Schüler/in
Puritan ['pjʊərɪtən] **1.** Puritaner/in; **2.** puritanisch
purpose ['pɜ:pəs] Absicht, Zweck
purse [pɜ:s] Geldbörse, Geldbeutel; AE *auch:* Handtasche
push [pʊʃ] schieben, stoßen, drücken
put [pʊt] stellen; legen; **put down** **1.** aufschreiben, eintragen; **2.** hinlegen, abstellen; **put in** einsetzen; **put on** anziehen *(Kleidung)*; **put out** *(Feuer, Licht)* löschen, ausmachen; **put up** aufhängen, anbringen
puzzle out [ˌpʌzl‿'aʊt] ausknobeln, austüfteln; **puzzled** ['pʌzld] verwirrt, verblüfft
pyjamas *(pl.)* [pə'dʒɑ:məz] (BE) Schlafanzug

D

Q

qualification [ˌkwɒlɪfɪ'keɪʃn] Qualifikation; Zeugnis
quality ['kwɒlətɪ] Eigenschaft; Qualität
quantity ['kwɒntətɪ] Menge, Quantität
quarter ['kwɔːtə] **1.** Viertel; **quarter of an hour** eine Viertelstunde; **2.** (AE) 25-Centmünze
queen [kwiːn] Königin
question ['kwestʃn] **1.** Frage; **ask a question** eine Frage stellen; **raise a question** eine Frage aufwerfen, vorbringen; **question mark** ['kwestʃn mɑːk] Fragezeichen; **2.** befragen, vernehmen; **questionnaire** [ˌkwestʃə'neə] Fragebogen
queue [kjuː] (Warte-)Schlange
quiche [kiːʃ] Quiche
quick [kwɪk] schnell; **quickly** schnell
quiet ['kwaɪət] ruhig, leise, still
quit [kwɪt] aufhören (mit); *(eine Arbeitsstelle)* aufgeben
quite [kwaɪt] ziemlich; ganz
quiz [kwɪz] Quiz; **quizmaster** ['kwɪzmɑːstə] Quizmaster
quotation [kwəʊ'teɪʃn] Zitat; **quotation marks** [kwəʊ'teɪʃn mɑːks] Anführungszeichen;
quote [kwəʊt] zitieren

R

rabbit ['ræbɪt] Kaninchen
race [reɪs] **1.** Rennen, Wettlauf; **have a race** ein Rennen veranstalten; **2.** Rasse; **3.** rennen, rasen
racism ['reɪsɪzm] Rassismus; **racist** ['reɪsɪst] **1.** Rassist/in; **2.** rassistisch
radical ['rædɪkl] radikal
radio ['reɪdɪəʊ] **1.** Radio; Rundfunk; **on the radio** im Radio; **2.** Funk(gerät)
rage [reɪdʒ] Wut, Zorn, Rage
raid (on) [reɪd] **1.** Razzia (in); **2.** Überfall (auf)
railroad ['reɪlrəʊd] (AE)/**railway** ['reɪlweɪ] *(meist* BE) Eisenbahn
rain [reɪn] **1.** Regen; **2.** regnen; **rainy** regnerisch
raise [reɪz] erhöhen; (hoch)heben; **raise a question** eine Frage aufwerfen, vorbringen
ranch ['rɑːntʃ] Ranch
rare [reə] selten; **rarely** selten
rate [reɪt] *(Wachstums-, Inflations- usw.)* Rate
raw material [ˌrɔː mə'tɪərɪəl] Rohstoff
razorbill ['reɪzəbɪl] Tordalk *(Seevogel)*
R.E. [ˌɑːr_'iː] (BE) (**Religious Education**) [rɪˌlɪdʒəs_edjʊ'keɪʃn] Religionsunterricht
reach [riːtʃ] erreichen; **reach for** greifen nach
react (to) [rɪ'ækt] reagieren (auf); **reaction (to)** [rɪ'ækʃn] Reaktion (auf)
read [riːd] lesen, vorlesen; **readable** ['riːdəbl] lesbar; **reader** Leser/in
ready ['redɪ] fertig, bereit; **ready-made meal** [ˌredɪmeɪd 'miːl] Fertiggericht
real [rɪəl] **1.** echt, wirklich **2.** (AE, infml.) sehr, äußerst; **realistic** [ˌrɪə'lɪstɪk] realistisch; **reality** [rɪ'ælətɪ] Wirklichkeit, Realität; **really** ['rɪəlɪ] wirklich, eigentlich
realize ['rɪəlaɪz] erkennen, merken
reappear [ˌriːə'pɪə] wieder erscheinen, wieder auftauchen
rearrange [ˌriːə'reɪndʒ] neu ordnen, ändern
reason ['riːzn] Grund, Begründung; **for this reason** aus diesem Grund, deshalb; **reasonable** ['riːznəbl] vernünftig, vertretbar
rebuild [ˌriː'bɪld] wiederaufbauen
recall sth. [rɪ'kɔːl] sich etwas in Erinnerung rufen
recap ['riːkæp] (infml.) zusammenfassen, rekapitulieren
receipt [rɪ'siːt] Beleg; Quittung, Kassenzettel
receive [rɪ'siːv] erhalten, bekommen; empfangen
recent ['riːsnt] jüngste(r, s), neueste(r, s); **recently** ['riːsntlɪ] vor kurzem; neulich
recognize ['rekəgnaɪz] erkennen
reconstruct [ˌriːkən'strʌkt] rekonstruieren
record **1.** ['rekɔːd] Schallplatte; **record-player** Plattenspieler; **2.** [rɪ'kɔːd] aufnehmen, aufzeichnen *(auf Band)*
recover [rɪ'kʌvə] wiederfinden, wiedergewinnen
recreate [ˌriːkrɪ'eɪt] wiederbeleben, neu erschaffen
recycle [ˌriː'saɪkl] wiederverwerten, wiederaufbereiten, recyceln; **recycled** Recycling-
red [red] rot
redo [ˌriː'duː] neu machen
reduce [rɪ'djuːs] verringern, reduzieren; **reduction** [rɪ'dʌkʃn] Verringerung, Reduzierung, Abnahme
reelect [ˌriːɪ'lekt] wiederwählen
refer to [rɪ'fɜː] sich beziehen auf
refill [ˌriː'fɪl] wieder füllen
reflect [rɪ'flekt] (wider)spiegeln; reflektieren
reform [rɪ'fɔːm] **1.** Reform; **2.** reformieren
refuse [rɪ'fjuːz] sich weigern; verweigern, ablehnen
region ['riːdʒən] Gebiet, Region; **regional** ['riːdʒənəl] regional
regret [rɪ'gret] **1.** bedauern, bereuen, **2.** Bedauern
regular ['regjʊlə] regelmäßig; **regularly** ['regjʊləlɪ] regelmäßig
regulate ['regjʊleɪt] regeln, regulieren; **regulation** [ˌregjʊ'leɪʃn] Vorschrift, Regel
related [rɪ'leɪtɪd]**: be related to** **1.** verwandt sein mit; **2.** zu tun haben mit, sich beziehen auf; **relations (with)** *(pl.)* [rɪ'leɪʃnz] Beziehungen (zu); **relationship** [rɪ'leɪʃnʃɪp] Beziehung; **relative** ['relətɪv] Verwandte(r)
relax [rɪ'læks] sich entspannen, sich ausruhen; **relaxed** entspannt, ruhig, locker; **relaxing** entspannend
relevance (to) ['reləvəns] Bedeutung, Relevanz (für)
religion [rɪ'lɪdʒən] Religion; **religious** [rɪ'lɪdʒəs] religiös; **Religious Education** [rɪˌlɪdʒəs_edjʊ'keɪʃn] (**R.E.**) Religionsunterricht
remain [rɪ'meɪn] bleiben; übrigbleiben; **remains** *(pl.)* [rɪ'meɪnz] Reste, Relikte
remember [rɪ'membə] sich erinnern an; daran denken *(, etwas zu tun)*
remind (of) [rɪ'maɪnd] erinnern (an)
rename [ˌriː'neɪm] umbenennen, neu benennen
renew [rɪ'njuː] erneuern; fortsetzen *(Angriff, Bemühungen)*; **renewable** [rɪ'njuːəbl] erneuerbar, regenerationsfähig
rent [rent] **1.** Miete, Pacht; **2.** mieten, leihen
reopen [riː'əʊpən] wieder (er)öffnen
reorganize [riː'ɔːgənaɪz] neu organisieren, umorganisieren
repair [rɪ'peə] **1.** Reparatur; **2.** reparieren
repay [rɪ'peɪ] zurückzahlen

D

repeat [rɪ'pi:t] wiederholen; **repetition** [ˌrepə'tɪʃn] Wiederholung
reply (to) [rɪ'plaɪ] **1.** Antwort, Erwiderung (auf); **2.** antworten (auf), erwidern
report [rɪ'pɔ:t] **1.** Bericht; BE *auch*: Schulzeugnis; **2.** berichten; **be reported to be** (angeblich sein) sollen; **reporter** Reporter/in
represent [ˌreprɪ'zent] vertreten, repräsentieren; darstellen
reproduction [ˌri:prə'dʌkʃn] Reproduktion, Nachbildung
Republican [rɪ'pʌblɪkn] **1.** Republikaner/in *(Mitglied der republikanischen Partei, einer der beiden großen politischen Parteien in den USA)*; **2.** republikanisch
request [rɪ'kwest] Bitte; Wunsch
reread [ˌri:'ri:d] erneut (durch)lesen
research **1.** [rɪ'sɜ:tʃ] (er)forschen, untersuchen; **2. research (into)** [rɪ'sɜ:tʃ, 'ri:sɜ:tʃ] Forschung (über)
reservation [ˌrezə'veɪʃn] (Indianer-) Reservation, Reservat
reserve [rɪ'zɜ:v] reservieren (lassen), buchen
resort: seaside resort ['si:saɪd rɪˌzɔ:t] (beliebter) Urlaubsort am Meer, Seebad
respect [rɪ'spekt] **1.** Respekt, Achtung; **2.** respektieren, achten
responsible (for) [rɪ'spɒnsəbl] verantwortlich (für); **responsibility (for)** [rɪˌspɒnsə'bɪlətɪ] Verantwortung, Verantwortlichkeit (für)
rest [rest] **1.** Rest; **2.** Ruhepause; **3.** ruhen; **rest (from)** sich ausruhen (von)
restaurant ['restərɒnt] Restaurant
restructure [ˌri:'strʌktʃə] umstrukturieren
result [rɪ'zʌlt] Ergebnis; **as a result** folglich; die Folge war, daß
retell [ˌri:'tel] nacherzählen
retrain [ˌri:'treɪn] umschulen
return [rɪ'tɜ:n] zurückkehren; **return journey** Rückfahrt, Rückreise; **returnable bottle** Mehrwegflasche, Pfandflasche
reuse [ˌri:'ju:z] wiederverwenden; **reusable** [ri:'ju:zəbl] wiederverwendbar
revise [rɪ'vaɪz] (BE) *(Lernstoff)* wiederholen; **revision** [rɪ'vɪʒn] (BE) Wiederholung *(des Lernstoffs)*
revolution [ˌrevə'lu:ʃn] Revolution
reward [rɪ'wɔ:d] **1.** Belohnung, Finderlohn; **2.** belohnen
rewrite [ˌri:'raɪt] neu schreiben, noch einmal schreiben

rhyme [raɪm] Reim
rice [raɪs] Reis
rich (in) [rɪtʃ] reich (an)
rid [rɪd]: **get rid of** loswerden
ride [raɪd] **1.** Fahrt; Ritt; **2.** reiten; **ride a bike** radfahren; **rider** Reiter/in; Radfahrer/in
right [raɪt] **1.** richtig; **be right** recht haben; **Are you all right?** Geht es dir (noch) gut? **2.** rechte(r, s), nach rechts; **on the right** rechts, auf der rechten Seite; **3.** *(adv.)* (infml.) direkt, genau; **4. rights** Rechte; **civil rights** [ˌsɪvl 'raɪts] Bürgerrechte
ring [rɪŋ] **1.** Ring; **2.** klingeln, läuten
riot ['raɪət] Aufruhr, Aufstand
ripe [raɪp] reif; **ripen** reifen
rise [raɪz] (an-, auf)steigen
risk [rɪsk] **1.** riskieren, wagen; **2.** Risiko; **take a risk** ein Risiko eingehen
rival ['raɪvl] Konkurrent/in, Rivale/ Rivalin
river ['rɪvə] Fluß
road [rəʊd] Straße, Landstraße
roast [rəʊst] geröstet, gebraten *(im Backofen)*; **roast beef** [ˌrəʊst 'bi:f] Rinderbraten, Roastbeef
rob [rɒb] berauben, ausrauben; **robbery** ['rɒbərɪ] Raub(überfall)
rock [rɒk] **1.** Fels(en); **2.** (AE) Stein; **rock (music)** Rock(musik); **rocky** felsig, steinig
role-play ['rəʊlpleɪ] Rollenspiel
roll [rəʊl]: **(bread) roll** Brötchen
Roman ['rəʊmən] **1.** römisch; **2.** Römer/in
romantic [rəʊ'mæntɪk] romantisch
roof [ru:f] Dach
room [ru:m] Zimmer, Raum; Platz
root [ru:t] Wurzel
rose [rəʊz] Rose
round [raʊnd] **1.** rund; **2.** (BE) um … (herum); in … umher, durch; **just round the corner** gleich um die Ecke; **turn round** sich umdrehen
route [ru:t] Route, Strecke
routine [ˌru:'ti:n] Routine
royal ['rɔɪəl] königlich
rubber ['rʌbə] (BE) Radiergummi
rubbish ['rʌbɪʃ] (BE) Abfall, Unrat
rucksack ['rʌksæk] Rucksack
ruin ['ru:ɪn] **1.** ruinieren, zerstören; **2.** Ruine
rule [ru:l] **1.** Regel, Vorschrift; **2.** regieren, herrschen über; **ruler** ['ru:lə] **1.** Herrscher/in; **2.** Lineal
run [rʌn] **1.** Lauf; **2.** laufen, rennen; **run after sb.** hinter jm. herrennen; **run out** knapp werden, ausgehen *(Vorräte)*; **We've run out of coffee.** Uns ist der Kaffee ausge-gangen. Wir haben keinen Kaffee mehr. **run sth.** etwas leiten, führen, verwalten; **runner** Läufer/in

S

sad [sæd] traurig; **sadness** Traurigkeit
safe [seɪf] sicher, gefahrlos
sail [seɪl] **1.** Segel; **2.** segeln; **sailing** ['seɪlɪŋ] Segeln; **sailor** Matrose, Seemann
salad ['sæləd] Salat *(als Gericht bzw. Beilage)*
salami [sə'lɑ:mɪ] Salami
salary ['sælərɪ] Gehalt
salt [sɒlt, sɔ:lt] Salz; **salty** salzig
same [seɪm]: **the same** der-/die-/dasselbe, dieselben; der/die/das gleiche, die gleichen
sand [sænd] Sand; **sandy** sandig
sandwich ['sænwɪtʃ] *(zusammengeklapptes)* belegtes Brot
Santa Claus ['sæntə klɔ:z] der Weihnachtsmann
satellite ['sætəlaɪt] Satellit
satisfaction [ˌsætɪs'fækʃn] Befriedigung; Zufriedenheit
Saturday ['sætədɪ, 'sætədeɪ] Samstag/Sonnabend; **on Saturday** am Samstag; **on Saturdays** samstags
saucer ['sɔ:sə] Untertasse
sausage ['sɒsɪdʒ] (Brat-, Bock-) Würstchen, Wurst
save [seɪv] sparen; retten
saw [sɔ:] Säge
say [seɪ] sagen; **Say hallo to …** Grüß(t) … (von mir); **the text says …** im Text steht …; **You can say that again.** (infml.) Das kann man wohl sagen! Das kannst du laut sagen! **be said to be** (angeblich sein) sollen; **saying** ['seɪɪŋ] Sprichwort, Redensart
scale [skeɪl] Skala
scared [skeəd]: **be scared (of)** Angst haben (vor)
scarf [skɑ:f], *pl.* **scarves** [skɑ:vz] Schal
scattered ['skætəd] verstreut; vereinzelt *(Regenschauer usw.)*
scene [si:n] Szene; **scenery** *(sing.)* ['si:nərɪ] (malerische) Landschaft(en)
schedule ['ʃedju:l] **1.** Zeitplan; AE *auch:* Stundenplan; **2.** anberaumen *(Sitzung)*, planen

D

school [sku:l] Schule; **at school** in der Schule; **schoolyard** ['sku:ljɑ:d] Schulhof
science ['saɪəns] (Natur-)Wissenschaft; **scientist** ['saɪəntɪst] (Natur-)Wissenschaftler/in
score [skɔ:] **1.** Spielstand, (Spiel-) Ergebnis; **2.** *(einen Punkt/Treffer)* erzielen, *(ein Tor)* schießen
Scot [skɒt] Schotte/Schottin; **the Scots** die Schotten; **Scottish** ['skɒtɪʃ] schottisch, Schottisch
scream [skri:m] **1.** Schrei, Aufschrei; **2.** schreien, kreischen
screw [skru:] Schraube; **screwdriver** ['skru:draɪvə] Schraubenzieher, Schraubendreher
sea [si:] Meer, *(die)* See; **seaside resort** ['si:saɪd rɪˌzɔ:t] (beliebter) Urlaubsort am Meer, Seebad
search (for) [sɜ:tʃ] **1.** Suche (nach), Durchsuchung; **in search of** auf der Suche nach; **2.** suchen (nach), durchsuchen (nach)
season ['si:zn] Jahreszeit; Saison
seat [si:t] Sitz, Sitzplatz; **Take a seat.** Nimm Platz./Nehmen Sie Platz.
second ['sekənd] Sekunde
second: second-hand [ˌsekənd 'hænd] aus zweiter Hand
secondary school ['sekəndrɪ sku:l] Oberschule
secondly zweitens
secretary [BE: 'sekrətrɪ, AE: 'sekrəterɪ:] Sekretär/in; 2. (US) Minister/in
section ['sekʃn] Teil, Ausschnitt
sector ['sektə] Sektor, Bereich
see [si:] sehen; besuchen, treffen; **See you later.** Bis dann. Bis später. **you see** weißt du, nämlich
seem [si:m] *(zu sein/tun)* scheinen
segregate ['segrɪgeɪt] *(nach Rasse, Sprache usw.)* trennen; **segregation** [ˌsegrɪ'geɪʃn] Rassentrennung
self-conscious [ˌself'kɒnʃəs] unsicher, gehemmt
self-government [ˌself'gʌvnmənt] Selbstverwaltung
selfish ['selfɪʃ] egoistisch, selbstsüchtig
sell [sel] verkaufen
semi-colon [ˌsemɪ'kəʊlən] Semikolon
semi-detached house ['semɪdɪˌtætʃt 'haʊs] (BE) Doppelhaushälfte
seminar (on) ['semɪnɑ:] Seminar (über)
send [send] senden, schicken; **send for** kommen lassen, holen
senior high school [ˌsi:niə 'haɪ sku:l] (US) *meistens die letzten drei Jahre der High School*
sensational [sen'seɪʃnəl] sensationell, Sensations-
sense [sens]**: a sense of humour** [ˌsens_əv 'hju:mə] (Sinn für) Humor; **make sense** (einen) Sinn ergeben, Sinn machen; **senseless** sinnlos
sensible ['sensəbl] vernünftig
sensitive ['sensətɪv] sensibel
sentence ['sentəns] Satz; (Gerichts-) Urteil
separate **1.** ['sepəreɪt] trennen; **2.** ['seprət] getrennt; einzeln
September [sep'tembə] September
serial ['sɪərɪəl] (Fernseh-, Hörspiel-)Serie; **series** (*sing.* and *pl.*) ['sɪəri:z] (Fernseh-)Serie; Reihe
serious ['sɪərɪəs] ernst, ernsthaft; **take sb./sth. seriously** jn./etwas ernst nehmen
serve [sɜ:v] (be)dienen, servieren; **service** ['sɜ:vɪs] Dienst(leistung); *(Bus-, Zug-, Flug-)*Verbindung(en)
set [set] (BE) Kursgruppe, Leistungsgruppe; **TV set** Fernsehgerät
setting [setɪŋ] Schauplatz
settle ['setl] sich niederlassen; *(Land)* besiedeln; **settlement** ['setlmənt] Siedlung; Besiedlung; **settler** ['setlə] Siedler/in
several ['sevrəl] einige, mehrere
sewing machine ['səʊɪŋ məʃi:n] Nähmaschine
sex [seks] **1.** Geschlecht; **2.** Sex
shabby ['ʃæbɪ] schäbig
shake [ʃeɪk] zittern; schütteln; **shake hands with sb.** jm. die Hand geben
shall [ʃæl, ʃəl]**: Shall I ...?** Soll ich ...? **I shall ...** Ich werde ..
shampoo [ʃæm'pu:] Haarwaschmittel, Shampoo
shape [ʃeɪp] *(äußere)* Form
share (with) [ʃeə] teilen (mit); sich *(etwas)* teilen (mit)
she [ʃi:] sie *(Singular)*
shed [ʃed] Schuppen
sheep, *pl.* **sheep** [ʃi:p] Schaf
shelf [ʃelf], *pl.* **shelves** [ʃelvz] Regal(brett), Bord
shine (on) [ʃaɪn] scheinen, leuchten (auf)
ship [ʃɪp] Schiff
shirt [ʃɜ:t] (Ober-)Hemd
shock [ʃɒk] Schock; **shocked** schockiert
shoe [ʃu:] Schuh
shoot [ʃu:t] schießen; (er)schießen; werfen *(Ball)*
shop [ʃɒp] Laden, Geschäft; **shopkeeper** Ladenbesitzer/in;
shoplifter ['ʃɒplɪftə] Ladendieb/in; **shopper** Käufer/in; **shopping** Einkaufen; Einkäufe; **do the shopping** einkaufen; **go shopping/go to the shops** einkaufen gehen; **window-shopping** ['wɪndəʊˌʃɒpɪŋ] Schaufensterbummeln
short [ʃɔ:t] kurz; klein *(von Gestalt)*; **shorten** kürzen, verkürzen; **short wave** Kurzwelle*(nsender)*; **shorts** *(pl.)* Shorts, kurze Hose
should [ʃʊd, ʃəd] sollte(n), müßte(n)
shoulder ['ʃəʊldə] Schulter
shout [ʃaʊt] **1.** Schrei, Ruf; **2. shout (at)** (an)schreien, laut rufen
show [ʃəʊ] **1.** Schau, Show; **2.** zeigen; sich zeigen, deutlich werden
showdown ['ʃəʊdaʊn] Showdown, Entscheidungskampf *(im Western)*
shower ['ʃaʊə] Dusche; **take a shower** duschen
shut [ʃʌt] schließen; **shut down** zumachen, schließen *(Fabrik usw.)*
shy [ʃaɪ] schüchtern, zurückhaltend, scheu
sick [sɪk] krank; **be sick** sich übergeben (müssen); **I feel sick.** Mir ist schlecht/übel. **sickness** ['sɪknəs] Krankheit
side [saɪd] Seite; **take sides with** Partei ergreifen für; **sidewalk** ['saɪdwɔ:k] (AE) Gehweg
sigh (with) [saɪ] seufzen (vor)
sights [saɪts] Sehenswürdigkeiten; **sightseeing** *(sing.)* ['saɪtˌsi:ɪŋ] (Stadt- usw.)Besichtigung(en), Sightseeing
sign [saɪn] **1.** Schild, Zeichen; **2.** unterschreiben
silence ['saɪləns] Stille, Ruhe; Schweigen; **silent** still; schweigsam
silliness ['sɪlɪnəs] Albernheit; **silly** ['sɪlɪ] albern, dumm
similar ['sɪmɪlə] ähnlich; **similarity** [ˌsɪmə'lærətɪ] Ähnlichkeit
simple ['sɪmpl] einfach; **simply** einfach, bloß, lediglich
since [sɪns] **1.** *(prep.; conj.)* seit; **2.** da, weil
sincerely [sɪn'sɪəlɪ]**: Yours sincerely, ...** (*meist* BE) Mit herzlichen/freundlichen Grüßen ...
sing [sɪŋ] singen; **singer** Sänger/in
single ['sɪŋgl] Einzel-; einzeln
sink [sɪŋk] **1.** sinken, untergehen; **2.** versenken
Sir, sir [sɜ:] mein Herr *(höfliche Anrede)*
siren ['saɪrən] Sirene
sister ['sɪstə] Schwester
sit [sɪt] sitzen; **sit (down)** sich setzen
site ['saɪt] Stätte; Stelle, Platz

situation [ˌsɪtʃʊ'eɪʃn] Situation
size [saɪz] Größe; **What size do you take?** Welche Größe haben Sie?
ski [ski:] Ski laufen, Ski fahren
skill [skɪl] Fähigkeit, Fertigkeit; Geschick(lichkeit); **skilled (in, at)** ausgebildet, erfahren, Fach-; geschickt (in); **skilled worker** Facharbeiter/in
skirt [skɜ:t] Rock
sky [skaɪ] Himmel; **in the sky** am Himmel; **skyscraper** ['skaɪskreɪpə] Wolkenkratzer
slave [sleɪv] Sklave/Sklavin; **slavery** ['sleɪvərɪ] Sklaverei
sleep [sli:p] **1.** Schlaf; **2.** schlafen; **sleeping-bag** ['sli:pɪŋ bæg] Schlafsack; **sleepless** schlaflos
slim [slɪm] schlank, dünn
slogan ['sləʊgən] Slogan, Wahlspruch
slow [sləʊ] langsam; **slowly** langsam
small [smɔ:l] klein
smell [smel] riechen; *(an etwas)* riechen
smile [smaɪl] **1.** Lächeln; **2. smile (at)** (an)lächeln; **smiling** lächelnd
smoke [sməʊk] **1.** Rauch; **2.** rauchen
snack [snæk] Imbiß; **snack bar** ['snæk bɑ:] Imbißstube
snake [sneɪk] Schlange
snob [snɒb] Snob, eingebildeter Mensch
snooker ['snu:kə] Snooker *(billardähnliches Spiel)*
snore [snɔ:] schnarchen
snow [snəʊ] Schnee; **snowy** verschneit
so [səʊ] **1.** so; **I hope so.** Ich hoffe es./Hoffentlich. **so (that)** damit, so daß; **so far** bis jetzt, bisher; **so-called** sogenannt; **2.** also; deshalb, daher
soap [səʊp] Seife; **soap (opera)** ['səʊp_ˌɒprə] „Seifenoper" *(sentimentale Hörspiel- oder Fernsehserie)*
soccer ['sɒkə] Fußball
social ['səʊʃl] sozial, gesellschaftlich; Sozial-
socialist ['səʊʃəlɪst] **1.** Sozialist/in; **2.** sozialistisch
society [sə'saɪətɪ] Gesellschaft
sock [sɒk] Socke, Strumpf
soft [sɒft] weich; **soften** weich machen; weich werden
sofa ['səʊfə] Sofa
software ['sɒftweə] (Computer-)Software
soil [sɔɪl] (Mutter-)Boden, Erde
solar ['səʊlə] Sonnen-, Solar-
soldier ['səʊldʒə] Soldat/in
solution (to) [sə'lu:ʃn] Lösung (für)
solve [sɒlv] *(Aufgabe, Problem)* lösen
some [sʌm, səm] **1.** einige, ein paar; **2.** etwas
somebody/someone ['sʌmbədɪ/'sʌmwʌn] jemand
somehow ['sʌmhaʊ] irgendwie
someone ['sʌmwʌn] jemand
someplace ['sʌmpleɪs] (AE, infml.) irgendwo(hin)
something ['sʌmθɪŋ] etwas
sometimes ['sʌmtaɪmz] manchmal
somewhere ['sʌmweə] irgendwo; irgendwohin
son [sʌn] Sohn
song [sɒŋ] Lied
soon [su:n] bald; **sooner or later** früher oder später
sore [sɔ:] wund, rauh, entzündet; **a sore throat** [ˌsɔ: 'θrəʊt] Halsschmerzen
Sorry. ['sɒrɪ] **(= I'm sorry.)** Tut mir leid. **I'm sorry about ...** Ich bedauere ..., Ich bin traurig über ...; **feel sorry for (sb./sth.)** (jn./etwas) bedauern; (etwas) bereuen
sort [sɔ:t] sortieren, ordnen
soul [səʊl] Seele
sound [saʊnd] **1.** Geräusch, Ton, Laut; Klang; **2.** klingen, sich *(gut usw.)* anhören
soup [su:p] Suppe
sour ['saʊə] sauer
source [sɔ:s] Quelle; Ursprung
south [saʊθ] **1.** Süden; **2.** nach Süden; **3. south (of)** südlich (von); **southern** ['sʌðən] Süd-, südlich
souvenir [ˌsu:və'nɪə] Souvenir, Andenken
space [speɪs] Weltraum; Raum, Platz; **spaceship** ['speɪsʃɪp] Raumschiff
span of time [spæn] Zeitspanne
Spanish ['spænɪʃ] Spanisch; spanisch
spanner ['spænə] (BE) Schraubenschlüssel
speak [spi:k] sprechen, reden; **speak out (against)** offen seine Meinung sagen (gegen); **speaker** Redner/in, Sprecher/in
special ['speʃl] besondere(r, s), Sonder-; **special offer** Sonderangebot; **specialist** ['speʃlɪst] Spezialist/in
species, *pl.* **species** ['spi:ʃi:z] *(Pflanzen-, Tier-)*Art
spectacular [spek'tækjʊlə] spektakulär, sensationell
speculate ['spekjʊleɪt] spekulieren; **speculation** [ˌspekjʊ'leɪʃŋ] Mutmaßung, Vermutung, Spekulation
speech (on, about) [spi:tʃ] Vortrag, Rede (über); **give/make a speech** eine Rede halten
speed [spi:d] Geschwindigkeit; **speed limit** ['spi:d ˌlɪmɪt] Geschwindigkeitsbeschränkung
spell [spel] buchstabieren, schreiben; **spelling** ['spelɪŋ] Schreibweise
spend (on) [spend] **1.** *(Geld)* ausgeben (für); **2.** *(Zeit)* verbringen (mit)
spirit ['spɪrɪt] Geist; **spiritual** ['spɪrɪtʃʊəl] Spiritual *(geistliches Lied der Schwarzen in Nordamerika)*
spite: in spite of [ɪn 'spaɪt_əv] trotz; **in spite of this/that** trotzdem
spoil [spɔɪl] *(Kinder)* verziehen; *(Personen)* verwöhnen; *(Landschaft, Stimmung usw.)* ruinieren, ver-derben; **spoiled** verwöhnt, verzogen
sponge [spʌndʒ] Schwamm
sponsor ['spɒnsə] **1.** Sponsor/in, Spender/in; **2.** durch Geldspenden unterstützen
spoon [spu:n] Löffel
sport [spɔ:t] Sport
spring [sprɪŋ] Frühling, Frühjahr
spy [spaɪ] Spion/in
square (sq.) [skweə] **1.** Quadrat; Quadrat-; **2. square** quadratisch, rechteckig
squash [skwɒʃ] Squash
stability [stə'bɪlətɪ] Stabilität
stadium ['steɪdɪəm] Stadion
stagecoach ['steɪdʒkəʊtʃ] Postkutsche
stairs *(pl.)* [steəz] Treppe(nstufen)
stamp [stæmp] Briefmarke
stand [stænd] stehen; **I can't stand ... .** Ich kann ... nicht ausstehen.
standard ['stændəd] Standard-, Norm-
stanza ['stænzə] Strophe *(eines Gedichtes)*
star [stɑ:] **1.** Stern; **2.** (Film-, Pop- usw.)Star; **the Stars and Stripes** [ˌstɑ:z_n 'straɪps] *US-Flagge („Sterne und Streifen")*
start [stɑ:t] **1.** Anfang, Start; **2.** anfangen, beginnen (mit); **start school** eingeschult werden
state [steɪt] **1.** Staat, (Bundes-)Land; **2.** Zustand; **state of mind** [ˌsteɪt_əv 'maɪnd] (geistige) Verfassung, (Gemüts-)Zustand
statement ['steɪtmənt] Aussage, Feststellung
station ['steɪʃn] **1.** Bahnhof; **2.** (Rundfunk-/Fernseh-)Sender
statistics *(pl.)* [stə'tɪstɪks] Statistik(en)
status ['steɪtəs] (gesellschaftliche) Stellung, Rang, Status

D

stay [steɪ] **1.** Aufenthalt; **2.** bleiben; übernachten
steak [steɪk] Steak
steal [sti:l] stehlen
steam [sti:m] (Wasser-)Dampf
steel [sti:l] Stahl
steep [sti:p] steil
stem [stem] (Wort-)Stamm
step [step] Stufe; Schritt
stereo ['sterɪəʊ] **1.** Stereo, Stereo-; **2. stereo (system)** ['sterɪəʊ ˌsɪstəm] Stereoanlage; **personal stereo** „Walkman"
stereotype ['sterɪətaɪp] Stereotyp, Klischee
stick [stɪk] Stock
still [stɪl] **1.** (immer) noch; **2.** trotzdem, dennoch
stink [stɪŋk] stinken
stomach ['stʌmək] Bauch, Magen; **stomach ache** ['stʌmək_eɪk] Bauchschmerzen, Magenschmerzen
stone [stəʊn] Stein
stop [stɒp] **1.** aufhören; stoppen, anhalten; **stop doing sth.** aufhören, etwas zu tun; **2. bus stop** Bushaltestelle
store [stɔ:] großes Geschäft, Kaufhaus; **department store** [dɪ'pɑ:tmənt stɔ:] Kaufhaus; **grocery store** ['grəʊsərɪ stɔ:] Lebensmittelladen
storey ['stɔ:rɪ] (BE) Stock(werk)
storm [stɔ:m] **1.** Sturm; Gewitter; **2. storm (into)** (hinein-)stürmen; **stormy** stürmisch
story ['stɔ:rɪ] **1.** Geschichte, Erzählung; **short story** Kurzgeschichte, Erzählung; **storyline** ['stɔ:rɪlaɪn] Handlung *(einer Erzählung)*; **storyteller** ['stɔ:rɪtelə] Erzähler/in; **2.** (AE) Stockwerk
straight *(adv.; adj.)* [streɪt] direkt, geradewegs; gerade
strange [streɪndʒ] **1.** seltsam, sonderbar; **2.** fremd; **stranger** Unbekannte(r), Fremde(r)
street [stri:t] Straße *(meist in einer Stadt)*
stress [stres] **1.** Betonung; **2.** betonen
stretch [stretʃ] sich erstrecken
strict [strɪkt] streng
strong [strɒŋ] stark
structure ['strʌktʃə] Struktur, Konstruktion
struggle (with, for) ['strʌgl] kämpfen (mit, um)
student ['stju:dənt] Student/in; Schüler/in
studio ['stju:dɪəʊ] Studio
study ['stʌdɪ] studieren; lernen
stupid ['stju:pɪd] dämlich, dumm, blöd
style [staɪl] Stil
subject ['sʌbdʒekt] (Unterrichts-)Fach
suburb ['sʌbɜ:b] Vorort, Vorstadt, Randbezirk
substitute ['sʌbstɪtju:t] (Stell-)Vertreter/in, Ersatz
subway ['sʌbweɪ] (AE) U-Bahn
succeed [sək'si:d] Erfolg haben; gelingen; **success** [sək'ses] Erfolg; **successful** [sək'sesfəl] erfolgreich
such (a) [sʌtʃ] solch, so (ein/e); solche; **such as** (wie) zum Beispiel
suddenly ['sʌdnlɪ] plötzlich
suffer (from) ['sʌfə] leiden (an, unter)
suffix ['sʌfɪks] Nachsilbe, Suffix
sugar ['ʃʊgə] Zucker
suggest [sə'dʒest] **1.** vorschlagen, anregen; **2.** nahelegen, andeuten; **suggestion** [sə'dʒestʃn] Vorschlag, Anregung
suit sb. [su:t] jm. stehen; **suitable** ['su:təbl] passend, geeignet
suitcase ['su:tkeɪs] Koffer
sum [sʌm] Summe, Betrag; **sum up** [ˌsʌm_'ʌp] zusammenfassen
summary ['sʌmərɪ] Zusammenfassung
summer ['sʌmə] Sommer
sun [sʌn] Sonne; **sunbathe** ['sʌnbeɪð] sonnenbaden; **sunny** sonnig; **sunshine** ['sʌnʃaɪn] Sonnenschein
Sunday ['sʌndɪ, 'sʌndeɪ] Sonntag
super ['su:pə] super, toll
supermarket ['su:pəmɑ:kɪt] Supermarkt
supply [sə'plaɪ] (be)liefern; versorgen; **supply ship** [sə'plaɪ ʃɪp] Versorgungsschiff
support [sə'pɔ:t] **1.** Unterstützung, Beistand; **2.** unterstützen; **supporter** [sə'pɔ:tə] Unterstützer/in, Befürworter/in
suppose [sə'pəʊz] vermuten, annehmen, glauben; **be supposed to** [sə'pəʊst] *(tun)* sollen; *(angeblich sein)* sollen
sure [ʃɔ:, ʃʊə] sicher; **make sure** sicherstellen, sichergehen; dafür sorgen *(, daß)*
surgery ['sɜ:dʒərɪ] (BE) (Arzt-)Praxis
surprise [sə'praɪz] **1.** Überraschung; **2.** überraschen; **surprised (at)** überrascht (über); **surprising** überraschend, erstaunlich; **surprisingly** überraschenderweise
survey (of) ['sɜ:veɪ] Umfrage, Untersuchung (über)
survive [sə'vaɪv] überleben
sweat [swet] **1.** schwitzen; **2.** Schweiß; **sweatshirt** ['swetʃɜ:t] Sweatshirt
sweet [swi:t] süß; **sweets** *(pl.)* [swi:ts] Süßigkeiten
swim [swɪm] schwimmen; **swimmer** Schwimmer/in; **swimming costume** ['swɪmɪŋ ˌkɒstju:m] (BE) Badebekleidung, Badeanzug; **swimming-pool** ['swɪmɪŋ pu:l] Schwimmbad
switch on/off [swɪtʃ] ein-/ausschalten
sword [sɔ:d] Schwert
syllable ['sɪləbl] Silbe
symbol ['sɪmbl] Symbol; **symbolize** ['sɪmbəlaɪz] symbolisieren
system ['sɪstəm] System

T

table ['teɪbl] **1.** Tisch; **2.** Tabelle; **table-tennis** ['teɪbltenɪs] Tischtennis
tablet ['tæblət] Tablette
tailor ['teɪlə] Schneider/in
take [teɪk] **1.** nehmen; mitnehmen, (hin)bringen; **take action** etwas unternehmen; **Take my advice.** Hör(t) auf meinen Rat. **take a chance/a risk** ein Risiko eingehen; es darauf ankommen lassen; **take sb. to court** jn. vor Gericht bringen, verklagen; **take a decision** eine Entscheidung treffen, fällen; **take an exam** eine Prüfung machen; **take part (in)** teilnehmen (an), mitmachen (bei); **take photos** Fotos machen, knipsen; **take place** stattfinden; **take sth. for granted** ['grɑ:ntɪd] etwas als selbstverständlich betrachten; **take sth. into consideration** etwas in Erwägung ziehen, etwas bedenken; **take sb./sth. seriously** jn./etwas ernst nehmen; **take a shower** duschen; **take sides with** Partei ergreifen für; **take sth. off** etwas ausziehen; **2. it takes** es dauert
talented ['tæləntɪd] talentiert, begabt
talk (to) [tɔ:k] **1.** reden, sprechen, sich unterhalten (mit); **2. talk (about, on)** Vortrag, Rede (über); **talks** *(pl.)* Gespräche; **give a talk** eine Rede halten

D

tall [tɔ:l] groß (gewachsen); hoch *(Bäume, Türme usw.)*
tape [teɪp] (Ton-)Band
task [tɑ:sk] Aufgabe
taste [teɪst] **1.** schmecken; probieren, kosten; **2.** Geschmack
tax [tæks] **1.** Steuer; **2.** besteuern
taxi ['tæksɪ] Taxi
tea [ti:] **1.** Tee; **2.** (BE) Abendbrot, Abendessen; **have tea** Abendbrot essen; **for tea** zum Abendbrot
teach [ti:tʃ] lehren, unterrichten; **teacher** ['ti:tʃə] Lehrer/in
team [ti:m] Mannschaft, Team, Gruppe
tear [tɪə] Träne
technology [tek'nɒlədʒɪ] Technologie, Technik; **technological** [ˌteknə'lɒdʒɪkl] technologisch; technisch
teenage ['ti:neɪdʒ] Jugend-, Teenager-; **teenager** Teenager, Jugendliche(r)
telephone ['teləfəʊn] Telefon; **on the telephone** am Telefon; **telephone box** (BE)**/telephone booth** [bu:θ] (AE) Telefonzelle
television ['telɪvɪʒn] **(TV)** Fernsehen
tell [tel] erzählen, berichten; sagen; **Can you tell me the way to ...?** Können Sie mir sagen, wie ich zu/nach ... komme? **tell sb. (not) to do sth.** jm. sagen, daß er/sie etwas (nicht) tun soll
temperature ['temprətʃə] **1.** Temperatur; **2.** Fieber; **I've got a temperature.** Ich habe Fieber. **take one's temperature** Fieber messen
tempting ['temptɪŋ] verlockend, verführerisch
tennis ['tenɪs] Tennis
tension ['tenʃn] Spannung(en)
tent [tent] Zelt
term [tɜ:m] **1.** (Fach-)Begriff, Ausdruck; **2.** Trimester, Semester
terraced house ['terəst] (BE) Reihenhaus
terrible ['terəbl] schrecklich, furchtbar
terrified ['terɪfaɪd]**: be terrified (of)** schreckliche Angst haben (vor)
terror ['terə] Terror; **terrorist** ['terərɪst] Terrorist/in; **terrorize** ['terəraɪz] terrorisieren
test [test] **1.** Test, (Klassen-)Arbeit; **2. test (on)** prüfen, testen (an *Tieren*)
text [tekst] Text
than [ðæn, ðən] als *(nach Komparativ)*
thank [θæŋk] danken; **Thank you.** Danke (schön). Vielen Dank. **Thanks.** (infml.) Danke. **thankful** ['θæŋkfəl] dankbar
that [ðæt, ðət] **1.** der, die, das (da), jene(r, s) (dort); **that is (i.e.)** das heißt (d.h.); **that's why** deshalb, darum; **You can say that again.** (infml.) Das kann man wohl sagen! Das kannst du laut sagen! **2.** der, die, das; die *(Relativpronomen)*; **3.** daß; **4. (not) that bad** [nɒt 'ðæt ˌbæd] (nicht) so schlecht/schlimm
the [ðə, ðɪ] der, die, das; die
theme [θi:m] Thema, Leitgedanke
theatre ['θɪətə] Theater
their [ðeə] *(poss. adj.)* ihr(e); **theirs** [ðeəz] *(poss. pron.)* ihre(r, s)
them [ðem, ðəm] sie, ihnen; **themselves** [ðəm'selvz] sich (selbst)
then [ðen] dann; damals, zu jener Zeit; **from then on** von da an
there [ðeə] da, dort; dahin, dorthin; **up there** dort oben; **there is** da ist, es gibt, es ist (vorhanden)
thermometer [θə'mɒmɪtə] Thermometer
these [ði:z] diese, die (hier); **these days** heutzutage
they [ðeɪ] sie *(Plural)*
thick [θɪk] dick; dicht
thief [θi:f], *pl.* **thieves** [θi:vz] Dieb/in
thin [θɪn] dünn
thing [θɪŋ] Ding, Sache
think [θɪŋk] denken; meinen; glauben; **think of 1.** denken an; **2.** halten von; **3.** sich ausdenken
third [θɜ:d] Drittel
thirst [θɜ:st] Durst; **thirsty** durstig
this [ðɪs] dies; der/die/das (hier), diese(r, s); **this morning/afternoon/evening** heute morgen/nachmittag/abend
those [ðəʊz] die (da), diese (da), jene (dort); **in those years/days** damals; in jenen Jahren/Tagen
though [ðəʊ] **1.** *(conj.)* obwohl; **2.** *(adv.)* jedoch; **even though** selbst wenn; obwohl
thought [θɔ:t] Gedanke, Einfall; **thoughtful** ['θɔ:tfəl] rücksichtsvoll, aufmerksam; nachdenklich
threat [θret] Drohung, Bedrohung; **threaten** ['θretn] (be)drohen
thrilled [θrɪld] begeistert
throat [θrəʊt] Hals, Kehle; **a sore throat** [ˌsɔ: 'θrəʊt] Halsschmerzen
through [θru:] durch, hindurch; **throughout** [θru'aʊt] während des/der ganzen; überall in
throw [θrəʊ] werfen; **throw oneself into one's work** sich in die Arbeit stürzen
thumb [θʌm] Daumen; **be under sb.'s thumb** (infml.) unter js. Fuchtel stehen
Thursday ['θɜ:zdɪ, 'θɜ:zdeɪ] Donnerstag
ticket ['tɪkɪt] **1.** Fahrkarte; Eintrittskarte; **ticket office** ['tɪkɪt‿ˌɒfɪs] Fahrkartenschalter
tidiness ['taɪdɪnəs] Ordentlichkeit; **tidy** ['taɪdɪ] **1.** ordentlich, aufgeräumt; **2. tidy (up)** aufräumen
tie [taɪ] Krawatte, Schlips; **bow tie** [ˌbəʊ 'taɪ] Fliege, (Frack-)Schleife
tiger ['taɪgə] Tiger
till [tɪl] bis *(zeitlich)*
timber ['tɪmbə] (Bau-)Holz
time [taɪm] **1.** Uhrzeit; Zeit; **What time is it?** Wie spät ist es? **What time is the film?** Wann fängt der Film an? **at one time or another** irgendwann (einmal); **at that time** damals, zu jener Zeit; **by this time** unterdessen, zu diesem Zeitpunkt; **have time on one's hands** viel freie Zeit haben; **in no time** (infml.) im Nu; **in time** rechtzeitig; **on time** pünktlich; **timeless** zeitlos; **timetable** Stundenplan; Fahrplan; **2.** stoppen; zeitlich abstimmen; **3. time(s)** Mal; -mal
tin [tɪn] *(meist* BE) Dose, Büchse
tip [tɪp] **1.** Tip, Hinweis; **2.** Trinkgeld; **3. tip sb.** jm. Trinkgeld geben
tired ['taɪəd] müde; **be tired of** genug haben von; **tiredness** ['taɪədnəs] Müdigkeit
title ['taɪtl] Titel
to [tu:, tə] **1.** (um) zu; **2.** nach, zu, in; **from ... to ...** von ... bis ...; **quarter to nine** Viertel vor neun (8.45/20.45); **Welcome to ...** Willkommen in ...
toast [təʊst] Toast(brot)
tobacco [tə'bækəʊ] Tabak
today [tə'deɪ] heute; **today's activities** die heutigen Aktivitäten, die Aktivitäten (von) heute
together [tə'geðə] zusammen; **get together** zusammenkommen
toilet ['tɔɪlət] Toilette; **toilet article** ['tɔɪlət‿ɑ:tɪkl] Toilettenartikel
tolerance (towards) *(sing.)* ['tɒlərəns] Toleranz (gegenüber); **tolerant (of)** tolerant (gegenüber)
tomato [tə'mɑ:təʊ], *pl.* **tomatoes** Tomate
tomorrow [tə'mɒrəʊ] morgen
tone [təʊn] Stimmung, Atmosphäre; Ton, Klang

D

tonight [tə'naɪt] heute abend, heute nacht

too [tu:] **1.** *(am Satzende)* auch, ebenfalls; **2. too good** zu gut

tool [tu:l] Werkzeug

tooth [tu:θ], *pl.* **teeth** [ti:θ] Zahn; **toothbrush** ['tu:θbrʌʃ] Zahnbürste; **toothpaste** ['tu:θpeɪst] Zahnpasta, Zahncreme

top [tɒp] oberes Ende, Kopfende; **top group** oberste/stärkste/beste Gruppe; Leistungskurs

topic ['tɒpɪk] Thema

total ['təʊtl] **1.** Gesamtbetrag, Summe; **2.** Gesamt-, absolute(r, s)

touch [tʌtʃ] berühren, anfassen

tour (of) [tʊə] Tour, (Rund-)Reise, (Rund-)Fahrt (durch); **guided tour (of)** [ˌgaɪdɪd 'tʊə] Führung (durch); **tourist** ['tʊərɪst] Tourist/in

towards [tə'wɔ:dz] **1.** auf … zu, in Richtung auf; **2.** gegen *(zeitlich)*; **towards sb./sth.** *(sich verhalten)* gegenüber jm./etwas, zu jm./etwas

towel ['taʊəl] Handtuch

tower ['taʊə] Turm

town [taʊn] Stadt; **in town** in der (Innen-)Stadt; **town hall** [ˌtaʊn 'hɔ:l] Rathaus; **town house** (AE) Reihenhaus

toxic ['tɒksɪk] giftig, Gift-

toy [tɔɪ] Spielzeug

track and field [ˌtræk‿n 'fi:ld] (AE) Leichtathletik

trade [treɪd] **1.** Handel; **2. trade with** Geschäfte machen, Handel treiben mit; **trade in sth.** mit etwas handeln

tradition [trə'dɪʃn] Tradition, Brauch; **traditional** [trə'dɪʃnəl] traditionnell; **traditionally** traditionell(erweise), üblicherweise

traffic ['træfɪk] Verkehr; **traffic congestion** *(sing.)* [kən'dʒestʃn] Verkehrsstau(s), verstopfte Straßen; **traffic jam** [dʒæm] (Verkehrs-)Stau; **traffic lights** *(pl.)* (Verkehrs-)Ampel(n)

tragedy ['trædʒədɪ] Tragödie, Katastrophe; **tragic** ['trædʒɪk] tragisch

trail [treɪl] Pfad; Wanderweg

trailer ['treɪlə] (AE) Wohnwagen

train [treɪn] **1.** Zug; **on the train** im Zug; **2.** trainieren, üben; ausbilden, schulen; **trained** ausgebildet, geschult; **training** Training

trait (of character) ['treɪt] (Charakter-)Eigenschaft, (Wesens-)Zug

tram [træm] Straßen-, Trambahn

trampoline [ˌtræmpə'li:n] Trampolin

translate [træns'leɪt] übersetzen; **translation** [træns'leɪʃn] Übersetzung

transport **1.** ['trænspɔ:t] Transport(mittel); Verkehrsmittel; **2.** [træns'pɔ:t] befördern, transportieren

trap [træp] Falle

trash [træʃ] (AE) Abfall

travel ['trævl] **1.** reisen; **2.** (das) Reisen; **travel-sick** ['trævl sɪk] reisekrank; **traveller** Reisende(r)

treat [tri:t] behandeln; **treatment** ['tri:tmənt] Behandlung

tree [tri:] Baum

trend [trend] Trend

trial ['traɪəl] Gerichtsverhandlung

tribe [traɪb] (Volks-)Stamm; **tribal** ['traɪbl] Stammes-

trick [trɪk] Trick, Streich, List; **play a trick on sb.** jm. einen Streich spielen; **tricky** knifflig, schwierig; heikel

trillion ['trɪljən] Billion(en)

trip [trɪp] Reise, Ausflug

trolley ['trɒlɪ] (BE) (Einkaufs-, Gepäck-)Wagen

trouble ['trʌbl] Schwierigkeit(en); **get in(to) trouble** Ärger bekommen, in Schwierigkeiten geraten; **give sb. trouble** jm. Ärger machen, bereiten; **trouble spot** ['trʌbl spɒt] „Achtung Falle!“

trousers *(pl.)* ['traʊzəz] (lange) Hose

truck [trʌk] *(meist* AE) LKW

true [tru:] wahr; **come true** Wirklichkeit werden, wahr werden; **truly** ['tru:lɪ] wirklich, wahrhaftig; **truth** [tru:θ] Wahrheit

try [traɪ] versuchen, (aus)probieren; **try and do sth./try to do sth.** versuchen, etwas zu tun; **try on** anprobieren *(Kleidung)*; **try-out** ['traɪaʊt] (AE) Probe(vorstellung)

T-shirt ['ti:ʃɜ:t] T-Shirt

tube [tju:b] **1.** Londoner U-Bahn; **2.** Rohr, Röhre

Tuesday ['tju:zdɪ, 'tju:zdeɪ] Dienstag

tuna fish, *pl.* **tuna fish** ['tju:nə] Thunfisch

tunnel ['tʌnl] Tunnel

turbo-brain ['tɜ:bəʊbreɪn] „Turbo-Gehirn“

turkey ['tɜ:kɪ] Truthahn, Pute

turn [tɜ:n] **1.** sich umdrehen; **turn away** [ˌtɜ:n‿ə'weɪ] sich abwenden; **turn into** (sich) verwandeln in, sich entwickeln zu; **turn left/right (into)** nach links/rechts abbiegen (in); **turn on/off** an-/ausschalten; **turn sth. over** etwas umdrehen, wenden; **turn round** sich umdrehen; **turn to** sich wenden an, sich zuwenden; **2. turn sth. into sth.** etwas in etwas verwandeln; etwas zu etwas machen; **3. turn green/red/…** grün/rot/… werden; **4. It's my turn.** Ich bin dran. Ich bin an der Reihe.

TV [ˌti:'vi:], **television** ['telɪvɪʒn] Fernsehen; Fernsehgerät; **TV set** Fernsehgerät; **on TV** im Fernsehen; **watch TV** fernsehen

twice [twaɪs] zweimal

twin [twɪn] Zwilling

type (of) [taɪp] Art, Sorte, Typ; **typical (of)** ['tɪpɪkl] typisch (für)

U

unable [ˌʌn'eɪbl] unfähig, nicht in der Lage

unanswerable [ʌn'ɑ:nsərəbl] nicht zu beantworten, unbeantwortbar

unavoidable [ˌʌnə'vɔɪdəbl] unvermeidlich, unausweichlich

unbearable [ʌn'beərəbl] unerträglich

unbeatable [ʌn'bi:təbl] unschlagbar

unbelievable [ˌʌnbɪ'li:vəbl] unglaublich

unborn [ˌʌn'bɔ:n] (noch) ungeboren

unbreakable [ʌn'breɪkəbl] unzerbrechlich

uncertain [ˌʌn'sɜ:tn] ungewiß, unsicher

uncle ['ʌŋkl] Onkel

uncomfortable [ʌn'kʌmftəbl] unbequem, unbehaglich

under ['ʌndə] unter

undergraduate [ˌʌndə'grædʒʊət] Student/in *(noch ohne akademischen Abschluß)*

underground ['ʌndəgraʊnd] (BE) U-Bahn

underlined [ˌʌndə'laɪnd] unterstrichen

understand [ˌʌndə'stænd] verstehen, begreifen; **understanding** Verständnis; **understandable** [ˌʌndə'stændəbl] verständlich

underwater tunnel [ˌʌndə'wɔ:tə] Unterwassertunnel

undrinkable [ʌn'drɪŋkəbl] untrinkbar, ungenießbar

unemployable [ˌʌnɪm'plɔɪəbl] als Arbeitskraft ungeeignet, nicht vermittelbar; **unemployed** [ˌʌnɪm'plɔɪd] arbeitslos; **unemployment** [ˌʌnɪm'plɔɪmənt] Arbeitslosigkeit

unfair [ˌʌn'feə] ungerecht, unfair; **unfairness** Ungerechtigkeit
unfit [ʌn'fɪt] ungeeignet
unforgettable [ˌʌnfə'getəbl] unvergeßlich
unfortunately [ʌn'fɔːtʃənətlɪ] leider, unglücklicherweise
unfriendliness [ʌn'frendlɪnəs] Unfreundlichkeit; **unfriendly** [ʌn'frendlɪ] unfreundlich
unhappy [ʌn'hæpɪ] unglücklich
unhealthy [ʌn'helθɪ] ungesund
uniform ['juːnɪfɔːm] Uniform
unimaginable [ˌʌnɪ'mædʒɪnəbl] unvorstellbar
unimportant [ˌʌnɪm'pɔːtnt] unwichtig, unbedeutend
uninteresting [ˌʌn'ɪntrestɪŋ] uninteressant
unit ['juːnɪt] Lektion, Einheit
unite [juː'naɪt] (sich) vereinigen, (sich) zusammenschließen
universal [ˌjuːnɪ'vɜːsl] universal, allgemein
university [ˌjuːnɪ'vɜːsətɪ] Universität
unkind [ˌʌn'kaɪnd] unfreundlich, gemein
unknown [ˌʌn'nəʊn] unbekannt
unless [ʌn'les] wenn nicht, außer wenn, es sei denn, daß
unlike [ˌʌn'laɪk] anders als, im Gegensatz zu
unlikely [ˌʌn'laɪklɪ] unwahrscheinlich; **be unlikely to do sth.** etwas wahrscheinlich nicht tun
unload [ˌʌn'ləʊd] aus-, entladen
unmarried [ˌʌn'mærɪd] unverheiratet
unnatural [ˌʌn'nætʃrəl] unnatürlich
unnecessary [ˌʌn'nesəsərɪ] unnötig, überflüssig
unpack [ʌn'pæk] auspacken
unpleasant [ʌn'pleznt] unangenehm
unpopular [ˌʌn'pɒpjʊlə] unbeliebt
unsafe [ˌʌn'seɪf] unsicher, gefährlich
unsuccessful [ˌʌnsək'sesfəl] erfolglos
unthinkable [ʌn'θɪŋkəbl] undenkbar
untidy [ˌʌn'taɪdɪ] unordentlich, unaufgeräumt
until [ən'tɪl] bis; **not … until** nicht vor/erst um; nicht … bevor
untouched [ˌʌn'tʌtʃt] unberührt
unusual [ˌʌn'juːʒʊəl] ungewöhnlich, außergewöhnlich
unwelcome [ʌn'welkəm] unwillkommen
up [ʌp] hinauf, herauf; **up there** dort oben; **up to** bis (zu); **It's up to you.** Es hängt von dir ab. Das überlasse ich dir.
upper ['ʌpə] obere(r, s), höhere(r, s)
upset [ˌʌp'set]**: be upset** aufgeregt, aufgebracht sein; betrübt sein; **upset stomach** Magenverstimmung
upside down [ˌʌpsaɪd 'daʊn] verkehrt herum, auf dem Kopf
upstairs [ˌʌp'steəz] oben (im Haus); nach oben, (die Treppe) hinauf
urban ['ɜːbən] städtisch, Stadt-
urgency ['ɜːdʒənsɪ] Dringlichkeit; **urgent** ['ɜːdʒənt] dringend
us [ʌs] uns
use 1. [juːz] gebrauchen, verwenden; **get/be used to sth./doing sth.** sich an etwas gewöhnen/an etwas gewöhnt sein
2. [juːs] Gebrauch, Verwendung; **useful** ['juːsfəl] nützlich; **useless** nutzlos, zu nichts nütze
3. it used to be … ['juːstə] es war früher (immer) …
usual ['juːʒʊəl] üblich, gewöhnlich; **usually** ['juːʒʊəlɪ] gewöhnlich, meistens, normalerweise

V

vacation [BE: və'keɪʃn, AE: veɪ'keɪʃn] (*meist* AE) Ferien, Urlaub
valid ['vælɪd] gültig
valley ['vælɪ] Tal
value ['væljuː] **1.** Wert; Nutzen; **2.** (hoch-)schätzen, achten
van [væn] Lieferwagen; Möbelwagen
variety [və'raɪətɪ] **1.** Vielzahl, Vielfalt; **2.** Sorte, Art
vase [vɑːz] Vase
vegetable ['vedʒtəbl] (ein) Gemüse
vegetarian [ˌvedʒɪ'teərɪən]**,** (infml. *auch:*) **veggie** ['vedʒɪ] Vegetarier/in
vehicle ['viːɪkl] Fahrzeug
verbal ['vɜːbl] verbal, mit einem Verb gebildet
verse [vɜːs] Strophe *(eines Gedichtes oder Liedes)*, Vers(zeile)
version ['vɜːʃn] Fassung *(eines Textes)*; Version *(eines Berichtes)*
very ['verɪ] sehr; **like/love/… very much** sehr mögen/lieben/…
via ['vaɪə] via, über
vice-(president) [ˌvaɪs 'prezɪdənt] Vize-(Präsident/in)
victim ['vɪktɪm] Opfer
video ['vɪdɪəʊ] Video(film); **video recorder** Videorecorder
view [vjuː] **1.** Ansicht, Meinung; **point of view** [ˌpɔɪnt‿əv 'vjuː] (Erzähl-)Standpunkt, (Erzähl-) Perspektive
2. view (over, of) Aussicht (über), Sicht (auf)
Viking ['vaɪkɪŋ] Wikinger/in
villa ['vɪlə] Villa
village ['vɪlɪdʒ] Dorf
vinegar ['vɪnɪgə] Essig
violence ['vaɪələns] Gewalt, Gewalttätigkeit; **violent** ['vaɪələnt] gewalttätig, brutal; heftig
vision ['vɪʒn] Vision
visit ['vɪzɪt] **1.** besuchen; besichtigen;
2. visit (to) Besuch, Aufenthalt (in); **visitor** ['vɪzɪtə] Besucher/in, Gast
voice [vɔɪs] Stimme
volleyball ['vɒlɪbɔːl] Volleyball
vote [vəʊt] **1.** Abstimmung;
2. Stimme *(bei Wahlen)*;
3. vote (for) stimmen (für), wählen; abstimmen; **voter** Wähler/in

W

wages *(pl.)* ['weɪdʒɪz] Lohn, Löhne
wagon, BE *auch:* **waggon** ['wægn] (Plan-)Wagen
wait (for) [weɪt] warten (auf); **I can't wait.** Ich kann es kaum erwarten.
waiter ['weɪtə] Kellner, Ober; **waitress** ['weɪtrəs] Kellnerin, Serviererin
wake up [weɪk] aufwachen; **wake sb. (up)** jn. (auf)wecken
walk [wɔːk] **1.** (zu Fuß) gehen, laufen; **2.** Spaziergang, Rundgang; **go for a walk** spazierengehen; **take the dog for a walk** mit dem Hund rausgehen; **walker** Spaziergänger/in; **walking shoes** Wanderschuhe; **walkman** Walkman
wall [wɔːl] Wand; Mauer
want [wɒnt] (haben) wollen; **want to do sth.** etwas tun wollen
war [wɔː] Krieg; **civil war** [ˌsɪvl 'wɔː] Bürgerkrieg
wardrobe ['wɔːdrəʊb] Kleiderschrank
warehouse ['weəhaʊs] Lagerhalle
warm [wɔːm] warm; **warmth** [wɔːmθ] Wärme
warn [wɔːn] warnen; **warn sb. not to do sth.** jn. ermahnen, etwas nicht zu tun; jn. davor warnen, etwas zu tun; **warning** Warnung

wash [wɒʃ] waschen; **wash the dishes** (das Geschirr) spülen, abwaschen; **washable** waschbar; **washing liquid** ['wɒʃɪŋ ˌlɪkwɪd] (BE) flüssiges Waschmittel; **washing machine** Waschmaschine
waste [weɪst] **1.** Abfall, Müll; **waste management** [ˌweɪst 'mænɪdʒmənt] Abfallbeseitigung, Abfallwirtschaft; **2.** Verschwendung; **3. waste (on)** verschwenden (für)
watch [wɒtʃ] **1.** (Armband-)Uhr; **watchmaker** Uhrmacher/in; **2.** sich *(etwas)* ansehen; *(jm.)* zuschauen, *(jn.)* beobachten; **watch TV** fernsehen
water ['wɔːtə] **1.** Wasser; **2.** bewässern, gießen; **water colour** Wasserfarbe; **water-power** Wasserkraft; **water-skiing** ['wɔːtəˌskiːɪŋ] Wasserski(laufen); **water down** verwässern, abschwächen; **waterfall** ['wɔːtəfɔːl] Wasserfall; **watering can** Gießkanne; **waterway** ['wɔːtəweɪ] Wasserstraße; **watery** ['wɔːtərɪ] wässerig
wave [weɪv] **1.** Welle; **2. wave (at)** (zu)winken
way [weɪ] **1.** Weg; **ask the way** nach dem Weg fragen; **Can you tell me the way to …?** Können Sie mir sagen, wie ich zu/nach … komme? **find the way back (to)** zurückfinden (nach, zu); **I'm going your way.** Ich fahre/gehe in deine/Ihre Richtung. **lose one's way** sich verirren, sich verlaufen; **We've come a long way.** Wir haben große Fortschritte erzielt. **2.** Art und Weise; **this way** auf diese Art und Weise; **in different ways** auf verschiedene Weise(n); **in the way of** (infml.) hinsichtlich; **way of life** Lebensstil, Lebensweise
we [wiː, wɪ] wir
weak [wiːk] schwach; **weaken** schwächen; schwächer werden; **weakness** ['wiːknəs] Schwäche
wealth [welθ] Wohlstand, Reichtum; **wealthy** ['welθɪ] wohlhabend, reich
weapon ['wepən] Waffe
wear [weə] *(Kleidung, Brille)* tragen, anhaben
weather ['weðə] Wetter
Wednesday ['wenzdɪ, 'wenzdeɪ] Mittwoch
week [wiːk] Woche; **weekday** ['wiːkdeɪ] Werktag, Wochentag; **weekend** [ˌwiːk'end] Wochenende; **at the weekend** (BE) am Wochenende; **weekly** Wochen-; wöchentlich
weigh [weɪ] wiegen
welcome ['welkəm] willkommen heißen, begrüßen; **Welcome to …** Willkommen in …; **You're welcome.** Bitte (sehr). Nichts zu danken.
welfare *(sing.)* ['welfeə] (AE) Sozialhilfe; **be on welfare** Sozialhilfe beziehen
well [wel] gesund, wohlauf; gut; **well-off** wohlhabend; **well-known** (wohl)bekannt; **as well as** und auch, ebenso wie; **just as well** genausogut; **Well!** Na so was! Du meine Güte! Wirklich? **Well, …** Nun, …
Welsh [welʃ] **1.** walisisch, Walisisch; **2.** Waliser/in
west [west] **1.** Westen; **2.** nach Westen; **3. west (of)** westlich (von); **western** ['westən] West-, westlich
wet [wet] naß; feucht
whale [weɪl] Wal
what [wɒt] was; **What …?** Was für ein(e) …? Welche(r, s) …? **What colour?** Welche Farbe? **What about …?** Wie wäre es mit …? Was ist mit …? **What is … like?** Wie ist …? **What time is it?** Wie spät ist es? **What time is the film?** Wann fängt der Film an? **What's your name?** Wie heißt du?/Wie heißen Sie? **whatever** [wɒt'evə] was (auch) immer
wheat [wiːt] Weizen
wheel [wiːl] Rad
when [wen] **1.** wenn, sobald; **2.** als; **3.** wann; **whenever** [wen'evə] wann (auch) immer
where [weə] wo; wohin; **where from?** woher? **whereas** [weər'æz] wohingegen, während; **wherever** [weər'evə] wo (auch) immer, wohin (auch) immer; überall wo
whether ['weðə] ob
which [wɪtʃ] **1.** der, die, das; die *(Relativpronomen)*; **2. which?** welche(r, s)? **which one?** welche(r, s)? **whichever** [wɪtʃ'evə] welche(r, s) (auch) immer
while [waɪl] **1.** Weile, Zeit(spanne); **2.** *(conj.)* während
whisky ['wɪskɪ] Whisky
white [waɪt] weiß
who [huː] **1.** der, die, das; die *(Relativpronomen)*; **2. who?** wer? wen? wem? **whoever** [huː'evə] wer (auch) immer
whole [həʊl] gesamte(r, s), ganze(r, s); **as a whole** als Ganzes
whom [huːm] **1.** den, die, das; dem, der, dem *(Relativpronomen)*; **2. whom?** wen? wem?
whose [huːz] **1.** wessen; **2.** deren, dessen *(Relativpronomen)*
why [waɪ] warum, weshalb; **that's why** deshalb, darum; **Why be sad?** Wozu denn traurig sein? **Why don't you ask …?** Warum fragst du nicht …? Frag doch … .
wide [waɪd] breit; **widen** verbreitern; *(Wissen)* erweitern
widow ['wɪdəʊ] Witwe; **widower** ['wɪdəʊə] Witwer
wife [waɪf], *pl.* **wives** [waɪvz] (Ehe-)Frau
wild [waɪld] wild
will [wɪl] werden *(Futur)*
win [wɪn] gewinnen, siegen; erringen, erwerben; **winner** Sieger/in, Gewinner/in
wind [wɪnd] Wind; **windsurfer** ['wɪndsɜːfə] Windsurfer/in; **windsurfing** Windsurfen; **windy** windig
window ['wɪndəʊ] Fenster; **window-shopping** ['wɪndəʊˌʃɒpɪŋ] Schaufensterbummeln
wine [waɪn] Wein
winter ['wɪntə] Winter
wish [wɪʃ] wünschen; **Best wishes** [ˌbest 'wɪʃɪz] Mit besten Wünschen; Viele Grüße
witch [wɪtʃ] Hexe
with [wɪð] mit; bei
within [wɪð'ɪn] innerhalb, in
without [wɪð'aʊt] ohne
woman ['wʊmən], *pl.* **women** ['wɪmɪn] Frau
wonder ['wʌndə] **1.** sich fragen, gern wissen wollen; **2. natural wonder** [ˌnætʃrəl 'wʌndə] Naturwunder; **wonderful** ['wʌndəfəl] wunderbar
won't [wəʊnt] **(= will not): I won't …** Ich werde nicht …
wood [wʊd] **1.** Holz; **wooden** hölzern; **2. wood(s)** [wʊd(z)] Wald
wool [wʊl] Wolle
word [wɜːd] Wort
work [wɜːk] **1.** Arbeit; **at work** bei der Arbeit, am Arbeitsplatz; **go to work** arbeiten gehen; **2.** arbeiten; funktionieren; **work on sb.** (infml.) jn. bearbeiten; **work out** (her)ausarbeiten, herausbekommen; ausrechnen; **get worked up** sich aufregen; **worker** Arbeiter/in; **working class** Arbeiterklasse; **worksheet** ['wɜːkʃiːt] Arbeitsblatt

world [wɜːld] Welt; **in the world** auf der (ganzen) Welt; **world-famous** [ˌwɜːld'feɪməs] weltberühmt
worry ['wʌrɪ] **1.** sich Sorgen machen; **worry oneself sick (about)** krank vor Sorge (um) werden; **worry sb.** jn. beunruhigen, jm. Sorgen machen; **be worried (about)** sich Sorgen machen (um); beunruhigt sein (wegen); **2.** Sorge; Unruhe
worse [wɜːs] schlechter, schlimmer; **(the) worst** [wɜːst] (der/die/das) schlechteste; am schlechtesten
worth [wɜːθ] wert; **be worth doing** wert sein, getan zu werden; **worthless** wertlos
would [wʊd, wəd] würde(n); **I'd like …** [aɪd 'laɪk] **= I would like …** ich möchte (gern) …, ich hätte … gern; **What would you like?** Was möchtest du? Was hättest du gern?
wrench [rentʃ] (AE) Schraubenschlüssel
wrestling ['reslɪŋ] Ringen, Catchen
write (to; about) [raɪt] schreiben (an; über); **write down** aufschreiben; **writer** Schreiber/in; Schriftsteller/in
wrong [rɒŋ] falsch; **be wrong** unrecht haben, im Unrecht sein; **go wrong** schiefgehen; **My watch is wrong.** Meine Uhr geht falsch. **There's something wrong with …** Etwas stimmt mit … nicht. **What's wrong?** Was ist los?

Y

Yankee ['jæŋkɪ] Yankee, Nordstaatler
yard [jɑːd] **1.** Yard *(= 91,4 cm)*; **2.** (AE) Garten
year [jɪə] Jahr; **all (the) year** das ganze Jahr über; **15-year-old** Fünfzehnjährige(r); **in fifty years (from now)** in fünfzig Jahren; **in the past few years** in den vergangenen/letzten Jahren; **in those years** damals, in jenen Jahren; **over the years** im Lauf der Jahre
yellow ['jeləʊ] gelb
yes [jes] ja
yesterday ['jestədɪ, 'jestədeɪ] gestern
yet [jet] doch, dennoch; **… yet?** … schon …? **not … yet** noch nicht
yogurt, yoghurt ['jɒgət] Joghurt
Yorkshire pudding [ˌjɔːkʃə 'pʊdɪŋ] *gebackener Eierteig als Beilage zum Rinderbraten*
you [juː, jʊ, jə] **1.** du; ihr; Sie; **2.** dich, dir; euch; Sie, Ihnen; **3.** man
young [jʌŋ] jung
your [jɔː, jə] *(poss. adj.)* dein(e); euer/eure; Ihr(e); **yourself** [jɔː'self] dich, dir (selbst); sich (selbst); **yourselves** [jɔː'selvz] euch (selbst); sich (selbst)
yours [jɔːz] *(poss. pron.)* deine(r, s); eure(r, s); Ihre(r, s); **Yours, …** Dein(e) …; Ihr(e) …; Euer/Eure … *(am Briefende)*; **Yours faithfully, …** ['feɪθfəlɪ] Mit freundlichen Grüßen …; Hochachtungsvoll …; **Yours sincerely, …** [sɪn'sɪəlɪ] (BE) Mit herzlichen/freundlichen Grüßen …
youth [juːθ] Jugendliche(r); Jugend; **youth club** ['juːθ klʌb] Jugendklub; **youth hostel** ['juːθ hɒstl] Jugendherberge; **youthful** ['juːθfəl] jung, jugendlich

Z

zero ['zɪərəʊ] Null
zoo [zuː] Zoo, Tierpark

D

Bildquellen:
Acaluso, Blumberg (S. 34 Flagge, S. 38 Kinder unten); Alexandria Conventions & Visitors Bureau, Alexandria, Virginia (S. 56 oben); Archiv für Kunst und Geschichte, Berlin (S. 15, S. 57 rechts, Mitte oben, S. 88, S. 92 alle außer Mitte rechts, S. 112); Arizona State Museum, University of Arizona, silkscreen by Robert Spray for Margaret Schevill Link (S. 108); Bavaria Bildagentur, Gauting (S. 21,S. 59 oben rechts); British Film Institute, London (S. 43 oben); J. Allan Cash, London (S. 24 Mitte, rechts, S. 25 oben, rechts, S. 29, S. 52/53 Landschaft); Close Up/Paul Alers, Washington (S. 25 unten); Close Up/Renee Bouchard, Washington (S. 24 links, S. 26); Columbia University, New York (S. 34 oben); David Dore, Guildford (S. 82 Mitte links, unten rechts); dpa, Frankfurt (S. 47 unten rechts, S. 57 Mitte unten, S. 91 oben rechts, S. 93 rechts); Europäische Kommission, Brüssel (S. 91 unten); Focus, Elisa Leonelli, Hamburg (S. 38 Mitte); Focus, Magnum, Hamburg (S. 35); David Graham, London (S. 8, S. 18 Mitte, S. 22, S. 59 Haus oben, S. 62/63, S. 71 Fenster, S. 82 oben rechts, unten links); Gruner + Jahr AG und Co, Hamburg (S. 16 links); Bildagentur Anne Hamann, München (S. 107); David Hissey, Oklahoma (S. 12, S. 18 alle außer Mitte); Hulton Deutsch, London (S. 47 oben links, S. 92 Mitte rechts, S. 93 links); Interfoto, München (S. 55); Kenji Kawano, Window Rock (S. 52 Mitte links, unten links, rechts, S. 53 oben rechts, unten links); Keystone, Hamburg (S. 98 unten); John Lally, York (S. 82 Mitte); Library of Congress, Washington (S. 43 unten); The Mansell Collection, London (S. 90); Tom Murray, Pittsfield (S. 11 oben links und rechts); Nottinghamshire County Library Service, Nottingham (S. 72); Okapia, Frankfurt (S. 71 Baum); Lewis Parker, The Warpath (S. 51); Bildarchiv Paysan, Stuttgart (S. 98 oben); Redferns, London (S. 47, oben rechts); Claudia Rothe, Berlin (S. 56 unten); Royal Mint, Wales (S. 73); Sportsphoto Agency, Stewart Kendall (S. 91 oben links); Stockfood, Eising Photos, München (S. 14, S. 16 rechts); Transglobe Agency, Hamburg (S. 38 oben, Frau unten, S. 41, S. 47 Mitte, unten links, S. 57 links); Gahan Wilson, from Gahan Wilson's America, Kirby McCauley Ltd., New York (S. 50); ZEFA, Düsseldorf (S. 11 unten).

Einband: Mauritius, Mittenwald

Textquellen:
Waiting by Eleanor Meek published in Just Seventeen; *A question of identity* based on "Lynn, a Navajo" from *To live in two worlds* by Brent Ashabranner, © Dodd, Mead & Company, Inc., New York; *Dreams* from *The Dream Keeper and Other Poems* by Langston Hughes © 1932 by Alfred A. Knopf, Inc. and renewed 1960 by Langston Hughes. Reprinted by permission of the publisher; *The Moth and the Star* © 1940 James Thurber. © 1968 Helen Thurber. From *Fables For Our Time*, published by Harper Collins; *The Winner* by Donald E. Westlake, © Donald E. Westlake. Reprinted by permission of Andrew Nurnberg Associates; *Dreampoem* by Roger McGough. Reprinted by permission of Peters Fraser & Dunlop Group Ltd.; *Key to the Door* by Alan Sillitoe, © Alan Sillitoe 1961 and 1989; *Just one of many stories in a park* by Angeles Manzaneque and *Out of the mouths of babes?* by Kathryn Clarke, © The Telegraph plc, London, 1994; *The Jaspistos Competition*, © The Spectator, London; *Sardines* by Spike Milligan, © Spike Milligan Productions Ltd.; *applaws)* reprinted from the *Complete Poems: 1904 -1962* by e.e. cummings, edited by George J. Firmage, by permission of Liveright Publishing Corporation, © 1944, 1972, 1991 by the Trustees for the e. e. cummings Trust; *Southbound on the freeway* from *New and Selected Things* by May Swenson, © Atlantic Monthly Press; *Charles* from *The Lottery* by Shirley Jackson © 1948,1949 by Shirley Jackson. Renewal © 1976, 1977 by Laurence Hyman, Barry Hyman, Mrs. Sarah Webster and Mrs Joanne Schnurer. Reprinted by permission of Farrar, Straus and Giroux, Inc.; *The All-American Slurp* by Lensey Namioka, from *Visions* edited by Donald R. Gallo. © Lensey Namioka; *Women of the West* by Cathy Luchetti and Carol Olwell, Antelope Island Press, Utah; *Oxford Advanced Learner's Dictionary of Current English, 1992* edited by A. P. Cowie, by permission of Oxford University Press; *The End* by Fredric Brown, © Fredric Brown and the publisher; excerpt from *The Hopi Chieftains' letter to the President of the USA (1949)* and an adaptation of *Which one are you? Five types of young Indians* in *The Way*, edited by Shirley Hill Witt & Stan Steiner, Vintage Books.

Nicht alle Copyrightinhaber konnten ermittelt werden; deren Urheberrechte werden hiermit vorsorglich und ausdrücklich anerkannt.

List of names

Girls/Women

Cora ['kɔ:rə]
Debbie ['debɪ]
Desiree [deɪ'zɪəreɪ]
Felicity [fə'lɪsətɪ]
Gail [geɪl]
Janice ['dʒænɪs]
Jenny ['dʒenɪ]
Kimberley ['kɪmbəlɪ]
Linda ['lɪndə]
Lynn [lɪn]
Marion ['mærɪən]
Pam [pæm]
Pat [pæt]
Patricia [pə'trɪʃə]
Sherri ['ʃerɪ]
Susie, Suzie ['su:zɪ]
Sylvia ['sɪlvɪə]
Vera ['vɪərə]

Boys/Men

Booker ['bʊkə]
Calvin ['kælvɪn]
Carl [kɑ:l]
Charles [tʃɑ:lz]
Ed [ed]
Enrico [en'ri:kəʊ]
Floyd [flɔɪd]
Jake [dʒeɪk]
Josh [dʒɒʃ]
Kevin ['kevɪn]
Leon ['li:ən]
Lloyd [lɔɪd]
Louis ['lu:ɪs]
Ray [reɪ]
Sonny ['sʌnɪ]
Steve [sti:v]
Tommy ['tɒmɪ]
Trampas ['træmpəs]
Warren ['wɒrən]

Family names

Allyn ['ælɪn]
Beale [bi:l]
Blackburn ['blækbɜ:n]
Brooks [brʊks]
Carlyle [kɑ:'laɪl]
Cruz [kru:z]
Davis ['deɪvɪs]
Dawson ['dɔ:sn]
Eastman ['i:stmən]
Evett ['evət]
Frank [fræŋk]
Goodrum ['gʊdrəm]
Henry ['henrɪ]
Holmes [həʊmz]
Hopp [hɒp]
Lanigan ['lænɪgən]
Maunders ['mɔ:ndəz]
Metz [mets]
Miller ['mɪlə]
Mitchell ['mɪʃtəl]
Parker ['pɑ:kə]
Peterson ['pi:təsən]
Petonita [ˌpetən'i:tə]
Porch [pɔ:tʃ]
Ramsey ['ræmzɪ]
Rand [rænd]
Revell ['revl]
Rigby ['rɪgbɪ]
Roberts ['rɒbəts]
Rosetti [rə'zetɪ]
Santi ['sæntɪ]
Sharpe [ʃɑ:p]
Spirropoulos [spɪ'rɒpələs]
Stoyak ['stɔɪæk]
Vance [væns]
Wordman ['wɜ:dmən]
Wu [wu:]

Place names*

Adams Building ['ædəmz ˌbɪldɪŋ]
Alexandria [ˌælɪg'zɑ:ndrɪə]
Anacostia [ˌænə'kɒstɪə]
Atlanta [ət'læntə]
Baltimore ['bɔ:ltɪmɔ:]
Boonetown ['bu:ntaʊn]
Canyon de Chelly [ˌkænjən də 'ʃeɪ]
Clayton ['kleɪtn]
Cleveland ['kli:vlənd]
Detroit [dɪ'trɔɪt]
Gary ['gærɪ]
Georgetown ['dʒɔ:dʒtaʊn]
Georgia ['dʒɔ:dʒə]
Illinois [ˌɪlə'nɔɪ]
Indiana [ˌɪndɪ'ænə]
Jamestown ['dʒeɪmztaʊn]
Jefferson Building ['dʒefəsən ˌbɪldɪŋ]
Lake Huron [ˌleɪk 'hjʊərən]
Missouri [mɪ'zʊərɪ]
Ohio [əʊ'haɪəʊ]
Paris ['pærɪs]
Placer County [ˌpleɪsə 'kaʊntɪ]
Raffestry Center ['ræfəstrɪ ˌsentə]
South Dakota [ˌsaʊθ də'kəʊtə]
St Louis [ˌseɪnt 'lu:ɪs]
Texas ['teksəs]
Uniontown ['ju:nɪəntaʊn]
Utah ['ju:tɑ:]
Vermont [və'mɒnt]
Window Rock [ˌwɪndəʊ 'rɒk]

Other names

Alan Sillitoe [ˌælən 'sɪlɪtəʊ]
Angeles Manzaneque [ˌændʒəlɪs mænzə'ni:k]
Apollo 11 [ə'pɒləʊ]
Black Knight [ˌblæk 'naɪt]
Brandermill School [ˌbrændəmɪl 'sku:l]
Brian Seaton [ˌbraɪən 'si:tn]
Carl Stokes [ˌkɑ:l 'stəʊks]
Carol Moseley-Braun [ˌkærəl ˌməʊzlɪ 'braʊn]
Charles Curtis [ˌtʃɑ:lz 'kɜ:tɪs]
Chief Joseph [ˌtʃi:f 'dʒəʊzɪf]
Chief Sitting Bull [ˌtʃi:f ˌsɪtɪŋ 'bʊl]
Close Up Foundation ['kləʊsʌp faʊnˌdeɪʃn]
CNN (Cable News Network) [ˌkeɪbl ˌnju:z 'netwɜ:k]
Colin L. Powell [ˌkɒlɪn‿ˌel 'paʊəl]
Columbus [kə'lʌmbəs]
David N. Dinkins [ˌdeɪvɪd‿ˌen 'dɪŋkɪnz]
David O. Selznick [ˌdeɪvɪd‿ˌəʊ 'selznɪk]
Douglas Wilder [ˌdʌgləs 'waɪldə]
Dunlap ['dʌnlæp]
Edgar Allan Poe [ˌedgər‿ˌælən 'pəʊ]
Edmond Clerihew Bentley [ˌedmənd ˌklerɪhju: 'bentlɪ]
Edmond Dantes [ˌedmənd 'dæntəz]
e. e. Cummings ['kʌmɪŋz]
Eleanor Meek [ˌelənə 'mi:k]
Elizabeth van Lew [ɪˌlɪzəbəθ ˌvæn 'lu:]
Frederick Douglass [ˌfredrɪk 'dʌgləs]
Hicktown Gazette [ˌhɪktaʊn gə'zet]
Highland Games [ˌhaɪlənd 'geɪmz]
Howard University [ˌhaʊəd ju:nɪ'vɜ:sətɪ]
James Madison [ˌdʒeɪmz 'mædɪsən]
James Smithson [ˌdʒeɪmz 'smɪθsən]
James Thurber [ˌdʒeɪmz 'θɜ:bə]
Jefferson Davis [ˌdʒefəsən 'deɪvɪs]
Jesse Jackson [ˌdʒesɪ 'dʒæksən]
John Alexander [ˌdʒɒn ˌælɪg'zɑ:ndə]
John Lavelle [ˌdʒɒn lə'vel]
Kathryn Clarke [ˌkæθrɪn 'klɑ:k]
Langston Hughes [ˌlæŋstən 'hju:z]
Louis Brandeis [ˌlu:ɪs 'brændaɪs]
Manuelito [ˌmænʊel'i:təʊ]
Margaret Mitchell [ˌmɑ:grət 'mɪtʃəl]
Marion Wright Edelman [ˌmærɪən 'raɪt 'eɪdlmən]
Mary Elizabeth Bowser [ˌmeərɪ ɪˌlɪzəbəθ 'baʊzə]
May Swenson [ˌmeɪ 'swensn]
Molly Wood [ˌmɒlɪ 'wʊd]
Morehouse College [ˌmɔ:haʊs 'kɒlɪdʒ]
Navajo ['nævəhəʊ]
O'Connell (High School) [əʊ'kɒnl]
Oscar ['ɒskə]
Owen Wister [ˌəʊɪn 'wɪstə]
Potomac [pə'təʊmæk]
Richard Hatcher [ˌrɪtʃəd 'hætʃə]
Roger McGough [ˌrɒdʒə mə'gɒf]
Saint Brendan [sənt 'brendən]
Samuel Morse [ˌsæmjʊəl mɔ:s]
Sioux [su:]
Skylab ['skaɪlæb]
Spectator [spek'teɪtə]
Spike Milligan [ˌspaɪk 'mɪlɪgən]
Sunday Telegraph [ˌsʌndeɪ 'telɪgrɑ:f]
Thomas Bradley [ˌtɒməs 'brædlɪ]
Tim Severin [ˌtɪm 'sevrɪn]
Toni Morrison [ˌtəʊnɪ 'mɒrɪsən]
Tuekakas [ˌtju:'kɑ:kəs]
Ulysses S. Grant [juˌlɪsi:z‿ˌes 'grɑ:nt]
Victoria Valle [ˌvɪk'tɔ:rɪə 'væl]
Washington Chronical [ˌwɒʃɪŋtən 'krɒnɪkl]
Winnetou ['wɪnətu:]
Wounded Knee [ˌwu:ndɪd 'ni:]

*Siehe auch S. 147 (Washington sights and institutions)

Countries and continents

Country/Continent	Person	People	Adjective
Africa ['æfrɪkə] *Afrika*	an African ['æfrɪkən]	the Africans	African
Asia ['eɪʃə, 'eɪʒə] *Asien*	an Asian ['eɪʃn, 'eɪʒn]	the Asians	Asian
Australia [ɒ'streɪlɪə] *Australien*	an Australian [ɒ'streɪlɪən]	the Australians	Australian
Austria ['ɒstrɪə] *Österreich*	an Austrian ['ɒstrɪən]	the Austrians	Austrian
Brazil [brə'zɪl] *Brasilien*	a Brazilian [brə'zɪlɪən]	the Brazilians	Brazilian
(Great) Britain ['brɪtn] *Großbritannien*	a Briton ['brɪtn]	the British ['brɪtɪʃ]	British
Canada ['kænədə] *Kanada*	a Canadian [kə'neɪdɪən]	the Canadians	Canadian
China ['tʃaɪnə] *China*	a Chinese [ˌtʃaɪ'ni:z]	the Chinese	Chinese
Costa Rica [ˌkɒstə 'ri:kə] *Costa Rica*	a Costa Rican [ˌkɒstə 'ri:kən]	the Costa Ricans	Costa Rican
Cuba ['kju:bə] *Kuba*	a Cuban ['kju:bən]	the Cubans	Cuban
Egypt ['i:dʒɪpt] *Ägypten*	an Egyptian [ɪ'dʒɪpʃn]	the Egyptians	Egyptian
El Salvador [el 'sælvədɔ:] *El Salvador*	a Salvadorian [ˌsælvə'dɔ:rɪən]	the Salvadorians	Salvadorian
England ['ɪŋglənd] *England*	an Englishman/Englishwoman	the English ['ɪŋglɪʃ]	English
Europe ['jʊərəp] *Europa*	a European [ˌjʊərə'pi:ən]	the Europeans	European
France [frɑ:ns] *Frankreich*	a Frenchman/Frenchwoman	the French [frentʃ]	French
Germany ['dʒɜ:mənɪ] *Deutschland*	a German ['dʒɜ:mən]	the Germans	German
Greece [gri:s] *Griechenland*	a Greek [gri:k]	the Greeks	Greek
Holland ['hɒlənd] *Holland*, the **Netherlands** ['neðələndz] *die Niederlande*	a Dutchman/Dutchwoman	the Dutch [dʌtʃ]	Dutch
India ['ɪndɪə] *Indien*	an Indian ['ɪndɪən]	the Indians	Indian
Ireland ['aɪələnd] *Irland*	an Irishman/Irishwoman	the Irish ['aɪrɪʃ]	Irish
Italy ['ɪtəlɪ] *Italien*	an Italian [ɪ'tæljən]	the Italians	Italian
Japan [dʒə'pæn] *Japan*	a Japanese [ˌdʒæpə'ni:z]	the Japanese	Japanese
Korea [kə'rɪə] *Korea*	a Korean [kə'rɪən]	the Koreans	Korean
Lebanon ['lebənən] *Libanon*	a Lebanese [ˌlebə'ni:z]	the Lebanese	Lebanese
Mexico ['meksɪkəʊ] *Mexiko*	a Mexican ['meksɪkən]	the Mexicans	Mexican
New Zealand [njʊ 'zi:lənd] *Neuseeland*	a New Zealander [njʊ 'zi:ləndə]	the New Zealanders	New Zealand[1]
Nicaragua [ˌnɪkə'rægjʊə] *Nicaragua*	a Nicaraguan [ˌnɪkə'rægjʊən]	the Nicaraguans	Nicaraguan
Pakistan [ˌpɑ:kɪ'stɑ:n] *Pakistan*	a Pakistani [ˌpɑ:kɪ'stɑ:nɪ]	the Pakistanis	Pakistani
Peru [pə'ru:] *Peru*	a Peruvian [pə'ru:vɪən]	the Peruvians	Peruvian
Poland ['pəʊlənd] *Polen*	a Pole [pəʊl]	the Poles	Polish ['pəʊlɪʃ]
Portugal ['pɔ:tʃʊgl] *Portugal*	a Portuguese [ˌpɔ:tʃʊ'gi:z]	the Portuguese	Portuguese
Russia ['rʌʃə] *Rußland*	a Russian ['rʌʃn]	the Russians	Russian
Saudi Arabia [ˌsaʊdɪ_ə'reɪbɪə] *Saudi-Arabien*	a Saudi ['saʊdɪ]	the Saudis	Saudi, Saudi-Arabian
Scotland ['skɒtlənd] *Schottland*	a Scotsman/Scotswoman, a Scot [skɒt]	the Scots	Scottish ['skɒtɪʃ]
Spain [speɪn] *Spanien*	a Spaniard ['spænjəd]	the Spanish ['spænɪʃ]	Spanish
Switzerland ['swɪtsələnd] *die Schweiz*	a Swiss [swɪs]	the Swiss	Swiss
Turkey ['tɜ:kɪ] *Türkei*	a Turk [tɜ:k]	the Turks	Turkish ['tɜ:kɪʃ]
the **United Kingdom (UK)** [jʊˌnaɪtɪd 'kɪŋdəm] *das Vereinigte Königreich*	a Briton ['brɪtn]	the British ['brɪtɪʃ]	British
the **United States (of America)** [jʊˌnaɪtɪd 'steɪts] *die Vereinigten Staaten (von Amerika)*	an American [ə'merɪkən]	the Americans	American
Vietnam [ˌvi:et'næm] *Vietnam*	a Vietnamese [vɪˌetnə'mi:z]	the Vietnamese	Vietnamese
Wales [weɪlz] *Wales*	a Welshman/Welshwoman	the Welsh [welʃ]	Welsh
West Indies [ˌwest_'ɪndɪz] *Westindische Inseln*	a West Indian [ˌwest_'ɪndɪən]	the West Indians	West Indian

[1] nur in attributiver Verwendung; vgl.: *New Zealand butter* – aber: *something is from New Zealand*

Grammatical terms

abstract noun ['æbstrækt]	*abstraktes Nomen, Abstraktum*
active ['æktɪv]	*Aktiv*
active infinitive [ɪn'fɪnɪtɪv]	*Infinitiv Aktiv*
activity verb [æk'tɪvətɪ]	*Tätigkeitsverb, Vorgangsverb*
adjective ['ædʒɪktɪv]	*Adjektiv*
adverb ['ædvɜ:b]	*Adverb*
of frequency ['fri:kwənsɪ]	*der Häufigkeit*
of indefinite time [ɪn'defɪnɪt]	*der unbestimmten Zeit*
of manner ['mænə]	*der Art und Weise*
adverbial [əd'vɜ:bɪəl]	*adverbiale Bestimmung*
of place	*des Ortes*
of time	*der Zeit*
adverbial sub-clause ['sʌbklɔ:z]	*Nebensatz in adverbialer Funktion*
article ['ɑ:tɪkl]	*Artikel*
aspect ['æspekt]	*Aspekt (= Wahl zwischen* simple *und* progressive form*)*
auxiliary (verb) [ɔ:g'zɪljərɪ]	*Hilfsverb*
clause [klɔ:z]	*Gliedsatz, Teilsatz*
of comparison [kəm'pærɪsn]	*des Vergleichs*
of concession [kən'seʃn]	*der Einräumung*
of place	*des Ortes*
of purpose	*des Zwecks*
of result	*der Folge*
of reason	*des Grundes*
of time	*der Zeit*
comparative [kəm'pærətɪv]	*Komparativ, erste Steigerungsform*
comparison (of adjectives/ of adverbs) [kəm'pærɪsn]	*Steigerung (der Adjektive/ der Adverbien)*
complex sentence ['kɒmpleks]	*Satzgefüge, zusammengesetzter Satz*
compound (word) ['kɒmpaʊnd]	*Kompositum, zusammengesetztes Wort*
conditional sentence [kən'dɪʃnəl]	*Bedingungssatz*
conjunction [kən'dʒʌŋkʃn]	*Konjunktion*
consonant ['kɒnsənənt]	*Konsonant, Mitlaut*
contact clause ['kɒntækt]	*Relativsatz ohne Relativpronomen*
coordinating conjunction [kəʊ'ɔ:dɪneɪtɪŋ]	*koordinierende Konjunktion, nebenordnende Konjunktion*
defining relative clause [dɪ'faɪnɪŋ]	*bestimmender Relativsatz*
definite article ['defɪnɪt]	*bestimmter Artikel*
direct object ['daɪrekt]	*direktes Objekt, „Sachobjekt"*
direct speech [spi:tʃ]	*direkte Rede*
dynamic verb [daɪ'næmɪk]	*Tätigkeitsverb, Vorgangsverb*
emphasizing pronoun ['emfəsaɪzɪŋ]	*verstärkendes Pronomen*
emphatic 'do' [ɪm'fætɪk]	*betontes* do
future ['fju:tʃə]	*Futur, Zukunft*
future perfect [ˌfju:tʃə 'pɜ:fɪkt]	*vollendete Zukunft, Futur II*
future progressive [ˌfju:tʃə prə'gresɪv]	*Verlaufsform des Futurs mit* will
genitive ['dʒenətɪv]	*Genitiv*
gerund ['dʒerənd]	*Gerundium (*-ing*-Form in der Funktion eines Nomens)*
going to-future	*Futur mit* going to
if-clause	*Nebensatz mit* if, if*-Satz*
imperative [ɪm'perətɪv]	*Imperativ*
indefinite article [ɪn'defɪnɪt]	*unbestimmter Artikel*
indirect object ['ɪndɪrekt]	*indirektes Objekt, „Personenobjekt"*
infinitive [ɪn'fɪnɪtɪv]	*Infinitiv*
-ing form ['ɪŋ fɔ:m]	-ing*-Form*
intransitive verb [ɪn'trænsətɪv]	*intransitives Verb*
inversion [ɪn'vɜ:ʃn]	*Inversion (= Wortstellung Hilfsverb – Subjekt)*
irregular verb [ɪ'regjʊlə]	*unregelmäßiges Verb*
long form ['lɒŋ fɔ:m]	*Langform*
main clause [meɪn]	*Hauptsatz*
main verb	*Vollverb*
material noun [mə'tɪərɪəl]	*Stoffname*
modal (auxiliary) [ˌməʊdl‿ɔ:g'zɪljərɪ]	*modales Hilfsverb*
modifier ['mɒdɪfaɪə]	*modifizierendes Element, Modifikator*
negative imperative [ˌnegətɪv‿ɪm'perətɪv]	*verneinter Imperativ*
negative statement [ˌnegətɪv 'steɪtmənt]	*verneinter Aussagesatz*
noun [naʊn]	*Nomen, Substantiv*
noun phrase ['naʊn freɪz]	*Nominalphrase*
object ['ɒbdʒɪkt]	*Objekt*
object form	*Objektform (eines Personalpronomens)*
of-phrase [freɪz]	of*-Fügung*
participle ['pɑ:tɪsɪpl]	*Partizip*
participle clause	*Partizipialsatz, -fügung*

passive ['pæsɪv]	*Passiv*
passive infinitive [ɪn'fɪnɪtɪv]	*Infinitiv Passiv*
past participle [ˌpɑːst 'pɑːtɪsɪpl]	*Partizip Perfekt*
past perfect [ˌpɑːst 'pɜːfɪkt]	*Plusquamperfekt*
past perfect progressive [prə'gresɪv]	*Verlaufsform des* past perfect
past progressive [ˌpɑːst prə'gresɪv]	*Verlaufsform der Vergangenheit*
personal pronoun [ˌpɜːsənəl 'prəʊnaʊn]	*Personalpronomen*
phrasal verb [ˌfreɪzl 'vɜːb]	*feste Verb-Adverb-Verbindung*
plural ['plʊərəl]	*Plural*
positive ['pɒzɪtɪv]	*Positiv, Grundform (eines Adjektivs/Adverbs)*
positive statement [ˌpɒzɪtɪv 'steɪtmənt]	*bejahter Aussagesatz*
possessive adjective [pəˌzesɪv‿'ædʒɪktɪv]	*adjektivisch gebrauchtes Possessivpronomen*
possessive form [pə'zesɪv]	*„besitzanzeigende Form", s-Genitiv*
possessive pronoun [pəˌzesɪv 'prəʊnaʊn]	*nominal gebrauchtes Possessivpronomen*
prefix ['priːfɪks]	*Vorsilbe, Präfix*
preposition [ˌprepə'zɪʃn]	*Präposition*
present participle [ˌpreznt 'pɑːtɪsɪpl]	*Partizip Präsens*
present perfect [ˌpreznt 'pɜːfɪkt]	present perfect *(Perfekt)*
present perfect progressive [prə'gresɪv]	*Verlaufsform des* present perfect
present progressive [ˌpreznt prə'gresɪv]	*Verlaufsform des Präsens*
progressive form [prə'gresɪv]	*Verlaufsform*
pronoun ['prəʊnaʊn]	*Pronomen*
prop-word ['prɒpwɜːd]	*Stützwort*
quantifier ['kwɒntɪfaɪə]	*Mengenbezeichnung*
question ['kwestʃən]	*Frage(satz)*
question tag ['kwestʃən tæg]	*Frageanhängsel*
question word	*Fragewort*
reflexive pronoun [rɪˌfleksɪv 'prəʊnaʊn]	*Reflexivpronomen*
reflexive verb	*reflexives Verb*
regular verb ['regjʊlə]	*regelmäßiges Verb*
relative clause ['relətɪv]	*Relativsatz*
relative pronoun	*Relativpronomen*
reported speech [spiːtʃ]	*indirekte Rede*
reporting verb	*die indirekte Rede einleitendes Verb, „berichtendes Verb"*
sentence ['sentəns]	*Satz, Satzgefüge*
short answer	*Kurzantwort*
short form	*Kurzform*
simple past [ˌsɪmpl 'pɑːst]	*einfache Form der Vergangenheit*
simple present [ˌsɪmpl 'preznt]	*einfache Form des Präsens*
singular ['sɪŋgjʊlə]	*Singular*
state verb / stative verb ['steɪtɪv]	*Zustandsverb*
stem [stem]	*(Wort-)Stamm*
sub-clause ['sʌbklɔːz], subordinate clause [sə'bɔːdɪnət]	*Nebensatz*
subject ['sʌbdʒɪkt]	*Subjekt*
subordinating conjunction [sə'bɔːdɪneɪtɪŋ]	*subordinierende Konjunktion, unterordnende Konjunktion*
substitute (verb) ['sʌbstɪtjuːt]	*Ersatzverb (für modale Hilfsverben)*
suffix ['sʌfɪks]	*Nachsilbe, Suffix*
superlative [suː'pɜːlətɪv]	*Superlativ, zweite Steigerungsform*
tense [tens]	*Tempus, Zeitform*
transitive verb ['trænsətɪv]	*transitives Verb*
verb [vɜːb]	*1. Prädikat, Satzaussage; 2. Verb*
verb of perception [pə'sepʃn]	*Verb der Sinneswahrnehmung*
vowel ['vaʊəl]	*Vokal, Selbstlaut*
will-future	*Futur mit* will
word class ['wɜːd klɑːs]	*Wortart, Wortklasse*
word order ['wɜːd‿ɔːdə]	*Wortstellung*
word stress ['wɜːd stres]	*Wortbetonung*
yes/no-question	*Entscheidungsfrage*

Irregular verbs

Infinitive	Simple past	Past participle	
(to) arise	arose	arisen	auftreten, entstehen
(to) be	was, were	been	sein
(to) beat	beat	beaten	schlagen
(to) become	became	become	werden
(to) begin	began	begun	beginnen
(to) bite	bit	bitten	beißen
(to) blow	blew	blown	blasen, wehen
(to) break	broke	broken	brechen; zerbrechen
(to) bring	brought	brought	(mit-, her)bringen
(to) broadcast	broadcast	broadcast	senden, ausstrahlen; übertragen
(to) build	built	built	bauen
(to) burn	burnt/burned	burnt/burned	(ver)brennen
(to) buy	bought	bought	kaufen
(to) catch	caught	caught	fangen, erwischen
(to) choose [uː]	chose [əʊ]	chosen [əʊ]	(aus)wählen, aussuchen
(to) come	came	come	kommen
(to) cost	cost	cost	kosten
(to) cut	cut	cut	schneiden
(to) deal [iː]	dealt [e]	dealt [e]	sich befassen (mit); handeln (von)
(to) do	did	done [ʌ]	tun
(to) draw	drew	drawn	zeichnen; ziehen
(to) dream [iː]	dreamt [e]/ dreamed [iː]	dreamt [e]/ dreamed [iː]	träumen
(to) drink	drank	drunk	trinken
(to) drive [aɪ]	drove	driven [ɪ]	*(ein Auto)* fahren
(to) eat	ate [BE: e, eɪ; AE: eɪ]	eaten	essen
(to) fall	fell	fallen	(hin)fallen
(to) feed	fed	fed	füttern
(to) feel	felt	felt	(sich) fühlen; empfinden; befühlen
(to) fight	fought	fought	kämpfen; bekämpfen
(to) find	found	found	finden
(to) fly	flew	flown	fliegen
(to) forget	forgot	forgotten	vergessen
(to) get	got	BE: got, AE: gotten	bekommen; (ab)holen, besorgen; (hin)kommen, gelangen; werden
(to) give	gave	given	geben
(to) go	went	gone [ɒ]	gehen; fahren
(to) grow	grew	grown	wachsen; anbauen; werden
(to) hang	hung	hung	(auf)hängen
(to) have (have got)	had	had	haben
(to) hear [ɪə]	heard [ɜː]	heard [ɜː]	hören
(to) hide	hid	hidden	(sich) verstecken
(to) hit	hit	hit	schlagen, treffen
(to) hold	held	held	(fest)halten
(to) hurt	hurt	hurt	verletzen, weh tun
(to) keep	kept	kept	behalten; aufbewahren
(to) kneel	knelt/kneeled	knelt/kneeled	(sich) knien
(to) know [əʊ]	knew [juː]	known [əʊ]	wissen; kennen

Infinitive	Simple past	Past participle	
(to) lead	led	led	führen, leiten
(to) leave	left	left	(zurück)lassen; verlassen; weggehen, abfahren
(to) let	let	let	(zu)lassen
(to) lie [aɪ]	lay [eɪ]	lain [eɪ]	liegen
(to) lose [uː]	lost [ɒ]	lost [ɒ]	verlieren
(to) make	made	made	machen, zubereiten
(to) mean [iː]	meant [e]	meant [e]	bedeuten; meinen
(to) meet	met	met	(sich) treffen, kennenlernen
(to) misunderstand	misunderstood	misunderstood	mißverstehen
(to) pay	paid	paid	(be)zahlen
(to) put	put	put	stellen, legen
(to) quit	quit	quit	aufhören (mit); aufgeben
(to) read [iː]	read [e]	read [e]	lesen, vorlesen
(to) ride	rode	ridden	reiten; (rad)fahren
(to) ring	rang	rung	klingeln, läuten
(to) rise	rose	risen	(an-, auf)steigen
(to) run	ran	run	laufen, rennen
(to) say [eɪ]	said [e]	said [e]	sagen
(to) see	saw	seen	sehen
(to) sell	sold	sold	verkaufen
(to) send	sent	sent	schicken, senden
(to) shake	shook	shaken	schütteln; zittern
(to) shine	shone [BE: ɒ; AE: əʊ]	shone [BE: ɒ; AE: əʊ]	scheinen, leuchten
(to) shoot	shot	shot	(er)schießen, *(Ball)* werfen
(to) show [əʊ]	showed [əʊ]	shown [əʊ]	zeigen
(to) shut	shut	shut	schließen
(to) sing	sang	sung	singen
(to) sink	sank	sunk	sinken; versenken
(to) sit	sat	sat	sitzen; sich setzen
(to) sleep	slept	slept	schlafen
(to) speak	spoke	spoken	sprechen
(to) spend	spent	spent	*(Geld)* ausgeben; *(Zeit)* verbringen
(to) spoil	spoilt/spoiled	spoilt/spoiled	verziehen; verwöhnen; verderben
(to) stand	stood	stood	stehen
(to) steal	stole	stolen	stehlen
(to) stink	stank	stunk	stinken
(to) swim	swam	swum	schwimmen
(to) take	took	taken	(mit)nehmen; (weg)bringen
(to) teach	taught	taught	lehren, unterrichten
(to) tell	told	told	erzählen, berichten
(to) think	thought	thought	denken, meinen, glauben
(to) throw	threw	thrown	werfen
(to) understand	understood	understood	verstehen, begreifen
(to) wake up	woke	woken	aufwachen; (auf)wecken
(to) wear	wore	worn	*(Kleidung, Brille)* tragen, anhaben
(to) win	won [ʌ]	won [ʌ]	gewinnen
(to) write	wrote	written	schreiben

Useful classroom phrases

Talking about texts

Giving your first impressions

I think the text/story/play/poem/song/excerpt/ … is interesting/funny/exciting/boring/sad/(un)realistic/ … because …	Ich finde, der Text/die Geschichte/das Theaterstück/das Gedicht/das Lied/der Auszug/ … ist interessant/lustig/ spannend/langweilig/traurig/(un)realistisch/ …, weil ..
The text made me feel sad/angry/concerned/confused/ happy/ …	Der Text hat mich traurig/ärgerlich/besorgt/verwirrt/ glücklich/ … gemacht.
I found the ending surprising/disappointing/annoying/confusing/predictable/ …	Ich fand das Ende überraschend/enttäuschend/ärgerlich/ verwirrend/vorhersagbar/ …
I enjoyed/didn't enjoy reading this text because it reminded me/made me think of …	Ich habe diesen Text (nicht) gern gelesen, weil er mich an … erinnert hat.
The text deals with/presents a humorous/serious/ current/ … theme.	In dem Text wird ein heiteres/ernstes/aktuelles/ … Thema behandelt/dargestellt.
I can/can't identify with the main character … because …	Ich kann mich mit der Hauptperson (nicht) identifizieren, weil …

Taking a closer look

• The author deals with the question why/criticizes/ analyses/comments on/compares/ …	Der Autor/Die Autorin behandelt die Frage, wieso/ kritisiert/analysiert/kommentiert/vergleicht/ …
At the beginning the author introduces the main character(s) … . Later on …	Am Anfang führt der Autor/die Autorin die Hauptperson(en) ein … . Später …
In the first paragraph the narrator describes the setting.	Im ersten Abschnitt beschreibt der Erzähler/die Erzählerin den Ort/Schauplatz des Geschehens.
The action takes place at/in/during …	Die Handlung spielt in/während …
• A is /is characterized as/seems to be a strong/weak/ aggressive/ambitious/thoughtful/thoughtless/ careful/brave/violent/creative/difficult/ … sort of person/character.	A ist/wird dargestellt als/scheint … zu sein/eine starke/schwache/aggressive/ehrgeizige/rücksichtsvolle/rücksichtslose/vorsichtige/mutige/ gewalttätige/kreative/schwierige/ … Person.
A's behaviour/reaction shows that/is a result of …	As Verhalten/Reaktion zeigt, daß/ergibt sich aus …
To give an example, in line X the text says …	Um ein Beispiel zu nennen: In Zeile X steht im Text …
• Another example of … is to be found in line X, where …	Ein anderes Beispiel von … findet man in Zeile X, wo …
This example/sentence shows/illustrates/suggests that/explains why …	Dieses Beispiel/Dieser Satz zeigt/veranschaulicht/legt nahe, daß/erklärt, warum …
In comparison with A, B is/seems to be …	Im Vergleich zu A ist B …/scheint B … zu sein.
• A is (very) similar to/(completely) different from/can(not) be compared to …	A ist … (sehr) ähnlich/(völlig) anders als/kann nicht verglichen werden mit …

Discussing different views

In my opinion/It seems to me that/As far as I can see …	Meiner Meinung nach/Mir scheint/Soweit ich sehe …
I think it is important to consider …	Ich finde, es ist wichtig zu bedenken …
I'm of the same opinion/also think that …	Ich bin der gleichen Meinung/finde auch, daß …
I agree with A's view that …	Ich stimme mit As Ansicht überein, daß …
I can't agree/don't agree/disagree with A's view that … because …	Ich kann As Ansicht, daß …, nicht zustimmen/stimme As Ansicht nicht zu, weil …
I'm not sure if/not convinced that …	Ich bin nicht sicher, ob/nicht überzeugt, daß …
I don't understand why/find it hard to believe that …	Ich verstehe nicht, wieso/finde es schwer zu glauben, daß …
In contrast to A, I believe/would say that …	Im Gegensatz zu A glaube ich/würde ich sagen, daß …